THE BLACKWELL GUIDE TO THEOLOGY AND POPULAR CULTURE

MW00454350

Blackwell Guides to Theology

Blackwell Guides to Theology offer cutting edge and imaginative coverage of the central themes, key works, important authors, and historical figures in the major subdisciplines of theology. The Guides will direct readers through the most recent research in a lively and accessible way, making them suitable for everyone from undergraduate level upwards.

The Blackwell Guide to Theology and Popular Culture

Kelton Cobb

Blackwell
Publishing

BLACKWELL PUBLISHING
350 Main Street, Malden, MA 02148-5020, USA
9600 Garsington Road, Oxford OX4 2DQ, UK
550 Swanston Street, Carlton, Victoria 3053, Australia

First published 2005 by Blackwell Publishing Ltd

1 2005

Library of Congress Cataloging-in-Publication Data

Cobb, Kelton.
    The Blackwell guide to theology and popular culture/Kelton Cobb.
        p. cm.—(Blackwell guides to theology)
    Includes bibliographical references and index.
    ISBN-13: 978-1-4051-0698-6 (alk. paper)
    ISBN-10: 1-4051-0698-0 (pbk. : alk. paper)
    ISBN-13: 978-1-4051-0702-0 (alk. paper)
    ISBN-10: 1-4051-0702-2 (pbk. : alk. paper)
1. Popular culture—Religious aspects—Christianity. 2. Popular culture—Religious aspects.
    I. Title. II. Series.

    BR115.C8C523 2005
    261—dc22

                                                                    2004029174

A catalogue record for this title is available from the British Library.

Set in 10/12pt Sabon
by Newgen Imaging Systems (P) Ltd, Chennai, India
Printed and bound in India
by Replika Press Pvt Ltd, Kundli

The publisher's policy is to use permanent paper from mills that operate a sustainable forestry policy, and which has been manufactured from pulp processed using acid-free and elementary chlorine-free practices. Furthermore, the publisher ensures that the text paper and cover board used have met acceptable environmental accreditation standards.

For further information on
Blackwell Publishing, visit our website:
www.blackwellpublishing.com

I dedicate this book to the memories of my father, William Cobb, and my uncle, Ernest Miller

"What have you that you did not receive?" I Cor. 4.7

Contents

Acknowledgments

Among the many gifts of St Augustine to theology is the idea that cultural signs have the power to facilitate our enjoyment of God. These pages are an attempt to unwrap that gift one more time. The signs that come under consideration here are scattered around in the detritus of popular culture – movies, novels, recorded music, prime-time dramas, wall art, the World Wide Web, theme parks, and advertising. But from Augustine I've also received a sober respect for sin. In the analysis undertaken here I've tried to keep both of these bequests in view and offer a measured assessment of select artifacts from among the onslaught of mass-produced images, sounds, and storytelling with which we, for the most part gladly, sometimes begrudgingly, fill our lives. So, my first word of gratitude goes to St Augustine.

But writing a book incurs many debts. I've had help along the way from the Louisville Institute, the Wabash Center, the North American Paul Tillich Society, the New Haven Theological Discussion Group, and a well-timed sabbatical from Hartford Seminary. I've benefited immensely from the insights and enthusiasm of students in my courses at Hartford Seminary and Wesleyan University who have been willing to lay their ears to the ground and listen for religious rumblings in popular culture. And I've received bountiful moral support from members of my family: Alverna, Lori, Henry and Elfriede.

I'm also mindful of what I have learned from my teachers and colleagues William Schweiker, David Klemm, Arthur Roberts, Doug Frank, Sam Alvord, Max Stackhouse, Langdon Gilkey, and Maria Antonoccio, each of them in league with Augustine's guarded endorsement of all things finite. My colleagues at Hartford Seminary, Clifford Green, Worth Loomis, and, particularly, Ian Markham, not only hounded me to write this book but also lightened my load to permit me to do so. My primary guides in determining what sounds, stories and images are worth paying attention to are my friends – Gary Erickson, Gayle Beebe, Scott Webb,

John Arndt, Steve Vaughan, Shann Cobb, Ned Edwards, Ed Horstmann, Graham Reside, Heng Wong, Lois Lorentzen and George McKinley – each attuned in different ways to the mysterious nuances of popular culture. They deserve both credit *and blame* for what materials come under scrutiny in this book.

Images and song lyrics have been reproduced in the book with permission of copyright holders. The difficulties involved in obtaining permissions are legion, but in a few cases permission was granted with exemplary graciousness – by the family of Joe Strummer, David McGinnis on behalf of Nick Cave, Dr Edison Amos on behalf of Tori Amos, and Vitaly Komar (who is equal parts iconoclast and iconographer). And both I and readers of this book owe thanks to Jennifer L. Geddes for her knowledge of the subject and gifts with language, and to Rebecca Harkin and Karen Wilson, my editors, who were encouraging throughout in allowing the book to become what it is.

To write this book, I've had to live among digitized, cathode ray, and newsprint artifacts more than I am ordinarily inclined to do. To my patient and long-suffering wife, Heidi Gehman, who wrote her own dissertation as I was writing this book, her desk beside mine, and to our puzzled though rarely neglected young sons, Henry and William, I can't begin to express the depth of my love and gratitude.

Introduction

In Battery Park in Lower Manhattan, next to a cart selling roasted pecans and hot pretzels, is a kiosk with Empire State Building pencil sharpeners, Statue of Liberty snow globes, and the standard-issue rack of souvenir postcards. On this rack are pictures of Grand Central Station, St Patrick's Cathedral, Central Park, the United Nations Plaza, the Chrysler Building, the American Museum of Natural History, the Guggenheim Museum, and Macy's Department Store. That each of these architectural marvels came to be built represents not only a confluence of political clout, engineering expertise, artistic craftsmanship and vast outlays of cash, but also a considerable level of public consent for what kinds of aspirations are worth enshrining in beautiful buildings.

This rack of postcards, like that at any tourist kiosk in any big city, can be read like a book that tells us what matters most to its citizens. The objects depicted on these postcards are human values that have been sheathed with rebar, stone, and glass and veined with romex and fiber optics. In this manner, they serve both as monuments to human values, and as instruments which can further extend the reach of those values into the community. They are *monuments* in that much creative genius has been lavished upon them to testify to the worthiness of a particular value; they are *instruments* in that they create a venue for that particular value to be pursued. We build magnificent buildings to provide physical bodies for our cultural values.

Thus, the landmark architecture pictured on New York City postcards can be read as an inventory of the particular human activities that are valued in American culture. Grand Central Station is a monument to and instrument of *freedom* (of physical movement); Central Park is a monument to and instrument of *leisure*; St Patrick's Cathedral is a monument to and instrument of *religion*; the Chrysler Building and Macy's are monuments to and instruments of the *economy*; the United Nations Plaza is a monument to and instrument of *politics*; the Guggenheim Museum is a monument to and instrument of *art*; the Museum of Natural History is a monument to and instrument of *knowledge*. It is in this respect that ecclesial terms are sometimes used as metaphors in relation to such landmark structures: Macy's is a "cathedral of commerce"; the Guggenheim is a "sanctuary of art"; the Museum of Natural History is a "temple of science," etc. Some discrete cultural value is being venerated and practiced within the walls of each.

The use of this sacred space metaphor in landmark architecture has a parallel in more general discussions of the value spheres that the buildings are built to enshrine. It has become common to say "art is religion," that we should have "faith in science," or that "the market is God." What is meant in these expressions is that something like faith and worship has come to be attached to art, science, and the economy. Just as the veneration of certain values may be expressed through the beauty of great architecture, these values can also become objects of a more generalized religious piety. Sociologists such as Max Weber and Michael Walzer have argued that at an earlier period in the history of the West, our ancestors conceived of their primary identity as tribal or religious (these typically overlapped), but that there has been a gradual differentiation or separating out of the cultural value spheres (religion, family, art, science, politics, economy, etc.) such that it is now possible for a person to claim that their *primary* identity derives from any one of these – e.g., profession, economic status, national origin, etc. – and to view religion as a secondary attribute. What is happening here is that the *good* for which one of these other value spheres exists to serve is being asserted as the *most* central or ultimate good in one's life.

The status of art as "religion" in some quarters is a good illustration of this. It is common today to view the artist as a prophet or seer. Wassily Kandinsky's 1911 manifesto, *Concerning the Spiritual in Art*, captured this notion of the artist who "is not born to a life of pleasure," but undergoing scorn and hatred must "see and point the way," dragging humanity forward. He wrote,

> Literature, music and art are the first and most sensitive spheres in which this spiritual revolution makes itself felt. They reflect the dark picture of the present time and show the importance of what at first was only a little point of light noticed by few and for the great majority non-existent. Perhaps they even grow dark in their turn, but on the other hand they turn away from the soulless life of the present towards those substances and ideas which give free scope to the non-material strivings of the soul.[1]

This attribution of prophetic insight to the artist who has the power to see behind the surface of things, to reveal what is otherwise hidden, developed into the prototype of the avant-garde artist who tells the truth of his feelings and sheds an unflattering light on a society's sins and the dangerous directions in which it is headed, and then pays the consequences for rendering this service. This is a modern conception in its assertion that art is an autonomous source of knowledge about the truth of reality. Previous to this, art was viewed as mediating an authority that was not its own, and in the West, this meant the authority of the religious tradition. As one author has described it, "Whatever moral passion a medieval artist brought to a fresco, contemporaries viewing it would regard the biblical story – not the artist himself or his illustration of it – as the source of authority."[2] The Renaissance was the turning point here. For a variety of reasons – disenchantment with corruption in the Church, diverging sources of patronage, the rediscovery of classical learning – iconography began to slide away from the monopoly of religion and re-root itself in other domains of culture – art and literature in particular. This had the effect of sacralizing art and literature as independent sources of wisdom and revelation.

Symbols once inseparable from religious myth and ritual thus began to wander, often in disguise, into other cultural spheres, carrying with them their inherent aura and an authority that was once derived from religion but became autonomous. Art is not unique in making this excursion. Science, politics, family, and the economy were also once acolytes of the religious sphere in the history of the West. Their justification as domains of human activity was that they served the good of religion – the knowledge of God and God's ways (science), the governance and the containment of sin in the kingdom of God (politics), the multiplication and nurture of souls on their journey to God (family), and management of the household of the children of God (economy). Here, too, it was with the Renaissance that these once dependent cultural spheres began a long protest that won their independence and progressed into the precious achievement of modernity, *viz.*, the refraction of our lives into multiple autonomous spheres of activity (art, science, politics, family, economy). In practice, we assume that each of these spheres stands on its own bottom – we presume a discrete good is being pursued within each one. There are clues to this assumption in slogans such as "art for art's sake," "science is the uninhibited pursuit of truth," "my country, right or wrong," "blood is thicker than water," and "the invisible hand of the market." Indeed, there is a distinct and legitimate good inside each of these spheres that each of the spheres exists to protect, proclaim, and foster – with all the instruments at their disposal: creeds, laws, institutions, poetry, monuments, schools, myths, and rituals.

This differentiation of the spheres has been an important achievement, one that ought not to be reversed. Nevertheless, it is worth noting a few implications of this brief archeology of the concept of cultural spheres. First, the differentiation itself was driven by the belief that some transcendent good is at the center of each sphere and that the activities and pursuits distinct to that sphere are authorized by the good that is being served through it. Second, there is what has been called a "sovereignty" to each of the spheres that ought not to be violated by the other spheres.[3] The good of the family, for instance, ought not to be violated by the good of the market. Frequent job transfers necessitated by one's desire to climb the corporate ladder would be an example of such a violation – at the point when these moves threaten to unravel the family. But from the other side, the good of the market ought not to be violated by the good of the family – nepotism would be an example here. Third, given that each sphere is oriented to a distinct good, each sphere develops its own norms of inquiry and analysis. Norms are always subordinate to the good they seek to protect – different goods give rise to different norms. Thus, each sphere can be identified with its own discipline of inquiry. For art there is aesthetics, for politics there is political science, for the economy there is economics, etc.

To illustrate this last point, take the phenomenon of the American lawn. The Puritans did not find neatly trimmed expanses of grass when they landed on these shores. The lawn is a social phenomenon with a cultural history that can be submitted to different kinds of analysis, each one of which gives us a fuller understanding of what a lawn "means." An *aesthetic analysis* might seek to better understand the peculiar notion of beauty or naturalism that inspires us to lay down yards of mown green grass on the landscape around not only our homes, but our factories, colleges, corporate headquarters, boulevards, municipal buildings, and graveyards. A *socio-political analysis* might concentrate instead on the City Beautiful Movement or the spread of Garden Clubs in the early twentieth century and their expressed desire to promote health and sanitation, civic pride, neighborhood stability and a work ethic among the urban poor through "beautification campaigns" designed to stimulate their desire for lawns and gardens. And an *economic analysis* might uncover the efforts of seed companies, mower manufacturers, and chemical producers to increase the national demand for lawns, or the lobbying of the US Golf Association, a private sector trade organization, for substantial government grants to develop turf-grass hybrids and to promote golfing and a grass aesthetic across the country.[4]

With this in mind, the purpose of this book is to undertake a *theological analysis* of ordinary cultural phenomena, such as the lawn, that will bring to bear concepts and norms that have been honed within the disciplines of theology and religious studies. It is not offered as a line of inquiry that replaces all others, but as a way of inquiring into aspects of these phenomena that the norms and methods of other disciplines, such as aesthetics, political theory, and economics, are not designed to detect. What might a theological analysis of the American lawn discover? It might draw attention to the systole and diastole one finds in the Bible between city and wilderness, with recurring admonitions of the Hebrew prophets for the faithful to return to the wilderness as a place they had once traversed and where they had been closer to God. Or it might draw a connection between the myth of Eden, a place where the footsteps of God could be heard in the cool of the evening breeze, which was not raw wilderness but a cultivated garden, and the blend of nature and horticulture that the modern lawn represents. Or, it might review the long and honored tradition in America of looking to nature for direction and purpose, with various permutations from the Puritans who undertook a divine "errand in the wilderness," to Emerson, Thoreau, and the Boston Transcendentalists who expected to find God more unobstructed in nature than in church, to various more contemporary deep ecologists who seek in the processes of nature a moral teacher and spiritual guide. In light of these more overt religious symbols and aspirations, what does it mean that we surround the lodgings of all our endeavors – our homes, schools, factories, corporate headquarters, government buildings, museums, highways, hospitals, and final resting places with green vegetation that someone has to fertilize and mow?

Again, while this line of inquiry is not meant to replace all others, it is my belief that it, in a literal sense, transcends them. It seeks to go beyond the limits of other inquiries, limits that they properly impose upon themselves (when they behave as they should). I am convinced that it is worthwhile to resume Paul Tillich's efforts to interpret cultural artifacts for the religious substance that rumbles in their deeper regions. As he proposed and argued repeatedly, beginning with his groundbreaking 1919 essay, "On the Idea of a Theology of Culture": while religions depend upon the cultures in which they find themselves for their forms of expression, cultures draw the meaning that they hold for those who inhabit them from an underlying substrate of religious faith. Without this, there is little passion for the culture's achievements and aspirations.

Christian theology is an old discipline which has been used to make sense of human life through twenty centuries and from within virtually every culture in the world today. It is ancient yet still active, experienced on many fronts, capable of learning from grievous transgressions of which it has periodically been guilty (anti-Semitism, *autos-da-fé*, slavery, misogyny, witchhunts) and from other moments in which it has been a historically effective instrument of grace (the rise of the universities, literacy, democratic movements, abolition, women's suffrage, prison reform, civil rights). In certain respects it is a large vessel into which its practitioners – who have been around to observe, learn from, and sometimes instigate all manner of historical experimentation and popular movements – have deposited their accumulated lessons. I view this vessel as a resource of paradigmatic plots, symbols, ideals, visions of good and evil – reference points upon which to draw in trying to make sense of our collective life. Christian theology has certain enduring – although not changeless – conceptions about an ultimate reality in response to which we are to measure our actions, intentions, and aspirations. For this reason, it is a valuable resource for interpreting our cultural life as it is unfolding, and offering commentary and guidance, dissent and endorsement.

One historian, Eugene McCarraher, has recently argued that most of the effective cultural critique in twentieth century America – effective in the sense that it actually precipitated social reform – originated from certain strains of progressive Christian theology (Dorothy Day, John Ryan, H. Richard Niebuhr), and not from their secular counterparts. Their effectiveness can be attributed, he argues, to three things: first, that they really believed in the possibility and imperative of redemption; second, that their critical capacities were informed by norms that had been formed outside the immediate *Sturm und Drang* of the cultural situation; and third, that they were inside members of organized cells of workers, *viz.*, congregations, cells which already had so permeated the society that they could transform class struggle into a historical movement. As a historian applying these lessons to the present, he ventures: in the face of "a brawny and agile capitalism, religion may well become the last refuge of hope for a world beyond the rule of Mammon."[5]

But theology could use some help, and coming to a better understanding of popular culture and its fascinations might assist theology to overcome some of its own prejudices and break through some of its impasses. It is worth noting that a great number of people are finding solace in popular culture, solace they find lacking in organized religion. Theologian Richard Mouw suggests that there is a middle range of concerns for ordinary people (health, financial resources, intimate relationships, loss of loved ones, depression, guilt) toward which "high theology" remains aloof. Consequently, people turn to things like folk religion, the New Age, superstition, belief in angels and demons, which offer an account of and techniques for dealing with these concerns.[6] Trusting that there is a practical wisdom to be found in ordinary people, Mouw advises that it will be worthwhile to examine popular culture for legitimate critique of the shortcomings of theology that have so distanced it from people struggling to believe. He writes, "We must probe the hidden places: looking for the signs of eloquence and grace to be found there; listening for deep calling unto deep; searching, not only for the Deeper Magic, but also for the Deeper Quests, the Deeper Pleasures, the Deeper Hurts, the Deeper Plots."[7]

Theologians in the past have tended to assume, correctly for the most part, that the believers they addressed had a basic working knowledge of the biblical stories, paradigmatic figures in the church, sanctioned ritual actions and symbols, and the essentials of the creeds. We are in a new era now, however, in which, for reasons that will be explored as we proceed, whole generations in the West have had their basic conceptions of the world formed by popular culture. Television, movies, a multitude of genres of music, amusement parks, fast food franchises, action heroes, Dr Seuss, Disney, DreamWorks, comic books, advertising, soundtracks, mail order catalogs, video games, contemporary fiction, sports, celebrities, journalism, wall art and science fiction have been the primary sources of the myths, parables, iconographies, hagiographies, devils and heroes that orient them in life. From this plethora of material whole generations now attempt through *bricolage* to invest life with meaning and find a justification for their lives. The mechanization of production, advances in communications technologies, and increased expendable wealth have made this possible. At least these are the material causes of this cultural development. They have not only made the artifacts of popular culture accessible to us, they have also altered the world of work and the demands of the household in ways that have shifted more of our time from work to leisure. And we spend more and more of our leisure time plugged in to the media-world[8] of popular culture.

This has meant, for many, shifting to a different arena in our search for our identities as human beings. As rock critic Simon Frith has suggested, it is in our leisure activities that we find our "pathways" through life, more so now than through our "paid employment." We find in pop music and other storytelling media the narratives about life that are most convincing to us, that best make sense of our lives, and we are persuaded that they express our "most deep-seated ethical views."[9]

The media-world has, in this sense, become a new cultural sphere with its own distinctive good and guiding norms, its own protective institutions, its own creeds, laws, monuments, prophets, myths and rituals, and discipline of inquiry (culture studies). We are coming to inhabit this sphere with as much comfort and conviction as we have inhabited the spheres of science, art, family, economy, and politics in the past. It is telling that when all of our obligations (to the other spheres) are met, when we can freely choose what we want to do – at the end of the day, at the end of the week, during holidays and vacations – the vast majority of us, at least in the US, choose to enter the media-world. In the words of the advertising motto for Play Station video games: "Live in your world, play in ours."

And we are finding more excuses to reduce our other obligations in order to spend even more time immersed in it.

What has been said so far is not intended to be a harangue, but rather a quick justification for what lies ahead in this book, and for why a theologian might venture into this territory, and why it is worthwhile to undertake a theological analysis of popular culture. Souvenir postcards, landmark architecture, Kentucky bluegrass – these and other cultural artifacts, properly interrogated, might divulge to us something about the ultimate yearnings of our culture. That's what this book is about.

Reading the Signs of the Times

The Second Vatican Council tract, *Gaudium et Spes*, among the more significant documents to emerge from the Council, was organized around the proposal that "At all times the Church carries the responsibility of reading the signs of the time and of interpreting them in the light of the Gospel, if it is to carry out its task." This trope, "reading the signs of the time," is an allusion to Matthew 16.3, in which Jesus criticizes religious leaders who can interpret the skies for tomorrow's weather, but cannot grasp the work of God in what is going on around them. The writers of *Gaudium et Spes*, in drawing on this trope, remind their readers that theological reflection which seeks to understand the ways of God must begin with an informed effort to ascertain the historical forces, convictions and hopes that are in play at a particular cultural moment. The paragraph goes on, "We must be aware of and understand the aspirations, the yearnings, and the often dramatic features of the world in which we live."[10] This admonition has become a standard feature of Catholic "social teachings," with every papal encyclical beginning with reflections on some fresh cultural development. Such signs are to be approached as registers of God's presence in the world, where God continues to be revealed.

This trope also echoes a question posed by the disciples to Jesus as he was issuing his apocalyptic warnings near the end of his life. "Tell us," they asked, "what will be the sign of your coming and of the end of the age?" (Mt. 24.3). What signs will alert us, in other words, to anticipate that a new order is at hand. Jesus went on to describe to them a bleak scenario of wars, famines, earthquakes, and widespread lawlessness. Great upheavals precede the unveiling of a new order, his message seemed to be. With this, Jesus gave us one of the most enduring plotlines of Western history, internalized in our consciousness and rehearsed in probably every generation since to make sense of the tumult that never really desists for long. The belief that the tumult of our present moment in modernity is foreshadowing a new order is a pervasive theme in our culture, inside and outside of the church, a preoccupation of sufficiently pressing importance that we have come to refer to our times as *postmodern.* This is a "sign" worth noting.

Antinomianism and Anarchy

In 1975, Robert Bellah, after reflecting on the cultural experimentation of the 1960s' counterculture, made the comment, "A period of great social change always produces a certain amount of antinomianism and anarchism."[11] Antinomianism is a rich term in Christian theology, referring to Gnostic sects in the early centuries of the church, some of them loosely Christian, who believed that spirit and matter were so opposed to each other that what one did with one's body was of no consequence to the condition of one's soul. This led to excesses of bacchanalian proportions among some sects. It found a justification in the Pauline view that because we are saved by God's gracious action on our behalf, we are freed from a strict observation of the law – a conclusion to which Paul strenuously objected. Anarchism is the belief that external laws and moral codes ought to be overthrown in order to allow people to govern themselves by their own best judgment.

Bellah's observation is a trenchant one, given that both antinomianism and anarchism have their advocates today, as much of the material that will be examined in the pages ahead will testify. Consumerism is a form of antinomianism, the therapeutic as a mode of life is anarchistic, and both antinomianism and anarchism travel well with the individualism that characterizes our time. If he is right that these two creeds are harbingers of "great social change," then we are right to be on the look out for what is next.

A similar account of what distinguishes our time is found in those who draw attention to our loss of faith. Not the loss of faith in God, or in transcendent reality – that loss was already sustained in the early twentieth century, as reported in advance by Nietzsche – but a second-stage loss of faith in the very things that compensated us for our loss of God. According to this view, our time is suffering from a loss of faith in progress, the great promise of the Enlightenment. Moreover, there has been a loss of faith in the capacity of modernity to provide our lives with a sense of meaning, whether through science, art, democratic institutions, or modern master narratives of global harmony. And most recently, there is a gathering disillusionment with the promises of material consumption, with the ideology of consumerism itself. This disillusionment has been deferred longer than Marx anticipated, due to the genius of marketers who learned how to harness the power of commodity fetishism and to insert brands into the sockets of our lives that were once filled with religious symbols and icons.

But there are multiple signs that our faith in the life-giving powers of commodities and even of the semiotic mythologies of brands and logos – the ethereal world that invests commodities with their meaning – is giving out, and that we are no longer satisfied by the compensation they offer. Take, for instance, the phenomenon of brands that have had virtually no marketing becoming the "underground darlings" of subcultures (like bike messengers and snowboarders) – subcultures whose strategy is not to avoid consumption, but to consume "square" and unknown brands as a form of protest. Recent beneficiaries of this loyalty to non-brands have been Doc Martens footwear, Pabst Blue Ribbon Beer, and Toyota's new and unadvertised Scion line of cars. These under-marketed brands have been elevated to the status of "fashion accessories" for aspiring anarchists, a way of registering solidarity with a "lifestyle of dissent" that resents the omnipresent brandscaping of our culture.[12] Some view this and other losses of faith in the various promises of modernity as revealing an aporia that will create an occasion for a re-enchantment of the world.[13] Others simply mark it as a feature of the malaise of the present that we must find a way beyond.

A poignant instance of this backlash is the 1999 film, *FightClub*.[14] *FightClub*, based on a novel of the same name by Chuck Palahniuk, is a parable about the life-sapping grip of commodities and brands on our identities. It is built around a character named Jack who works for an automobile maker as a recall coordinator who flies around the country investigating gory car wrecks in order to determine whether mechanical failure was at fault, and, if so, to calculate, on behalf of his employer, the expense of initiating recalls versus the anticipated costs of out-of-court settlements. This macabre line of work has distanced him somewhat from his feelings. Jack (Edward Norton) is in his early thirties, calm, likable, but a bit bland, without friends or family. He lives in a stylish high-rise condo outfitted entirely with designer-name furniture, kitchenware, and wardrobe that he has acquired from mail order catalogs. Suffering from insomnia and a vague longing for something to matter in his life, he seeks solace in support groups for a variety of ailments he does not have. Then one night, returning from the airport, he discovers his condo has been blown-up, and out of the blue he calls a soap salesman he had just met on the plane, a character named Tyler (Brad Pitt) who is half Good Samaritan, half sociopath.

Tyler invites Jack to meet him at a nearby bar, and over beers Jack tries to size up his loss:

> *Jack*: I don't know, it's just that when you buy furniture you tell yourself, "That's it, that's the last sofa I'm going to need. Whatever else happens,

I've got that sofa problem handled." I had it all. I had a stereo that was very decent, a wardrobe that was getting very respectable. It was close to being complete.

Tyler: Shit, man, now it's all gone.

Jack: All gone.

Tyler: All gone. Do you know what a duvet is?

Jack: It's a comforter.

Tyler: It's a blanket. Just a blanket. Now why do guys like you and I know what a duvet is? Is this essential to our survival, in the hunter-gatherer sense of the word? No. What are we then?

Jack: Consumers...

Tyler: Right, consumers. We are by-products of a lifestyle obsession. Murder, crime, poverty – these things don't concern me. What concerns me are celebrity magazines, television with 500 channels, some guy's name on my underwear. Rogaine, Viagra, Olestra...

Jack: Martha Stewart.

Tyler: F – k Martha Stewart. Martha's just polishing the brass on the Titanic. It's all goin' down, man. . . . But that's me, I could be wrong, maybe it's a terrible tragedy.

Jack: Naw, it's just stuff. It's not a tragedy.

Tyler: Well, you did lose a lot of versatile solutions for modern living. . . . Look, things you own end up owning you.

Thus begins Jack's apprenticeship to an ad hoc twelve-step program that Tyler devises to free Jack from his bondage to the dominant paradigm of consumerism. It involves Jack in making a lot of bad choices, and escalates to "Project Mayhem," a guerilla war on corporate America with missions ranging from bashing luxury cars parked on the street with a baseball bat, to "Operation Latté Thunder" (dislodging an elephant-sized bronze sphere from its pedestal above a corporate fountain and aiming it to roll down an embankment to crash through a franchise coffee bar), to the culminating assignment of a coordinated detonation of explosives in the skyscraper headquarters of every credit card company in the US, thereby completely erasing everyone's debt record, and ensuring that "we all go back to zero – total chaos."

This is a movie that has tremendous cachet with Generation Y. It has been compared to *The Graduate* as a work of popular art that speaks of the frustration and resentment that at least a large segment of this generation harbors toward their predecessors for the world they have been handed. The story does not advocate the measures it depicts, but it does intend to be a scathing critique of the ubiquitous branding of our lives. Palahniuk has said that his intention with the book was to offer people "the idea that they could create their own lives outside the existing blueprint for happiness offered by society." And this blueprint that is circulating has the logos of corporate sponsorship limned onto every square inch.

FightClub is a parable about the emptiness of a life full of consumable products. It commends, at least on the surface, a solution replete with aggressive anarchism and antinomianism. We do, it seems, live in a hinge period between eras. The anarchism and antinomianism that Bellah reminds us is to be expected in such a time has proven fruitful for much experimentation in both critiques and overarching visions of what life might mean in the new era we are just entering. Such experimentation tends to be fractal in the sense that it tends to generate clear alternatives that themselves come to impasses, and then new alternatives emerge. The counterculture movement of the 1960s, for instance, which was itself an assertion of freedom against post-war consumerism, has been charged with becoming the very "bourgeois bohemianism"[15] or "therapeutic consumerism"[16] – a freedom to consume whatever one wishes for the lofty ideal of personal fulfillment – that a film like *Fight-Club* protests. Here, Generation Y is openly criticizing the depthlessness of the world they have been handed by the generation who registered its complaint in *The Graduate*. The Hegelian movement of Spirit may be at work here – thesis, antithesis, synthesis. We seem conditioned with each rising generation to subvert the dominant paradigm, but then find some novel way to reconcile our rebellion with the enticements to consume.

Shades of Faith and Broken Faith

M. Night Shyamalan is a filmmaker who uses his craft to openly raise issues of religious faith. In the movie, *Signs* (2002),[17] which he wrote and directed, crop circles are reported to have begun appearing all over the world and rumors are circulating of UFOs hovering in the earth's orbit. When a crop circle appears in the corn field of their family farm, the lead character in the story, Graham Hess – a disillusioned and recently widowed Episcopal priest played by Mel Gibson – is asked by his brother what all of this means. He replies,

> There are only two kinds of people. [The first] see the lights and they see a miracle. They believe there is someone watching out for them and they feel hope. [For the second] everything is chance. They see the lights and their chances are 50/50. Could be bad or good. Deep down they feel whatever happens they are alone. And they feel fear.

The choice, as Hess boils it down for his brother, is between believing that there is an intelligence and purposefulness that underwrites the universe *or* conceding that we are alone in a randomly operating universe where the best we can hope for is a little good luck. As a place to start, this division of two ways that people respond to some anomaly in their experience offers two categories for analyzing overarching visions of the world that are now playing in popular culture.

But for the sake of capturing some important nuances in the prevailing visions of the world at the beginning of the twenty-first century in America, it might be helpful to consider some thicker terms by way of a detour through the work of two religious thinkers who have reflected on the phenomenology of faith: H. Richard Niebuhr and William James.

In his lectures on the nature of faith, published posthumously as *Faith on Earth: An Inquiry into the Structure of Human Faith*, Niebuhr describes a basic fault line to be found within faith. According to Niebuhr, virtually all of us, at least subconsciously, believe that our existence is worthwhile and that the whole world of being is meaningful. He writes, "There is in the background of existence, whether as memory of childhood, or as Platonic recollection of something heard in another existence, or as the echo of an inner voice, the sense of something glorious, splendid, clean and joyous for which this being and all being is intended." But in the normal course of life this fundamental faith is interrupted by "the great disillusionment," whether "in childhood or adolescence or later." A tragic chord is heard, a chord that reverberates through literature, art, and philosophy, which Niebuhr describes as the discovery "that things are not what they seem and that what they are is infinitely sadder, darker and more disappointing than what they appear to be . . ." This, he claims, is a constant in human experience.[18] Each generation finds itself in a web of dissimulations spun by its forebears that its more contrary members must expose. They expose it, then begin to spin their own, and on it goes. For at least the last 40 years, we have become so accustomed to the great schemes and loyalties of our time being exposed as deceptions, or, at least, as "partly fictions," that we have developed a keen sense of irony in the way we regard all cultural conventions and all great causes.[19]

But it is important, Niebuhr insists, to understand that *both* fundamental faith *and* disillusionment do justice to reality. There *is* something "glorious, splendid, clean and joyous for which this being and all being is intended." For Niebuhr, drawing on a central theological symbol, this is a description of our innocent trust in God before the Fall that remains at the edges of our consciousness. But life in this world is post-Fall. We only know lives that have broken trust with the great and mysterious goodness at the center of all things, and generations of broken trust have built up massive defenses against it and diversions from it. Moreover, a profound disillusionment with "that One from which we all proceed" is not entirely unjustified – how, after all, could things have been allowed to become this sad and cruel and wretched? Has not this One who ought to have been loyal *to us* failed us? Our disillusionment stems from an understandable "distrust toward a being which...ought to be loyal, yet is not."[20] Niebuhr goes on to parse our disillusionment into three manifestations of "broken faith."

- *Defiance* – Our broken faith in the Transcendent One gives rise to resentment and hostility. It may be a conscious defiance of God, or of the godless Nature of Things. "If the nature of things is the creation of a transcendent God," Niebuhr writes, "then that God is our enemy, and if it is not then the world itself is our enemy, and must be resisted though the fight may be carried on without personal hatred." In its noblest form, it begins out of a love for humanity, and particularly for the victims of cruelty, on whose behalf it "raises its voice against Omnipotence." Its complaint is raised in "the name of humane feeling or of spiritual values."[21]

- *Fear* – Overwhelmed by our awareness that human power is no match for the forces of reality that take so little regard of us, our broken faith expresses itself by trembling before "the powerful enemy." Niebuhr draws the distinction: "Defiance says, 'I am against God.' Fear says, 'God is against me.'" Such fear typically manifests itself through the terrors of conscience, the awareness of "an angry Otherness in the world which hunts out every secret fault." The terrorized conscience is most ill-at-ease with an unknown Otherness, and so goes to work churning out objects it can picture or conceptualize – "ghosts and wraiths and demons and vindictive deities." Once reified, these enemies are not resisted, but appeased. We bargain, grovel, and honor them in fear.[22]

- *Escape* – Weary of so much metaphysical distrust, broken faith can also move one in the direction of isolating oneself from the aggravation of it all. Here, "the effort is made to put all thought of that Other out of the mind while the self devotes itself to the little struggles and victories of life."[23] Retreating to an imaginary world of penultimate concerns to which we can attach our ultimate loyalties, the "bright gods," as Niebuhr calls them, we can pretend to be at peace. Some who have opted for this mode of broken faith proceed to people their world with "kindly, beneficent powers." Others simply place the sense of transcendent reality out of bounds and become Epicureans who "interpret the world as superficial, without depth or meaning, without foundation or superstructure." Like Epicurus, they seek whatever satisfactions and pleasures can be had from those things that are within reach. The consolation here, Niebuhr suggests, is that "if you are very wise and do not attract its notice [the world] will not hurt you."[24]

I suggest that these three manifestations of broken faith constitute three distinguishable subcategories for ascertaining the meaning of life in the larger category of lost faith. Many current works of popular culture that probe the meaning of existence can be organized into one of these three subcategories.

But there are also nuances within the larger category of faith itself. Just as not all faith*less*ness is the same, not all faith*ful*ness is the same. In his 1901–2 Gifford Lectures, which were subsequently published as the now classic *Varieties of Religious Experience*, the philosopher William James proposed the terms "once-born healthy-minded souls" and "twice-born sick souls" to differentiate between different dispositions among religious believers.

- *Once-born* – The healthy-minded soul is preoccupied with God's kindness and mercy, is impressed with the beauty and harmony of the world which God has made, and takes solace in the conviction that ours is the best of all possible worlds, overseen by the benevolent providence of a loving God. All that happens is for the best. Such souls are not distressed by their own imperfections, nor by the energetic efforts of the sinners around them. Preachers in this camp avoid "magnifying our consciousness of sin," and instead "seem devoted to making little of it."[25] Sin and evil are imperfections that can be overcome. Healthy-minded souls are, as it were, temperamentally predisposed to cheerfulness, and forbid themselves "to linger . . . over the darker aspects of the universe."[26] James refers to those with this type of faith as the "once born" because they embrace the world into which they were born, and persist in their belief that the God who oversees it is trustworthy. James gives as examples of the once-born: Ralph Waldo Emerson, Walt Whitman, and turn-of-the-century liberal Christianity.
- *Twice-born* – The sick soul, on the other hand, is the believer whose faith in the goodness of the world and the kindness of God has stumbled into one of three obstacles: the vanity of our attachment to mortal things which spill through our fingers like grains of sand, the irresistibility of personal sin, or the fear of a hostility of the universe toward our happiness, to the effect that their "original optimism and self-satisfaction get leveled with the dust."[27] The disequilibria this causes is akin to seasickness, a condition in which one contemplates all things with disgust. Sadness, dread, despair, and melancholy overtake the sick soul. But what impressed James was the testimony of

those who, like Leo Tolstoy and John Bunyan, had transcended these dark nights of the soul and, without denying the reality of the causes of their despair, had found a way to reaffirm their faith. James calls those who have undergone such anguish and come out the other side, confident of the goodness of existence and the meaningfulness of life, "the twice-born."[28]

So, under the guidance of James, it is possible to conceive of two subcategories for faith: the *once-born* and the *twice-born*. Add to these the three subcategories of broken faith and we have a useful template for sorting out different overarching visions of the world that are now playing in popular culture. The scripts of many songs, novels, movies, advertisements, television shows and music videos – at least those that purport to comment on what matters in life – enact these variations on the theme of faith.

To return to Niebuhr for a moment, it is worth noting that he views each of the three manifestations of *broken* faith (defiance, fear, and escape) as appearances of the Transcendent in our lives.[29] In fact, these forms of broken faith parallel the very obstacles to faith that James elaborates as necessary way stations *en route* to the sobered faith of the second birth. Niebuhr insists that each one is a response to a preceding trust that has been disturbed. Distrust and disbelief presuppose a previously established trust and belief. A primordial faith in the Power that has thrown us into existence is affirmed in the very disappointment that expresses itself through defiance, fear, and escape. Each kind of brokenness contains a testimony, in other words, to a Reality that is being defied, feared, and escaped. Let us consider each of these subcategories of faith as it is realized in scripts that can be found in popular culture.

Scripts of defiance

The theme of hostile resentment toward God or toward the metaphysical order of things is not hard to spot in popular culture. The classic example of this is Ivan Karamazov in Fyodor Dostoevsky's *The Brothers Karamazov*. After rehearsing a litany of grievances, from the soldiers who amused themselves by "cutting the unborn child from the mother's womb, tossing babies up in the air, and catching them on the points of their bayonets before their mother's eyes," to the savage beating of an old and feeble cart horse, to the jagged disembowelment of a peasant boy by a pack of hounds set upon him by a Russian general, Ivan proclaims: even if there will be ultimate justice, whereby the perpetrators of these crimes are cast into hell and all wrongdoing will be rectified by an avenging God – or made right through the restoration of harmony by a loving God – the suffering of these innocents cannot be undone. No divine scheme of justice can compensate for an earth "soaked from its crust to its center" with human tears shed on behalf of such extravagant cruelty toward innocents. The very idea of such a justice is so perverse, he declares, that he must "respectfully return God the ticket." To accept a world like this is to endorse its misery. This is conscious defiance of God, protesting the nature of things on behalf of the countless victims who have suffered because of it.

This script of defiance, common in the mid-twentieth century, was an understandable response to two world wars. While it was seldom as explicit a rejection of God as Ivan's was, it was a pointed questioning of the worthwhileness of living in an absurd universe that has already been vacated by God. This is seen particularly in the existentialist-tinged novels of Ernest Hemingway, Albert Camus and Joseph Heller, the plays of Jean Paul Sartre and Samuel Beckett, and the films of Alfred Hitchcock and Stanley Kubrick. Hitchcock used the genre of suspense to film a Nietzschean world in which God is dead or missing and the moral universe has lost its bearings. Many of his killers had nothing to gain from their actions – short of the exercise of their liberated genius or the pure sport of pushing on a universe that doesn't push back. More recently, we've seen this defiance carried forward by Woody Allen, whose *Crimes and Misdemeanors* was a brilliant parable about how we are adjusting to the disintegration of the fanciful idea that the universe has a moral order, and also under the banner of postmodern "anti-narrative" fiction, such as that found in films like *Memento* (2000) and *Mulholland Drive* (2001).

Scripts of fear   GOD'S ANGER TOWARD US!

Convinced as it is that the Powers that dominate reality are at best indifferent toward us, and at worst opposed to us, works of popular culture in this vein depict our helplessness in the face of unknown forces – forces both external to us and inside of us. The Gothic is the purest variety of this subcategory of broken faith. Slasher movies, vampire tales, films like *Silence of the Lambs, Kalifornia* and *Natural Born Killers* about the sociopaths among us, the work of Stephen King (who has 250 million books in circulation), a generous portion of music videos and rock star fashion, even comedy films such as *Beetlejuice* and *Edward Scissorhands* by director Tim Burton – terrify us with supernatural foes and, perhaps more interestingly, with the lingering effects of past human transgressions that haunt us with a vengeance. Mary Shelley's *Frankenstein* is the ur-text of this genre. She established the archetype in which some humanly initiated reordering of nature, often done with noble intentions, went awry and circled back upon its creator and any innocents who stood in its way. We can expect punishment for our hubris. This is a versatile idiom, and it is particularly useful for its identification of which specific acts of hubris dominate our collective consciousness at any given time. Apocalyptic novels and movies rise out of this Gothic fear script, warning us of the unforeseen and horrible consequences of our manipulations of atoms, genes, viruses, and the temperature of the atmosphere.

Scripts of escape

There are multiple ways to script escape, some of which provide invaluable lessons in how to live. One is to devote oneself to the immediate concerns of life and to view mundane struggles, achievements, and commitments as the most sacred plane of existence to be had. The novelist John Irving is very skilled at scripting escape, and his blend of tragedy and comedy teaches us that neither sorrow nor happiness are endless, that one will necessarily and inevitably prepare us for the other, and that the wonder of life is to be found in this ebb and flow. Nick Hornby (*About a Boy, High Fidelity*) is also good at this in his own way, inviting highly isolated individuals into the mysteries and deep satisfactions of human community, with all the attendant risks. Both Irving and Hornby are soft Epicureans, however, in that while they sacralize the ordinary, they don't absolutely foreclose on a reality that transcends it.

This is different from a more disciplined Epicurean escape route of *withdrawing* one's demand that life have depth or meaning, and seeking ultimate satisfaction from what is close at hand. The door on depth must first be closed, a bona fide Epicurean maneuver, before one can find grace in the surface of things. Sam Mendes' 1999 movie, *American Beauty*, takes this perspective.[30] This story is narrated by its central character, Lester Burnham (Kevin Spacey), in the minutes after his murder. As his consciousness leaves his body, rises from the scene of the crime, and floats down the suburban streets of his neighborhood, he recounts events of the past year that led to this simultaneous moment of death and awakening. It was a year in which he realized his money-smitten wife, Carolyn, hated him, that his sullen and self-loathing teenage daughter, Jane, was embarrassed by him, and that his employer had concluded he was overpaid and obsolete. He plunged into a yearlong regimen of self-indulgence, chasing down every adolescent fantasy he had deferred in order to lead a respectable life in the suburbs. His conscientious pursuit of each passing desire, the "new me" as he described it, further alienated him from his family but, the story wants to tell us, also served as a kind of catechism for the sudden epiphany he was to experience in the minutes before his neighbor shoots him in the head. Standing in his kitchen he catches sight of a framed photograph of his wife and daughter leaning into him on a spinning teacup ride, taken many years earlier at an amusement park and, as if scales were lifted from his eyes, he is startled at how happy they each look. The picture transfixes him. Sitting down, he rests his elbows on the kitchen table and folds his hands as if in prayer. Then he smiles – a knowing, sated smile – as if he has in this moment understood what it was all about. At this instant of *satori*, his next-door neighbor who has stealthily crept up behind him and raised a revolver to Lester's head, pulls the trigger. The screen goes white, we hear the sound of rushing wind, then we see Lester in his pajamas rising to the sky. In a voice over, he confides:

> They say your entire life flashes in front of your eyes when you die. It's not really your entire life. It's just the moments that stood out. And they're not the ones you'd expect, either . . .
>
> The moments you remember are tiny ones, some you haven't thought of in years, if you've thought of them at all. But in the last second of your life, you remember them with astonishing clarity because they're just so . . . beautiful that they must have been imprinted, on like a cellular level.
>
> For me it was lying on my back at Boy Scout camp, watching falling stars. Or my grandmother's hands, and the way her skin seemed like paper. And the first time I saw my cousin Tony's brand new GTO . . . Carolyn . . .

He pictures his wife sitting across from him in the spinning teacup ride from the photograph, laughing as she spins the wheel.

> And Janie . . .

He sees his daughter when she was seven years-old, dressing as a princess for Halloween and smiling at him.

> I guess I could be pretty pissed off about what happened to me. But it's hard to stay mad, when there's so much beauty in the world. Sometimes I feel like I'm seeing it all at once, and it's too much, my heart fills up like a balloon that's about to burst.

We see Lester now, flying above the clouds and laughing.

> And then I remember to relax, and stop trying to hold on to it, and then it flows through me like rain and I can't feel anything but gratitude for every single moment of my stupid little life.

He is soaring higher and higher.

You have no idea what I'm talking about, I'm sure ... but don't worry ...

He floats out of sight.

You will someday.

The screen fades to black.

The epiphany he has undergone in the instant of his death is the astonishing optical beauty of so many forgotten moments of his "stupid little life." This vision is reinforced as the scene cuts to the final appearance of a white plastic bag wafting and falling in a gentle, swirling breeze, captured on video. This shot has appeared at intervals throughout the movie. We receive the instruction at its first appearance that it represents a beauty so stunning that it suspends all fear. Like a visual Greek chorus, the dancing bag coaxes us to pause over the ineffable wonder of such mundane beauty, whereby the image of a discarded grocery sack, swirling fairy-like, can take away all fears, even the fear of death. *American Beauty* directs us to invest much in beauty, a beauty captureable in photographs and on video, a beauty of surfaces. To derive happiness from ready-to-hand aesthetic delight is the "bright god" that Mendes offers. No need to be perturbed further with the meaning of life, nor to impose duties or disciplines upon oneself to acquire a deeper wisdom. Be content with modest aesthetic pleasures and the world will not hurt you. Even if you are shot in the head by a deranged neighbor in your own kitchen.

A final direction to push within this subcategory of escape is the impulse to project "kindly and beneficent powers" into one's world, lesser gods who exist to make our lives come out right. These may be angels (*Touched by an Angel*), the recently departed (Alice Sebold's *The Lovely Bones*), the fool (*Sling Blade, The Green Mile*), cyber-technologies (the omniscient Internet, the omnipresent wireless network), space aliens (*ET*), superheroes, Mayan deities (*Chocolat*), product brands and totems (Levis, Ronald MacDonald, the Jolly Green Giant), dumb luck (*Forrest Gump*), or even the simple power of romantic love, which can overcome all obstacles (country-western music).

Scripts of the once-born

According to James, the healthy-minded soul trusts in divine providence and, while not ignoring the sin and evil in the world, trusts sufficiently in the benevolent intent of providence to not be intimidated by them.

Figure 1   Angels Damiel and Cassiel briefing each other on the captivating behavior of the citizens of Berlin in Wim Wenders 1987 film, *Wings of Desire* (used with the kind permission of Reverse Angle Library, GmbH, all rights reserved).

A common religious and literary symbol for divine providence is angels. In the past decade we have seen an explosion of interest in angels, and ample media outlets providing them. When angels are presented as actively intervening in human affairs, they fit best in the escape script described above. But there are artists who take a more minimalist view of angels – reflecting a more minimalist view of divine providence. One of the most poignant stories told of angels in recent memory is the 1988 Wim Wenders film, *Wings of Desire*.[31] In this film we learn that angels live in our midst (although we cannot see them), and devote their time to watching us, recording in diaries what impresses them – dispatches from the front, as it were. Near the beginning of the movie, two angels, Damiel and Cassiel, are sitting in a convertible in an auto showroom in Berlin, reading to each other from their diaries (Figure 1). Their tone is admiring and curious with respect to the antics of the humans they have observed: A woman who folded her umbrella while it was raining, and let herself get drenched. At the U-Bahn station, instead of announcing the station's name, the conductor suddenly shouted, "Tierra del Fuego." In the hills, an old man read the *Odyssey* to a child and the young listener stopped blinking his eyes. These are the things that delight the angels. Damiel, who is pining to become human himself, confesses,

It's great to live only by the spirit, to testify day by day for eternity only to the spiritual side of people. But sometimes I get fed up with my spiritual existence. Instead of forever hovering above I'd like to feel there's some weight to me, to end my eternity and bind me to earth. At each step, each gust of wind, I'd like to be able to say, "Now, and now and now." And no longer say "since always," and "forever" ... Not that I want to beget a child or plant a tree right away. But it would be quite something to come home after a long day and feed the cat, to have a fever, to have blackened fingers from the newspaper, to be excited not only by the mind, but, at last, by a meal, the curve of a neck, an ear. To lie! through the teeth! To feel your skeleton moving along as you walk. Finally to suspect, instead of forever knowing all. To be able to say, "Ah!" and "Oh!" and "Hey!" instead of "Yes" and "Amen." For once, to be enthused over evil.

This is the confession of the faith of a once-born soul. It has all of the elements of gratitude for the wondrous routines of ordinary life, a trait it shares with broken faith in the escape mode. But here it is a disposition formed out of the deep trust in divine benevolence and the corresponding view that we live in the best of all possible worlds. Its elevation of the ordinary is sacramental – receiving the simple pleasures of gravity, sensuality and the passage of time as tokens of transcendent grace. These words come, after all, from an angel, a self-aware agent of grace – at least of graceful observation. Damiel's seeming endorsement of evil in his last remark is folded into his privileged awareness that the Good will have the final word.

Scripts of the twice-born

The faith of the twice-born is distinguished by its having passed through the dark night of the soul and transcended it to gain what Paul Ricoeur has called a "second-naiveté." This is a faith sobered by the awful grace of God, the faith of many saints – perhaps the primary requirement of sainthood, although not the only one. This script can be found hidden within the sometimes prurient humor of the movie, *Dogma*, by the young filmmaker Kevin Smith.[32] Like *Wings of Desire, Dogma* is a story about angels, but of the sick-soul type, which requires a shift of locale from Berlin to New Jersey. The movie opens with a cardinal in New Jersey launching a campaign he's named "Catholicism, Wow!" in an effort to freshen up the image of his Church and increase its appeal to a younger crowd. As part of the festivities surrounding the launch of the campaign, he invokes the ancient rite of plenary indulgence, whereby the Church draws on the accumulated merit of the saints to cancel in its entirety the punishment due to sinners to whom it is granted. Cardinal Glick gets the word out through a press conference that all who pass under the arches of the cathedral in Red Bank on the opening day of the campaign will be granted a plenary indulgence.

Meanwhile, we learn that two angels, Loki (Matt Damon) and Bartleby (Ben Affleck), have been whiling away the last 4,000 years in Wisconsin, where they were banished by God following a small act of rebellion in the wake of the destruction of Sodom and Gomorrah. Loki was the very Angel of Death whom God had ordered to open the sluice gates of heaven in the time of Noah and, later, to rain sulfur on Sodom and Gomorrah. Bartleby was a Gregorian Angel, one of the choir of angels, and a trusted friend of Loki. Loki had misgivings about the destruction of Sodom, and quietly raised the question with Bartleby about how it is that a loving God could be so full of wrath. Commiserating with each other, the two got drunk and gave God the finger. As punishment they were banished to Wisconsin, where they were to remain until the end of time itself, when they will be destroyed.

They are resigned to their fate and their tedious life in Wisconsin until they read a press report of the offer of plenary indulgence that has been extended by Cardinal Glick. Finally, a window of opportunity – to flee Wisconsin, escape their pending destruction, and "go home" to the God who rejected them. They board a train bound for New Jersey.

En route, however, they encounter one of Jesus' apostles, Rufus, who has been sent to stop them. What they had not realized is that if they return to heaven it will force a reversal of God's decree on their transgression, which was binding until the end of time. The reversal of any of God's decrees entails a metaphysical paradox that will result in the total negation of the whole of creation. All of existence will unravel in the instant they re-enter heaven. Rufus and his companions throw them off the train, and, reassessing the situation, Loki and Bartleby have the following conversation:

> *Loki*: Look there is more to this than we thought about. That guy said there will be consequences.
>
> *Bartleby*: You know what? My eyes are open. I had an epiphany. In the beginning it was just us and him, angels and God. Ours was designed to be a life of servitude and worship and bowing and scraping and adoration. But he gave [humans] more than he ever gave us. He gave them a choice. They choose to acknowledge God; they choose to ignore him. All this time we've been down here I've felt the absence of the divine presence and it's pained me, as I'm sure it must have pained you. And why? Because of the way he's made us. Had we been given free will we could choose to ignore the pain like they do. But no, we're servants.
>
> *Loki, alarmed at Bartleby's agitation*: Look, all I'm saying here is that maybe one of us could use a nap.
>
> *Bartleby*: Wake up! These humans have besmirched everything he has bestowed upon them. They were given paradise, they threw it away. They were given this planet and they destroyed it. They were favored best among all his endeavors, and some of them don't even believe he exists. And in

spite of it all, he has shown them infinite f – g patience at every turn. What about us? I asked you, once, to lay down the sword because I felt sorry for them. What was the result? Expulsion from paradise. Where was his infinite f – g patience then? It's not right, it's not fair. We paid our debt. Don't you think it's time? Don't you think it's time we went home? And to do that I think we may have to dispatch our would be dispatchers.

The astonishing revelation here is that these two long-suffering angels desire to "go home" at all, to return to bask in the divine presence of the One whose justice they doubt and whose judgment of them had been their undoing. After 4,000 years of stewing on God's wrath and their own rejection, they want back in. Behind the strange empyrean world of the film is the further revelation that Kevin Smith, a filmmaker who turned 30 the year the film was released, appears to agree with them, given the way he directs our sympathies on behalf of these two characters in his telling of the story. The story seems to concur with the idea that even a God whose exercise of justice is faulty is worthy of the longing of creatures who scramble to return to the divine presence. This is different from an earlier generation that, as William James observed, so objected to the image of a wrathful God that they either exorcised this attribute from God's countenance or abandoned their belief in God altogether. Like Tolstoy and Bunyan, Loki and Bartleby have undergone the depths of despair, suffered the dark flank of God, and come out the other side through a second birth. Smith, their creator, displays his own twice-born, sick soul in making use of arcane Catholic rites and symbols to explore a range of theological conundrums – theodicy, divine transcendence and immanence, God's wrath and mercy, human sin and divine forgiveness – conundrums he takes seriously. His use of these arcana suggests that there is still life in them, that their power to interpret our existence has not been exhausted.

Conclusion

Paul Ricoeur has described the present as a "period of mourning for the gods who have died," an intermediate time in which the ancient gods of morality have died of obsolescence and exhaustion. An essential theological task demanded in this period of mourning, he goes on to suggest, is a long recuperative wandering, a detour through the texts of our culture. In this detour we might discern a new way of being-in-the-world in response to a new understanding of divinity.[33] I suggest that the five scripts just assembled (defiance, fear, escape, once-born, twice-born) are the products of some of the most creative minds of our time in

American culture. Within each type assertions are made about where trust ought to be placed or withheld, and about what may be fairly expected of the powers upon which our lives depend. This is a good place to begin in reading the signs of our time, a task that I believe, in good company, theology has a responsibility to undertake.

Aware, however, that a discipline for investigating popular culture already exists and hoping to stand on its shoulders in the investigation that is undertaken in this book, I turn first to examine the field of cultural studies in its various paths.

I

Theories of Popular Culture

1

Popular Culture

Our world is drenched with images. Knick-knacks, plaques, shirts, art prints, tattoos, coffee mugs, wall calendars, newspapers, greeting cards, book covers, magazines, billboards, murals, television, movie and computer screens, comic books, coffee table books, cereal boxes, neckties, scarves, toilet paper, wrapping paper, grocery sacks, and the chipboard, polystyrene and paper that everything we consume comes packaged in – we are swimming in images. How different this is from the world of our European predecessors – at least the vast majority of them who were not members of the privileged classes.[1] In that long window of time between tribal life and the Renaissance, the spaces inhabited by peasants – their huts, barns, taverns – were image free. Art and cultural historians tell us that even folk art was virtually unknown until the recent past. City-dwellers might have seen the occasional stone arch, monument or fountain with relief engravings, but they could not enter the palaces, burial grounds, and assembly halls where the aristocracy displayed the paintings, tapestries and sculptures produced by the guilds and academies of artists. There were no public museums or galleries. Public murals were uncommon, particularly in areas with peasant traffic. Until the invention of woodblock printing in the fifteenth century, which made it possible to reproduce images, the only place where common folk could see visual art was in places of worship. Historian Luc Sante underlines the exuberant significance of this exception:

> The church or temple was not only the most notable piece of architecture around; it also concentrated in a single place all the sculpture, painting, mosaic work, tapestry and metallurgy available to the public eye. Churches and temples were in effect the first museums. Consider, for example, the Gothic cathedral, with its array of side chapels, each containing some combination of statues, paintings, carvings, reredoses, tombs, baptismal fonts and sacristies.[2]

Given the desert of images everywhere else, this exception helped to imbue these worship spaces with an atmosphere of otherworldly resplendence. But this was it, the single place where images could be viewed, and solidly associated with the idea of worship. It was only with woodblock printing that images became more plentiful and portable so that they began appearing outside of the sanctuary, most typically in the form of illustrated broadsheets depicting scenes from the Bible, or propagandistic pamphlets containing early cartoons etched by leading artists of the day (Cranach, Dürer, Holbein) and displaying the turpitude of the clergy and nobility. This was very likely the birth of mass media in the West, as Jacques Barzun has observed.[3] But the real ascendance of imagery came in the eighteenth century with two developments: the turning over of royal art collections to the public in the political revolutions across Europe and the invention of offset lithography which made it possible to reproduce more images at low cost and with greater precision. In time, photography and color lithography were developed, and the floodgates opened – from inspirational pictures of saints and newspaper photography, to nationally circulated magazines, advertising, greeting cards, coffee table books, family photo galleries, art prints, celebrity posters and wallpaper. Images inundated the homes, workplaces and retail spaces of the masses.

The Popular

In 1936, Walter Benjamin wrote a seminal essay reflecting on the impact that the new technologies of mechanical reproduction (lithography, photography, sound recording, movies) were having on Western culture.[4] What distinguished a work of art before these technologies was its "aura," the sacred, one-of-a-kind quality that inheres in a painting like the *Mona Lisa* or the live performance of a Beethoven symphony. The genius and originality of *this* paint on *this* piece of canvas hanging on *this* wall in *this* city, the unrepeatable inflection reverberating on *these* strings in *this* concert hall – demand a kind of reverence to which we intuitively assent. Benjamin speculated that we extend this recognition out of a cultural memory of the fact that the earliest works of art originated as rituals in the service of religion, as means by which our ancestors made the gods present in icons, told their stories through drama, and worshipped them through music. With the Renaissance, artists began gaining autonomy from religion, but the residual sense of reverence for cultic works of art persisted, reattaching itself to "the secular cult of beauty" – now no longer reflecting divine powers, but instead the archetypal form of beauty-itself, which sustained the sense of aura associated now with any work of art. The authority that had derived from the sacred realities depicted in art was transferred to the genius of the artist herself, who still conveys transcendent knowledge through the work of art, but of a different sort.

With the advent of mechanical reproducibility, Benjamin continued, the aura of the individual work of art is shriveling. When the same image or sound can be multiplied endlessly, the uniqueness of the original, its mystical power and the ordeal undergone to come into its presence, disappears. The authenticity of art gives way to the commodification of art, readily accessible through the conduit of technology. Like the pipes and wires that bring water, gas, and electricity into our homes at the flip of a switch, these reproduction technologies deliver visual and auditory images with ease. Instead of undergoing an ordeal to reach and contemplate a work of art, a sea of art washes over us.

Benjamin then made the interesting move of refusing to lament this development. The proliferation of art – its being liberated from museums, cathedrals, and mansions and taken out into the streets – will have two positive effects, he predicted in 1936: it will make art connoisseurs out of a broader public, equipping them with the potentially revolutionary habits of criticism, and it will alter the objectives of the artists, who will seize this opportunity to use art as a medium to mobilize the masses for political (i.e., Marxist) reform. Both consumer and producer will be transformed. And film, he concluded, the very artistic medium that had to await the invention of reproduction techniques, will be the most emancipatory art form of all.

In the subtle argument of this landmark essay, Benjamin was offering a critique of the highbrow/lowbrow distinction of aesthetic taste that was common among his colleagues in the Frankfurt School in the 1930s. There is some irony in the elitism that is found among this Marxist-oriented school of culture criticism. While new forms of popular art were not produced by the proletariat (popular art is not folk art), popular art was having some genuine leveling effects on society. Commercial forms of entertainment like amusement parks and World Fairs, phonograph records, radio and film were blurring the boundaries between upper and lower class leisure, creating occasions for people of different walks of life to be thrown in together to consume entertainments that had broad appeal. As a nascent phenomenon in America it wasn't foremost in Benjamin's thinking, but there was a populist movement underway in the US in the 1930s (an echo of the populist revolt of the 1880s) that was being supplied with salvaged mythological material coming from the story boards of a film studio in Hollywood.[5] Throughout the 1930s, Walt Disney Studios churned out a steady stream of animated short films with strong egalitarian messages and social satire, manufacturing some of the most enduring folk heroes in the mythology of American culture. Mickey Mouse was the quintessence of "the little guy" who struggled against ferocious odds and through pluck and an underlying sense of fairness triumphed over whatever forces were arrayed against him (cats, autocratic boat captains, corrupt sheriffs). This established a David and Goliath theme that was one of Disney's trademarks, evoked through a series of transmutations through the 1930s, including Donald Duck, Snow White, Pinocchio, Dumbo, Bambi, and numerous characters in the *Silly Symphony* series – the Ugly Duckling, Tortoise and the Hare, the Country Cousin, the Grasshopper and the Ants, and the Three Little Pigs. Aimed at all ages of theatergoers, these animated features and shorts were enormously popular, and Disney was the recipient of 13 Oscars between 1932 and 1941.

This was the period of the Great Depression, and a ready explanation offered by some of a more Marxist-tilt was that these simple stories of plain folk conquering formidable adversaries provided the pacifying reassurance that the meek shall inherit the earth. This message, delivered via such a mesmerizing vehicle of entertainment as moving pictures in Technicolor and high-fidelity sound, served as the opiate *de jour*. The leitmotif of these little stories was that if you work hard (on the farm or in the factory), exercise self-discipline and moral virtue, and if you can celebrate ordinary satisfactions as your reward, your current hardships will surrender to a happy ending. In the refrain of the 1941 smash hit *Dumbo*, "Persevere! Don't give up!"[6] In this analysis, Disney offered pure escapism to the masses, reinforced their false-consciousness, and did its part to divert American society away from class revolution.

However, a different analysis is possible. If Disney's cartoons were reinvigorating an atrophied memory of the David and Goliath story, as well as forgotten assurances of the Beatitudes, he was drilling into a deep layer of biblical advocacy on behalf of the victims of political oppression and tyranny. He accomplished this by casting folktale characters in the crucial roles – plodding tortoises, lithe fairies, diligent ants, elves, dwarves, wise old trees, talking crickets, flying elephants – in effect, repopulating the disenchanted world of modernity with otherworldly avatars of a proven message of resistance to oppression. While Disney was not the sort of avant-garde filmmaker that Benjamin had in mind, it is possible that the masses were mobilized sufficiently by culture producers like Disney to demand the sort of social reconstruction that was initiated through Franklin Roosevelt's New Deal. It is possible to see this decade of Disney's work as providing stories and characters that were used by a cross-section of Americans to interpret their lives in ways that restored their dignity and empowered them to demand at least incremental justice. There were elements of social critique in this body of work from the 1930s that would lend themselves to a moderate subversiveness for anyone who soaked them in. The *Silly Symphony* short, *Three Little Pigs*, released in 1933, became a cultural phenomenon in economically depressed America. With so many in the country losing their homes to bankers and dust storms, this little fable about a voracious wolf depriving rural farmers and craftsmen of their homes struck a chord. In the end it was by taking in the weak, hard work, the denial of self-indulgence and collective resistance that the big, bad wolf was defeated. Many theater operators reported that the cartoon was a bigger draw than the feature movie it preceded, and its theme song, "Who's Afraid of the Big, Bad Wolf?" became a hit song on the radio and a best-selling piece of sheet music.[7]

Disney was fluent in the ideas common to populism, such as the pitting of rural values and an agrarian way of life against urban industrialism, the innate goodness, wisdom and dignity of plain folk, the importance of hard work, the sanctity of the family, and the communitarian sense of civic obligation, which are found in abundance in these films. They contain a strong undercurrent of resentment toward the "survival of the fittest" ethos that dominated the US economy at the time, and a corresponding assurance that the viciousness of the powerful ultimately exhausts itself if its victims refuse to acquiesce. The socialist activist and cultural historian, C.L.R. James, compared Donald Duck to Charlie Chaplin in *Modern Times*, for his "perpetual exasperation with the never-ending irritations of modern life" – its authoritarianism, inhumane technology, alienating bureaucracies and insults to human dignity – to which Donald responds with anger and acts of sabotage. In the view of James, Donald Duck came across as a model liberator.[8]

Another feature of Disney's populism that has had a lasting impact on the aesthetics of popular culture was his mission to bring "high art" to the people. This was the driving force behind *Fantasia*, the 1941 masterpiece that blended classical music and animated shorts that was produced by Disney in collaboration with the highly acclaimed conductor of the Philadelphia Orchestra, Leopold Stokowski. Disney structured *Fantasia* like a formal symphony concert, including the gathering of the musicians, tuning the instruments, and inserting an intermission. Stokowski was the on-screen and actual conductor of the 100-piece studio orchestra, and a prominent musicologist at the time, Deems Taylor, served as the narrator, providing the audience with bits of biographical, aesthetic, and musicological clues to educate them as listeners to classical music. Disney set out to bring not only the high art of orchestral music to the people (Tchaikovsky, Stravinsky, Beethoven, Moussorgsky, Schubert), but also the reigning form of visual arts – abstract expressionism. The first piece in the film is Bach's "Toccata and Fugue in D Minor," which is accompanied by a mix of abstract and lightly representational images cavorting across the screen – violin bows and reverberating harp strings, starbursts, geometric shapes, hieroglyphs, and sizzling jet streams, reminiscent of the paintings of Kandinsky and Joan Miro. In its interpretation of other pieces, the film evoked images and narrative elements from Greek, Russian, and Celtic mythology, European fairytales, medieval Christian ritual procession, and even an epic visual telling of the modern cosmogonic myth of the fiery origin of the earth and its evolutionary generation of the dinosaurs. In its effort to enable its audience to *see* the music and *hear* the pictures, *Fantasia* produced a hybrid of high and low art forms.[9]

But the groundwork had been laid for this earlier in the *Silly Symphonies* series. Feeling confined by the Mickey Mouse formula, Disney and his associates had introduced *Silly Symphonies* in 1929 with *The Skeleton Dance*, an eerie tarantella of the dead with black cats, spiders and bats scattering at midnight as skeletons rose from their churchyard graves and jitterbugged each other's bones into tidy stacks, set to music reminiscent of Edvard Grieg's "March of the Dwarves." The *Silly Symphony* concept was to develop animated shorts that were designed primarily to illustrate music, both classical and jazz. There would be no recurring characters to constrain the generation of new ideas, and the animators were encouraged to use the series as a forum to experiment with new techniques in animation and film production, such as Technicolor – the first three-tone Technicolor film out of Hollywood was a 1932 *Silly Symphony, Flowers and Trees*. The series coheres as various shorts blending comforting images of nature and rural life and traditional fables and other simple narrative plots with arrangements of classical music lifted from Mendelssohn, Wagner, Schubert, etc. It was here that Disney first hit upon the use of the low culture medium of animation to introduce his movie theater audience to classical music. In the visual solace of pastoral scenery, accompanied by the reassurance of traditional folktales (with a populist twist), and in the plebeian comfort of the movie theater, the highbrow music of Europe's great composers was not as intimidating as it would be in the hushed reverence of a Carnegie Hall concert. In time, the series matured to include the use of jazz as well, as is found in *Woodland Café*, a Harlem Cotton Club for the insect world, where ants, beetles, spiders and snails jitterbug to the music of Fats Waller performed by thick-lipped grasshoppers in tuxedos playing trumpets fashioned from honeysuckle blossoms and drums made of acorns.

This blending of high and low cultures was raised to the level of social commentary in the 1935 short *Music Land*. The story opens with a map of two islands, the Land of Symphony and the Isle of Jazz, separated by the Sea of Discord. As the camera zooms toward the Land of Symphony, it passes through the gates of an elegant palace situated in the center of spacious formal gardens and into a great hall where living harps, violins, and flutes are playing a delicate minuet and waltzing before the throne of the queen and the princess, each with shapely violin bodies. The queen is asleep and the princess is obviously bored and distracted, and sneaks off to a balcony to gaze over the Sea of Discord toward the Isle of Jazz. Over on the Isle of Jazz, which has the appearance of early twentieth century Coney Island, a pile of buildings built entirely of brass instruments is pulsating with jiving jazz. Inside the drum-shaped dance hall the king and his son, both with saxophone bodies, are entertained by swinging trumpets, French horns, tenor saxophones, saws, ukuleles, tambourines, and ragtime pianos banging away in syncopated rhythm. While the king thumps his drums, the prince slips away to a balcony overlooking the Land of Symphony. Catching sight of the violin princess as she signals to him with her handkerchief, he leaps to the dock, boards his xylophone raft, and paddles with his musical note-shaped oar across the Sea of Discord to rendezvous with his forbidden lover. Once ashore the Land of Symphony, he is caught by the queen who has her soldiers imprison him in a giant metronome. When word of this reaches his father, the Isle of Jazz launches a blitzkrieg of free-form jazz, firing red-hot musical notes out of trombone canons. The pipe organs on the Land of Symphony retaliate with a barrage of Wagner's "Flight of the Valkyries." The princess attempts to cross the ocean in her violin dingy to surrender, is struck by musical ordinance, sinks, is rescued by the prince, whose xylophone raft is then pierced by falling debris, the battle is halted, the queen of Symphony and the king of Jazz motor out to their drowning children, look each other in the eye, and fall in love themselves. A double wedding follows, the wedding of the queen of classical music and the king of jazz and their two children, and as Mendelssohn's "Wedding March" plays in a lovely arrangement of violins, a jazzy horn section gracefully rises and merges with the strings, while the camera shows us that a stone bridge has been erected between the two islands, across the Sea of Discord, and engraved with the words, "Bridge of Harmony."

This synthesis of lowbrow and highbrow cultural materials was so quintessentially Disney that any rendering of high culture into accessible forms of popular entertainment has come to be described as "Disneyization." Merchandising of this hybrid aesthetic soon followed, adding an additional layer of meaning we generally associate with Disney's name. Merchandising of this hybrid aesthetic has come to be a very thick layer of contemporary popular culture, indeed. Paging through several museum shop catalogs turns up the following sample: a pillow sham silk screened with Leonardo da Vinci's *Mona Lisa*, a wrist watch based on a Frank Lloyd Wright window, a necktie imprinted with a variation of one of Kandinsky's *Composition* masterpieces, a four-foot wooden totem pole "inspired by" the art of the Tlingit Indians of British Columbia, a hieroglyphics tea towel, and a Chagall wall calendar. The 1997 feature, *Bean: The Movie*, in which the actor Rowan Atkinson brings his Mr Bean character from British television to the big screen playing an inept museum guard who is mistaken for an eccentric art critic, builds its storyline around the merchandising of the painting, Whistler's *Mother*, which is on exhibit at a Los Angeles art museum. The cups and towels and figurines in the image of the dour woman in the rocking chair generate more of a sensation than the painting itself. While the original painting is displayed to accentuate its Benjaminian "aura," these facsimiles are what engross the stampeding crowds of art connoisseurs.

And then there is the great reservoir of high culture icons that have become vernacular images – "visual quotations and aural images," in the expression of cultural historian Thomas Hine, who argues that certain *visual* images like Edvard Munch's *The Scream*, Whistler's *Mother*, Stonehenge, the planet earth floating in space, Ansel Adams's photographs of Yosemite Valley, the fingers of God and Adam touching on the ceiling of the Sistine Chapel, the Eiffel Tower, the tilting Titanic, the Manhattan skyline, filmmaker John Ford's Monument Valley scenery, Einstein, Che Guevara, the lone protester stopping the tank in Tiananmen Square, the collapsing World Trade towers, and certain *aural* "images" like Beethoven's Fifty Symphony, the Shaker hymn "Simple Gifts," Chopin's *Funeral March*, "Amazing Grace," Rossini's *William Tell Overture*, and the eerie staccato theme song of *The Twilight Zone* – are widely recognized. And over time, as they are imitated, reproduced, repackaged and adapted, again and again, each of these fragments of art, music, cinema and news footage accumulates a thicker profile of semiotically loaded meanings. Visual quotations and aural images become one of the most exercised languages of popular culture, traversing the spectrum from high art to consumable merchandise, and back again. In this historically novel, but now widely practiced manner, Hine argues, "high" Western culture is far from dead. "Quite the contrary," he claims, "we're swimming in it."[10]

As Hine points out, human beings have always imitated the images, sounds, and gestures – the meaning-rich symbols – that were available to them. Mimesis of the symbolic material around one is fundamental to communication and self-expression. What has changed is the sheer number of the symbols and their range. In an earlier age – before the boom in the machinery of reproduction and broadcasting – the symbols available to one for imitation would have been produced by a relatively local community, reflecting its historically acquired traditions and ways of knowing. One would imitate, absorb, and build one's world around the words, images, sounds, and gestures of one's family, neighbors, and local figures and institutions. The invention of the printing press was the first serious breach in this highly localized sphere of mimetic communication of our ancestors. Printing presses made it possible to reproduce texts and images – and the symbolic worlds they reflected – in large numbers and to deliver them across multiple communities. The production and circulation of books and newspapers were tremendously important in the eighteenth and nineteenth centuries for creating the national cultures that ultimately made modern nation-states feel like natural and obvious ways of organizing ourselves. The empathy that extends naturally to family and local community opened out to a larger domain when the printed word spoke of the achievements, hardships, and thoughts of more far-flung neighbors – and the fresher the news, the more immediate the effect. Alexis de Tocqueville, who visited the US from France in the 1830s, in puzzling over the proliferation of newspapers here, concluded that newspapers persuade individuals that their private interests are enmeshed with the common interest, and encourage people to become involved in common actions with strangers they will never meet. "Only a newspaper," he wrote, "can put the same thought at the same time before a thousand readers." For this reason, he decided, newspapers are necessary for maintaining the kind of small associations that hold American democracy together, and ultimately, for the maintenance of civilized life itself.[11] Without them, free citizens are more inclined to devolve into a war of all against all.

Still, the impact of print had its limits. Economic conditions, shipping difficulties, literacy rates, national boundaries and language barriers pinched the circulation of the print media. With respect to the flood of words, images, sounds, and gestures that now freely cross every cultural boundary to wash over us every day, the invention and refinement of telecommunications technology has been a quantum leap beyond the printed page. Telephones, radio, television, the cinema, videocassettes, video games, compact disks, fax machines, computers, the Internet, cable, satellite, broadband and digital technologies, along with newspapers, magazines, catalogues, and books, are essentially instruments we have for throwing words, images, sounds and gestures – meaning-bearing symbols – to one another from a distance and at great speed, crossing all traditional boundaries that once prevented, slowed, or regulated such traffic.

Taken together, these instruments of delivery are what is meant by the term "media." But the media are not neutral instruments; they are not simple pipelines that deliver symbols produced elsewhere in the traditional spheres of culture (art, science, state, market, family, etc.), serving their ends. The rapid expansion of media technologies has raised media to the level of being a cultural sphere itself – a media-world – complete with its own central organizing good and all the supporting symbols, rituals, codes, secondary goods and institutions that are necessary to maintain and promote it. The media-world is more than a messenger. The media, in Marshall McLuhan's well-known phrase, is the message. Yes, the media-world delivers the goods of other spheres, but only when doing so corresponds with serving its own ends. And that inevitably means modifying whatever other goods it handles.

A simple example of this was the appearance of the 3-minute hit song in the 1950s, a formula that was necessitated by the physical limitations of the 45 RPM record disks that juke boxes required and had become the recording industry standard. Everything a song was meant to accomplish had to be pulled off before the stylus hit the hub of the platter. It is hard for love or war or death or whatever other experience the lyrics set forth to be probed very deeply in 3 minutes.

A more damaging example is found in the heavy hand that television has had on the information that it mediates. It has accentuated the horse race aspect of politics to the point where there is little else left. Practically every election and every policy deliberation is outfitted by the evening news as a contest between self-serving egoists who keep their eye on the camera, special interests, and the next election. Substantive social visions are set out of view. In her telling study of news coverage of the 1968 and 1988 presidential elections, sociologist Kiku Adatto discovered that in 1968 the average television sound bite from a candidate was 42.5 seconds; in 1988 it was only 9.8 seconds.[12] Three tendencies inherent in television contributed to this evaporation of substance. First, the image takes precedent over the word. Second, television thrives on spectacle because spectacle holds viewers – so a tedious policy debate gets juiced up into a clash of the titans. Third, news divisions work with a finite number of plotlines in reporting on politics, and the athletic race is one of them. Some scripted plot must be imposed upon much messier real life in order to fit the report into the minute or two that is assigned to it.

Another effect of television is how it flattens out the momentous and the trivial. In one weekend of television viewing, one can see more drama, human tragedy, comedy, feats of spectacular achievement, and sexual escapades than most of our ancestors would have seen in a year or even in their lifetimes. And these highs and lows flow out of the set in a steady stream, interrupted only by ad pitches to buy the sponsors' products. The flow itself, Bill McKibben points out in *The Age of Missing Information*, his rich little book on how television narrows our picture of the world, "means that if something exceptional happens it hardly matters – it is quickly forgotten, averaged out, eroded by this ceaseless flood."[13]

What is unsettling about these effects of television is that their distorted representations of reality are so pervasive that reality becomes these representations. As the British moral philosopher, Iris Murdoch, has suggested, "Man is a creature who makes pictures of himself and then comes to resemble the picture."[14] Politicians *become* racehorses, and politics comes to attract individuals who value winning more than they do any particular social vision. And, too much television viewing *does* numb our capacity to feel joy and grief, and can be correlated to diminished participation in the life of our communities.[15]

The very capacity of the combined technologies of the media to store and basically never lose a text, image, or sound that has been entrusted to them has remade our world into a cacophonous place that will never again have the built-in coherencies our forebears experienced. The *bricolage* that postmodernism celebrates as the "little bit from here, little bit from there" process through which we now grab and assign meaning to the world and improvise in an ad hoc manner our own deepest identities has become a possibility only because of the new media. This has far-reaching repercussions on the way our imaginations work in each of the other cultural spheres. It alters our consciousness and cognitive processes, much the way these were altered in an earlier era when Western societies were transformed from oral to print cultures.

As Peter Horsfield has described this, the media form the matrix "where most people now get most of their insight, influence, values, and meaning." A power shift has occurred, and now instead of various social institutions using the media to convey *their own* "reality," they "are placed by the media on the web of culture in different positions and for different purposes." We no longer view the media through the lenses of various other social institutions; media are "so pervasive and such an inextricable part of people's lives and culture that we now see all other social collectives (including religious faith) through the lens of our enculturation in media."[16]

In effect, the media have colonized the other spheres of life, and now extract the riches found in them and put those riches into circulation in whatever combinations are most suitable to the media's own processes and the most conducive to achieving its own ends – disseminating information, accelerating communication, finding, creating and enlarging audiences, rendering borrowed ideas and symbols accessible, making its categories and genres the dominant forms with which our minds and imaginations grasp, classify, and interpret reality. The success of media can be measured both by how much knowledge they put within our reach, and the degree to which they become the gatekeepers for us knowing anything.

Douglas Rushkoff has suggested that the term "media" no longer really fits this phenomenon of communications technology. What we are dealing with is bigger and more extensive than media ever were, and he gives it the name "datasphere."[17] At some point in the middle of the twentieth century, he suggests, the technology "got too big and too complex for any one group to control," and the media grew into the datasphere, which is much more autonomous, adaptable and unruly than all preceding media.[18] He describes it as "the circulatory system for today's information, ideas, and images,"[19] and to emphasize his point about how it has come to permeate our lives, he draws attention to the fact that, "The average American home has more media-gathering technology than a state-of-the-art newsroom did ten years ago."[20] Looking back, the 1960's appear to have been the point of no return:

> By the sixties, the media had become a world of its own. Kids could grow up spending more time in the media world than the real world. The datasphere became our new natural environment. ... We compared our own lives to those of Marcia Brady on "The Brady Bunch" or Will Robinson on "Lost in Space." Television characters filled our discussions, our fantasies, even our dreams. Social engagements were structured around television schedules. Our cultural references had more to do with what cartoons we admired than which sport we played or which church we belonged to.[21]

In subsequent years, the datasphere has spread far beyond American society, and "has become our global society's weather system, touching us all with the same (if superficially inane) iconography and spectacles."[22] And it touches us *inside* of our homes, through all the media utilities that carry through screens, speakers, headphones, and the printed page versions of the world that might corroborate our own, or pose serious threats to them. While this sometimes has the positive effect that de Tocqueville praised, broadening the horizon of our private interests to take into account the needs, hardships and achievements of others, it can also have a bewildering, alienating effect. The parade of alternative worlds that the privacy of the home once provided haven from now has around the clock privileges.

Another alteration of our consciousness that can be attributed to the media-world is that it has conditioned us to expect that exposure to the stream of knowledge should be accompanied by pleasure. Visual images, music, skilled narration and plot construction, titillation, humor, style, hipness, quick resolution of ambiguities, action, spectacle, catharsis – we will gravitate toward the sources of knowledge that best perfect these delivery mechanisms, that best entertain us. As film critic Neil Gabler has explained it, "More and more, American life [will] come to resemble entertainment in order to survive."[23] Politicians, economists, preachers, scientists, educators, moral teachers, novelists and journalists all come under the spell, and must modify their message if they hope to have an audience.

Popular/culture is the amalgamation of these delivering media *and* the delivered cultural symbols. The media remold what they *mediate*; they colonize and extract cultural materials that they have not produced. But how are we to understand this encompassing thing called "culture" that supplies them with their materials?

The Culture Concept

The use of the word "culture" to refer to distinctively human ways of being is of relatively recent vintage. The term comes from the Latin, *cultura* and its root, *colere*, which means to till or cultivate the soil, conjuring the image of human labor massaging nature into crops. With this root meaning it has always held great promise as a metaphor for thinking about any conversion of raw nature into a habitable world through the exercise of human labor and attention. The metaphor was reified into a concept during the Enlightenment, when it was first put to good use in the writings of the German theologian, Johann Gottfried Herder in the late eighteenth century. In the 1780s, Herder, who stands in the Romantic branch of the German Enlightenment, wrote a work called *Outlines of a Philosophy of the History of Man*, in which he reflected on the processes through which people assimilate and apply the learnings of their forebears. He suggested calling this process "culture" (*Kultur*), "for it is like the cultivation of the soil," and goes on to claim that the "chain of culture ... stretches to the ends of the earth. Even the natives of California and Tierra del Fuego learned to make and use the bow and arrow; they learned their language and concepts, practices and arts, just as we learn ours." In this sense, they, too, are "cultured."[24]

The difference between cultures, Herder proposed, lies in the workings of divine providence, according to which God has seen fit to appoint to each people a particular kind of happiness, which each people then organizes itself around as a way of life. In this and other essays, Herder develops a second and related concept that later became influential on cultural anthropology (a discipline that did not yet exist): the notion of the *Volkgeist* (folk spirit). According to his notion of the *Volkgeist*, every people has a unique genius with which it pursues, under the influence of its inherited arts, language, folksongs, and religion, as well as the natural climate in which it finds itself, an aspect of "humanity" which providence has entrusted to them to develop. Thus, in surveying human societies around the world, one can expect to see a great variety of experiments in how to be human, and to grant each experiment the respect owed to its having exercised the peculiar genius and mode of happiness assigned to it by God.

> In all the institutions of peoples from China to Rome ... we can recognize
> the main law of nature: Let human beings be human beings! Let them shape
> their situation according to what they hold to be best. ... In all the different
> parts of the earth, marriage, the state, slaves, clothing, houses, recreation,
> food, science, and art have been made into what people thought was best
> for their own or for the general good.[25]

Herder stops short of granting equal validity to all societies, but he does
counsel that goodwill be extended even to those diverse ways of living that
his readers cannot understand. Those cultures that endure over time, he
proposes, have lived responsibly toward God's "holy, eternal laws," and
been genuine "images of God on earth."[26] Cultures are spiritual entities,
each embodying and carrying forward their portion of God's ideas. And
those that have failed have simply suffered their own effects.[27]

Given that the meaning of the term culture is a hotly contested one
in academic circles, both within and between the three disciplines for
which it serves as the central object of study (the humanities, cultural
anthropology, and cultural studies), a brief consideration of these
divisions of opinion is essential. One way of parsing the prevailing theories
is to break them down into three rather clear understandings of culture:

- *Culture as a standard of excellence* – Here culture is viewed as an
  ideal to which individuals and societies ought to aspire. We become
  "cultured" by being exposed to and struggling to understand certain
  touchstones of literature, philosophy, poetry and art, works that represent great achievements of the human spirit, and by internalizing
  the values that have produced them – aesthetic, moral, philosophical and religious values. Familiarity with such luminaries as Plato,
  Virgil, St Thomas, Dante, Michelangelo, Shakespeare, Francis Bacon,
  John Locke, Immanuel Kant, Freud, Tolstoy, Picasso, T.S. Elliot,
  and Martin Heidegger, and training in the arts, cuisines, athlet-
  ics, proper apparel and social manners are the means by which we
  become cultured persons. Each great civilization has a culture, and
  while the canon of artifacts that carry it will be different, it will point
  to the same values and ideals to which the cultures of other great
  civilizations aspire. This approach is associated with the field of studies traditionally referred to as the humanities. While it is sometimes
  written off as an elitist view of culture, the same dynamic is at work
  in a multitude of transmuted forms. Wherever the belief is found that
  some artifacts of a culture are intrinsically more valuable than others
  (e.g., that the music of singer-songwriters is a more authentic expression of the human spirit than that of singers who buy their songs and
  are backed by studio musicians, or that independent films are more

attuned to life than Hollywood blockbusters), or that certain genres, writers or performers are more capable of allowing us to transcend our small selves and be carried into communion with some great truth or dimension of reality that makes us better persons, a cultural ideal is in play. Thus, most forms of culture criticism – from *New Criterion* to *Spin* – demonstrate the continuing strength of the view that culture is a standard of excellence.

- *Culture as a way of life* – In this understanding, sometimes referred to as "the modern anthropological view of culture" (with a clear debt to Herder), the idea is that there are multiple cultures in the world, each of them self-contained and internally coherent, each one a homogeneous, functioning organism driven by its own peculiar genius. This conception of cultural wholes is often traced back to Edward B. Tylor, the curator of the University Museum at Oxford, who published a paradigm-setting book in 1871 called *Primitive Culture*. The opening sentence reads: "Culture or civilization, taken in its wide ethnographic sense, is that complex whole which includes knowledge, belief, art, morals, law, custom, and any other capabilities and habits acquired by man as a member of society."[28] This is the concept of culture that is found in the classic period of the discipline of cultural anthropology (roughly 1910–70), associated with such figures as Franz Boas, Bronislaw Malinowski, and Ruth Benedict. It is the presumption found in the ethnographies that were written by these scholars and their students, who would travel to remote parts of the world to live among and observe the people of "primitive cultures," to record their various exotic (to us) family arrangements, child-rearing techniques, religious beliefs, arts and technologies, political structures, and economic practices. Upon returning to their university departments, they would write up their field notes and add reflections on what underlying views about reality integrated this people into a cultural whole, distinct among the multitude of cultures around the world. This is the view of culture most of us received who grew up reading *National Geographic*, and some version of it is still prevalent in cultural anthropology, although it is eroding.
- *Subaltern cultures* – This view rejects the understanding of cultures as monolithic and integrated wholes, and proposes instead that the integrated system of values that pass as cultural wholes are actually ideologies of power by means of which the dominant segments of a society seek to maintain their power over its subaltern, or subordinate, communities. Subaltern communities are constituted by age, race, ethnicity, gender, etc., and often develop into "subcultures," in the sense that they share a way of life, and particularly a use of speech, common values, solidarity in suffering and a shared self-image, that

distinguishes them from the dominant culture. Subcultures have an arsenal of ways to resist their oppression, including a fluid semiotics of "style," by means of which they shield themselves from and undermine the dominant culture through the guerilla tactics of slang, ironic practices of consumption, and the development of gestures, codes of conduct, and icons with meanings impenetrable to all but the cognoscenti. This view is central to the field of cultural studies.

Given that these three competing uses of the term "culture" are at the heart of three flourishing disciplines (the humanities, cultural anthropology, cultural studies), they are important to distinguish as theories of culture. Each of them isolates something crucial about this thing we call culture. Rather than get bogged down in choosing sides in these debates, it is possible to work with a broad theory that borrows a little from each.

Culture as a standard of excellence suggests that human beings objectify into concrete artifacts certain enduring ideals and values that they believe have the power to lift us outside of ourselves and make us better persons. *Culture as a way of life* recognizes that human beings seek a coherence in their pursuits that includes the whole sweep of our activities – from the most mundane to the most elevated. Theorists of *subaltern cultures* instruct us in the maneuverings of power for which culture offers cover, and the class interests and resentments for which cultural artifacts serve as instruments.

Incorporating the central insights of each of these competing theories leads to this three-fold understanding of the concept of culture: Through culture we seek to grasp, consolidate, and transmit a coherent order of values that we perceive to be transcendent and therefore worthy of pursuit. These values are discernible in the whole range of cultural artifacts, from poetry, music, and moral beliefs to economic practices, technology, and cooking utensils. The values that organize a culture are never static, but always struggling into new configurations. Each of these insights can be found in at least seminal form in Herder, who managed to hold them together.

It has been suggested by some that the *idea of culture* has replaced religion as the preferred abstraction into which we have stashed our most sacred truths, the vessel into which we place our fetishes to be guarded and revered. Literary critic, Terry Eagleton, believes that the *concept* of culture has come for many in the West "to substitute for a fading sense of divinity and transcendence."[29] Reading the leading theorists representing each of the definitions of culture above, it is not hard to sense that, respectively, refinement of taste, integrated wholeness, and subordinated peoples function as objects of veneration. Perhaps this is the wild ride that has been taken by Herder's assertion that cultures are the embodiments of God's ideas in subsequent generations of scholars, who have distanced themselves from God-language but not from the desire to find something transcendent within culture.

The Frankfurt School

The earliest concerted effort to theorize *popular* culture is to be found in the Frankfurt Institute for Social Research, which was founded in Germany in 1923 by neo-Marxist sociologists who pioneered the field of "critical theory." Walter Benjamin, Theodor Adorno, Max Horkheimer, Leo Lowenthal, Herbert Marcuse, and Erich Fromm were among its celebrated roster of intellectuals. Expelled from Germany by the Nazis, all of them migrated to the US in the early 1930's and temporarily relocated the School to New York and California. Their founding problem was the puzzling fact that the working class failed to see the wretched conditions in which it labored and consequently failed to overthrow its oppressors. Indeed, the underclass had grown rather comfortable with capitalism. Marx had predicted that capitalism was an unstable system, on the verge of crisis and a revolution from below. What the Frankfurt theorists concluded was that the masses had so deeply imbibed the ideology of the ruling class that they were operating out of it and sustaining it without protest. They had been deluded with what Marx called a "false-consciousness." According to Marx,

> The ideas of the ruling class are in every epoch the ruling ideas, i.e., the class which is the ruling force of society, is at the same time its ruling intellectual force. The class which has the means of material production at its disposal, has control at the same time over the means of mental production, so that thereby, generally speaking, the ideas of those who lack the means of mental production are subject to it.[30]

In Marxist thought, that is to say, ideology refers to the presence in a society of a set of ideas and values that organize people's perceptions and vision of life. These ideas and values are so deeply embedded in their consciousness that they are taken for granted as reflecting what is most true about reality. The prevailing ideology in a society reflects the interests of the ruling class in maintaining their dominance. It is built into a society's myths and philosophy, and when the proletariat adopts it as their own view of the world, they have been co-opted by a false consciousness that hides from them the desperate condition of their lives under the capitalist system. In the twentieth century, the capitalist ideology circulated through what the Frankfurt theorists came to refer to as "the culture industries."

The culture industries churn out art and entertainment that lull the oppressed into believing that they are actually happy with their lot in life. These industries are overseen by the powerful heads of economic, political, and military establishments who hire specialists to reiterate through various media the ideology of capitalism. Charlie Chaplin's 1936 film, *Modern Times*, is a well-told Frankfurt parable – in it, the owners of industry are portrayed as using the media to exercise power over the laboring masses. Reading essays from the Frankfurt critics, we learn that through the diversions of such popular pastimes as baseball, jazz, Hollywood movies, radio, television, best-selling novels, comic books, and Disney's animation, the masses are distracted from the unbearable conditions in which they live, and their resentments and rage are dissipated. It is a kind of bread and circus effect. Their real need for political and economic liberation is transmuted into a "false need" for the freedom of choice between a plethora of consumer goods and brands that the great engines of capitalist production are ready to satisfy. Lured into the endless pursuit of satisfying their desires as consumers, the masses are diverted from becoming politically enlightened and also from devoting their energies into the production of a genuinely *folk* culture – which, if they put their minds to it, would allow them to give artistic expression to their resentments and thus make them aware of their condition. In this vein, Lowenthal wrote in a 1950 article, "Historical Perspectives of Popular Culture":

> There is considerable agreement that all media are estranged from values and offer nothing but entertainment and distraction – that, ultimately, they expedite flight from an unbearable reality. Wherever revolutionary tendencies show a timid head, they are mitigated and cut short by a false fulfillment of wish dreams, like wealth, adventure, passionate love, power, and sensationalism in general.[31]

In one of the Institute's most influential essays, "On Popular Music," Adorno, inspired by his recent discovery of American popular music and Broadway musicals, attempted to articulate the way the culture industry manipulates mass psychology. After examining the work of performers such as Benny Goodman, Guy Lombardo, Artie Shaw, and Ginger Rogers, Adorno converges on the "releasing element" of popular music that reconciles people to their unhappiness: "It is katharsis for the masses," he writes, "but katharsis which keeps them all the more firmly in line."[32] He then concludes that the energy expended on the weekends to master the frenzied histrionics of "jitterbugging," or "simply to 'like' popular music," depletes the reserves of energy that might otherwise further one's social transformation "into a man."[33]

This criticism of the hypnotizing effect of mass culture, driven by the culture industries, is the central assertion of the Frankfurt School. A second important feature of their dismissal of popular culture is its affinity for *kitsch*. They refined the notion of kitsch into a technical term with both aesthetic and political import. Unlike genuine art, which is difficult to experience, the reception of kitsch is effortless. According to Adorno, a genuine work of art requires effort to understand – *substantively*, because it explores the dialectic of the beautiful *and* the ugly, and *formally* because it portrays this dialectic through abstract and complex media, all of which demand sustained and disciplined reflection in order to grasp the inspiration behind them. Kitsch, on the other hand, is "sugary trash," which presents "the beautiful minus its ugly counterpart."[34] By concealing the ugly, Adorno argued, kitsch panders to our longing to "feel on safe ground all of the time," gratifying our "infantile need for protection."[35] Moreover, it is "pre-digested" art, which, as in the case of popular music, offers a "composition which hears for the listener" and "promotes conditioned reflexes," thus leaving the imagination dormant.[36]

A third feature of the Frankfurt School's disparagement of popular culture is found in its insistence that art – and specifically *avant-garde* art – is the cultural activity where the resources necessary to revolutionize the consciousness of the masses can be expected to arise. It is through such experimental and uncompromising artists as James Joyce and Picasso, Horkheimer insisted in 1941, that the appropriate responses of grief and horror to the "gulf between the monadic individual and his barbarous surrounding" is expressed.[37] According to Adorno, an Expressionist work such as Picasso's *Guernica* evokes a public outcry that testifies to its power to "bring to light what is wrong with present social conditions."[38] In contrast to the entertainment industry, Adorno proposed, modernist art "respects the masses," in that, "It puts before them an image of what they might be, rather than adapting to their dehumanized condition."[39] Genuine art, he reasoned, is always ahead of the commonly subscribed values in a culture, turning on them in protest.[40]

Horkheimer, in his influential 1941 essay, "Art and Mass Culture," argued that genuine art always has a utopic dimension. "Art," he wrote, "since it became autonomous, has preserved the utopia that evaporated from religion." This is achieved in the way that art erects a world above the familiar world, and true works of art thus "harbor principles through which the world that bore them appears alien and false." When this effect is achieved, the experience of art can recall one to a "freedom that makes prevailing standards appear narrow-minded and barbarous." In inciting this judgment, true art – avant-garde art – enables one, then, to imagine a world different from that in which we live.[41]

These are the three most forceful criticisms of popular culture proposed by the Frankfurt critical theorists: popular culture is an instrument for maintaining class privilege, its heavy use of kitsch panders to people's infantile wishes for how the world ought to be, and it does not present to its audience a vision of the world that is different, and morally better, than the one in which we live. Only the art of the avant-garde can do this.

A fourth criticism of popular culture that can be found in the Frankfurt School, but which was further developed by a similarly-minded group of New York intellectuals who were associated with the journal *Partisan Review*, is found in the distinction they draw between "folk art" and "mass culture."[42] Folk art in this schema is a precious achievement that arises authentically from "the people," and is a genuine expression of the insight they have into their own condition. Mass culture, on the other hand, is a new phenomenon made possible by new technologies of mechanical reproduction, a new set of artifacts that have been inserted between the old and discrete categories of highbrow and lowbrow art. Mass culture is a debasement of highbrow culture, diluting it for mass consumption – filling people's stomachs with objects that look like real art but are just empty calories. Ultimately, this dulls everyone's appetite for real high culture and the social benefits it conveys. In the words of Dwight Macdonald,

> Folk Art grew from below. It was a spontaneous, autochthonous expression of the people, shaped by themselves, pretty much without the benefit of High Culture, to suit their own needs. Mass Culture is imposed from above. It is fabricated by technicians hired by businessmen; its audiences are passive consumers, their participation limited to the choice between buying and not buying. The Lords of *kitsch*, in short, exploit the cultural needs of the masses in order to make a profit and/or to maintain their class rule.[43]

Macdonald reaches the absolute conclusion that "Mass Culture is not and can never be any good."[44] What is particularly insidious about it is the way it compromises both high culture and folk art. It usurps folk art by drying up the energies of the folk for producing their own artifacts, thus rendering them into a passive audience for mass culture – which is not art, but a commodity produced for profit and manipulation. And it vulgarizes the aesthetic and moral values that have traditionally been borne by high culture, even high culture in its avant-garde manifestations, leveling taste and moral sensibility down to the lowest common denominator. Disney, of course, came under sharp criticism from this point of view. He desecrated folk tales, symphonies, and abstract expressionist art by turning all of it into cartoons.

Eagleton has noted how various schools of cultural criticism have presumed an affinity between high and folk culture. "Whenever one hears admiring talk of the savage, one can be sure that one is in the presence of sophisticates. ... The overbred and the underdeveloped forge strange alliances."[45] This is particularly the case in Marxist circles, where it serves as a means to demean the middling tastes of the bourgeoisie. Here, viewing "the habits of the majority" with distaste "is an abiding feature of 'high' or aesthetic culture. The patrician and the dissenter can thus link hands over the heads of the petty bourgeoisie."[46]

It is easy to dismiss the Frankfurt and Mass Culture critiques of popular culture as being shrill and elitist. The insistence that only the expressions of art that most people find alienating contain the truth – the assertion, that is, of the prophetic role of avant-garde modernism – is a bit haughty and overly pessimistic with respect to common tastes; and the idea that there are agents of culture industries who operate as a cabal, plotting the oppression of the masses, comes across as a bit paranoid. When one considers the hundreds of names that roll by in the credits following a movie, for instance, all of whom are employed in the culture industries, one must wonder what kind of power at the top would turn them all into collaborators. A movie represents so many layers of creative input – film editors, director, screenplay writer, book author, set designer, actors – that, even given the current small club of media conglomerates, it is hard to imagine all these notoriously cranky artists would consent to only telling stories that keep the masses hypnotically happy with their oppression. Particularly today, while there is a genre of formula blockbusters that may justify the suspicions of the Frankfurt School to some extent, the movie industry is not now the standardized entity that it may have been in the 1930s when the studio system was still operating and the Frankfurt School was developing these theories.

But there are still plenty of theorists in the Frankfurt camp, although the central critique that popular culture is an opiate of the masses is now blamed more on impersonal forces that have taken on a life of their own than on powerful individuals. Jürgen Habermas, Noam Chomsky, Neil Postman, and Jacques Ellul are among the more persuasive thinkers along these lines.[47] And the effects of media and retail conglomerates like Time Warner-CNN and Wal-Mart do raise the specter of centralized control in the distribution of popular culture. There are now a handful of corporations that are approaching a monopoly on media properties, combining under a relatively small number of executives' control the country's dominant newspapers and magazines, radio stations, cable suppliers, Internet providers, television networks, record labels, and movie studios. The big retail chains like Wal-Mart have considerable clout in determining the books, music, and videos that Americans buy. Authors, musicians, and filmmakers have gone public with complaints that Wal-Mart's buyers are screening what they make available in the stores, and given that 100 million people shop at Wal-Mart each week, and that the big chain stores together now account for roughly 50 percent of the sales of all best-selling books, albums, and DVDs sold in the US, they are effectively becoming the arbiters of popular culture in this country. If Wal-Mart will not carry it, the studios and publishing houses may become less inclined to produce it. While this does not necessarily make chain stores the agents of subduing the masses, it does have a homogenizing effect on the popular culture materials that manage to attain broad circulation.[48] Another unsettling statistic: according to sociologist Michael Dawson,

> Big business in the United States now spends well over a *trillion* dollars a year on marketing. This is double Americans' combined annual spending on all public and private education, from kindergartens through graduate schools. It also works out to around four thousand dollars a year for each man, woman, and child in the country.[49]

Spending of this magnitude makes one consider again the seriousness with which the Frankfurt School believed that the vested interests of the economically powerful dominate the public consciousness with messages that generate profit and valorize the capitalist system.

Another reason to avoid hastily dismissing the Frankfurt critique: there is a curious fractal effect in the way most of us view popular culture that owes a debt to the Frankfurt School. Their distinction between genuine art and manufactured kitsch – art as an authentic expression of some unsettling truth, which can be fully appreciated only by the initiated, and kitsch as a form of commerce that panders to our illusions about ourselves and that prettifies reality – continues to serve as a norm familiar to most of us. Even within the hermetic world of popular music, judgments along these lines abound about both what music is good and who is worthy of listening to it.

This roving high art/low art norm is what was expressed in the boos from the crowd when Bob Dylan fired up his amplifier at the 1966 Newport Jazz Festival. It is the default norm of every music critic who has praised the pure authenticity of the sometimes off-key singer-songwriter (Woody Guthrie, Joni Mitchell, Stevie Wonder, Van Morrison, Joe Strummer) and dismissed the overly engineered sounds of the pop performer (Paul Anka, Wayne Newton, Three Dog Night, Madonna, Britney Spears). It is what drives the distinction between the fresh, avant-garde innovation of musicians like Pink Floyd, the Velvet Underground, Moby, and the Flaming Lips in contrast to the stale, predictable formulations of performers like the Osmonds, Aerosmith, Garth Brooks, the Spice

Girls and Backstreet Boys. It is the aesthetic differentiation that separates "underground" radio from Top Forty. Assessments tend to follow these fractal lines with each new genre that appears – the blues were more authentic than jazz, jazz was more authentic than soul, black soul was more authentic than white soul, the Rolling Stones, who blended the harshness of blues with the hooks of rock, were more primitive, truer to the grittier side of life, and therefore better artists than the Beatles, whose themes of simple romance, brotherly love, and utopianism were sung in harmonious melodies. While the Frankfurt critics would not have shared these judgments, the mix of affection for autochthonic folk art, exaltation of the eccentricities of the avant-garde, and revulsion toward any manufactured enhancements that characterized their aesthetic persist as reference points for judgment in contemporary music.

It may be said that the Frankfurt theorists were more elitist than they realized. Sociologist Pierre Bourdieu would argue that this moving edge of art which is forever being domesticated for mass consumption can itself be explained by the efforts of the highly privileged to preserve their status and the bourgeoisie to get a piece of it. Bourdieu argues that the economically privileged classes always manage to stay one step ahead as the aesthetic tastes of the lower classes approach their own. So, it is precisely in the constant motion of the content and norms of good taste that the cultural markers that maintain class privilege are preserved.[50]

This is not to say that the Frankfurt aesthetic has given us a faulty cluster of standards. My point here is that it is a highly versatile aesthetic that has been deeply absorbed into our culture, yet it was sufficiently ambiguous to be deployed in ways the Frankfurt theorists would never have sanctioned, allowing for concrete judgments that have wandered far from what they intended. It has been transformed from an aesthetic elitism that absolutely dismissed all manifestations of popular culture into an elitism that is internal to popular culture. Thus, Ray Charles is an artistic genius, the real thing, while Michael Bolton is a mawkish crooner, a singing commodity. Stanley Kubrick is a virtuoso filmmaker; Stephen Spielberg is neo-colonialist ideologue. These judgments may be valid. Nevertheless, consistent with Eagleton's acerbic remarks, they evoke an elitism that is used to distance the critic from the tastes of the bourgeoisie, at least the demographic center of the bourgeoisie. As that center moves, judgments in the Frankfurt lineage follow.

Conclusion

Another, simpler explanation for the fractal quality of aesthetic judgments made *within* popular culture is found in what several writers have described as a "cultural pessimism" that follows the aging process. Our most formative years for acquiring knowledge of popular culture are ages 15–25. It is then that our cultural tastes are shaped. In time, due to various commitments (marriage, children, jobs), the time we once had for reading books and browsing music in stores or online diminishes. In the view of economist Tyler Cowan, "In many lives the rate of cultural discovery starts at a high clip and gradually diminishes so that, to the individual, culture appears to be drying up and declining, creating yet another pessimist."[51] Thus, the music and art of one's youth becomes normative, and everything that follows is mediocre or abrasive.

There is some merit in this common sense analysis. But that cannot be all there is to it. Popular culture is a market, and wherever there is a market, moneyed interests do contrive to increase their profits and maintain their control over the means of production behind the scenes. But there is a surplus of condescension in the Frankfurt view of the "masses," the duped consumers of what the culture industries produce. To better appreciate this, we turn now to one of the heirs of the Frankfurt School, the Cultural Studies approach to popular culture that originated at the University of Birmingham.

2

Cultural Studies

Similar to the Frankfurt School in its Marxist leanings, the Centre for Contemporary Cultural Studies at the University of Birmingham in Britain has been an important influence on the evolving discipline of theorizing about popular culture – arguably generating the most trenchant concepts for thinking about popular culture that are now in use.[1] Founded by Richard Hoggart in 1964 (reportedly with money contributed by Penguin Books in appreciation for Hoggart's then recent assistance in their legal defense of the *Lady Chatterly's Lover* obscenity case), the Centre has launched the discipline of "cultural studies" and the careers of several significant culture critics: Stuart Hall, Paul Willis, Angela McRobbie, Dick Hebdige, and John Hartley.[2]

While Hoggart, in his landmark book, *The Uses of Literacy* (1957), adopted a Frankfurt-style nostalgic romanticism about the folk culture of the people, what he called the "lived culture" of the working-class – the culture that is found in the pubs, singalongs, fairgrounds, miracle cure advertisements, etc. – and lamented the banality of popular culture that was then pouring into Britain from the US, he did make some observations that became groundbreaking insights that were later developed by his colleagues in the Centre. Hoggart found a moral earnestness in the self-made folkways of the working-class that was then being threatened by the moral vacuousness of the "candy-floss" pop music, science fiction comic books, and crime and sex dimestore novels that were being imported from America following World War II. Referring to these imports, Hoggart wrote,

> Most mass-entertainments are in the end what D.H. Lawrence described as "anti-life." They are full of a corrupt brightness, of improper appeals and moral evasions. To recall instances: they tend towards a view of the world in which progress is conceived as a seeking of material possessions, equality as a moral leveling, and freedom as the ground for endless irresponsible pleasure.[3]

Despite this nostalgia and cultural pessimism, however, he did two things in this book that had a lasting impact on cultural studies. First, he experimented in the book with using the tools of literary criticism, originally developed for the analysis of classical literature, to interpret popular magazines, fiction, pop songs, and advertisements. He did this out of the conviction that popular culture contains and conveys insights about the meaning of life that these tools are designed to ferret out. Second, he argued that working-class people exercise some agency in their reception of the products of popular culture that are pressed upon them by the culture industries. "Working-class people," he wrote, "though they are being in a sense exploited today, at least have now to be approached for their consent. The force of environment and the powers of persuasion count for a great deal but are not irresistible, and there are many instances of the power of free action."[4]

This was a crucial departure from the Frankfurt fixation on the production side of popular culture, and opened up a whole new field for investigation: how do the consumers receive and make use of the magazines, movies, television shows, fashions and music that they are enticed to buy? While it may be true that "mass-entertainments" coax their audiences to equate progress with the acquisition of stuff, equality with moral indifference, and freedom with uninhibited hedonism, do these messages enter the consciousness of the consuming public unabridged? Following trends in literary criticism, Hoggart raised the possibility that as with great works of literature, "readers" of popular culture "texts" renegotiate the meanings that were intended by the texts' authors through the exercise of active reading. The meaning of the text is thus reworked in every act of reading. Consumption of the output of the culture industries can be expected to be just as selective and creative.

Hegemony

Like the Frankfurt School, the Birmingham Centre was driven by strong Marxist undercurrents. But, again like the Frankfurt School, its Marxism was selective. It retained the view that the ruling class seeks to impose its ideology on the rest of society, and remained committed to the priority of *praxis* in the way it analyzed popular artifacts – that is, that the purpose of scholarly analysis is to change the order of society and the power relations that exist between social classes. But, as Michael Bérubé has pointed out, it rejected many of the fundamentals of Marxism, e.g., the historical inevitability of class struggle, the primacy of class, the faith in an intellectual vanguard, the belief that the material base determines the superstructure, the notion that "the ruling class owns the ruling ideas," and that "ideology is just false consciousness."[5]

Much of this subversion of Marxism came by way of Antonio Gramsci, an Italian Marxist whose posthumously published *Prison Notebooks* appeared in English in 1971 and were eagerly read by Stuart Hall and Angela McRobbie. Gramsci objected to Marx's absolutizing of the material base of a society (its economic conditions and processes of production) as determinative of its superstructure (its ideas and values). Marx believed that class struggle is precipitated by catastrophes in the material base of a society, which shatter the false consciousness of the oppressed in the ruling ideology and empowers them to revolt. Gramsci found this to be depressingly pessimistic and unrealistically deterministic, and sought an alternative concept to the Marxist coupling of ideology and false consciousness, a coupling that both devalued the importance of ideas as effective agents in class struggle and demeaned the critical mental powers of the working class. What he offered in its place was the concept of "hegemony."

Hegemony is the process whereby the dominant groups in a society seek to win the consent of subordinate groups through all means of persuasion short of coercion and force. True enough, there are coercive agencies in every society – the police, military, courts and prisons. And these *are* used to repress the working class. But the class structure is also maintained through other institutions, and more effectively; institutions like organized religion, schools, labor unions, marketplaces, and the media – the institutions of civil society. These are the real transmitters of ideology in Western democracies; these are the places where the ideas and values of the dominant groups are presented to the subordinate groups for their consent. Hegemony is the process of negotiation through which the oppressed are presented with the ideas around which they are expected to organize their lives, to which they respond with counter demands and alternative ideas, and in light of which concessions – both material and ideological – are made by the dominant groups who wish to pacify them. Maintaining equilibrium here requires ongoing demands, counter-demands, and compromise. In the words of Gramsci, "the fact of hegemony presupposes that account be taken of the interests and the tendencies of the groups over which hegemony is to be exercised, and that a certain compromise equilibrium be formed."[6]

Hegemony, in short, provides us a way for thinking about the reciprocity between the production of popular culture and its consumption. As described by John Storey, "Because hegemony is always the result of 'negotiations' between dominant and subordinate groups, it is a process marked by both 'resistance' and 'incorporation'; it is never simply power imposed from above."[7] Popular culture is a vital hegemonic zone of this reciprocity. As an example, Storey offers the example of reggae music and the Rastafarian culture that is inseparable from it:

> Bob Marley, for example, had international success with songs articulating the values and beliefs of Rastafari. This success can be viewed in two ways. On the one hand, it signals the expression of the message of his religious convictions to an enormous audience world-wide; undoubtedly for many of his audience the music had the effect of enlightenment, understanding and perhaps even conversion to, or bonding for those already convinced of, the principles of the faith. On the other hand, the music has made and continues to make enormous profits for the music industry, promoters, Island Records, etc. What we have is a paradox in which the anti-capitalist politics of Rastafari are being "articulated" in the economic interests of capitalism: the music is lubricating the very system it seeks to condemn; and yet the music is an expression of an oppositional (religious) politics, and may produce certain political and cultural effects.

Given that society has not yet been turned upside down, hegemony does ensure that the dominant groups maintain the upper hand – just not an absolutely free hand. They do, however, have subtle strategies to contain more extreme forms of resistance, as this example illustrates. The recalcitrant subcultures that a dominant culture finds attempting to undermine the social order are countered first by "a wave of hysteria in the press," a hysteria that "fluctuates between dread and fascination, outrage and amusement."[8] But actions of the subversives that begin to spread into society must either be definitively rejected by branding them as a form of deviant behavior to be handled by the police and legal system, or else de-fanged, absorbed and incorporated. These are the means by which the dominant culture maintains the coherence of its own grasp of reality. Incorporation is typically done through market mechanisms, manufacturing dissent into desirable commodities, demonstrating that this new irritant does not threaten the dominant culture. And so Bob Marley was given a record contract and his anti-capitalist message was transformed into a consumer good, thus enriching the very capitalist system he detested.

In a similar manner, the dominant culture has incorporated many waves of dissent that have arisen in the past as radical critiques of its premises – religious separatists, Romanticism, surrealism, existentialism, Marxism, the 1960s' counter-culture, anarchism. The Amish in Pennsylvania are remade into a tourist attraction; their farms surrounded by belts of quilt and candle shops, buffet restaurants and souvenir shops that sell figurines and postcards depicting Amish life. In a racy twist on separatism as entertainment, they are not even off-limits to the voyeurism of reality TV, with real Amish young people relocated to a camera-outfitted house in Hollywood for weekly episodes of *Amish in the City* (UPN). Existentialism winds its way through the Beat poets into books from big publishing houses, poetry readings with steep gate fees, lucrative lecture circuits, appearances on the *Tonight Show*, television sitcoms (*The Many Loves of Dobie Gillis*) and dramas (*The Twilight Zone, Johnny Staccato*), and Hollywood movies. Music of the Beatles, the Rolling Stones, Nick Drake, Led Zeppelin and Iggy Pop is used to score commercials for sports utility vehicles (SUVs) and luxury cruises that are pitched to aging baby-boomers, seeking to relive their bolshevist youth on a Princess Cruise. According to Hebdige, "It is through this continual process of recuperation that the fractured order is repaired and the subculture incorporated as a diverting spectacle within the dominant mythology from which it in part emanates."[9]

Writer Thomas Frank has argued that the aesthetic of "cool" was discovered long ago by advertisers as a strategy to keep the wheels of recuperation running smoothly. The cultural rebel who is out there sub-verting the system is a beloved cliché, and a highly effective figure when used by those who are trying to sell us cars, cigarettes, computers, pants, and soft drinks.[10] It is well-known in the ad industry, Frank makes clear from trade seminars and publications he cites, that the successful brands are those that identify themselves with liberation, and the handiest way to do this is to identify some easily recognized social convention and then position the brand in opposition to it, e.g., Benetton and racism, Apple and technocracy, Nike and modest exercise, Isuzu and "coloring within the lines," Mountain Dew and the laws of physics. Many brands scramble to identify themselves with authority-defying individualism and radical politics.[11] Frank, nostalgic for the Frankfurt theorists, views this as evidence for how wily the culture industries are, neutralizing dissent wherever it flares by harnessing it to the engine of commerce. But the model of hegemony offers a better account, it can be argued, given its built-in recognition of the negotiations and compromises that the eco-nomically and culturally powerful groups in Western societies are willing to enter to maintain their privilege.

Style

Second generation Birmingham scholars took an interest in rebellious youth cultures as phenomena that did not square with the old culture industries model. For his book, *Profane Culture*, which originated as his 1972 dissertation under Hoggart and Hall, Paul Willis went under-ground to conduct a field study of motorcycle gangs and hippies. He produced a work that was half Margaret Mead's *Coming of Age in Samoa* and half Hunter S. Thompson's *Hell's Angels* – a pure gonzo ethnography.

He opened the book by taking a hard swipe at the Frankfurt School's view of consumer passiveness under the onslaught of the culture industries: "[O]pressed, subordinate or minority groups can have a hand in the construction of their own vibrant cultures and are not merely dupes: the fall guys in a social system stacked overwhelmingly against them and dominated by capitalist media and commercial provision."[12] Dick Hebdige's 1979 book, *Subculture: The Meaning of Style*, easily the most widely cited work of the Birmingham school, reached the same conclusion but went much further in theorizing how youth subcultures in industrialized societies defy the culture industries. *Subculture* is an ethnography of skinheads, hipsters, mods, punks, rastas, beats and teddy-boys – youth tribalisms of note in Britain in the 1970s.[13] Having heard the instruction Hoggart and Hall had given him to pay close attention to the lived practices of consumption, Hebdige found that these subcultures exercised their agency through a practice he called "style."

Style in this context refers to the way people use commodities in ways that were not intended by their producers and, further, how they assemble consumable goods into clusters of deeply encoded meaning. Subcultures with low incomes, in particular, will scavenge for articles that others have discarded and rehabilitate them with new uses and meanings. Everyday objects like safety pins or combat boots, manufactured to have a strictly utilitarian use, are conscripted and assigned a prestige that both baffles and grates on the nerves of the dominant groups in a society, a kind of patois of consumable goods. It is not simply that they are put to alternative practical uses, but they are thrust into alternative semiotic universes. Thus, according to Hebdige, safety pins and other humble objects can be "magically appropriated; 'stolen' by subordinate groups and made to carry 'secret' meanings: Meanings which express, in code, a form of resistance to the order which guarantees their continued subordination."[14] And this can be done not only with such mundane objects, it is also frequently done with fashions whose day has come and gone, like beehive hairdos, tennis skirts, Converse high-tops, tattoos and pomade, which make a resurgence as an act of rebellion against the mainstream culture that is more obedient in dressing itself in the newest wares of the culture industries. Also eligible for appropriation are bottom-feeding artifacts of popular culture like soap operas, tabloids, aging teen idols, and romance novels, which can be treasured by subordinate groups to the same degree they are despised by the culturally sophisticated.

What Hebdige discovered was that each of the youth subcultures he examined exploited the consumer goods, advertising images, entertainments and fashions of popular culture in the same manner: as raw materials that they first emptied of their common significations, and then attributed alternative meanings and accessorized them in novel combinations. They remanufactured mass-produced commodities into signs and symbols. As Hebdige describes it,

> Hollywood films, advertising images, packaging, clothes and music – offer a rich iconography, a set of symbols, objects and artifacts which can be assembled and re-assembled by different groups in a literally limitless number of combinations. And the meaning of each selection is transformed as individual objects – jeans, rock records, Tony Curtis hairstyles, bobby socks, etc. – are taken out of their original historical and cultural contexts and juxtaposed against other signs from other sources.[15]

And they did this in order to proclaim their tribal identity in opposition to the dominant order. Given all the semiotic connivance that this involves, digging below the "glossy surfaces" of style will be rewarded with something worth knowing, Hebdige directs us to expect – "maps of meaning" that are otherwise hidden.[16] Style is, then, a ritualized form of consumption through which groups within a culture divulge their own grasp of reality in opposition to the ideology that is handed to them.

Hebdige was aided in developing his theory of style through the concept of *bricolage*, which he borrowed from the French anthropologist Claude Levi-Strauss. Literally, *bricolage* means a makeshift repair, making something work by patching it together with whatever materials are at hand, a kind of ad hoc improvisation. Levi-Strauss used it as a way to describe how primitive peoples "think" their world, elaborating classificatory schemes that relate concrete objects in the world around them to certain powers and meanings that, to an insider, constitute a coherent system. When some new or strange phenomenon appears that cannot be readily absorbed into the scheme, adjustments are made; the scheme with which they think their world is modified to accommodate it. For Hebdige, the improvisations found in style are precisely this sort of activity – subcultures handling each thing that is thrown in their path as an occasion to divest it of its intended meaning, invest it with their own, and incorporate it into the ever-evolving scheme of meaning with which they interpret the world. This results in idiosyncratic assemblages of signs and symbols, combining the available symbols, images, cultural codes and texts into novel semiotic systems.

Poaching

Another gift from French social theory for the study of popular culture is the concept of *braconnage*. This is a term that was introduced by Michel de Certeau, and it means "poaching." According to de Certeau, consumers of television, magazines, and popular fiction practice "an art of using" that is like poaching in "its clandestine nature, its tireless but quiet activity."[17] These readers of popular texts "are travelers; they move across lands belonging to someone else, like nomads poaching their way across fields they did not write, despoiling the wealth of Egypt to enjoy it themselves."[18] Like Robin Hood, the consumer of popular culture poaches deer on the king's land because there is no other meat to be had, and uses those deer to satisfy ends other than those for which they were intended. This deprives the king of his wealth, but even more significantly, it aggravates him because the rules he has promulgated to serve his own ends are being flagrantly violated.

Style is all about poaching. Subaltern groups scrounge around in the vast fields of popular culture and put its symbols to uses for which they were not intended. There are also more overt practitioners of *braconnage*. The monkeywrenching tactics of the group EarthFirst!, inspired by the writings of Edward Abbey, are classic poaching techniques. Felling billboards with chainsaws, staging tree sits to deter the cutting of redwoods, disrupting timber barons' trade meetings by dumping barrels of sawdust on their cocktail parties, reseeding timber access roads – are all forms of "ecotage" designed to foil the production of wealth that is done at the expense of other cultural values. Computer hacking has become a strategy of poaching; free downloadable music servers like the chastened Napster and DVD Macrovision encryption ripping software from companies like 321 Studios use the king's technology to bust into his treasury and redistribute his wealth.

Even more sophisticated and media savvy are the actions of the loosely organized, self-styled anarchists who have been putting in appearances at World Trade Organization (WTO) and G-8 summits in the past few years. One of their meeting grounds is The Media Foundation, which puts out the magazine *Adbusters*. The Foundation is described on their website as:

> a loose global network of artists, writers, environmentalists, ecological economists, media-literacy teachers, reborn Lefties, ecofeminists, downshifters, high school shit-disturbers, campus rabble-rousers, incorrigibles, malcontents and green entrepreneurs. We are idealists, anarchists, guerrilla tacticians, pranksters, neo-Luddites, poets, philosophers and punks.

Their modest aim is to "unbrand" America through a variety of "culture jamming" campaigns that will "topple existing power structures" and

> change the way information flows, the way institutions wield power, the way the world keeps the peace, the way the food, fashion, automobile, sports, music and culture industries set their agendas. Above all, we want to change the way we interact with the mass media and the way in which meaning is produced in our society.[19]

Writers for *Adbusters* are shrewd about the semiological systems that sustain corporate interests, such as the train of inferences that couple coolness to freedom to democracy to individuality and ultimately to capitalism. They offer sophisticated critiques of current ad campaigns, create ads to promote their own vision for a less consuming society, and offer spoof ads on their website that they encourage people to print out and surreptitiously post in the offending stores and corporate headquarters. These spoofs cleverly demystify the brands' own advertised images with messages that disclose dirty secrets about the production process or about the environmental or health effects that result from consuming the product. One ad shows a picture of a Volkswagen Beetle airbrushed in aqua blue and covered with colorful fish; the caption reads: "Less cars. More world. Drivers wanted." (Figure 2) Another ad shows the crusted feces and feathers on the bottom of a chicken cage. The caption, attributed to one of McDonalds' laying hens, is an expression of gratitude for recently passed guidelines that have added twenty square inches to the cages at factory farms, and concludes, "let me tell you, when you're crammed into a cage with five other surly hens, an extra 20 inches means a lot."

This is very smart *braconnage* – pilfering corporate ads and logos, digitally morphing their trademark images, cleverly dressing them up

Less cars, more world. **Drivers wanted.**

Figure 2 Adbusters Media Foundation has produced an archive of spoof ads like this one, "Less Cars, More World," in a highly skilled campaign of "poaching" corporate images and putting them to anti-corporate uses (www.adbusters.org. Reprinted with permission).

with a complaint about the company's effects on society, then disseminating them for public consumption – a gesture fully in the spirit of Robin Hood delivering to a royal banquet one of the king's own poached deer, freshly dressed and ready to roast. The culture jammers know the magical power of images, and bend it to their own ends. They poach state-of-the-art advertising technique itself, utilizing the same irreverent hipness that advertising agencies have perfected over the years to undermine the mystifications they have promoted on behalf of their clients.

The movie, *FightClub*, itself a parable in the battle against consumerism, offers a gruesome illustration of *braconnage* in a sequence that shows Jack and Tyler breaking into the dumpster at a cosmetic surgery clinic to retrieve sealed packets of human fat that had been liposuctioned from patients earlier in the day. This is the source of the fat out of which Tyler makes his luxurious soaps that he sells to boutiques for twenty dollars a bar.

> *Tyler*: The best fat for making soap comes from humans.
>
> *Jack*: What is this place?
>
> *Tyler*: Liposuction clinic. The richest, creamiest fat in the world, the fat of the land.
>
> *Jack* [in voiceover]: It was beautiful. We were selling rich women their own fat asses back to them.

Umberto Eco has given us an expression that is widely used to describe these acts of poaching by which consumers appropriate the symbols and merchandise of popular culture and subvert them to their own ends. He calls it "semiotic guerilla warfare."[20] A full analysis of the meaning of a cultural artifact involves interpreting not only the code of the artifact's intended message, he argues, but also the oppositional decoding, the ripping of the code that has been done through the guerilla operations of various consumers. For example, rock music lends itself to receiving very opposite decodings. Ronald Reagan requested that Bruce Springsteen's song, "Born in the USA," be played at the 1984 Republican Convention. Reagan was reportedly enchanted by the uplifting chorus line, but oblivious to the irony in a song protesting the meaningless of the war in Vietnam and a dead end refinery job. The Rolling Stones' song, "Sympathy for the Devil," intended ironically as a warning about the cunningness of evil, forever connected Mick Jagger in the minds of many listeners with satanic aspirations, given such singable lines as "Just call me Lucifer." And the songs of such left-leaning lyricists as John Lennon and Lou Reed of the Velvet Underground were instrumental in inspiring dissidents in Czechoslovakia under Soviet rule to organize on behalf of a capitalist alternative to East European communism. Nelson Mandela has given MTV and Nike ads some credit for emboldening the youth of South Africa to join the political struggle against apartheid. They may not have become consumers of Nike air trainers or the multitude of hip products that MTV serves as musical packaging for, but they did buy into MTV's siren call of individualism and disdain for authority.

Simulacrum and the hyperreal

A final useful and important concept that is common in cultural studies is the notion of the simulacrum, which is generally attributed to the French sociologist, Jean Baudrillard. According to Baudrillard, the postmodern era has witnessed the end of the naïve belief that signs, language, and images refer to reality, the end of the idea that, as a mirror reflects an original, we represent reality as it actually is, to some degree of accuracy, through the symbols we use to speak about it. The history of Western thought, according to Baudrillard, has gradually drifted away from this innocent view. First it was acknowledged that our words and images may reflect the real, but only in a distorted way – distorted by our physical senses and limited intellects. This was the view of Plato, of the Bible, and of Kant. Next, it was believed that our words and images reflect and mask the *absence* of a basic reality, that they are stories we tell ourselves and images we conjure up to substitute for the incomprehensibility of what is really out there – a sort of whistling in the dark. This was the view of some strains of mysticism and apophatic theology, of Nietzsche, and of much twentieth century philosophy.

Now, however, we have moved to the next stage of estrangement of image from reality, according to Baudrillard, and that is the realization that words and images bear no relation to any reality whatsoever; words and images reflect only other words and images. All the images that surround us are nothing more than reflections of other images; all of the symbols reflect only other symbols. All of our images and symbols are copies for which no original ever existed. This is pure simulation, the simulacrum, for which belief in any original was always an illusion; we have attained a level of culture in which all images, all representations, are copies of copies. Once this is acknowledged, he writes, "the whole system becomes weightless, it is no longer anything but a gigantic simulacrum . . . an uninterrupted circuit without reference."[21] There is no originary ground or foundation for our simulations. There is no reality out there in light of which to measure the veracity of our representations of it.

With our hands empty of an original reality against which to validate our simulations, the new standard of measurement becomes "hyperreality," which is the excrescence of our images to a degree of perfection that results in fabricated images that are more real than reality itself. Hyperreal objects reverse the old Platonic idea that all concrete things and values dimly mirror an archetype that preexists them in the transcendent realm, the idea that hovering in the noumena are the singular archetypes of chairness, horseness, and beauty-itself, which all real chairs, horses, and beautiful objects dimly reflect. Replacing this ideal model is the hyperreal model according to which the human intellect has been striving all this time through its image-making to produce simulacrum that are even better than the real thing could ever have been. And we are finally at the point where it has become apparent, according to Baudrillard, that our simulacra do not reflect any originals, but just other images. Our world is a hall of mirrors, images imitating images.

Hollywood can be excavated for the last layers of this development. The earliest films were about real historical characters and events (*The Passion Play* [1898], *The Temptation of St Anthony* [1902], *Birth of a Nation* [1915]). Then movies were made that were based on characters from literature – folk tales, dimestore fiction and comic books – characters like Robin Hood, Snow White, Tarzan, the Virginian, Superman, the Lone Ranger. A newer trend has been to base movies on characters that have neither a historical nor literary point of origin, but arise from pure simulation. In the 1980s Steven Spielberg began with his *Raiders of the Lost Ark* franchise, which was an amalgam of action heroes and cliffhanger plot developments that the filmmaker recalled from the matinees of his childhood, to make movies that were generated out of movies. Now we have the *Lara Croft: Tomb Raider* movies featuring a character borrowed from a video game that was invented in 1996. The game's inventor, Adrian Smith, was surprised soon after the game hit the market to receive inquiries from players who wanted to know when Lara's birthday was, and listservs and websites started cropping up to speculate and talk about her character. When the character was optioned for a movie, the screenwriters had to invent her life story, a mixture of elements from James Bond, Indiana Jones, and Batman – she was born on a Valentine's Day, an orphan in a mansion with a generous trust fund, driven in her superheroism less by a sense of justice than a desire to cheat death and complete her father's work. In the sequel, *Lara Croft: Tomb Raider – The Cradle of Life* (2003), the story explores her more human side, even bordering on a spiritual quest for meaning. And the latest twist on the simulacrum comes from the Disney Studios, with two feature films, *Pirates of the Caribbean: The Curse of the Black Pearl*, and *The Haunted Mansion* – both of which have their genesis in Disneyland amusement park rides.

With this hall of mirrors in mind, simulation upon simulation, consider what a strange world we have entered if one accepts the view that movies constitute a primary source for our collective efforts to sort out how to live and what we might fairly expect from life. Nearly 100 years ago, the Christian reformer and sociologist of urban life, Jane Addams, observed that:

> "Going to the show" for thousands of young people in every industrial city is the only possible road to the realms of mystery and romance; the theater is the only place where they can satisfy that craving for a conception of life higher than that which the actual world offers them. In a very real sense the drama and the drama alone performs for them the office of art as is clearly revealed in their blundering demand stated in many forms for "a play unlike life." The theater becomes to them a "veritable house of dreams" infinitely more real than the noisy streets and the crowded factories.

She goes on, "what they hear there, flimsy and poor as it often is, easily becomes their actual moral guide. In moments of moral crisis they turn to the sayings of the hero who found himself in a similar plight. The sayings may not be profound, but at least they are applicable to conduct."[22] It was clear to Addams, even then (1909), that popular theater does more than entertain, it teaches us how to think, act and feel. When the movies are themselves simulacra of video games and amusement park rides, the whole process by which our culture is receiving its moral formation begins to feel a bit bizarre.

For Umberto Eco, America is the epicenter of the hyperreal, and it is much bigger than the movies.[23] To verify his theory, Eco took a road trip across America, dropping in at many of the usual tourist traps (wax museums, marine parks, historical mansions, art museums, theme parks). He was enthralled with a visit to the Palace of Living Arts in Buena Park, California, a museum that displays three-dimensional wax figures of great masterpieces of art, often extrapolating beyond the frame to include not only the artist painting in his studio, but also a fuller depiction of the figure on the canvas. So a life-size wax facsimile of Leonardo da Vinci is found standing at his easel, paints in hand, with the mysterious Mona Lisa before him, sitting in a chair, with all of her unpainted limbs in perfect poise. Eco comments, "The Palace's philosophy is not, 'We are giving you the reproduction so that you will want the original,' but rather, 'We are giving you the reproduction so you will no longer feel any need for the original.'"[24] Then it is on to Disneyland, America's "Sistine Chapel" of the hyperreal. Reflecting on the Jungle Ride through the swamps of Adventureland, it dawns on Eco why, when they could go to any zoo and see a real crocodile, anyone would prefer to take this ride instead:

> A real crocodile can be found in the zoo, and as a rule it is dozing or hiding, but Disneyland tells us that faked nature corresponds much more to our daydream demands. Disneyland, where the wild animals don't have to be coaxed. Disneyland tells us that technology can give us more reality than nature can.[25]

While it is at Disneyland that "imitation has reached its apex and afterwards reality will always be inferior to it,"[26] the effect Eco is describing is one found throughout popular culture. We have developed a decidedly hyperreal aesthetic in our capacity to appreciate ordinary reality. We don't want nature in its undisturbed form; we want it hyped-up, performing a spectacle of pursuing its prey, being hunted down, wrestling to the death, mating, molting, suckling, and parading its colors. Nature shows on television pack more stealth, fornication, fecundity, and tragedy into their 30-minute treatments than most of their wildlife subjects see in a year. Seeing the *real* animal in the wild is pure tedium by comparison. In our minds, the image of a polar bear we see on the small screen is more definitive of polar bear reality than any real polar bear lumbering on the ice will ever be.

In Las Vegas, another apex of hyperreality, there is a casino resort with its own active volcano and tropical rainforest called the Mirage that opened in 1990. Reporting on this new wonder on the Strip, a *New York Times* reporter queried two women guests who had just witnessed one of the regularly timed eruptions of volcanic fire and steam. "It's absolutely gorgeous," said one. "It takes your breath away. It makes you feel like you're in another world," said her friend. The two women had traveled in the past to real tropical rainforests in the Caribbean. Their verdict: "This one is better, everything is in its proper place." When the reporter asked Stephen Wynn, the operator of the Mirage, if the developers of the casino were attempting to tap into the growing social awareness of disappearing rainforests, he retorted, "No, no, no, it has nothing to do with that. The real rainforest, they'd hate it to death."[27] Just imagine the bugs, sweltering heat, amoebic dysentery, and all that molten lava they would have to dodge.

Then there are the travel brochures, postcards, magazines, TV shows – all of the image-producing instruments of the travel industry – pouring out picturesque views of staggering beauty: ribbony waterfalls, emerald pools, glaciers cutting through granite juggernauts, charming medieval villages built along winding canals. So breathtakingly beautiful in airbrushed, filtered lens, digitally enhanced splendor that getting there can be a sad disappointment. As a society, over the years, we've had enough of these image-treatments of reality that we begin to prefer them. We have developed habits of perception that prefer to view the world through technologies of image-making through which the experience can be framed, captured, and manipulated as an image. Nature, history, art, life passages, politics – really only become real when they've found their way into some form of media, captured in images, a spectacle of hyperreality.

Events in the world only become real for us when they get worked up for television, which, ironically, has become the most important authority of the real. Those world events that are assigned the full spectacle treatment – their own graphics, musical score, and byline, such as "Desert Thunder" and "America Strikes Back," and return every evening with their familiar visuals and sounds – are the most real, the most captivating. This packaging encourages viewers to tune in each night to whatever war America is fighting as if we are tuning into a serialized primetime drama. These manufactured images are more real than reality in the way they dominate our attention, move our emotions and steer them into life-orienting attitudes that have lasting social and political effects. The 1997 movie *Wag the Dog* explored this phenomenon by pushing it to the cynical extreme. A beleaguered US president, on the verge of a breaking story about being caught in the Oval Office with a girl scout, turns to a political consultant who enlists the help of a Hollywood movie producer to fabricate a war in Albania. The war takes place entirely in a California soundstage and daily footage is transmitted to CNN, complete with a patriotic soundtrack and story logos. The news media runs with it and the viewing public plops down in front of their TV sets to watch it unfold. Yellow ribbons appear across the nation and the president's polls rise. Even the Albanians half believe it – it has the veracity of moving images on the screen. Eco remarks, "the American imagination demands the real thing and, to attain it, must fabricate the absolute fake."[28]

Eco clearly has reservations about this headlong plunge into hyperreality, while Baudrillard, in the postmodernist spirit, celebrates it. The point worth retaining here has to do with the dizzying love of images in popular culture. As the effect of the simulacrum generates more layers of images, decorating more square inches of our lives, it seems that we do live more and more through second-hand images rather than through experiences we have undergone ourselves. That must be taken into account in any analysis of popular culture.

Reflections on Cultural Studies

To review, the achievements of the post-Frankfurt School approach to cultural studies, which have been treated in this chapter largely as elements within research associated with the Birmingham Centre (although the concepts have been used by many outside the Birmingham circle), are as follows:

First, there is an *affinity with the disenfranchised in society*. This is the legacy of the Frankfurt School that persists in cultural studies. Hoggart romanticized the working class; his students, with a more textured understanding of society, refined this into a concern for *subaltern groups* like teenage girls, punks, motorcycle gangs, skinheads and Rastafarians. This affinity with the disenfranchised extends to advocacy on their behalf. Cultural studies has embraced the view that scholarship should be engaged – both in its research methods (thus the shift toward ethnography) and in its desire for its analyses to move society in a direction that levels out existing power relations.

Second, they built a bridge between the field of *literary criticism* and the "texts" of popular culture. This is significant given that literary criticism arose originally as a variety of methods for reading the great literary masterpieces of Western culture, primarily for the purpose of discerning what profound insights they contained about matters of import for human life. Extending these methods to working-class novels, popular music, film, and magazines demonstrated an expectation that they, too, might contain profound insights. This had the effect of blurring many of the old distinctions between high and low culture.

Third, attention is directed away from the *production* of mass culture and toward the *actual practices of consumption.* The working class, the subjugated subcultures, all consumers of the culture industries, are not passive dupes. They exercise some agency in the manner in which they receive the commodities that are pressed upon them through the market. The forms this agency takes is complex and worthy of study.

Fourth, the concept of *hegemony* better captures the dynamics between the dominant and subordinate groups within a society than does the concept of the culture industries. According to the culture industries concept, the masses are infiltrated with an ideology that they absorb from popular culture without resistance and eventually internalize deeply enough that they oppress themselves through false consciousness. With hegemony there is a more realistic understanding of the struggle that occurs inside of popular culture, reflecting the ongoing negotiation, compromise, retrenchment and resistance that occur as the ruling classes seek the consent of the masses they seek to rule. It also recognizes that the values and ideas of the ruling classes can be affected for the better through this process of negotiation that occurs in popular culture and the institutions of civil society.

Fifth, the cluster of *style, bricolage, poaching,* and *semiotic guerilla warfare* that reflects the influence of Continental theorists on culture studies and was drawn together so effectively by Hebdige and his heirs, explains much that would otherwise make little sense. Style is a ritualized form of consumption, a reception of manufactured goods that empties them of their intended symbolism and invests them with different and often subversive meanings. This is done through *bricolage*, the creative, ad hoc improvisation that assembles richly encoded symbols systems out of poached materials, symbol systems that baffle outsiders, sustain the solidarity of insiders, and serve as highly effective "sites of resistance." At the extreme, this becomes what Eco has called "semiotic guerilla warfare," expressing itself in various forms of monkeywrenching and culture jamming.

Finally, the long drifting away from representational understandings of symbols and images and toward the funhouse of mirrors called the *simulacrum* is a fair description of how the image-generating propensities of popular culture appear to work. We grant an authority to images that hardly seems warranted given our knowledge of how easily they can be manipulated, and how their field of reference is more and more a thick deposit of preceding "visual quotes." The displacement of noumenal reality with the enticements of the *hyperreal*, which has accompanied the exuberant increase of simulacra, also helps us to make sense of the strange aesthetic that seems to prevail in how we choose to entertain ourselves and our flagging attention span for and easy disappointment with simple pleasures. While this explains much, it is also one of the most disturbing features of what cultural studies has uncovered in its reflection on popular culture.

Some important lines of critique have been lodged against cultural studies. Jennifer Daryl Slack and Laurie Anne Whitt have taken it to task for absorbing too much postmodern anti-theory and trying to sustain its advocacy for the disenfranchised without a coherent ethical theoretical basis for doing so. Without some reference to a reality that transcends appearances, there is little reason to assert that any human being is intrinsically valuable or worthy of respect.[29]

Thomas Frank has criticized cultural studies for becoming so enamored with the agency of the audience and with the consumer's powers of creative resistance that they have lost the greatest insight of the Frankfurt School: that autocratic moneyed interests can masquerade in a multitude of ways to ensure that their power is maintained. The sustained fascination of cultural studies with the guerilla tactics of consumers has drifted in the direction of a "market populism" that effectively conflates democratic freedom with consumer choice. Graduates of cultural studies programs have become so expert in the secret rituals of consumption, Frank argues, that they are being vigorously recruited by the culture industries themselves. In fact, there could not be a better preparation for overcoming the creative resistance of the underclass than an intensive program of studies in their strategies. Thus, more and more, departments of cultural studies are training the next generation of manufacturers of consent. "The point now," Frank writes, isn't "so much to celebrate 'resistance' as to work around it, preparing students to make commercials (like the Nike skateboarder spots) that flatter a subculture's paranoia or that use the more standard techniques of prude-dissing or let-you-be-you-ing to get, as the admen put it, under the radar."[30]

From a different angle, cultural studies is criticized for becoming so preoccupied with the subversive element in the use that subcultures make of cultural goods that the only attribute the discipline is capable of seeing in any artifact is the degree to which it is either liberating or oppressive. Commenting on a 1992 set of essays that has become the gold standard of the field of cultural studies in the US (Lawrence Grossberg et al.'s *Cultural Studies*), anthropologist Stefan Collini remarked on what he found to be the common thread:

> The suspicion is that most forms of cultural activity are essentially a disguise for the fact that Somebody is Trying to Screw Somebody Else ... hardly a page of this fat volume goes by without our being told that somebody who possesses some kind of power ... is trying to "dominate," "suppress," "occlude," "mystify," "exploit," "marginalize" ... someone else, and in response it is the duty of those engaged in Cultural Studies to "subvert," "unmask," "contest," "de-legitimize," "intervene," "struggle against."[31]

Thus, there is a reductionistic tendency in much of cultural studies that would lead one to conclude that the only thing worth noting about popular culture are the political and economic power struggles that its production and consumption represents. Particularly under the influence of Michel Foucault, who is ubiquitous in cultural studies of the early 1990s, the discipline tended to adopt a method of deconstruction, which always led to the same conclusion: cultural practices are to be unmasked in order to reveal the spiraling conspiracy of power and knowledge that they facilitate. This leaves little room for considering other aspects of popular culture – for example, the aesthetic, theological, and moral aspirations it might contain.

These three criticisms are suitable warnings for various temptations and transgressions that one can find in the field of cultural studies. Nevertheless, they are not inevitable outcomes. The concepts and lines of inquiry I have summarized above are quite perceptive about the phenomenon of popular culture, and ought to guide any earnest effort to understand what kind of work popular culture does in a society. The trick is to heed the real insights of cultural studies into the operations of popular culture without surrendering to the cynicism, reductionism and aversion to transcendence one can find at its outer edges.

In an essay he wrote 8 years after the publication of his landmark book, *Subculture*, and in the aftermath of having suffered a mental breakdown, Dick Hebdige lamented the loss that the great celebration of the simulacrum, this relishing of life on the surfaces, represents:

> There can be no more . . . trawling for hidden truths, no more going behind appearances of or "against the grain" of the visible and the obvious. . . . In short, no more (Book of) Revelations. Instead what is left, to use another postmodernist key word, is a "fascination" with mirrors, icons, surfaces.[32]

Hebdige was commenting more generally here about the surrender of "the depth model" by so many of the scholars of cultural studies, including himself. Cultural artifacts were once believed to have teleological undercurrents entrusted to them by their creators that thoughtful analysis could reveal. To presume this and look for it is now off limits. Hebdige was genuinely lamenting this, criticizing himself and his colleagues for allowing this fascination with surfaces to crowd out all other considerations. Cultural studies is intent on overcoming depth with a flat world without a "behind . . . with length and breadth but no thickness," because it is only by banishing metaphysics that we will finally achieve a world that is free of debilitating distinctions and hierarchies.[33]

It is probably fair to say that in the current academy, only theologians are brazen enough to openly trawl for hidden truths, to persist in believing in revelation, to seek in their reading of texts some guidance regarding transcendent ends and purposes. Theologians, by trade, believe in a reality behind the appearances. To this bit of audacity, let us now turn.

3

Theology and Culture

The media-world is the shelter where the vast majority of those of us who live in the West dwell and from which we draw the material out of which we make sense of our lives. It is under the canopy of the media that we imbibe, speculate about and negotiate the meaning of love, friendship, beauty, happiness, truth, hope, pain, grace, luck, work, sacrifice, and death. The mediated world of electronic images, sounds, and printed words provides us with our most broadly shared symbols, icons, myths and rituals – the signs with which we enlighten ourselves, search for consolation, and establish our bearings. In some ways organized religion has failed us; but in other ways this is simply due to the emergence of the datasphere and our exposure through it to other workshops of meaning in the world, other ways to assemble stories and symbols that give weight and direction to our existence. Many of these stories and symbols sprang originally from authentic religious traditions, but now float free, available for the taking.

As a theologian reflecting on culture, my sympathies lie with Johann Gottfried Herder. With Herder, I concur that it is not off-limits to speak of culture, and of diverse cultures, in terms of divine providence or as embodiments of God's ideas – at least cautiously. That is a working hypothesis for the remainder of this book, to be explored in this chapter through a survey of classic theological treatments of popular culture, to be followed, in Chapter 4, with an inventory of theological concepts that are particularly useful to cultural inquiry.

One preliminary caution: It is important to acknowledge that the arts and the media are not the only artifacts that tell us about a culture. And simply disclosing and interpreting the symbols, semiotics and values of a culture's arts and media does not exhaust what needs to be said and investigated with respect to social processes that operate within a culture, particularly those processes that lead to oppression and discrimination against age, gender, race, class, etc. Ideological critique is also a worthwhile way to examine a culture. While it is not entirely outside the scope of a theology of culture, it is not the primary focus.

Theologians and the Study of Culture

Christian theologians are notorious for either preemptively dismissing theory that is making the rounds outside their discipline, or rushing headlong to embrace it. The work of cultural studies has caught the attention of many of us, and, true to form, some view it as yet more evidence for the decline of godly civilization, while others, at the opposite end, herald it as the key to understanding all past failures of godly civilization.[1] What has caught the interest of its heralds, in particular, are its twin emphases on the importance of material culture over the standard big ideas, classic texts, and towering personalities when looking for indicators of how people actually construe reality, and the valorization of popular culture as the most vibrant site of creative resistance and liberation of subordinate peoples within Western societies today.[2]

One particularly striking example of this is found in the work of Anthony Pinn, a professor of religious studies at Macalester College. Pinn has offered some trenchant analyses of blues and rap music, sorting them out into various sub-genres and articulating the theological experimentation, social criticism, and envisioning of liberation to which they give voice.[3] Pinn approaches blues and rap as exemplary sites of resistance within popular culture where a subordinate people "tell it like it is" about the hostility of the world toward "Black life" – a reading of their experience that he calls "nitty-gritty hermeneutics." In often uncompromising roughness, blues and rap artists unmask the "nitty-gritty" reality of their suffering and carry their bitterness into convention-breaking music and lyrics that speak aloud their defiance and advocate a variety of strategies of rebellion to their audience. Anyone who listens to them, Pinn argues, cannot help but rethink the social order and the ideological and religious assumptions that perpetuate it. In this, Pinn has followed the lead of the Birmingham theorists to privilege subaltern communities and attend to the grasp of reality that expresses itself in their ad hoc creativity – complete with the elements of *bricolage* and poaching that typify the sampling so characteristic of rap.

Other writers have done as much – James Cone, Michael Eric Dyson, and Jon Michael Spencer have written perceptively on blues, soul, rap and hip hop as forms of community self-affirmation and prophetic critique that have extended the long-standing efforts of the Black churches to empower their people.[4] But Pinn goes further, and divides these musical sites of resistance against the Black churches and their preachers and theologians. As much as blues and rap rhymes object to the dominant culture in American society, he argues, they heave contempt at the Black churches and their God. A persistent message of blues and rap is that Black Christianity perpetuates Black suffering. The crucial insight that Pinn finds in blues and rap to oppose to this is a theological one, namely, that there is no God and that holding onto theistic beliefs keeps subjugated people in their chains. It will not be until they realize that there is no "Being outside of the human realm" who takes an interest in their liberation that they will take the situation in hand and struggle fully against the structures that oppress them.[5] If religion is to become "usable" it must abandon the crutches of theism and all notions of redemptive suffering and rally the people to take matters into their own hands. He writes:

> Only a religiosity that participates in and affirms the cultural life of the community, and speaks plainly to pressing issues without paying tribute to unproved theological assertions – no new wine in old wineskins – is in keeping with the meaning of religion.[6]

Pinn, in other words, privileges the "hermeneutic" of one segment of a subordinate community over the hermeneutic of its own mainstream. He pits the *sub*-subaltern against the subaltern, in effect, and favors the former. He privileges this segment to the extent of claiming that until the Black churches concur with the theological atheism, strong humanism, and no-holds-barred social realism of the rappers, they have no legitimate claim to true religiosity. This is a use of cultural studies that overextends its real value. Cultural studies directs us to understand that a fuller appreciation of the vital and complex life of a society requires an examination of the semiotic guerilla tactics of its subcultures, and that studying their agency in the realm of popular culture is a reliable means to do this. Pinn borrows the concept, produces an eloquent account of two genres of popular culture within the Black community, isolates a hermeneutic of life within these two genres, and then uses it to pass judgment on the central tenets of faith of the Black churches.

Pinn is right to look outside the churches and organized religion to other places where people are making and finding meaning and hope for their lives. But he makes the mistake of concluding that the subaltern rappers have emerged because organized religion has gotten the essentials wrong. While normative judgments have a place in the theological analysis of popular culture, and while religious beliefs ought to come in for some criticism in light of insights that are discovered through cultural studies, Pinn's unilateralism lacks subtlety. His work so privileges the insights generated by one site of resistance within popular culture that it misses the kind of reciprocity of judgment that ought to characterize the enterprise of theology of culture. He has turned the sound guidance of cultural studies to listen respectfully to deviant uses of popular culture into a prejudice that presumes deviance is where the truth will be found. This is an error to be avoided. The relationship between the discipline of theology and the theological improvisation that occurs in popular culture should be characterized by more thoughtful reciprocity than this. As the theologian Jürgen Moltmann has advised, the reason it is important to grasp "the *implicit theology* of this modern world of ours, and understand why and how it was born," is "so that we can recognize *both* its vitality *and* its congenital defects."[7]

While it is true that the media-world is still relatively new, popular culture is not. Theologians have had to advise the churches for centuries on how they should relate to popular culture. Moltmann's distinction between an openness to the vitality of a culture and a suspicion of its congenital defects is a good one for identifying two opposing schools of thought vis-à-vis culture in the history of Christian theology. Both have solid pedigrees going back to the church fathers, and both have their advocates on the scene today. Because the writings of Tertullian and Augustine on how Christians should view the gladiatorial games, athletic contests, theater and poetry of the ancient world offer the basic arguments of both sides in this debate, it will be instructive to begin with them.

Popular Culture's Congenital Defects: Tertullian's *de Spectaculus*

Tertullian was a church father from Carthage, a Roman city on the north coast of Africa, who lived from 160–225 CE. Born a pagan, he studied law in Rome, converted to Christianity in his thirties and had a long career as a theologian and apologist for the Christian faith. He stands out for the moral rigor he expected of Christians, and for his vigorous defenses of the minority Christian community against charges of atheism, cannibalism, and treachery toward the state that circulated in the second century, depicting Christians instead as good citizens of the empire who posed no threat to its well-being. He is also remembered for his colorful rhetoric, and left us with such enduring declarations as "What has Athens to do with Jerusalem?" and, "The blood of the martyrs is the seed of the Church."

In the second century Christians were a common scapegoat when plagues, barbarian invasions and natural disasters struck. To bring an end to such calamities, a provincial or imperial decree would typically be issued, dictating that all inhabitants must offer sacrifices to placate the gods of the empire. Many Christians would refuse, the public would blame them for the latest troubles, and mob violence would ensue, only to be calmed by magistrates who would round up Christians and sentence them to various sorts of torture and death in the coliseums.

Coliseums and arenas throughout the Roman Empire were the sites of ceremonial games that performed a number of functions in Roman society – religious, penal, and patriotic. The games originated as rites of the imperial cult, which honored the pagan gods and were thought to be modeled after the festivals of the gods themselves. It was believed that the more spectacular the games, and the greater the loss of life, the higher the tribute being paid the deities.[8] More immediately practical, however, the games had become an effective way to dispose of enemies captured in Rome's skirmishes at its frontiers (Gauls, Spaniards, Arabs, Germans), as well as enemies within (Christians and other minorities who had proven difficult to assimilate), displaying up-close to residents of the provincial centers of the empire that their adversaries were being destroyed.

The games featured gladiators, dwarves, women warriors and wild animals, sometimes matched against each other, sometimes matched against the enemies of the state. Criminals would be "purchased" from city jails by wealthy donors who would then send them in to be dramatically massacred by expertly trained fighters and wild beasts. Gladiators were themselves typically slaves or condemned criminals who could extend their lives and gain a sort of heroic celebrity through swearing the gladiator's oath and consenting to beatings, combat and, eventually, death. The wealthiest donors could supply combatants for games lasting several days, gaining favor with state officials whose authority was connected to the games, and earn public recognition and gratitude.[9] This financing end of the whole operation can be seen as an early form of corporate sponsorship.

Ridley Scott's movie, *Gladiator* (2000), set during the reign of Emperor Commodus, the son of Marcus Aurelius, opens in 180 CE, the year Commodus assumed power. The real life Commodus was particularly fond of the games, required the senators to attend as a sign of their loyalty, and is recorded by the third-century historians Herodian and Dio Cassius as displaying his own warrior prowess by descending to the floor of the coliseum to fight subservient gladiators and slaughter hippopotami, elephants, rhinoceroses, and ostriches in the hundreds. A favorite trick was to cleanly decapitate ostriches and send their headless bodies scurrying aimlessly around the amphitheater to the roaring approval of the crowd. Scott's movie does justice to the politics, economics, combatants, brutal violence, and public acclaim for the games.

This was the context of Tertullian's treatise *de Spectaculus* (197 CE), in which he condemns "the spectacles," or shows, as degrading to all who come into contact with them.[10] For Tertullian, the shows included the gladiatorial games, but also the circus, the theater and the races – all manner of public entertainment of his time.[11] In this treatise we have a classic articulation of one strain among several that have emerged in Christianity regarding the attitude that believers should adopt toward popular entertainment. "The laws of Christian Discipline," he writes, "forbid among the other sins of the world the pleasures of the public shows."[12] In the treatise, Tertullian claims that the shows are demonic and he offers three arguments to prove this: their pagan origin, their conduct, and their social consequences.

The festival days around which the shows are arranged have their roots in paganism, he argues, as can be plainly seen in that they are dedicated to such false gods as Venus (patroness of lust), Bacchus (patron of drunkenness), Circe (the enchantress), and Neptune (ruler of the surging passions of the soul). The gladiatorial games retain elements of ancient rites of human sacrifice, which can be detected in the cruelty they are known to have perfected toward their victims. Perhaps they mete out a kind of justice, but it is a perverse justice. True, Tertullian allows, they provide a mechanism for the guilty to be punished; nevertheless, God commands us to love our enemies and show them mercy. Consequently, "the innocent can find no pleasure in another's sufferings: he rather mourns that a brother has sinned so heinously as to need a punishment so dreadful." Besides, it is not always the guilty who are thrown to wild beasts or drawn on racks.[13] Instead of teaching us mercy, these spectacles of combat "lead to spiritual agitation," and thus to inward rivalries, which give rise to "rage, bitterness, wrath, and grief, with all bad things which flow from them."[14]

Furthermore, the games encourage their audiences to adopt a socially destructive sense of irony, given that the very brawls that are reproached in the streets are rewarded in the arena, "making that which is good in one place evil in another, and that which is evil in one place in another good." The combatants and performers, who have been deprived of their rights as citizens, are exploited; their souls and their bodies are prostituted. This, plus the violence to which they are submitted, so "disfigures the human countenance" that it amounts to "nothing less than the disfigurement of God's own image."[15]

So much for the games. Tertullian's charges against the theater are no less reviling, if differently nuanced. What the theater lacks in actual violence, it substitutes for in immodesty, buffoonery, the incitement of violence, and lies. The theater offers a harbor to harlots and fools in women's clothes who, in enacting tragedies and comedies before susceptible audiences, are "bloody and wanton, impious and licentious inventors of crimes and lusts." They instruct their audiences in social pathologies and encourage them to go and do likewise. Even if they don't inspire immediate mayhem, the plays so titillate theatergoers with images that they "store up in their souls," in the words of John Chrysostom – another church father who took a low view of the theater – that when they return home, they find the humdrum reality of their lives unbearable. In competition with these images, "your wife seems rather distasteful, your children seem rather tiresome, your servants a nuisance and your house too much, and the usual cares associated with running the necessary affairs of the household appear troublesome, and everyone who belongs to it is tiresome and a nuisance."[16]

Furthermore, Tertullian finds the donning of masks that occurs onstage to be in violation of the biblical prohibition against "making every kind of likeness." God, to the contrary, who is the very author of truth, does not approve of "any putting on of voice, or sex, or age; He never will approve pretended loves, and wraths, and groans, and tears."[17] For Tertullian, acting is a form of image-making that falls under the prohibition against graven images found in the first of the Ten Commandments.

In a broad stroke, Tertullian dismisses everything that even appears to be virtuous in the circus, theater, athletic contests, and gladiatorial spectacles: "Everything there, then, that is either brave, noble, loud-sounding, melodious, or exquisite in taste, hold it but as the honey drop of a poisoned cake."[18]

In making his case, Tertullian raises what he takes to be the best argument of his opponents.

> [E]veryone is ready with the argument that all things, as we teach, were created by God, and given to man for his use, and that they must be good, as coming all from so good a source; but that among them are found the various constituent elements of the public shows, such as the horse, the lion, bodily strength, and musical voice. It cannot, then, be thought that what exists by God's own creative will is either foreign or hostile to Him; and if it is not opposed to Him, it cannot be regarded as injurious to His worshippers, as certainly it is not foreign to them. Beyond all doubt, too, the very buildings connected with the places of public amusement, composed as they are of rocks, stones, marbles, pillars, are things of God, who has given these various things for the earth's embellishment; nay, the very scenes are enacted under God's own heaven. How skillful a pleader seems human wisdom to herself, especially if she has the fear of losing any of her delights . . .[19]

In short, since all that exists in nature has been willed into existence by God, and since, following the account of creation in Genesis 1, God has proclaimed each level of creation "good," the various creatures (horses and lions), activities (bodily strength and musical voice), and architectural elements (rocks, stones, marbles, pillars) found assembled for our entertainment at the coliseum are intrinsically good. What can be the harm in our enjoyment of them?

Tertullian concedes that there are no explicit prohibitions of the shows in the Bible. Nevertheless, he counters this sanguine view with the argument that there is a "hostile power" in the world that works against God and "perverts to wrong uses the things His hand has formed." We must differentiate, he insists, between the original purpose for which a thing was created and the perverted use to which it may be put. He writes: "There is a vast difference between the corrupted state and that of primal purity." True, all things are God's, "but in offending Him, it ceases to be His."[20] The shows pervert elements of creation that are designed to testify to their Creator by recasting them into a great cacophony of noisy idols. He describes this as a desecration of good nature, which, once desecrated, is itself polluted and defiles all who come into contact with it. It is through such human actions of desecration reverberating upon the horses, the lions, the music, marble and architecture that serve as the constituent elements of the spectacles that Satan and his angels are invited to fill the world and to exercise their power.

In an earlier treatise, *On Idolatry*, Tertullian went so far as to say that one need not be so brazen as to "burn incense, immolate a victim, or give a sacrificial banquet" to be guilty of idolatry. Even artisans who enter contracts with the architects of pagan temples, altars, shrines, or statues – artisans at any stage of production, from quarrymen to plasterers to masons, bronze workers, gold-leaf manufacturers, incense-makers, and painters – corrupt their art if the work of their hands is knowingly destined for cultic practices, and should not be admitted into the church. Likewise the teacher of literature who even utters the names or delineates the genealogies of the gods to his students.[21]

Finally, in a move that offers to restore what he has just disparaged, Tertullian admits the need humans have for the delights of drama, music, intrigue, and even violence. But he invites his reader to pick up the Bible and its stories, and to attend to the liturgy of the church and the dramas that it enacts through ritual:

> If the literature of the stage delights you, we have literature in abundance of our own – plenty of verses, sentences, songs, proverbs; and these not fabulous, but true; not tricks of art, but plain realities. Would you have also fightings and wrestlings? Well, of these there is no lacking, and they are not of slight account. Behold unchastity overcome by chastity, perfidy slain by faithfulness, cruelty stricken by compassion ... [T]hese are the contests we have among us, and in these *we* win our crowns. Would you have something of blood too? You have Christ's.[22]

Tertullian had such a high regard for divine revelation as found in scripture that he discounted the value of all things pagan, even its best literature. The poets and playwrights, along with the actors, charioteers and wrestlers, he concludes, are destined for that greatest of spectacles, the fierce fires of divine judgment. This treatise, aimed at the Christian community to admonish it to minimize contact with the surrounding pagan culture, was Tertullian's way of instructing Christians that, "you have your joys where you have your longings." If one longs for the excitement of the shows, one longs to be satisfied by a crass imitation of the deeper excitement of a life lived for God, where true drama consists in the struggles that overcome sin. In this, Tertullian established for Christianity one pattern of response to the surrounding culture – it is a land of alluring idols to be avoided. Contact with the culture on its terms is defiling. As H. Richard Niebuhr concluded, Tertullian serves as "one of the foremost illustrations of the anticultural movement to be found in the history of the church."[23] The Church, for Tertullian, is an alternative society, an ark of redemption drifting upon a sea of roiling sin.

Popular Culture's Religious Vitality: Augustine

While he lived there about 150 years after Tertullian had died, Saint Augustine was familiar with Carthage. In his *Confessions* he recalls this city where he was sent to be educated at the age of sixteen, and where he spent most of the decade of his twenties, first as a student, later as a teacher: "I went to Carthage, where I found myself in the midst of a hissing cauldron of lust." As the largest cosmopolitan city in the Roman territory of Africa, Carthage was an epicenter of popular entertainment in the empire, famous for its circus, amphitheater and gladiatorial shows – a fourth-century Las Vegas. As a libidinous teenager, Augustine's particular weakness was for the theater, he tells us, "because the plays reflected my own unhappy plight and were tinder to my fire." He was a fan of romantic tragedies, and the more the actors moved him to pity, the more delight he derived. The uniting and then distressing separation of lovers was an exquisite pleasure to witness, he admits, although he had "no wish to endure the sufferings which I only saw on the stage."[24] But the sweet tears these imaginary fictions brought to his eyes absorbed him and strangely ramped up from friendly feelings toward the victims of love, he confides, into full-force torrents of lust.

While not much of a fan of gladiators himself, Augustine describes at length the experience of his close friend, Alypius, who was "caught in the whirl of easy morals at Carthage, with its continual round of futile entertainments, and had lost his heart and his head to the games in the amphitheater." For a time Alypius was able to overcome his craving for the games, but then on a trip to Rome he set out to prove his mastery of his former obsession by accompanying friends to the arena for a gladiatorial show, determined to keep his eyes clamped shut and thus serve as a model of virtue to his companions. In a gripping passage, Augustine describes the scene:

> An incident in the fight drew a great roar from the crowd, and this thrilled him so deeply that he could not contain his curiosity. ... So he opened his eyes.... When he saw the blood, it was as though he had drunk a deep draught of savage passion. Instead of turning away, he fixed his eyes upon the scene and drank in all its frenzy, unaware of what he was doing. He reveled in the wickedness of the fighting and was drunk with the fascination of bloodshed. He was no longer the man who had come to the arena, but simply one of the crowd which he had joined. ... [W]hen he left the arena, he carried with him a diseased mind which would leave him no peace until he came back again.[25]

From these accounts, we get a sense for the perverse appeal Augustine finds in the popular forms of entertainment of his day. It is an appeal he knows first-hand; when one succumbs, the will is overcome with a craving that cannot be controlled. Although Augustine's reservations about the spectacles did have something to do with their pagan elements and with the work of demons for whom they offered cover, criticisms he shared with Tertullian, they had even more to do with their irresistible attractiveness to human cupidity – to our proclivity to surrender our will to unrestrained cravings for objects that are less than God.

It is worth noting that much had changed in the Roman Empire in the years that separated Augustine from Tertullian. After Emperor Constantine's conversion to Christianity in 312 CE, pagan society had begun feeling pressure from edicts granting greater tolerance for the Church and less tolerance for pagan religion. During Augustine's life, laws were issued by Emperor Theodosius I directing local officials to remove idols and altars from pagan temples and to destroy them, to confiscate property on which pagan rites were performed, to prohibit visits to pagan temples, and to exclude pagans from imperial employment. Because the Roman senate and army remained largely pagan, these laws were resisted by local officials, but intense and violent pressure from bands of Christian vigilantes such as the Circumcellions in Egypt was very effective in curbing the open practice of pagan religion. Still, the games held on; they had a firm grasp on the popular imagination – for both pagans and Christians.

Given the ebb and flow of pagan devotion in the late fourth century, the time was ripe for someone to discern what this meant. Augustine stepped up to the challenge. In his *Confessions*, *On Christian Doctrine*, and his monumental *City of God*, he marked the passing of pagan culture by distinguishing between pagan poetry, temple cult, and philosophy. For the most part, he favored its philosophy but wrote abusively about its poetry, myth, and cult. The philosophers, and particularly the Platonists, he wrote in *On Christian Doctrine*, "have said things which are indeed true and are well accommodated to our faith."[26] In the *City of God*, he lays down a sweeping criticism of the work of the poets and their stories of the gods – stories frequently performed at the theater – insisting that these stories are "foolish things" that cannot be rendered into real wisdom with any amount of interpretation.

But as is often the case with Augustine, these declarations do not tell the whole story. On the opening page of the *City of God* he transcribes a stanza from the pagan poet Virgil – the author of the epic poems about the ancient gods that became primary source material for the dramas upon which Augustine heaped so much scorn – to summarize the basic dialectic of his own argument in two brief lines:

> Show pity to the humbled soul,
> And crush the sons of pride.

In these two lines of poetry Augustine draws on the authority of the pagan Virgil to introduce his Christian argument about the city of God (the humbled soul) and the earthly city (the sons of pride). In fact, the *City of God* contains frequent transcriptions of Virgil, accompanied by such endorsements as "the most famous poet speaks truly ... "[27] In the *Confessions* he suggests that while the fables of the poets are not "true," they nevertheless "provide real food for thought."[28] Following a long examination of the myriad corruptions of nature and miseries that have been introduced as a result of original sin and the curse, he pauses to consider the "blessings of God" which have persisted in spite of it all. Among these blessings he lists such "astonishing arts" as weaving, navigation, architecture, painting, sculpture, the theater, song and musical instruments, each of which owes its existence to God's providence – God who has filled the human mind with exuberant inventiveness, vigor and a marvelous nimbleness, and not removed these as punishment for our sin. "The little spark of reason," Augustine assures us, "which was the image of God in him, has not been quite quenched." Even the theater receives a guarded endorsement here. "What wonderful spectacles," he writes, "are exhibited in the theaters, which those who have not seen them cannot credit!"[29] While Augustine, like Tertullian, was a pagan who had been recast into a Christian, unlike Tertullian he retained a real affection for the world he had turned his back on – a world that was now itself threatened both internally by the growing Christian influence, and externally by the incursions of barbarians from northern Europe – and took the view that aspects of pagan culture ought to be preserved and put into the service of the church.

In effect, Augustine softened the boundary between the church and the surrounding culture that had been erected by Tertullian and other church fathers. In Augustine's terms, while the earthly and heavenly cities had two different ultimate destinies, for the present, they "are mingled together from the beginning down to the end."[30] The two cities, he wrote, "are entangled together in this world, and intermixed until the last judgment effects their separation."[31] Citizens of both cities inhabit overlapping spaces for the duration of history, and spend their lives passing through the same buildings, participating in the same institutions, witnessing the same works of art, and engaging in many of the same social practices that constitute the earthly city. The difference between them is not in the external accoutrements of their lives, but in the quality of their love and attachment to these things. We are citizens of the earthly city to the extent that we love the earthly city as an end in itself; we are citizens of the heavenly city to the extent that we make use of the earthly city – including its astonishing arts and cultural attainments – as a way of loving God.

With respect to cultural phenomena that functioned in the ancient world as popular culture – such as the games, the theater, pagan philosophy, myth and ritual – Tertullian readily associated the bulk of it with false gods and idolatry. As such, he insisted that participating in them at any level would draw Satan and his demons into the world to do their work. Augustine, on the other hand, suggests that while idolatry is bad and to be avoided in every case, idols and their stories can be examined for what they can tell us about various attributes and actions of God. The various mysterious powers attributed to the gods, by which particular things are caused to be, by which seeds germinate, diseases are healed, eloquent speech is uttered, wars are fought and won, the waters are governed, the light of the sun is sustained, and human minds acquire knowledge of the arts that are necessary for life – the very powers that had been distributed among the gods in the pagan imagination – "these are the things the one true God makes and does."[32] Examining the powers of the gods can be viewed as a primitive form of metaphysics that accurately analyzes the forces that operate in the universe, even if it fails to determine their true source.

And so, Augustine urges, the pantheon of pagan gods should not be spurned out of hand given what they might teach us about how the world works and, moreover, about the attributes of the true God. "We ought rather to seek to know what gods these are, and for what purpose they may appear to have been selected." Augustine then lists, among others, the gods whose specialized powers are well known: Jupiter, Saturn, Mercury, Mars, Neptune, and Venus. It is important to note, first, he suggests, that despite their rivalries, these gods work for the most part in concert. The pantheon is at least a distorted recognition that the cosmos is unified and coherent. Furthermore, the ancients who "invented the images, badges, and adornments of the gods" did so, he speculates, out of a humane desire to provide people with vessels they could see with their own eyes, vessels that contain real mysteries. And while this took away some of their fear of cosmic mysteries, a worthy achievement in Augustine's view, it also added error.[33] But for Augustine this is worth sorting through; there is much to be gained from an investigation of the invented symbols and fabulous deities of the pagans regarding knowledge of an array of powers that are in reality the work of the one true and supreme God who is the great mystery deep below the surface. Given that humans are made to long for God, and given the inescapable fact that even proper worship requires the use of signs, it is to be expected, Augustine argues, that humans will discover in earthly and celestial forces a rich supply of "symbols of mystery ... which increase our mystical knowledge." Thus, even in the scriptures God is called lamb, calf, lion and rock, which are all sanctioned ways to signify God, provided God is treated as that to which these things point.[34]

Behind this view of a true religion which adores the world as a means to worship God is Augustine's fundamental principle of the human condition, namely that the heart is restless until it finds peace in God. It is with this recognition that Augustine framed his *Confessions*, his autobiographical examination of his own restless life. Looking back he understood that his life had been a succession of grasping for some enduring consolation – ideas, bodily gratifications, social esteem, friendships, metaphysical schemes – to which he became attached, eventually grew weary, then moved on. Driving this restlessness, he concluded, was an unslakable desire for the true God, a desire that kept pressing him to fix onto some aspect of reality larger than himself. God alone can satisfy this longing; the world can function only as a set of signs through which God is encountered.

One can find in Augustine two norms that guide his judgments regarding which elements of pagan culture deserve to be preserved. First, he claims that "Wherever we may find truth, it is the Lord's."[35] With this norm in mind, he makes such observations as:

> We should not think that we ought not to learn literature because Mercury is said to be its inventor, nor that because the pagans dedicated temples to Justice and Virtue and adored in stones what should be performed in the heart, we should therefore avoid justice and virtue.[36]

He goes on, "If the philosophers have said things that are indeed true and are well accommodated to our faith, they should not be feared; rather, what they have said should be taken from them as from unjust possessors and converted to our use." Just as the people of Israel took vases, ornaments, garments, gold and silver from the Egyptians when they fled, "as if to put them to a better use," Christians should plunder the philosophers.[37]

The second norm is charity. Augustine writes: "Knowledge which is used to promote love is useful."[38] In his handling of pagan religious symbols and forms of devotional practice, Augustine adamantly rejects those that have arisen from collusion with demons. But this does not exhaust all pagan symbols and practices; there are many that the Romans had borrowed from nature and history, which are for Augustine legitimate sources for symbolizing the divine, and only become problematic when observed in an idolatrous manner. This misuse, however, does not invalidate them as potentially useful religious signs that can be used in understanding or worshipping the one true God. To test their usefulness as genuine religious symbols, Augustine proposes that they be interpreted in the chamber of the conscience. If in a particular interpretation of an appropriated pagan symbol the interpreter is aware of himself becoming more proficient at loving God and neighbor, then there is something worthy of retrieval in the symbol. By proficiency in love, Augustine has in mind "the motion of the soul toward the enjoyment of God for God's own sake."[39]

This understanding of love as the "enjoyment" of God is a technical definition in Augustine. He frequently distinguishes between the terms "enjoyment" (*frui* – as in the word fruition) and "use" (*uti* – as in the word utilize). To *enjoy* something is to love it for its own sake. To *use* something is to employ it in moving closer to that which is loved. But both enjoyment and use are ways of loving. The first is appropriate to human love for God and the second is appropriate to human love for other creatures. In this distinction, Augustine prescribes the proper attitude one is to take regarding religious symbols. "In this mortal life," he writes, "wandering from God, if we wish to return to our native country where we can be blessed we should *use* this world and not *enjoy* it ... so that by means of corporal and temporal things we may comprehend the eternal and spiritual."[40] Or, expressed differently: "Love those things by which we are carried along for the sake of that toward which we are carried."[41] Thus, any sign, whether it is a symbol or a custom, may be appropriated by a Christian provided one's application of it propels the soul in this movement toward God which Augustine calls charity.

This is precisely the shortcoming of the pagans in their poetic and theatrical portrayals of the gods. The pagan gods are presented as moral criminals. Augustine is fond of citing the example of Jupiter, who is "painted, cast, beaten, carved, written, read, acted, sung, and danced" in the act of committing adultery.[42] This sort of behavior attributed to the gods can only inspire similar immorality in humans, who know instinctively that they are to imitate the divine. Consequently, these religious symbols and performances make people unfit for society and depraved, and thereby fall short of the criteria of charity. In any legitimate representation of the divine, it is incumbent, according to the very idea of divinity, "to publish in plain terms the laws of a good life."[43] The theater, then, is not intrinsically evil; all depends upon the love of God and neighbor that it inspires.

Even the artistry and ornamentation that is incorporated into the most mundane objects can be an occasion for gratitude to God. In *Confessions*, Augustine writes,

> By every kind of art and the skill of their hands men make innumerable things – clothes, shoes, pottery, and other useful objects, besides pictures and various works which are the fruit of the imagination. They make them on a far more lavish scale than is required to satisfy their own modest needs or to express their devotion, and all these things are additional temptations to the eye, made by men who love the worldly things they make themselves but forget their own Maker and destroy what he made in them. But, O my God, my Glory, for these things too I offer you a hymn of thanksgiving. I make a sacrifice of praise to him who sanctifies me, for the beauty which flows through men's minds into their skilful hands comes from that Beauty which is above their souls and for which my soul sighs all day and night.[44]

Thus, Augustine offers a strategy for the appropriation of pagan religious symbols and all varieties of popular art. They may be appropriated if they can be pressed into the service of charity, into the journey of the soul to God, as a *means* of devotion rather than as *objects* of devotion, if they can be "used" rather than "enjoyed." Pagan customs, figures, metaphors, fables, precepts, poetry, theater, paintings, sculptures, clothing, shoes, and pottery may be plundered if they can be put to use in such a way as to enable one to enjoy God and imitate divine goodness.

Furthermore, Augustine *encourages* this appropriation. First, by pointing out that it is the fitting thing to indulge the human need for tangible signs, and, second, by claiming that truth artfully adorned is more persuasive, comprehensible, and conducive to stirring human beings to charity. Augustine, for these reasons, is receptive to a Christian use of elements of popular culture from outside of the church. The treasures of the pagans and even conventional ornaments may be plundered and converted to a better use in the worship of the one true God.

Open Resistance or Cautious Compromise?

So, between Tertullian and Augustine we have two different views of culture, both of which have had enduring influence on Western Christianity. *From Tertullian* we have inherited a view of culture and the church as discrete realities, in which the surrounding culture is essentially a great expanse of human activity riddled with idolatry that beckons as a sweet poison to the pious. *From Augustine* we have received a view of culture and church as two intertwined cities with many common spaces and activities. Where and when the earthly city grasps truth and promotes charity, it may be used by the pious as a means to know and love God and neighbor. Religious movements in the lineage of Tertullian promote the idea of withdrawal from, if not open resistance to, the world and its snares; those in the lineage of Augustine seek compromises with the surrounding culture, leveraging the good where it is found, and acknowledge their participation in the general life of the world. Ernst Troeltsch, a German theologian writing at the beginning of the twentieth century, identifies these two trajectories as distinct models of religious community, which he calls "sect" and "church," each promoting a different social theory. The sect type, he explains, views the world with indifference, if not active hostility, is suspicious of institutions, even those it creates, and demands purity of heart in all things. The church type maintains an openness to the world, accepting the political order as a remedial form of grace that mitigates the grosser effects of sin.[45] The church-type endorses the participation of Christians in the secular world as agents of reform, and accommodates itself to prevailing practices of scientific inquiry, artistic expression, and modes of communication.

Troeltsch had certain affinities for the church-type, but recognized that over the centuries it was in the interaction and tension of church and sect that Christianity had sustained its vitality. Both types, he argued, have their point of origin in the Bible. The sect seeks to follow the strict teachings and example of Jesus in the Gospels; the church is a response to the message of Paul, who in his efforts at bringing the Gospel to the Gentiles had found it necessary to reach compromises, adjusting the radicalism of the kingdom of God teachings to the political and social realities of the diverse communities he encountered in his travels. Visiting Athens, Paul entered discussions with Stoic and Epicurean philosophers and acknowledged that even this city full of idols had not been without a witness to the one true God, and he acknowledged with the Stoics that a divine Logos pervaded everything in the universe and that a universal moral law had been written on the human heart (Acts 17). Theologians like Augustine and Thomas Aquinas would develop this concession to

Stoicism into a full-blown doctrine of natural law, rich with possibilities for understanding how divine grace and providence persist in guiding, sustaining and sometimes overthrowing the political and social order, convinced that the close inspection of the secular order will uncover the work of God operating deep in its proceedings.

Tertullian's heirs are found in a great variety of Christian movements and individuals who have made it central to their piety to promote a way of life separate from, and standing in judgment of, the surrounding culture. The early monastic movement, Anabaptists, radical Baptists, Quakers, and Adventists are movements that at least began with this impulse. Leo Tolstoy was a powerful advocate for those who would withdraw from the world and erect alternative societies, and an incisive critic of the means by which cultures stupefy people into perpetuating violence and oppression. On the present scene are North American theologians like George Lindbeck, John Howard Yoder and Stanley Hauerwas, whose theological views have been described as "postliberal," and British theologians like John Milbank and Catherine Pickstock, who have adopted the banner of "radical orthodoxy." Postliberalism and radical orthodoxy claim that biblical language and narratives – and theologies that are consistent with them – offer a cohesive world that stands as an alternative to the "Enlightenment project" of modernity, an alternative world that faithful Christians are called to inhabit.

Hauerwas is particularly adamant about this.[46] In his view, the church is "an alternative *polis*, a countercultural social structure," and the history of the true church, or, using his term, the "confessing church," is at odds with the history of the West. He treats the church and its practices and narratives as if they were the products of an independent development in the midst of Western history. While he denies that the confessing church aspires to withdraw from the world, he insists that it will, if true to itself, reject modern culture "with a few exceptions."[47] When the church is the church, it is composed of "people who live here as aliens," a "colony of heaven" that does not recognize the sovereignty of nation-states nor easily acquiesce to the grasp of reality asserted by the surrounding culture. The confessing church has been shaped according to a different story and by a different set of values than the stories and values of the surrounding culture. What it offers to the world is an alternative vision and a community to which exiles from the culture can come to be converted, detoxified and transformed. Hauerwas's view, in short, is that the Christian community represents a counter-history to the history of the emergence of modernity, and it is this counter-history which ought to be a Christian's deepest moral and metaphysical framework. Theologies of culture, along the lines of the work of Paul Tillich, Hauerwas claims, are engaged in the "Constantinian enterprise of making the faith credible to the powers-that-be so that Christians might now have a share in those powers."[48] Such theologies are, in the end, he says, hard "to distinguish from journalism."[49]

Echoes of Tertullian resound in Hauerwas, as they do in postliberalism and radical orthodoxy in general. Tertullian's question, "What has Athens to do with Jerusalem?," his searing critique of the seductive idolatries that divert Christians from worshipping the true God, and his insistence that our economies are inextricably dependent upon the manufacturing of idols are central themes in the writings of these thinkers. And as Tertullian appealed to those who had a taste for the "literature of the stage" by tantalizing them with the alternative literature of the church, a literature full of "fightings and wrestlings" that are narrated toward radically different endings, these contemporary Tertullians invite their listeners to enter the Gospel as an adventurously alternative way of thinking the world and acting upon it.

Augustine's heirs have been more sympathetic to the continuities between Christianity and culture than have Tertullian's. Indeed, Augustine *was* a post-Constantinian thinker who was trying to understand the place of Christian faith in a culture where Christianity had finally gained legal standing. While Augustine thought the course of history through in terms of the unending tension between the heavenly and earthly cities, he allowed at the outset that the underlying desire that kept both in play was a love for the metaphysical goodness of being – a goodness of being which can be found in both cities. According to Augustine, "there cannot be a nature in which there is no good."[50] Every being, insofar as it exists, is good. It is human concupiscence – our boundless, pulsating, heedless desire – that corrupts this goodness by latching onto creatures to satisfy our craving for God. By desiring finite goods (e.g., power, friendship, romantic partners, food, material goods, comfort) for more satisfaction than they can deliver, and organizing our lives around them, it is as if we suck the goodness out of them. When the inherent goodness of something is in this way desiccated, its being is diminished, although it retains something good until the point that it ceases to exist.

The earthly city is the world we create through our concupiscence, attaching greater expectations to the finite world than it is designed to uphold, seeking in creation a degree of fulfillment that can only be found in God. With Augustine, finite goods exist to facilitate our enjoyment of God. Loading our friends, possessions, families, political institutions, artists, scientists, or entertainments with the full weight of our boundless longing results in their recoiling under the pressure and our resentment that they have disappointed us. Concupiscence sets in motion burdens and disappointments that spiral out of control, which is the core of the human condition for Augustine. We are all already born into this earthly city which sizzles with the dissatisfactions and betrayals of misplaced and inordinate desire. Nevertheless, where being is found, goodness is found. And our world is *earthly* to the extent that we enjoy it as an end in itself; it is *heavenly* to the extent that it is loved as an exercise in our enjoyment of God.

In league with Augustine's guarded endorsement of all things finite, Martin Luther popularized the leveling formula of *finitum capax infiniti* (the finite has the capacity for the infinite) according to which divine goodness is understood to have the power to appear wherever God wills and a believer is receptive – in the basic sacramental elements of water, bread and wine, but also in the humble phenomena of a crib, a cross, skin, muscle and bones, parental love, and the tools of one's trade. Indeed, according to Luther, "God in his essence is present everywhere, in and through the whole creation in all its parts and in all places, and so the world is full of God and he fills it all, yet he is not limited or circumscribed by it."[51] John Calvin, whose severe views on the corrosive effects of the Fall of Adam and Eve are well known, still insisted that a "common grace" continues to work outside of the church, both in nature and in human affairs. Friederich Schleiermacher located an opening onto the infinite in the very structure of human consciousness, through a deeply residing awareness that he called the "feeling of absolute dependence," an aperture in all of us through which the constant presence of God enters the world. The fundamental insight which each of these thinkers has handed on is that even the most common productions of human creativity can be interpreted theologically as indicating the presence and activity of God in the midst of human existence. Paul Tillich attempted to transform this insight into an actual discipline of inquiry to which he gave the name "theology of culture." At the heart of this inquiry is his formulation: "Religion is the depth of culture, culture is the form of religion."

Paul Tillich's Theology of Culture

Paul Tillich was born in 1886, the son of a Lutheran pastor in a village near Berlin, Germany. By the age of 28, he had received his doctorate in philosophy, been ordained as a Lutheran pastor, and had served for several years in a church in a working-class neighborhood of Berlin. Within months of the outbreak of the First World War in 1914, Tillich volunteered for military service and was appointed to serve as a chaplain in the Army. His first orders took him to the western front, where for 4 years he led services of worship, prayed with the dying, dug graves and buried the dead, and comforted troops whose faith and patriotism were corroded by the horrors of the war. As he propped up the faith of others during these years in the trenches, he made the discovery that he could restore his own faith in God and humanity through the unlikely medium of reproductions of great paintings in art books and magazines that he purchased at field bookstores. He described thumbing through these in candle and lantern light to distract his mind during lulls in the bombardments on the front, and, as his division moved about, he would decorate the walls of their temporary quarters with art lithographs cut from magazines. At the end of the war, Tillich, who had only begun paying attention to art as a diversion from the fighting, resolved to go see some original paintings at a museum in Berlin. Once there he found himself standing before Sandro Botticelli's fifteenth-century painting, *Madonna with Singing Angels*, a painting from one of his books that had comforted him at the front. Years later, Tillich wrote of this moment at the museum:

> Gazing up at it, I felt a state approaching ecstasy. In the beauty of the painting there was Beauty itself. It shone through the colors of the paint as the light of day shines through the stained glass windows of a medieval church.
>
> As I stood there, bathed in the beauty its painter had envisioned so long ago, something of the divine source of all things came through to me. I turned away shaken.
>
> That moment has affected my whole life, given me the keys for the interpretation of human existence, brought vital joy and spiritual truth. I compare it with what is usually called revelation in the language of religion.[52]

He went on to acknowledge that he wouldn't put this moment of revelation on the same level as that experienced by the biblical prophets, but he insisted there was an analogy between their experience and his that he had never appreciated before. "In both cases, the experience goes beyond the way we encounter reality in our daily lives. It opens up depths experienced in no other way." Looking back on the experience 36 years later, he admitted that this particular painting is not really exceptional, that he has subsequently seen much more lucid expressions of the "Divine Presence" in other paintings – paintings by Cézanne, Van Gogh and Picasso, in particular, which are religious in "style" if not in "content." Nevertheless, he confided, the strength of that one "moment of ecstasy" as he stood transfixed before Botticelli's *Madonna* in 1918, was overwhelming to a degree that he would never experience again. That crystalline moment opened up for Tillich a new way of seeing cultural productions as potential bearers of divine revelation.

In the spring of 1919, a few months after this experience, Tillich was invited to offer a lecture to the Kant Society in Berlin. He was in the middle of teaching his first university course, "Christianity and the Social

Problems of the Present," a course built around Troeltsch's recently published *The Social Teachings of the Christian Churches* (1914) and seeking to sort through the cultural trauma that was on everyone's mind in the circumstances of the still fresh military defeat and political humiliation of Germany. In the aftermath of the war, Berlin was drawing such experimental talent as Wassily Kandinsky, Paul Klee, Franz Marc, Bertolt Brecht, Fritz Lang, Rainer Maria Rilke, and Walter Benjamin. Tillich used the occasion of his Kant Society lecture to ascertain the religious stirrings he could discern in the depths of various new experiments in art, science, politics, and morality. From these bohemian edges of early Weimar Germany, he sought some guidance for the church – a church which, as he had learned during the years he had just spent in the trenches with soldiers drawn largely from the working class, was viewed by most Germans as the spiritual auxiliary to the bankrupt bourgeois values that were responsible for the war.[53] The lecture, "On the Idea of a Theology of Culture,"[54] introduced an approach and themes that were to become a charter for Tillich's work in the years ahead.

In this lecture, Tillich distinguishes between "theology of the church," which consists in interpreting materials found in the overt religious sphere (sacred scriptures, doctrines, the architecture of worship, symbols and rituals), and "theology of culture," which consists in searching for religious "substance" within the other spheres of culture (science, art, morality, politics, economy). He uses the term "religion" in two ways here. First, religion is a discrete sphere within a culture in which revelatory experiences are openly transmitted through texts, liturgies, stories, clergy, and institutions. Second, religion is a primordial source of meaning, what Tillich calls an "unconditioned" source of meaning, or simply "the unconditioned," the "ground and abyss of everything that is" that seethes beneath the surface of all cultural spheres and sustains our conviction that participating in them is worthwhile. In this second sense, Tillich is suggesting that religious substance is embedded in every cultural phenomenon in which meaning can be detected.

Because this distinction between the two meanings of religion is crucial to appreciating what is assumed in theology of culture, a form of shorthand will be used in what follows to keep the two meanings clear: religion$_1$ and religion$_2$.[55] Religion$_1$ will refer to religion as the substance of culture; religion$_2$ to religion as a recognizable institution. Religion$_1$ is the province of "theology of culture"; religion$_2$ is the province of "theology of the church."

In the course of this early lecture and in other writings from this period, Tillich experimented with a pattern of examining each of the great cultural spheres in turn, inquiring into how religious substance manifests itself in each one. In *Art*, Tillich saw in the work of expressionist painters of the time (1920s) an effort to recapture the revelatory power of symbols. The primitivism and shattering of surfaces that characterized their paintings was an invitation to glimpse "the depth-content of the world ... that shines through things," to experience "the immediate revelation of an absolute reality in the relative things."[56] Tillich saw in the fractured style of expressionism a creative tension between an overwhelming sense of "the guilt of sheer existence" and a mystical love longing for the union of all living things.[57] Expressionism is religious art in that it exposes an array of religious feelings – primal anxiety, guilt, sin, redemption and love. As far as Tillich was concerned, at the beginning of the twentieth century, this recognition of the divine "No" and "Yes" was coming to expression more powerfully in the paintings of Cézanne, Van Gogh, Franz Marc and Edvard Munch than it was in any of the art that was being commissioned by the churches.

In the sphere of *Science*, Tillich discerned the makings of a new movement of resistance against both "the materialistic shadow of idealism" and against exclusively autonomous approaches to the sciences. He saw a dawning recognition among scientists that there is both an elegant, enduring structure that sustains the universe and, under the influence of Henri Bergson, a growing awareness of a boundless vitality that renews it – a dialectic that, for Tillich, disclosed something essential about the eternal ground of our being (God). In *Ethics*, Tillich saw in writers like Nietzsche, Rilke and Tolstoy the shattering of bourgeois morality with its limitations on the scope of love and its motivations oriented to the categories of reward and punishment. In these thinkers, he made out a "higher order" for the possibilities regarding the formation of personality and a recovery of the metaphysical love that embraces and reunites all things. And in the sphere of *Politics*, Tillich identified expressions of religious substance in Nietzsche's critique of politics driven by power and justified by a calculating utility, and in socialism's impulse toward "the mysticism of love, which produces not for the sake of production but for the sake of the human being."[58]

In his first book-length treatment of theology of culture, *The Religious Situation* (1926), a book that became a best seller in Germany and was the first of his books to be translated into English (by H. Richard Niebuhr) and published in the US in 1932, Tillich again surveyed each of the spheres of culture to discern in what ways they were testifying to "the shaking of our time by eternity." Here he reiterated the contention that, in the years following the war, the sphere of religion$_2$ was largely mute as a voice of revelation. The support of the churches in Germany for the war had devastated their credibility and cost them this voice. But fortunately, Tillich proposed, "Human religion ... is not the only phenomenon which bears witness to the ultimate and in some periods it is not even the most important of the witnesses or the most effective in expression and symbolism."[59] The voice of eternity moves where it will, and like the sovereign God whose voice it is, it will not be confined to organs controlled by religion$_2$. In this Tillich stirred back to life Luther's insistence that the infinite makes itself known to us through plain finitude, and that where and when this occurs depends upon the freedom of God, and in a manner that will certainly scandalize us. When it does occur, it is an occasion of "theonomous" revelation, according to Tillich, by which he meant a glimpse of God – of the abyss and ground of reality – which has been had through the ordinary processes of life. In all of the innovations he observed among artists, scientists, politicians and economists in the early 1920s, Tillich suggested that "a new theonomy" was breaking into "an exhausted culture."[60]

The theology of culture that Tillich formulated in this period evolved over the years. As Hitler rose to power in the 1930s, Tillich grew disillusioned with his once eager hopes regarding theonomous developments in German culture outside of the church. Shortly after emigrating to the US in 1933, a move made necessary by his public opposition to Hitler, his writings began to make clear that his enthusiasm for the positive revelatory power of culture had dimmed. The cultural spheres in Germany had served as powerful instruments of destructive, "demonic" forces that had Germany in their grip. Art, science, politics, voluntary associations, and the economy had all succumbed to becoming agents of National Socialism. It was at this time that Tillich began to move away from describing secular culture as a place where "the unconditioned" was making its presence known, and to move toward viewing it as a place where the doubts and anxieties of human existence rise to the surface, existential questions which are revelatory only in the negative sense that they make us aware of our fragile contingency in life. Theology of culture, in his view, was becoming less about inquiring into the divine substance rumbling in the depths of cultural activity, and more about investigating culture for its more revealing expressions of its own deepest absences, its raw ends seeking reconnection with some kind of meaning-giving substance.

In an essay he wrote in 1946, in the immediate aftermath this time of the Second World War, Tillich referred to his earlier theonomous interpretations of culture as overly romantic. "This has come to an end," he wrote, because with World War II, "the end itself has appeared like a flash of lightning before our eyes." Now when he surveyed the products and formations of culture he saw a "sacred void." Thus:

> A present theology of culture is, above all, a theology of the end of culture, not in general terms but in a concrete analysis of the inner void of most of our cultural expressions. Little is left in our present

civilization which does not indicate to a sensitive mind the presence of this vacuum, this lack of ultimacy and substantial power in language and education, in politics and philosophy, in the development of personalities, and in the life of communities ... One gets the impression that only those cultural creations have greatness in which the experience of the void is expressed.[61]

His profound disappointment moderated somewhat in the years following the war, but it remained in his conviction that what was to be found through theology of culture was primarily the ringing questions of the day, a kind of nagging activity of divine revelation alerting us to our fallenness, to our estrangement from our divine ground, to which symbols from the treasury of Christian theology could be retrieved as answers. This was the *apologetic*, or "answering," theology he developed in his *Systematic Theology*.

It was during this period (1950s) that Tillich, who had developed a reputation as an amateur art critic and gave opening addresses at several exhibition openings for modern art, began in different settings to describe Picasso's painting, *Guernica*, as the most Protestant painting ever made (Figure 3). This enormous cubist mural of chunks of human bodies, animals and inorganic objects jumbled together, was Picasso's graphic rendering of the 1937 air bombing of the village of Guernica in the Basque region of Northern Spain. What makes this a Protestant painting, he claimed, is that "it shows the human situation without any cover. It shows what is now in the souls of many Americans as disruptiveness, existential doubt, emptiness and meaninglessness."[62] *Guernica* corroborates Luther's experience of *Anfechtung*, of the desolation of sinful humanity forsaken by God, but now tuned into the frequency of the twentieth century. *Guernica* is, in this sense, in the lineage of the art of the crucifixion.

Although Tillich remained more attentive to culture than most theologians – and this continues to be his legacy[63] – over time his expectations contracted regarding culture's power to express its own meaning-giving depths. He moved from expecting these depths to arise like artesian waters through the aquifer of cultural forms, to expecting, at best, a lucid expression of the dryness of the human spirit – and thereby its demand for waters of meaning from outside of itself – by the most gifted and honest artists, thinkers, and community leaders.

In short, Tillich had once believed that a theology of culture conducted outside the bounds of the church could discriminate appearances of the unconditioned in material culture. In his later work he no longer did.

The reconceived task of theology of culture in the later work of Tillich, then, consisted in drawing together materials from the most refined expressions of novelists, poets, painters, architects and philosophers for

Figure 3 Pablo Picasso, *Guernica* (1937, Museo Nacional Centro de Arte Reina Sofía, Madrid). Tillich called this a great "Protestant painting," because "it shows the human situation without any cover." (©2005 Estate of Pablo Picasso/Artists Rights Society (ARS), New York. Used with permission).

the purpose of articulating the prevailing human predicament, which Tillich concluded in the 1950s was the feeling of meaninglessness, the sense of separation from the ultimate source of meaning. It was a negative disclosure of human being in estrangement, and not, as he had once believed, a positive revelation of the actions of divine reality upon the forms of human culture.

Tillich and the Frankfurt School

There is an interesting and enduring connection between Paul Tillich and the Frankfurt Institute for Social Research. From 1929 to 1933 Tillich taught at the University of Frankfurt. As a professor of philosophy at Frankfurt, Tillich oversaw Theodor Adorno's dissertation on Kierkegaard's aesthetics, and later helped him secure a teaching position at the university. It was with Tillich's support as dean that Max Horkheimer was appointed in 1929 to a new chair in social philosophy at Frankfurt, and then in 1930 was made the director of the Institute for Social Research. Tillich was a close associate of Horkheimer, Adorno, Leo Lowenthal, and the circle of intellectuals connected to the Institute during the years when it was shaping the unique blend of Marxist social analysis and Freudian psychoanalysis that became the legacy of Frankfurt critical theory. This continued when all of them converged in New York City in the early 1930s, sharing the honor of being among the first academics expelled by the Nazis – Tillich relocated to Union Seminary and Horkheimer and the Institute across the street at Columbia University.[64] Once in New York, they resumed their discussions, collaborations, and dinner parties.

Understanding Tillich's relationship with the Frankfurt theorists provides an important key to his writings on culture. The Frankfurt critique of kitsch, the prophetic status they granted to the artists, poets, and philosophers of the avant-garde, their distinctive blending of Marx and Freud, and their suspicions of the "culture industry" are all found in Tillich. They had all worked out their thinking on these matters in conversation with each other, and reached many of the same conclusions. Taken together, these elements of critical theory help to explain Tillich's dismissal of popular culture as material that deserves to be taken seriously for its religious content. His aversion toward popular culture was one constant in Tillich's theology of culture in both its early and later phases.

In a tract he wrote in 1945, "The World Situation," Tillich examined the myriad ways in which communities have disintegrated into masses under the demands of the "all-embracing mechanism of capitalist economy," and he insisted that "it must be recognized that standardized communication through radio, movies, press, and fashions tends to create standardized men who are all too susceptible to propaganda for old or new totalitarian purposes." Like the Frankfurt theorists, Tillich had formed a distrust of the mass media after seeing how effectively Hitler had used it in the years leading up to the war. Writing this tract at the end of the war, and 12 years into his sojourn in America, he saw similar forces at work here – a culture industry infiltrating the minds of the masses to bolster their embrace of capitalism. In contrast to these mass arts, which idealized existing reality and reinforced inherited economic arrangements, Tillich gravitated toward the avant-garde artists of the Expressionist and Bauhaus movements – this was already the case in his earliest writings on culture, even before he had entered the circle of the Frankfurt School.

Tillich's frequent references to kitsch as a "beautifying sentimentalism" which is fundamentally dishonest, likewise, reflect the Frankfurt judgment against art that conceals the ugliness of reality from view.[65] The response of horror to the "gulf between the monadic individual and his barbarous surroundings" that Horkheimer saw in Picasso's work is echoed in Tillich's observation in 1946 that "One often gets the impression that only those cultural creations have greatness in which the experience of the void is expressed,"[66] and in his frequent declarations that *Guernica* is the great contemporary Protestant painting because it displays the human situation in its depths of estrangement. For Tillich, as for others in the Frankfurt School, genuine art necessarily absorbs one into the dialectical ambiguity of the beautiful and the disturbing.

Finally, Tillich's assessment of the revolutionary power of modern art is one he shares with members of the Institute. In his 1951 lectures on "The Political Meaning of Utopia," he rejects the idea that those "who stand on the lowest rung of the economic ladder, whose discontent is basically economic and nothing more," are the "real bearers of utopia." The bearers of utopia are, instead, those "who have sufficient power of being to achieve advance" – the highly cultivated bourgeoisie of the French Revolution, for instance, or those whom Marx referred to as the "avant-garde."[67]

Consideration of Tillich's theology of culture and his connection to the Frankfurt School is important for the following reasons. First, in my view it is incumbent upon anyone attempting to do a theological or religious analysis of culture in the present to check in with Paul Tillich. Whether they realize it or not, the numerous scholars in the broader field of theological and religious studies who are now examining popular culture for its religious elements are indebted to him. He was the one who created the discipline "theology of culture," and influenced a whole generation of theologians and sociologists of religion to look for religion outside the sphere of organized religion. It is stunning how infrequently he is cited in many of the books on popular culture that have been written by scholars in religious studies in the last 10 years. The irony is how frequently the Frankfurt social theorists are acknowledged as precursors in these same books. The neglect of Tillich, the single theologian within the Frankfurt circle, is a strange kind of amnesia and a wasted resource.

Second, while Tillich essentially invented the discipline of theology of culture, he had a strong aversion to *popular* culture. In concert with the Frankfurt School, he dismissed American popular culture as little more than a vehicle for capitalist ideology and the engendering of a false consciousness in the working class, containing nothing of religious substance other than further evidence of human estrangement of a capitalist sort. If Tillich was right about this, there is really very little to be gained from using theology of culture to examine popular culture – once it is determined that this underlying ideology is all that will be found.

However, in his most mature formulation of it, Tillich defined theology of culture as "the attempt to analyze the theology behind all cultural expressions, to discover the ultimate concern in the ground of a philosophy, a political system, an artistic style, a set of ethical or social principles." The key to discerning the ultimate concern that underlies the philosophy, politics, art and ethics of a culture, he goes on, is found in acquiring the ability to "read styles," to penetrate through the surface of a culture's artifacts and preoccupations "to the level where an ultimate concern exercises its driving power."[68] Extrapolating from the root of the word in *stylus*, which is an instrument for writing, Tillich uses the term "style" to refer to the creative ways in which a culture inscribes or expresses itself; the style of a culture is the patterned ways in which it interprets itself across its various domains (art, science, ethics, politics, etc.). It has been argued earlier in this book that it is toward the production of popular culture – films, novels, advertising, theme parks, television, music, etc. – that much of the creative genius of our time is gravitating. With respect to theology of culture, a fascinating clue that it might be necessary to transcend Tillich's *prejudice* against popular culture by applying Tillich's own *method* is found in his endorsement of the importance of style, his suggestion that it is in reading the style of a culture that its most honest self-interpretation and its dominant religious concerns will be uncovered. As he describes it,

> Style is a term derived from the realm of the arts, but it can be applied to all realms of culture. There is a style of thought, of politics, of social life, etc. The style of a period expresses itself in its cultural forms, in its choice of objects, in the attitudes of its creative personalities, in its institutions and customs.[69]

Recall the similar claim by Dick Hebdige, who, in his field research of subaltern communities, concluded that the primary way in which they exercise their agency is through style. For Hebdige, style is a practice, it is the way people use commodities in a manner unintended by their producers for the purpose of stitching together an alternative semiotics that serves as their own self-interpretation of what matters to them. With this new understanding of style, borrowed from cultural studies, it is possible to extend Tillich's method in the direction of popular culture, in spite of his own resistance to doing so.

Finally, it is worth reconsidering Tillich in light of his connection to the Frankfurt School because as one traces out the route that critical theory has taken through cultural studies, as was done in the previous chapter, it turns out that the attention to style, *bricolage*, and semiotic surfaces have led many cultural theorists to a celebration of simulacra that is so thoroughly enchanted with surfaces that, as Hebdige has concluded, there can be no more trawling for hidden truths. What Tillich still offers is a language for the conviction that there is a reality below the surfaces, a reality that is not reducible to power and social conflict. Over the years Tillich compiled a lexicon for talking about this underlying reality, a set of concepts that can still be of service to any theorist who hasn't foreclosed on "the depth model," or on the belief that our cultural creativity occurs in response to religious anxieties, dispositions, insights, dodges, and longings. To these concepts, and others like them, we now turn.

4

Theological Tools

In order to begin building a vocabulary for how to isolate the religious dimension of popular culture, this chapter will introduce several key concepts from Paul Tillich's theology of culture. These concepts will serve as scaffolding from which to reach into the work of other theologians and scholars of religious studies who offer deft refinements of the concepts, both dependent upon and independent of Tillich's formulations. Only the most basic concepts will be assembled here, pulling together some essential tools to conduct the inquiry that lies ahead. The concepts: ultimate concern, the holy, moral and ontological faith, ecstatic revelation, religious symbols, myths, liminality, and three different modes of religion.

Ultimate Concern

There are certain things in life that we value even though they don't make us feel good or benefit us in any obvious way. That there is wilderness remaining on this planet in remote parts of Canada, Siberia and Brazil is something most of us value, even though we are unlikely to ever go there to experience its wonders, and even though leaving it as wilderness means its natural resources will not be extracted to produce manufactured goods for us to consume. We have this idea that we would find the world to be a poorer place if these great stretches of wilderness were to disappear. Similarly, there are genres of music that we may not enjoy or benefit from in any tangible way that we would still defend if all record of them were about to be wiped clean. Outside of movie soundtracks, for instance, most Americans do not listen to classical music; nevertheless, most would feel deprived if the world suddenly found itself bereft of Beethoven's Fifth Symphony. There is something about wilderness and Beethoven, about endangered species, city skylines and Miles Davis, about great writers and thinkers, about distant cultures, about the life of others – even strangers we will never meet and creatures we will never see – there is something about these things that leads most of us to grant them value, even though they might bring us no first-hand pleasure or practical advantage. In recognizing their value, in granting them worth in the great scheme of things, we commit an act that is really very complex.

Why, after all, should it matter that a piece of music not vanish, or an ecosystem not degrade to the point of irreversibility, or a child in Sierra Leone not have her arms hacked off by a guerilla soldier? Assuming it is music one doesn't listen to, an ecosystem one will never set foot in, or a child one will never meet, if pressed for an answer for why one is nevertheless concerned about these things, the response is typically to resort to a handful of aesthetic and moral abstractions to explain the concern. The music, while not one's cup of tea, is a beautiful and elegant composition; the ecosystem has an integrity that ought not be spoiled, and it sustains forms of life that are deserving of respect; the child's well-being is a matter of justice, of rights, of concern for the weak, respect for innocence.

Good reasons, but it could be pressed further – why should one care about beauty and elegance, integrity, life, justice, rights, and innocence? On what grounds do these abstractions acquire the obvious authority that we grant them? In Hindu mythology, the universe is understood to rest on a platform that sits on the backs of four elephants, and the elephants all stand on a turtle's back. Clifford Geertz tells the story of an Indian who, when asked what the turtle rested on, answered, "Ah, Sahib, after that it is turtles all the way down."[1] The turtle, here, is a symbol for the last reality that can be conceptualized, beyond which is a mystery that our consciousness cannot articulate but our faith still affirms. In a similar vein, Augustine followed a chain of inquiry, chasing down leads in search of God, from land to sea to living things to air to heavenly bodies – each, at the time, the embodiment of some cosmic power or metaphysical principle:

> But what is my God? I put my question to the earth. It answered, "I am not God," and all things on earth declared the same. I asked the sea and the chasms of the deep and the living things that creep in them, but they answered, "We are not your God. Seek what is above us." I spoke to the winds that blow, and the whole air and all that lives in it replied, "I am not God." I asked the sky, the sun, the moon, and the stars, but they told me "Neither are we the God whom you seek." I spoke to all the things that are about me, all that can be admitted by the door of the senses, and I said, "Since you are not my God, tell me about him. Tell me something of my God." Clear and loud they answered, "God is he who made us."[2]

Tillich proposed that within the consciousness of every person the reality beyond the last principle and beneath the last turtle is something called "ultimate concern." Out of the multitude of things we value in life – food, shelter, pleasure, truth, beauty, integrity, love, justice, etc. – something makes an unconditional claim upon us, and we organize our lives and all of our other values in accordance with it. For each of us, there is something of supreme worth, a concern in-light-of-which and for-the-sake-of-which we order everything else we care about. This is an old idea in theology. Augustine put the idea thus: "All agree that God is that thing which they place above all other things."[3] It is this concern that sustains us through our lives. As Jack Kerouac said to his friend, Carlo Marx (Allen Ginzberg) in *On the Road*, "That last thing is what you can't get, Carlo. Nobody can get to that last thing. We keep on living in hopes of catching it once for all."[4]

Etymologically, "con-cern" means to sift or separate (*cerne*) with (*con*). It is by means of a concern that one is able to sort through the cares that constitute our lives. An *ultimate* concern is one's weightiest conviction, loyalty, or interest that assigns the relative gravity to all other convictions, loyalties, and interests that one holds. It is not accidental that the word "concern" is both a verb and noun. It is both a subjective act (we concern ourselves with something) and the object of that act (we have concerns). Tillich seizes upon this gerund-like quality of "concern," and suggests that ultimate concern in the subjective sense is what is meant by faith; in the objective sense it is what is meant by God. Thus, ultimate concern is a synonym both for faith and for God. Faith is the experience of being grasped by an ultimate concern. And insofar as everyone has a central conviction that organizes his or her life, everyone has faith. In this there is little difference between those who understand themselves as religious and those who do not. For Tillich, there are no unbelievers. Everyone is religious; everyone has an ultimate concern (with the exception of those who are suicidal or chronically depressed). But with respect to the object of ultimate concern, with respect to what functions for each of us as "god," there is great divergence. He writes: "Faith is the state of being ultimately concerned. The content matters infinitely for the life of the believer, but it does not matter for the formal definition of faith."[5] The interesting question is not whether a person has faith, but in what that faith is lodged.

A concern that claims ultimacy in one's life has a triadic character, according to Tillich. It makes a demand, a threat, and a promise. First, it *demands* absolute loyalty and the willingness to surrender all of one's other concerns, if necessary, for its sake. Second, it *threatens* to exclude one from its benefits and from the fellowship of others who revere it if surrender to it is not complete. Third, it *promises* to fulfill one's being, to guide one into the best and most satisfying existence that is possible, if one remains faithful to it.

Tillich suggests that his concept of ultimate concern is nothing more than an "abstract translation" of the great commandment: "The Lord our God, the Lord is one; you shall love the Lord your God with all your heart, and with all your soul, and with all your mind, and with all your strength" (Mk 12.29). With Augustine, Tillich held that human beings are driven by a restless heart that seeks "the infinite because that is where the finite wants to rest."[6] Therefore, the only *genuine* ultimate concern is one that is attuned to God, who is infinite. But while, in the words of Havelock Ellis, "It is the infinite for which we hunger," we "ride gladly on every little wave that promises to bear us towards it."[7] In our restlessness, we clutch onto idols. "Idolatry," Tillich writes, "is the elevation of a preliminary concern to ultimacy."[8] We commit idolatry when we treat something that is conditioned as if it is unconditioned, when we treat an elephant or even a turtle as if it is the infinite mystery. The genuinely infinite will always be what resides below the lowest turtle.

Candidates for idolatrous ultimate concerns that Tillich frequently identified include one's nation (this was fresh on his mind given the ultimacy of blood and soil in Nazi Germany), economic well-being, health and life, family, beauty, truth, justice, or some abstract idea of humanity (think of the French Revolution, or of a free-standing concept of human rights). One could add other candidates: work, sports, education, romantic love, pleasure, physical fitness, self-fulfillment, political power, or freedom.

In a similar manner, William James, after describing "piety" as a surrendering to the feeling that one exists in "a wider life than that of this world's selfish little interests," suggested that this "wider life" might be personified as God, or it might be identified with "abstract moral ideals, civic or patriotic utopias, or inner visions of holiness," each of which can function as "the true lords and enlargers of our life." When one surrenders to such an enlarger of life, the religious effect is one of "an immense elation and freedom, as the outlines of the confining selfhood melt down."[9]

For James, as for Tillich, these "true lords and enlargers of our life" can lead to commendable acts of self-sacrifice and disciplined devotion that lend one's life to the well-being of others. But for Tillich, an ultimate concern that is, in reality, finite or transitory, and therefore less than ultimate, will eventually culminate in existential disappointment. This is a shattering experience that might be deferred for a long time, because even transitory ultimate concerns can function to orient and enlarge one's life. But it will, he assures us, finally break down.[10] When this happens, one will feel some combination of forsakenness, betrayal, foolishness, self-loathing, deep disorientation, alienation, bitterness or despondency.

Eventually, another ultimate concern will rise in one's consciousness as an axis around which to order one's life. When this happens it is commonly described as conversion. It can be a conversion from one finite good to another, or from a finite good to a good that is genuinely ultimate. It can also be a conversion from one apprehension of God to another, say from faith in a God who hustles to satisfy the desires of the faithful to a view of God as indifferent to human desire. As Tillich suggests, the best literature moves its characters through such shifts and reversals in ultimate concerns.

While this account might make it sound relatively easy to identify one's ultimate concern, for most of us our ultimate concern does its work unnoticed and unexamined, unobtrusively pressing and pulling us in the ways we look upon and value the world. Nevertheless, it is a rich concept for shedding light on the religious dimensions of popular culture. As Tillich himself noted, "Pictures, poems, and music can become objects of theology ... from the point of view of their power of expressing some aspects of that which concerns us ultimately."[11]

The Holy

Art theorists and cultural critics sometimes describe certain works of art as being expressions of the sublime. Etymologically, sublime means below (*sub*) the threshold (*limen*), suggesting a deeper reality than what at first meets the eye. In the eighteenth century, the Irish writer Edmund Burke and the German philosopher Immanuel Kant both wrote treatises that explored the peculiar relationship between the sublime and the beautiful, and developed aesthetic theories to explain the satisfying mix of passions that are activated within us when we read certain works of literature or stand inside of spacious and magnificent buildings or before vast natural landscapes.[12] Both described the sublime as the experience of a kind of delightful terror.

When we are in the presence of something sublime, we perceive a greatness in the face of which we feel exceedingly small; we sense we are in the presence of something that has absolutely no need for us, and that humiliation propels us into a state of wonder. We find the sublime in objects that are high, deep, immense, gloomy, rugged, powerful, or dark. We hear it in the cries of animals, observe it in a raging storm, feel it in moments of abandonment, confront it in our conscience. We are frozen in fear in such moments, but then, when we discover that we have outlasted the terror and are returned to our senses, the fear is followed by a deep joy. As Philip Hallie has described it, "Sublimity is an experience of terror and exaltation rendered tranquil by *our* actual safety."[13] This arc is the meaning of the sublime. And we are drawn to it, Burke and Kant suggest, both because it rejuvenates us and because through repeated experiences of such survivable mystery, our imaginations are invited to extend to unknown frontiers. The sublime thus drives the aesthetic imagination.[14]

The evocative power of the sublime became a central theme in both German and British Romanticism through the nineteenth century. The Protestant theologian Friedrich Schleiermacher, a central figure in German Romanticism, identified a sense of absolute dependence within human consciousness, an "intuition and feeling of the infinite" through which we become aware of the permanent dependence of all finite reality upon the infinite. He called this our "God-consciousness," a point of contact between the finite and the infinite which enters our awareness through our consciousness of sin and grace – a fluctuating sense of our alienation from God and our fellowship with God. This twin consciousness is never had without something to mediate it – music, literature, friendships, storytelling, family, nature, scriptures, religious rituals – each of which can trigger a moment of original awareness, an impression of our absolute dependence inflected with either alienation (sin) or fellowship (grace).[15] The similarities of this divided God-consciousness to then current reflections on the sublime are worth noting, particularly because of the work of Rudolph Otto on the idea of the holy.

Otto's book, *The Idea of the Holy*, which first appeared in 1917, describes the holy as having the double character of the *mysterium tremendum et fascinosum*, a mystery that is simultaneously terrifying and fascinating. Objects, places, persons, and events that register with one as holy are experienced, on one hand, as repulsive, unnerving, demanding and full of a searing judgment, and, on the other hand, as attractive, alluring, mesmerizing and consoling – all at once, though not necessarily in equal amounts. One might find oneself speechless and shuddering, with blood running cold as one's body intercepts these twin frequencies of the holy. Long before Otto, Augustine captured this experience in describing the effect he felt in reading scripture:

> How wonderful are your Scriptures! How profound! We see their surface and it attracts us like children. And yet, O my God, their depth is stupendous. We shudder to peer deep into them, for they inspire in us both the awe of reverence and the thrill of love.[16]

Otto was a great synthesizer. He viewed himself as an heir of both Kant and Schleiermacher, and sought to secure a sense for the infinite as one of the faculties of human consciousness, a religious *a priori* universally present in human beings, on account of which we can recognize the numinous where it appears. He also drew upon the more recent discussions of *orenda*, *mana*, and *wakanda* – words describing a raw, undifferentiated power thought to reside in natural phenomena – that had been outlined in the reports of missionaries who had observed the religious beliefs of indigenous peoples of North America and the South Pacific. Back in Europe, those who reflected on this primitive sense of raw supernatural power described it as an amoral force, unconnected to any notions of good or evil. It was more properly understood as simply a power that one would be wise to appease and make effective. Protecting oneself from it and putting it to positive uses gave rise to magic, it was theorized; magic which, in time, evolved into religion.

This became an influential theory of religion in general – speculating that the religions of the world had all evolved from a belief that the world operates under the power of *mana*, that this power must be regulated, and, eventually, the theory claims, it occurred to the shamanic handlers of this power that a framework of good and evil is the most effective way to regulate it. This then gave rise to divergent rituals, myths, officials, and institutions that distinguish the world's religions. Otto, a Christian theologian, reworked these ideas into his concept of the holy, and conjectured that while our first response to an encounter with the holy is to be overwhelmed by it, to sense our own insignificance in the face of its awful majesty, we also realize we are willingly captivated by it. Standing in its presence, our sense of our own relative nothingness evolves into a sense of uncleanness, and eventually into an awareness of sin and our need for atonement. This, for Otto, better describes the origin of the great religions. But at their fountainhead is this *mysterium tremendum*, which inspires dread, a dread from which we generally choose not to flee, a dread that fascinates us. And this experience of numinous power can be expected to be encountered through virtually any medium.

According to Tillich, who adopted this concept of the holy from Otto, when we have an encounter with holiness, it is a signal that we have entered into the presence of our ultimate concern. While we commonly use the term "holiness" to refer to moral purity, this captures only part of its meaning, and can even be a distortion of its meaning. We also become aware of holiness through holy "objects," elements within the world that represent or draw us nearer to our ultimate concern, and anything "can become a vehicle of one's ultimate concern."[17] Obviously, this is why religious art and icons have such power – they serve as channels through which people encounter what they believe to be ultimate. Tillich had just such an experience when he stood before Botticelli's painting, *Madonna with Singing Angels*, in 1918. For him this became the paradigm for how subjectivity and self-awareness are momentarily suspended as one becomes the receptacle of a power that reaches through the holy object and overwhelms one with a sense of numinous mystery.

While some objects are more inclined to produce an experience of the holy in people than other objects, Tillich was cautious to explain that the holy does not inhere in the objects in which it is perceived, but that its appearance is a phenomenon in the strict sense – it is an experience co-produced by the external object *and* the internal disposition of the subject who encounters it.

Tillich sometimes describes the two poles of the holy as the ground and abyss of being. The *ground* refers to the positive, attractive element, the creative power with which we sense reality is maintained, which bubbles up as if from an artesian well. The *abyss* refers to the negative, repelling element, our feeling of our own paltriness in the face of the infinite, "the 'stigma' of finitude which appears in all things and in the whole of reality and the 'shock' which grasps the mind when it encounters the threat of nonbeing."[18] The abyss is the source of the "dark night of the soul" described by St John of the Cross, an experience corroborated by other mystics who, having probed the divine presence, have been left feeling undone. We vacillate between feeling elevated and annihilated when we are in the presence of that which we experience as holy.

It is not difficult to imagine experiencing the holy through a religious icon like Botticelli's *Madonna*. Less obvious, however, is the way in which more "profane" or secular phenomena can serve as conduits of the holy. Tillich was particularly taken with Van Gogh's artistry in this regard. In a painting like *Starry Night*, Van Gogh was tuned to the enchanting side of the holy, and used his paints to pierce the surface of nature and reveal its creative energies, while in his *Night Café* he gave us a picture of "late emptiness," where, with the waiter gone and one man sitting alone we are confronted with the emptiness of our own loneliest moments, a loneliness from which we flee in futility, aware that it is an unsettling truth of the human condition that follows us wherever we go.

Great public spaces can also be occasions of the holy. Beautiful buildings and structures like the interior of Grand Central Terminal, Gaudí's Park Güell in Barcelona, Wrigley Field in Chicago, the Golden Gate Bridge, or the Mirage Casino in Las Vegas – engineered marvels in which we enshrine and recognize our common aspirations – can be holy objects or places. Natural phenomena, likewise, can be sites of the holy. Niagara Falls, Yosemite Valley and Big Sur can have a religious effect upon visitors, who are overtaken by a sense of having entered a sanctuary of numinous beauty and power, and a corresponding sense of their own smallness. Well-told stories, poems, and films, whose subject matter is not overtly religious, can also momentarily transport one into an experience of the holy.

Tillich makes two important moves with Otto's concept of the holy. First, he develops the notion that while the experience of the holy is evanescent and quite unpredictable where and when it will arise, it makes a lasting mark on the person who has felt its presence by permanently altering their perception of the world. Having brushed against a reality that is so emblematic of one's ultimate concern, the face of one's world is washed with a fresh spray of the utterly meaningful. Second, he refines the twin effects of the experience of the holy, the abyss and the ground, into two ways that religions construe how the holy enters the world – through a divine judgment on our moral actions and a corresponding demand for justice, on one hand, and through a divine consolation that sustains our wonder at the sacramental texture of life, on the other.

Ontological and Moral Faith

According to Tillich, we respond to the two faces of the holy with these two types of faith: ontological faith and moral faith. *Ontological faith* finds itself enchanted by the fascinating face of the holy, by the moments in which the numinous shines through existing beings[19] and the unconditional endorsement of being-as-it-is that this signifies. That plain, finite reality is found adequate to serve as a receptacle for the transcendent beauty of the divine is deeply reassuring. Ontological faith gravitates toward sacramental and mystical types of piety. In sacramental religions, ultimate reality is *expected* to be encountered through concrete things, persons, and events – this particular jar of water, piece of bread, tree, or building. The experience of being grasped and stilled in the presence of something that strikes one as being charged with mystery and power is key here. The Catholic Mass is such an event. Here, after the consecration of the elements, the bread and wine are transubstantiated into God who becomes physically present in this space. Awareness of this has influenced the architecture of worship spaces in the Catholic Church – flying buttresses were invented in the Middle Ages in order to accommodate these divine visitations.

Moral faith, on the other hand, is attuned to the terrifying side of the holy, picking up on how, in the presence of the infinite, all finite reality falls short of what it ought to be. Sensing that the holy in its purity stands over against us, measuring us and our world by standards of perfect justice and love that far exceed our best achievements, the ears of faith hear a relentless moral demand to *make* the world a more fit receptacle for God. Aware of their shortcomings, those with moral faith occupy themselves with constructing a *way of life* that is just and compassionate. Only then will we be found fit for the presence of the divine. Moral faith gravitates toward law-generating, activist, and utopian expressions of piety.[20]

A helpful way to think about these two types is by posing the simple question: How is it that the holy enters the world? Is it through the portals of those things that are beautiful – natural phenomena like waterfalls and shooting stars, noble thoughts, elegant poetry, and great works of art – which due to their grandeur and magnificence inspire in us a sense of awe? Or is it through moral action, the sacrificial and sustained efforts of people to act lovingly and with justice toward others? The word "holy" is commonly used in both senses. We say of Yosemite Valley, "This is a holy place"; we say of Mother Theresa, "She lived a holy life." Onto-logical and moral faiths are two ways we ascribe meaning to the finite world – it is through its abundant beauty, on one hand, and through its approximations of justice, on the other, that a point of contact is made between it and the infinite reality that transcends it. If the finite world is to have meaning for us, it must have some points of contact with the infinite.

In short, with ontological faith, one anticipates encountering God in the *beautiful*; with moral faith, one anticipates encountering God in the *good*. And while these two types of faith tend to pull in different direc-tions, Tillich insists that each one is in need of the counterbalancing effect of the other. For religious faith to thrive, it must strike a balance between the moral and the ontological. Because God is *both* beautiful *and* good, at least as evoked in the experience of the holy, the human response of faith must take account of both. But also, in very practical terms, a desire for beauty that is cut free from moral goodness can descend to the worst sorts of cruelty, as can be seen in the eras of Caligula and Nero, Lorenzo de Medici, Louis IX, Ivan the Terrible and, more recently, Saddam Hus-sein – regimes characterized by the erection of lavish palaces and the patronage of art, yet surrounded by a vast and impoverished under-class. The subversive fiction of the Marquis de Sade, Nietzsche's assertion that aesthetics, not ethics, is the only human achievement that will ultimately justify our existence,[21] Antonin Artaud's "theater of cruelty," modern aesthetic hedonism of the sort that "worships pure experience without restraint of any kind,"[22] and the proliferation of sex and violence with all the ramped up special effects that characterize current Hollywood cinema (think of a movie like *Natural Born Killers*) are all instances of the worship of beauty untethered from any moral faith.

The opposite danger is a moral faith that dismisses any trust in the sacra-mental capacities of being. An ardently secular humanism that abandons the religious symbols and myths that originally gave rise to it runs the risk of losing its way and depleting its passion for justice. "I think that history has shown – and it is my personal experience, too," Tillich told a group of students in 1963, "that only the vision of the holy itself, of that ground of our own being on which we depend, can make us take the moral law with ultimate seriousness."[23] For moral faith to endure it must be sustained by ontological faith, by symbols with transcendent power that testify to the goodness of being.

These two concepts – moral and ontological types of faith – are in operation within Western culture, and are amply expressed through popular culture outside of the sphere of religion2. In fact, they are often used as rostrums from which the culture criticizes organized religion. Religion1 critics often resort to their own moral faith when they disparage religion2 adherents for being hypocrites who do not practice what they preach, or reach into their own ontological faith when they dismiss religion2 adherents for always harping on about sin and guilt and thereby failing to live their lives more abundantly. To charge anyone else with "Puritanism" is to confess to one's own ontological faith.

Revelation and Ecstasy

William James relates the testimony of a man who, while hiking in a coastal range, experiences the momentary obliteration of "all the conventionalities which usually surround and cover my life":

> [F]rom the summit of a high mountain I looked over a gashed and corrugated landscape extending to a long convex of ocean that ascended to the horizon, and ... I could see nothing beneath me but a boundless expanse of white cloud. ... What I felt on these occasions was a temporary loss of my own identity, accompanied by an illumination which revealed to me a deeper significance than I had been wont to attach to life. It is in this that I find my justification for saying that I have enjoyed communication with God. Of course, the absence of such a being as this would be chaos. I cannot conceive of life without its presence.[24]

This combination of self-annihilation and communion with God that he attributes to peering out over an immense and rugged landscape richly illustrates the double-effect of the holy. But there is an additional element, which Tillich would say flows naturally from an encounter with the holy, namely, "an illumination which revealed to me a deeper significance than I had been wont to attach to life." In Tillich's terms, the young man underwent a moment of *revelation* by momentarily losing himself in the divine ground of being (God) through the medium of some part of the finite world.

"Revelation," Tillich writes, "is the manifestation of what concerns us ultimately."[25] At its root it means to remove the veil, exposing to view the depth of reality. It has both an objective side and a subjective side. Its *objective side* is what Tillich calls "miracle": the unconditioned ground and abyss of being (the holy) makes an appearance. The *subjective side* is "ecstasy": for the receiver of revelation, the normal cleavage between subject and object that is present in all ordinary experience is briefly overcome. The person who receives the miracle of revelation is thrown beyond herself, transcends herself, as she is grasped by the mystery of being. Etymologically, "ecstasy" means standing (*stasis*) outside (*ex-*) of oneself, and, Tillich adds, this occurs without one's ceasing to be oneself.[26] In a few shining moments, one's consciousness converges with the object, mixes with it, then returns to oneself convinced that reality, in some large or small way, is not what one had thought it to be. Tillich writes:

> It is as in a thunderstorm at night, when the lightning throws a blinding clarity over all things, leaving them in complete darkness the next moment. When reality is seen in this way ... it has become something new. Its ground has become visible in an "ecstatic" experience.[27]

Virtually any object, person or event can serve as a medium of revelation – oceans, stars, plants, animals, mountains, natural catastrophes. Since all of reality receives its power of being from the ground of being (God), in the moments when any bit of finite reality becomes transparent, it reveals "the ground of its power." But because revelation of the infinite is always mediated by something finite, what is disclosed is always a distortion. Even when finite objects become transparent, they retain a certain opacity. As the apostle Paul put it, "we see through a glass darkly," even in the instant of ecstasy. Or, to think of it in terms of an old Javanese proverb, we are like water buffaloes trying to comprehend a symphony. Our powers of comprehension are miniscule in relation to the majesty that confronts us.

Revelation is not so much new knowledge as it is a new perspective on the world. It repositions the world in a new light. It does not add to our knowledge about the structures of the natural world, history, or humanity. It deepens our conviction that these things matter, that existence itself is meaningful. This is the difference between ecstatic understanding and more ordinary ways of acquiring knowledge.[28]

In his description of revelation Tillich has given us a versatile tool for locating eruptions of religion₁ in popular culture. The ecstatic experience is a signal that one has come into the presence of one's ultimate concern. When many report that they are undergoing experiences of ecstasy around a common concern, a theological analysis of the culture should pay attention. Keeping in mind that an ultimate concern may not be genuinely ultimate, but merely functioning in that capacity for individuals or communities, it is not hard to appreciate that a phenomenon such as patriotism, which can generate in people intense feelings of ecstasy, might indicate the presence of nationalism as one's ultimate concern. The stirring of hearts when patriotic anthems are sung, or when tales of heroism and sacrifice are told, or at the sight of a flag hoisted in a battlefield or amidst the ruins of the World Trade Towers can occur at the level of ecstasy, and does indicate the extent to which the nation is revered. Simply having these emotions does not mean that the nation *is* one's ultimate concern, but it does provide a measure of the relative weight of one's concerns. What other events or circumstances give rise to ecstatic experiences of this intensity – family gatherings, alpine vistas, weddings, funerals, the birth of a child, news reports on children starving in sub-Saharan Africa or on children who are victims of violence in our own cities, pictures of wild animals suffering from the pursuit of commerce, pornography, the celebration of religious holidays, entering a shopping mall or a big box electronics store? Monitoring the sources that activate this experience of losing oneself in an ecstatic moment is a way to map one's concerns, and to draw conclusions about which concern serves as ultimate.

Religious Symbols

American patriotism is surrounded by a latticework of symbols: the stars and stripes, the Liberty Bell, the Declaration of Independence, the White House, fireworks, the Washington Monument, the Statue of Liberty, Gettysburg, Apollo, cowboys and the Supreme Court, to name a few. An outsider would see a flag, a bell, a parchment, a building, an explosive, an obelisk, a statue, a battlefield, a rocket, a herdsman, a courthouse. But to an insider each of these objects is a vessel in which something sacred is stored. Each one of these ordinary objects transcends itself and rises to the status of being a religious symbol.

According to Tillich, we encode our ultimate concerns in the language of religious symbols. In order to speak of the ultimate, we must borrow from our experience of ordinary reality. Thus, in the Bible, God is referred to as creative, compassionate, powerful, good, abiding, just, wrathful, steadfast, fatherly, loving, etc. These terms all describe a range of attributes and actions drawn primarily from human behavior, and then, by analogy, extended to describe God. This has the dual effect of making the mystery of the divine comprehensible *and* valorizing certain human traits. "Religious symbols are double-edged," Tillich writes, "they force the infinite down to finitude and the finite up to infinity." For example, to speak of God as father makes the divine approachable by diminishing the infinite to a finite, familiar condition, while at the same time it consecrates parent – child relationships.[29]

Even the exalted words we use to describe the classic attributes of God – that is, transcendent, eternal, omnipresent, omnipotent, and omniscient – are derivative and symbolic. They are negations of things with which we are very familiar, the standard markers of finitude – our boundedness to physical substance, time, space, and causality, and the conditionedness of all knowledge. None of these words for God's attributes tell us anything except that the divine is not like us. The divine is not limited by the things that limit us and the world as we know it. Our words for God are either extensions of our own powers, or negations of our own limitations. To borrow a Buddhist image, human efforts to describe transcendent reality is like fish trying to explain dry land. We use a watery vocabulary to speak of things dry. But again, this is what we must do if we are going to say anything at all.

Tillich enumerates six characteristics of religious symbols that help both in identifying them and in understanding how it is they work.[30]

First, *symbols point beyond themselves.* Symbols draw attention to something other than themselves. They are like frosted panes of glass – not crystal clear, but still revealing of shapes and shades of light and color on the opposite side. Like an old song that plays on the radio, triggering memories of people, places, and earlier phases and events in one's life, symbols have the power to transport one beyond the immediate sensory data of the symbol to other mental associations and memories. In this capacity, symbols are like signs, in that one thing signifies another.

Second, symbols are different from signs because they *participate in that to which they point.* Symbols are not arbitrarily related to what they signify. A simple sign would be a traffic light, for which we have agreed, by social contract, that green means go and red means stop. It would be hard to argue that there is any obvious connection between these colors and the actions they mandate. The opposite might even be argued, namely, that green conjures up feelings of tranquility and suggests that one might slow down or pause, while red indicates energy and heat and suggests that one get moving, and fast. Symbols, in contrast to signs, *participate* in what they signify; there is some resemblance of properties between the symbol and the reality it represents. A few examples: trees are common religious symbols. Cosmic trees that allow traffic between the heavens and the earth are found in religious symbolism with some frequency – think of the Yggdrasil tree in Norse mythology, or the cross of Christ. That ordinary trees have roots plunging deep into the earth and branches ascending far into the sky, and that they provide homes to birds who do not seem bound by gravity, lend credence to this image of trees serving as a conduit between the world above and the world below. Or the notion that there is a tree of life where fruit or leaves grow that, if eaten, will rejuvenate life, can be seen as an extension of the observable rejuvenation of the tree itself, dying each winter and reviving each spring. Water is another prevalent symbol in religious traditions. It is found as an element in most creation myths, as might be expected from anyone who knows that water is essential for life, or who has observed the discharge of water before the birth of a child. It is also a common ingredient in initiation rituals, and just as a flood obliterates everything in its path then recedes to permit a new season of crop growth, initiates are dipped in water to obliterate their old identities and emerge to begin anew. Water, like other objects or processes that lend themselves to symbolism, has certain inherent powers that evoke the power they point toward, the power of being in the depths of reality.

Third, *symbols open up for us levels of reality that are otherwise hidden*. Science, history, and philosophy are forms of discourse that investigate and speak about reality at different levels with the aim of reducing our dependence upon symbolic forms of expression. The long history of their establishment as disciplines autonomous from religion$_2$ is largely a story of their rejecting religious symbols as the currency of their inquiry, and developing more precise nomenclatures. This, as has been said above, is a genuine achievement in the history of the West. Nevertheless, Tillich insists, there are layers of reality, particularly at the level of the grounding of the meaningfulness of existence itself, that cannot be apprehended or spoken of adequately without religious symbols. Perhaps the clearest case for this can be made by considering the power of artistic symbols to delve into regions of meaning untouched by science, history and philosophy. Music, poetry, visual arts and architecture interpret reality through symbols that enable us to experience the world in ways that are not possible through these other kinds of expression. Paint and canvas in the hands of Franz Marc and Van Gogh, Tillich liked to point out, can capture dimensions of the ground and abyss of being, the "depth-content" of the world, and allow the sacred to shine through even simple paintings of animals or the sky at night.

Fourth, *symbols unlock dimensions of our own being*. This is an extension of what has just been said of the power of symbols to disclose levels of reality otherwise hidden, except that here the emphasis is not on the outward structures of reality but on the inward dimensions of the soul. For Tillich, musical rhythms and melodies are particularly effective at this, as is the theater. The Bible, of course, is a vast repository for symbols that shed light on the soul. Returning to the opening chapters of Genesis, for example, one can find the following: At the outset of creation, "the earth was a formless void and darkness covered the face of the deep." This compact string of symbols describes reality before there was reality; it describes the nothingness out of which the cosmos was called into being. But as the story is told, this nothingness is not eliminated. It is simply distinguished from the ordered cosmos as a chaos that persists, hovering at the edges of being. It is the nothingness from which we were snatched, and the nothingness we remain on the brink of returning to but for the ongoing creative activity of God. As such, it is an awareness deep within us of our dependence upon a power that sustains us;

we do not give existence to ourselves, and we are at all moments at the edge of returning to the nothingness from which we have come. These symbols – the void, darkness, the deep – illuminate impulses felt in the subterranean regions of all human beings, impulses that touch upon our anxieties, yearnings and hopes, which these symbols have endured for ages to help us name and manage.

Fifth, *symbols cannot be artificially produced.* Clifford Geertz has written: "Meanings are 'stored' in symbols: a cross, a crescent, a feathered serpent. Such religious symbols, dramatized in rituals and related in myths, are somehow felt to sum up, for those for whom they resonate, what is known about the way the world is."[31] Such summary symbols, rich and teeming with significations, are limited in any given culture, limited to guard their value as sacred referents. Because the reliability of sacred symbols is taken for granted in a culture, as self-evident windows onto meaning, "individuals who ignore the symbols," Geertz notes, "are regarded not so much as evil as stupid."[32]

The process by which symbols take on meaning and carry this meaning over time is not one that is easily contrived. Geertz highlights two important features of this process. First, the capacity of symbols to carry meaning is reinforced through their appearance in rituals and myths. In rituals our bodies internalize the symbols through repeated performance; in myths our imaginations learn to conceive of the world by relying on symbols as fundamental reference points. Second, symbols are effective in orienting our lives because they are "felt to sum up, for those for whom they resonate, what is known about the way the world is." Gathering this kind of authority does not happen overnight, but is a long process, and it requires, according to Tillich, the consent of both the individual and the collective unconscious. Tillich cites for evidence the claim of psychoanalysis that we even dream in symbols, the same symbols that appear with frequency in religious myths, iconography, and liturgy. Living symbols serve as a code between the conscious and unconscious self, and between the individual unconscious and the collective unconscious. This code is the consolidated (and evolving) memory of a people or a tradition that has been entrusted to its symbols.

Finally, *symbols are organic, they are born, grow and die.* A symbol emerges when the situation for it is ripe. It grows and matures, unfolding over time as succeeding generations use it to interpret their lives and devote themselves to reflect on the meaning that is encoded in it. Jesus would be the best example of this in Christianity. Over the centuries layers of meaning have been accruing, so that from the vantage of the twenty-first century we can look back and see a multitude of images through which Jesus has been viewed: carpenter, miracle worker, friend of children, suffering servant, teacher of Gnostic wisdom, ruler of the universe, crusading warrior, moral teacher, divine Logos, revolutionary, prince of peace, CEO.[33] The fecundity of Jesus as a symbol is an indication of how potent the situation of revelation was in which he first appeared. The same could be said of Moses, the Buddha, Lao Tzu, and Muhammad. This fecundity is a feature of the founding figure of any religion.

A symbol can also die. History is strewn with dead symbols, and those which die usually do so at the hands of the religions that gave birth to them in the first place. In time, the revelatory situation that produced them can become obsolete and have nothing to say any longer. When this happens, the symbols that represented that revelation grow silent and eventually lifeless, either disappearing or persisting only as clichés. "In this way," Tillich claims (perhaps prematurely), "all of the polytheistic gods have died; the situation in which they were born has changed or does not exist anymore, and so the symbols died."[34] It is in this manner that Mary as a symbol of devotion has died for most Protestants, although she remains as a less potent symbol of a sort of faithfulness to God that ought to be emulated.

And a symbol can go into hibernation, ready to be awakened when the conditions are right, although this is not a possibility Tillich seems to have anticipated. The resurgence of goddess worship and druidic cults, of Celtic "spirituality," or of the use of medieval spiritual disciplines, icons, and speculation about purgatory that can be found among Protestant Christians in recent years would be examples of this. The ever-percolating centrality of various images of Jesus would be another instance. Jesus as rabbi, as stoic philosopher, and as lover of the soul in mystical rapture are making a comeback. And ever since the late nineteenth century there has been in the West a fascination with primitive myth, fetishes and sacred symbols from Africa, Asia, Australia and the indigenous peoples of the Americas, which coincided with a flagging interest in traditional Western religions among the educated classes. Even when this has been pursued out of aesthetic interest, it carried an undertow of expectation that a reconnection to raw primordial powers is possible through these symbols.

For Tillich, symbols that cease pointing beyond themselves become idols. John Calvin contended that while human beings were created to find their "chief delight" in God, the Fall signaled our relocating this delight into some fragment of reality, and often some work of our own hands, absolutizing or deifying nature or our own powers. Thus, for Calvin, human nature "is a perpetual factory of idols,"[35] and this is the heart of apostasy, the origin and perpetuation of our brokenness. Like Calvin, Tillich believed that there is a human tendency to coax symbols into becoming opaque to the reality "to which they are supposed to point, and to become ultimate in themselves. And in the moment in which they

do this, they become idols. All idolatry is nothing else than the absolutizing of symbols of the Holy, and making them identical with the Holy
itself."[36] Symbols, intended to be instruments, are transmuted into ends
in themselves, graven images before which we worship. When this occurs,
religious symbols become "demonic," leading us astray from worship of
the true God.

Nevertheless, it is our divinely given capacity for ultimate concern,
according to Tillich – the very homing device that keeps us restless until
we find rest in God – that craves symbols. In a cultural situation in which
the inherited symbols have lost their power, this craving can be either
rejuvenating or destructive. Hitler was disturbingly brilliant in this regard.
In the 1930s he "realized that an empty space existed in the whole German
nation, and this empty space had to be filled." He filled it with the symbol
of "the German race." Communism did something similar, producing a
great new set of symbols that put in motion a social movement which
drew on these symbols for its meaning. "[E]mptiness drives the human
mind toward certain strong reactions," Tillich argued, "and if they are
not creatively good ones they can become very evil indeed."[37]

But our proclivity for religious symbols need not be at either extreme
of good or evil. There is a vast middle ground in which we exercise
our facility with symbols with ambiguous results. A phenomenology of
symbols, which Tillich outlines for us, can be useful in identifying this
great middle range of symbols that are emerging and the values in which
they participate.

So, Tillich provides us with these instruments for scanning the culture
for images and figures that are functioning as religious symbols. They
point beyond themselves, participate in that to which they point, open
up otherwise hidden dimensions of reality, and cannot be artificially contrived or forced. When something can be determined to be operating
in all of these ways, it indicates that an ultimate concern is making its
presence known. Tillich's demarcation of what constitutes a religious
symbol has been influential on both theologians and anthropologists of
religion, but it is not absolutely unique. Others have used other terms to
describe similar phenomena. The historian of religions, Mircea Eliade, for
instance, suggests that the *hierophany* is the basic element of religion. In a
hierophany something sacred (*hiero*) shows itself (*phanía*) to us. Religions
are composed of great numbers of hierophanies, which, for Eliade,
include "rites, myths, divine forms, sacred and venerated objects, cos-
mologies, theologoumena, consecrated men, animals and plants, sacred
spaces, and more."[38] But archaic symbols are first order hierophanies.
For the religious person, "every cosmic fragment is transparent; its own
mode of existence shows a particular structure of being, and hence of
the sacred."[39] Whenever human beings brush up against something that

seems to manifest the structure of reality itself, of what is what, that something impresses us as a vessel of the sacred. The phenomena we encounter every day, for example, the sunrise, dirt, seeds, food, water and vegetation, are common hierophanies in the historical religious traditions because we are aware that our existence depends upon them.

To push this inquiry into symbols in a direction that neither Tillich nor Eliade would have been likely to pursue, but fully in keeping with their theories, consider the lowly hamburger. British sociologist Mike Featherstone has commented on the iconic potency of the hamburger and other symbols of the American way of life as it is introduced around the world through globalization. While it is generally acknowledged that McDonald's represents a certain corporate ethos of standardization and efficiency, it represents more than this as a symbol in the cultures where it has set up operation. As anyone can testify who has stood in line with eager patrons at a McDonald's outside of North America, and witnessed or heard reports of vandalism of McDonald's franchises in these same places, the hamburger both attracts and repels. What is the holy reality to which it points that elicits this response? According to Featherstone,

> [T]he burger is clearly American and it stands for the American way of life. It is a product from a superior global center, which has long represented itself as *the* center. For those on the periphery it offers the possibility of the psychological benefits of identifying with the powerful. Along with the Marlboro Man, Coca-Cola, Hollywood, Sesame Street, rock music and American football insignia, McDonald's is one of a series of icons of the American way of life. They have become associated with transposable themes which are central to consumer culture, such as youth, fitness, beauty, luxury, romance, freedom. American dreams have become transposed with those of the good life.[40]

Youth, fitness, beauty, romance and freedom are not necessarily bad things. Bound together in a gestalt of corporate logos, American power, and consumption, however, they begin to resemble a religious system organized around an ultimate concern. The hamburger can be both a symbol and a sacrament of this emerging religion. Eating it is a way of participating in a pantheon of powers to which it points.

Myth

"Myth" is a strange concept in that it has had considerable prestige among scholars for more than 200 years, but is often used in ordinary language as a pejorative term to indicate that a given account is untrue or mistaken. This is an old discrepancy. With the rise of the Enlightenment there emerged an effort to separate the reasonable elements of Christianity from its implausible elements, namely its miracles and myths. John Locke, David Hume, and Immanuel Kant were key figures in this critique of religion. In 1785, in reaction to this accelerating critique of religion's mythical elements, Johann Gottfried Herder contended that "If we consider the mythologies of peoples to be merely teachings about false gods, lapses of human reason, or lamentable cases of blind superstition, then in my opinion our outlook is too narrow." In his estimation, myths began as elementary exercises of human reason seeking to ascertain the natural and moral order of reality and the feelings that it elicits, which were then secured for future generations by suturing the images and ideas together into stories. Myths increased in their refinement over time, each generation testing and retelling them, and should, in light of this, be viewed as a treasury of symbols, limited in some ways, but full of genuine wisdom about what matters in life. Because of this, the myths of the different peoples of the earth should be "observed and treated with humanity," for although each people went its own way, in some manner and to some degree "God ... revealed himself to them all,"[41] much of which was captured in their myths. Through myths, we are inducted into strains of wisdom thousands of years in the making.

Throughout the nineteenth and into the twentieth century, while there was a sustained dismissal of myth by a variety of philosophers and biblical scholars, there was a parallel line of defense that followed Herder. Among the defenders of myth can be found three broad arguments. For some, myths are to be read *literally* for what information they provide us about what happened a very long time ago and for the explanations they offer about the origin of certain phenomena and customs. Others argue that myths are not intended to give information at all, but are intended instead to encourage and console, to render the world a habitable place where human beings can be oriented to *transcendent* meaning. Schleiermacher and Troeltsch, for instance, offered theological arguments for *mythos* as essential for replenishing the deepest energies of religion, a need that the human race will never outgrow, and for orienting believers to God and the world in a trustworthy way. A third group, arising outside of the churches, claim that myths are not true in either the literal or transcendent sense, but that they are true in a *functional* sense, performing the essential function of ordering the world for the purpose of gaining some level of control over it. For them, myths have provided an indispensable template for instructing us how to wrestle what is necessary for life out of nature (James Frazer), organizing ourselves into moral communities (Emile Durkheim), and calming our psychic anxieties (Freud and Jung).

Tillich was an heir to the second and third groups of these defenders of myth. Parallel to his accounts of both ultimate concern and religious symbols, he insisted that "One can replace one myth by another, but one cannot remove the myth from man's spiritual life."[42] There is no substitute for myths, which, for Tillich, are the natural repositories of religious symbols; they are necessary to the ongoing vitality of religious symbols in that discrete symbols only have meaning when they are lodged within stories and thus connected to the other symbols, spinning out, as one myth is hooked onto others, until the world in all its parts is sacralized by a great narrative of symbols. In this way religious symbols find their way into myths that guide us in determining our relationship to the world.

Furthermore for Tillich, myths are stories in which divine figures appear as characters. True, myth "puts the stories of the gods into the framework of time and space although it belongs to the nature of the ultimate to be beyond time and space."[43] Myths, that is, submit the infinite divine to the same finite limitations and ambiguities that we are mired in, which is problematic. Nevertheless, as both Tertullian and Augustine recognized, human beings need images and stories. Our imaginations demand concrete symbols and master plots that are thick and rich enough for us to insert our own lives into as they are retold through the generations. Bare metaphysical schemes and moral codes have little longevity outside of narratives. Moreover, myths are a religious and cultural trust that matures over time. As they age, and as the historical conditions in which they are received change, different insights and emphases that were formerly unseen in them can rise to the surface.

But Tillich insisted that myths must be "broken" in order to release their revelatory power. A myth must be broken open, as an egg is broken open, to allow the nourishment it contains to be poured out. An unbroken myth is read as a literal account of past events, as if it were a journalist's report of what actually occurred. A broken reading interprets the myth for what it might illuminate regarding the structure of human nature, the human task, or the forces and limitations that we can expect to encounter in life.

Perhaps the person most associated with the study of myth in the twentieth century is Mircea Eliade. Like Tillich, Eliade contended that we are mythmakers because there is a mythic space in human consciousness that demands to be filled. But Eliade enables us to think more thoroughly about what it is we do with our myths, what it is that makes them indispensable. Myths provide us with the templates we need to conduct our most significant activities. "The supreme function of myth," he writes, "is to 'fix' the paradigmatic models for all rites and all significant human activities – eating, sexuality, work, education, and so on."[44] Myths narrate for us how it is that the cosmos and everything in it came to be what it is, laying before us a blueprint of its structure and telling us about the specific actions that brought it all into existence.

According to Eliade,

> Myth narrates a sacred history; it relates an event that took place in primordial Time, the fabled time of the "beginnings." In other words, myth tells how, through the deeds of Supernatural Beings, a reality came into existence, be it the whole of reality, the Cosmos, or only a fragment of reality – an island, a species of plant, a particular kind of human behavior, an institution.[45]

The creative process narrated in myths is often ritualized into human creative activity. When it comes time to do something, particularly to build something, for example, a house, canoe, or the tools of one's trade, or to install a new political leader or constitution, or to plant crops at the beginning of the growing season, myths are either recited or ritually enacted to consecrate the new creation.[46] Two reasons can be given for this.

First, the adage "as above, so below," is a fixture in the archaic understanding of creativity. The creation of the cosmos established a procedural precedent. If the cosmos was created according to a particular procedure, that procedure must be the only effective recipe for any creation. If, for instance, the universe was made from the slaughtered body of a primeval god, as in the Norse myth of Ymir and the Babylonian myth of Tiamat, the building of a new house or the planting of a new field might be ritually supplemented with a blood sacrifice. In whatever fashion reality itself was created, subsequent additions to reality must be prepared in a similar manner.

A second reason for this is, as Eliade describes it, that "they hope to recover the vital reserves and the germinal riches which were made manifest for the first time in the majestic act of creation."[47] Recitation of the creation myth conjures up the compost from the outset of time, when undifferentiated energy could barely be contained, bursting at its seams for a chance to be and to breed. At that time of the beginnings, vitality charged the atmosphere. Anything was possible because "the species were not yet fixed and all forms were fluid."[48] The creation narrative returns the matter at hand (the wood or stones for the house, the soil and seeds for the field) to its pre-differentiated, chaotic state, and narratively escorts it through a consecrated sequence to new creation on a smaller scale.

Reciting the myth opens up the immediate situation to powers of transcendent origin. The recitation of the myth is itself a hierophany, bringing all within the range of its utterance into the presence and rejuvenating powers of the sacred. After entering the mythic story and re-encountering its symbols and plot, we can ourselves be rejuvenated and re-equipped with fresh insights into who we are and what we are for, revived for our return to regular time. Only upon returning the world is bathed in mythical meanings – an effect that dissipates with the passage of time, then is restored with the next ritual interruption.

Eliade derives his account of myth from what can be observed, he claims, in "archaic" societies – societies in which people conscientiously model their lives according to their myths. He admits that this archaic veneration of myth is broken in the modern period. Nevertheless, he argues, myths are still operating – just not in plain sight. As Eliade sees it, although they have been driven underground they still carry on the work they have always done, shaping and empowering the prevailing world-views. Pushed down to the depths of the psyche, lurking at the bottom of the unconscious, are the rejected plots, personages, and symbols of myth that once disclosed the nature of reality to our ancestors. From there, they continue doing their work, as best they can, in a variety of disguises.[49]

So, our myths feed us our scripts. We imitate the quests and struggles of the dominant figures in the myths and rehearse our lives informed by mythic plots. We awaken to a set of sacred stories, and then proceed to apprehend the world and to express ourselves in terms of these stories. They shape us secretly at a formative age and remain with us, informing the ongoing narrative constructions of our experience. They teach us how to perceive the world as we order our outlooks and choices in terms of their patterns and plots.

When religious$_2$ myths are on the wane, other myths appear to take their place. For the purpose of doing a theological analysis of culture, the assumption is that there are myths in place, and that they can be found in popular culture. Identifying them is a matter of determining which of our cultural stories are performing this function of providing the plots and exemplary figures and actions around which we form our identities, measure the dignity of our own actions, and derive the sense of meaning we grant to the world. Because they feed us our scripts, myths are the stories that we never get tired of hearing; consequently, discerning which plotlines and exemplary figures recur with great frequency is a way to discover the operative myths in our culture. Given the prominence of television, advertising, and movies today as our culture's most prolific generator of exemplary figures and visions of the good life – our preeminent storytellers – it will prove worthwhile to turn to these media for an understanding of the myths we are circulating.

Novelists, poets, filmmakers, and painters are reliable indices to the currently vital myths in a culture, as will be explored later. But so are astronomers, political scientists, sociologists, and historians. We moderns and postmoderns do have metaphysical plots with which we tell the story of the forces that have made the world what it is: survival of the fittest, rational choice, secularization, globalization, the war of all against all, dialectical materialism, chaos theory, the cunning collusion of power and knowledge, the triumph of the therapeutic, the decline of civilization, the "end of history," the "clash of civilizations," the Big Bang, and Murphy's Law ("Anything that can go wrong, will")[50] to name a few – all have their adherents, and all have their heroic figures and rituals through which the forces they reveal are enacted, displayed, resisted and placated. These grand plots function as myths ᴄ indeed they are often re-warmed archaic myths, as has frequently been pointed out in the case of biblical millennialism and Marx's dialectic materialism, or as might be argued in the cases of Eden and the decline of civilization, Odysseus and the Big Bang, Dionysus and the will-to-power, or Narcissus and the triumph of the therapeutic.[51]

Liminality

Arnold van Gennep was a Dutch anthropologist who wrote an important study in the early twentieth century on patterns he had detected across cultures in the rituals that marked life transitions. He began his book, *The Rites of Passage*, describing what he took to be the more obvious phenomenon of territorial passage, noting the way human beings in archaic societies divide land into a patchwork of domains with boundaries that they mark with sacred stones, trees, or rivers. Passage across these boundaries is always risky and requires observing various formalities. Those who pass from one domain to another, he claims, find themselves in a precarious situation for a certain length of time, wavering between two worlds. Compiling field research from Africa, Australia, China and Europe, he extended this observation by noting that it is common in ritual observances that conduct human beings between precarious *stages of life* to make a ceremonial use of doors – symbols of territorial passage borrowed for the purpose of illuminating the cycle of a human life. As a central part of ceremonies surrounding coming of age, marriage, entrance into secret societies, royal enthronements, and death, doors are solemnly sprinkled with blood, water and perfume, and festooned with sacred objects, often bearing images of fantastic creatures like dragons, griffins, and monsters. Crossing a threshold as part of these initiation rituals signifies the gravity of one's passing from one world to another.[52]

Van Gennep argues that a common progression can be discerned in the rites of initiation he has examined, a sequence consisting of three stages:[53]

- separation from a previous world;
- ordeals of liminality;
- ceremonies of incorporation.

First, those undergoing the initiation are separated out from everyone else for a determined span of time – either alone or in the company of others undergoing the same transition. Second, they are subjected to great physical and mental ordeals designed to make them forget the phase of life they are exiting, and then exposed to totem ceremonies, recitations of sacred myths, instruction in tribal law, etc., which they had never witnessed before. Finally, a processional is held in which the neophyte is elevated to a new status in life, and ceremonially marked in some way that is typical of members of that station. Actual marking of the body is quite common here: circumcision, tattoos, scarifying, perforating the ear lobe or nasal septum, cutting the hair, pulling a tooth.[54]

Drawing on the work of van Gennep when he set out to do his own fieldwork among the Ndembu people of Zambia in the 1960s, anthropologist Victor Turner observed the same sequence in Ndembu rites of passage.[55] But Turner has gone further than van Gennep in two respects: in reflecting on what larger social purpose is served by this pattern, a dialectic he describes as an interplay between structure and anti-structure that is essential to the ongoing vitality of a culture, and in identifying its survival in contemporary Western culture.

Turner found the middle phase of liminality to be fascinating for the remarkably statusless condition into which it thrusts the persons undergoing the rite. The root of the term "liminality" was seen earlier in the etymology given for the term "sublime": *limen* means "threshold." People who are crossing through a ritual threshold slip between their society's normal categories of classification. They shed the structure in which their identities, social class, and community responsibilities have been embedded and linger in a "betwixt and between" condition, for the duration of which they are "neither-this-nor-that, neither here-nor-there," and during which any new assignment of structure is suspended until the ritual has been concluded and they are reincorporated into the society.[56] In Ndembu ritual this threshold state is expressed in a rich variety of symbols: darkness, wilderness, womb, grave, and bisexuality. The initiands are cast into what Turner describes as "the limbo of statuslessness."[57]

Rituals undergone during this phase emphasize dissolution. Initiands are commonly buried, stained black, or forced to lie motionless, as if dead. They strip off their clothing to signify their loss of identity. They may be chased into the wilderness where they become caked with dirt and, as it were, blend into the earth, disintegrating into the wild and primal matter from whence they came. Turner describes it as a "grinding down process" that is accomplished by ordeals:

> circumcision, subincision, clitoridectomy, hazing, endurance of heat and cold, impossible physical tests in which failure is greeted by ridicule,

unanswerable riddles which make even clever candidates look stupid, followed by physical punishment, and the like.[58]

All of these symbolic actions contribute to their awareness of starting over from scratch, in preparation for their pending re-entry into their society with a new status and identity. During the threshold phase they are introduced to the *sacra* of their people. They are shown icons and diagrams, told sacred myths and the names of their deities. Turner suggests that the information communicated to the initiands during this display of the *sacra* is the most fundamental stuff of their culture, the elemental symbols out of which the culture is built; it is the most prized wisdom of the tribe.[59] In this liminal time they are relieved of their everyday labors and given the opportunity to reflect on the symbols that signify their culture's ultimate concerns and references, and to assume a position with respect to these things. And as they reflect, they deepen their loyalty to their culture's grasp of reality, appropriating it as their own, and perhaps begin to improvise on it now that the symbols are entrusted to their hands. Knowing what they have undergone, knowing of their fresh exposure to the cherished symbols of the tribe, the society that has sent them into this ritual process prepares itself to receive them back in a transformed status.

Something occurs during the phase of liminality that Turner calls communitas. Communitas is the deep bonding that develops between initiands. The experience of dissolution, of being stripped of status and structural roles, allows them to relate to one another with a spontaneity and rawness that endures long after the ritual has concluded, often connecting them for life. They discover each other without the trappings of rank, property or kinship positions.[60] Communitas is a quality of profound interpersonal communion that Turner believes human beings instinctively long for. Through the contrivance of the shared ordeal, initiands glimpse new ways for structural relations to be arranged among themselves, and then re-enter their societies prepared to implement what they have glimpsed, experienced, and so deeply enjoyed. If the visions that were generated while they were held in thrall by communitas have sufficient power and durability, they can actually carry over into permanent changes in the way their society classifies reality and the social relations within it.[61] In this way cultures are reoxygenated by these rituals.

The central rite of initiation in Christianity is baptism. In the early church, before the practice of infant baptism became the standard, baptisms were generally done once a year at Easter, following daily instruction on the creeds and the mysteries of the faith in the preceding weeks of Lent. Baptismal fonts in settled Christian communities were ornately decorated, with paintings or mosaics of key biblical scenes: Adam and Eve with the serpent in the garden, David and Goliath, the good shepherd and his sheep, the Samaritan woman at the well, Peter walking on water, the women mourning at the tomb of Jesus. Baptism was a solemn affair in which a priest invoked the Holy Spirit to come upon the water and then, one by one, the catechumens disrobed, publicly renounced Satan, were anointed with oil, then descended into the water. Confessing their faith, they were immersed and the prayer of baptism recited. Emerging from the waters, reborn, the new Christian was robed and then proceeded to the Eucharist to be joined by the whole local community of believers.

All of the components of liminality were present here. The naked descent into the water (a symbol of dissolution into the primal matter), the death and rebirth of the initiand, exposure to the *sacra* of the biblical stories and liturgical prayers, and the first participation in the Eucharist.

While baptisms today are more streamlined than this, much lighter affairs, vestiges of all of these elements persist. But it is worth wondering whether the fundamental components of the rite of passage captured by van Gennep and Turner may have wandered elsewhere in our culture. This will be explored more fully in chapters below, but for now, three lessons can be drawn for where this concept of liminality suggests we might look.

First, thresholds are important. Passageways that are delineated by strange markers like sculpted figures from myths and legends, gargoyles, and inscriptions in ancient languages, or well-tended natural barriers like lagoons and gardens, or dazzling signage, particularly neon – may well be there to regulate traffic between two worlds, one profane and the other sacred.

Second, the spaces and times in our culture that are "betwixt and between" our more routine obligations are important. Where do we go to suspend our normal identities and responsibilities? What occasions do we anticipate will allow us that peculiar kind of anti-structure that rejuvenates us ostensibly for the sake of rejuvenating our society? Where and when do people in our culture experience liminality and communitas?

And third, activities that combine the elements of ordeal with exposure to icons, totems, myths, densely compressed symbols, and communal values are significant. Where are our ritualized ordeals, and what secret knowledge is associated with them?

Religion

Up to this point two modes of religion have been denoted – religion$_1$ (religion as the surging of unconditioned forces beneath the surface of a culture) and religion$_2$ (religion as a discrete sphere within a culture). Religion$_1$ refers to religion as ultimate concern. This is our for the most part pre-conscious faith that existence is worthwhile, the faith that can be found in the depths of each of the spheres of culture – art, science, politics, family, economy, religion, and the media-world – sustaining our conviction that it is a meaningful act to participate in them. Religion$_1$, as Tillich described it, "is the life-blood, the inner power, the ultimate meaning of all life. The 'sacred' or the 'holy' inflames, imbues, inspires, all reality and all aspects of existence."[62]

Religion$_2$, on the other hand, refers to overt religion, with its scriptures, myths, symbols, rituals, officials, prayers, places of worship, etc., through which people seek to comprehend, respond to, and communicate in an explicit manner the ultimate realities upon which their faith rests. Religion$_2$ relies upon "all forms of meaningful expression" – such as language, music, art, philosophy, architecture, ritual, ethics, and technology (writing, printing presses, telecommunications). Without these cultural forms, religion$_2$ "cannot express itself even in a meaningful silence."[63] Human beings "would not be spiritual," Tillich claims, "without words, thoughts, and concepts," which are the gifts of culture.[64]

These are the two senses of religion captured in Tillich's formula: "Religion is the substance of culture and culture is the form of religion." Religion$_{(1)}$ is the substance of culture; culture is the form of religion$_{(2)}$.

But there is also a third mode of religion – one that Tillich did not distinguish, and therefore did not give the attention it deserves – a mode that can be designated as religion$_3$. Religion$_3$ refers to the way that the ideas and values of a particular religion$_2$ come to be absorbed – but not lost – by the culture in which that religion is or has been dominant. As a variation on Herder's notion that each culture may be viewed as the embodiment of an idea of God, it is possible to make some generalizations about different cultures and civilizations based on the religious traditions that have been most active and enduring within them. The way that a culture ages and matures is influenced to a great extent by the religious$_2$ forces that prevailed in its formative periods. While no culture is monolithic, it is still possible to find within modern Arab nations powerful "secular" institutions and enduring moral habits that are inconceivable without the historical influence of Islam. Similarly with China and Taoism, and India and Hinduism. Legal systems, political cultures, aesthetic sensibilities, family structures, modes of entertainment, and educational practices bear the lingering effects of religion$_2$ influence even when it has long ceased to be direct. This is not to say that the institutions and moral habits are explicitly "Islamic," "Taoist," or "Hindu"; it is only to say that ideas and moral predilections that originated in these religions have been sown in the cultures in which they made their home and have germinated and mutated over long stretches of time in ways that are different from, yet resonant with, the development of the same ideas and moral predilections that occur inside the religion traditions themselves. This renegade activity of once explicit religious influences outside the sphere of religion$_2$ is what is meant by religion$_3$. It is not a kind of spontaneous eruption of religion$_1$ inspiring the culture from its ontological depths, but a derivative emergence from religion$_2$.

To offer a more familiar example: in the history of Western cultures, religion$_2$ has established a multitude of institutions to reflect its values and ideals that were subsequently dispersed throughout the West and have come to be taken for granted as elements Westerners expect to find in any livable society. Think about such institutions as universities, hospitals, social service agencies, art patronage, public libraries, urban cemeteries, public parks and playgrounds, the constitutional form of government, family law, and homes for orphans, the destitute and elderly. Each one can be traced back to the founding efforts of organized religion. True, most universities, hospitals, social service agencies, and the rest are now independent non-profit, for-profit, or state-run institutions. But the historical record is that their first appearance in Western civilization in anything like their modern form came by way of the agitations of religious communities who were motivated by religious ideas to launch an institution-producing moral crusade.[65]

That we largely concur that these institutions and the values they promote are good and for the most part assume that any society we would wish to be members of will address these values through similar institutions and laws, is one of religion$_2$'s great achievements. It shows the extent to which the moral habits that have been refined within overt religion have been adopted and internalized by Western secular culture, even though the religious pedigree of these institutions and laws is forgotten and, in some quarters, strenuously denied. Religious$_2$ tendencies, values, and ideals continue to develop and organize life within religious denominations and congregations, but they have also been entrusted to a process of development that is independent of the oversight of religion$_2$. Moral habits that originated in religious communities now travel down two different roads, one still within religion$_2$ and one in its secular diaspora of religion$_3$.

With respect to doing a theological analysis of culture, it is important to remember that the moral habits that now travel in secular diaspora in the West were originally conceived as responses to theological convictions about the nature of God, the human condition, covenant, grace and salvation. This raises the possibility that if one digs around in our culture's moral habits – which are found in the non-profit institutions it supports, the mythic stories it tells itself, its founding documents, and the exemplary persons it promotes as worthy to emulate, among other things – a theological layer might be uncovered.

That we value democracy has its historical roots in the Puritan struggles for popular sovereignty, the Calvinist belief that those who have power will inevitably abuse it, and an even deeper root in the biblical admonitions that promoted a feeling of obligation for the poor and humble. The Bible has much to say about championing the side of victims, being suspicious of wealth, refusing to be "respecters of persons," and condemning the delusions of the powerful, all prejudices inclined toward social leveling that persist as moral reflexes in the West, as can be seen in the insistence upon due process in Western legal practice, and the different permutations of the anti-globalization movement of the last decade. In addition to its role in the emergence of human rights, the concept of a higher law that arose in the natural law tradition and was a franchise of Roman Catholicism for centuries has had repercussions in science and art, where it has served to embolden many thinkers and artists to question conventions and common wisdom. The practice of critical interpretation of culture that permeates the West – in journalism, literature, cinema, and higher education – rests at some level on faith in a higher law in relation to which everything falls short, and to which everything is accountable, a law that medieval theologians conceived as emanating from the mind of God.

That the three great American sports – football, baseball, and basketball – were invented by New England Protestants, a pedigree about which few are aware, suggests that they are features of popular culture ripe for analysis as religion$_3$ phenomena. They became organized sports in the eighteenth and nineteenth centuries through the efforts of students studying for ministry at Yale, Princeton, and Harvard, and later as an explicit effort of the Massachusetts-based YMCA, promoted for the purpose of disciplining the excess vitality of youth and cultivating such moral values as cooperation, fair play, and sacrifice.[66] They have taken a route in our society surely unintended by their founders. While the mythic, ritual, and moral elements of each of the three still bear vestigial traces of their origins, they have appropriated and given rise to a full-fledged religious$_3$ system that competes with Christianity as much, if not more than, it reinforces certain Christian values. While there is still some impulse to cheer on the underdog, and with the possible exception of Cubs' fans, there is little survival in these sports of Jesus' admonition that "the last shall be first."

Still, one of the ironies is that, in many cases, the very same values that were conceived within religion$_2$ fare better once they have been released to do their work outside the religious sphere. This can be seen in the sluggish pace with which women have been admitted into leadership within many Christian churches relative to what has occurred within the political, academic, and business spheres of Western culture. Liberation from bondage is a biblical legacy in the West, one that is only gradually coming to be realized. The slow emancipation of women that we have achieved owes its inspiration to the rogue journey of this particular biblical ideal into the wider culture. There is a conservative inertia within religious traditions that can hold back the potential of certain homegrown values within the tradition itself. Because of this, the tradition that gave the culture such a treasured ideal often comes under criticism from those who are indebted to it, *viz.*, the recipients of the ideal who have fostered its development outside the tradition. The full power of many of the symbols that originate in religion$_2$ can remain ineffective until they are bequeathed to the culture outside the religious community and undergo the refinement that the frictions of history force upon them.

What has thus germinated outside of the religious sphere can be understood as a genuine enlargement of reality, a bringing of a revelatory insight into real life tensions and conflicts that has produced subsequent revelations that would have remained dormant but for having entered this secondary track and the conditions that awaited it there. However, this is not a religion$_1$ kind of revelation that breaks through directly into the culture from its underlying substance. It is a revelation occurring by means of the historical process itself, with religion$_2$ emptying itself out into its home culture.

Religion$_1$, religion$_2$, and religion$_3$, then, are three different modes in which culture reveals, takes hold of, and develops an apprehension of unconditioned reality. Each one mediates the sacred in a different manner. And while theology of the church develops methods for reflecting on religion$_2$, theology of culture is intended to investigate the apprehensions of the sacred in religion$_1$ and religion$_3$. The specific benefit of analyzing a culture for its religion$_3$ elements is two-fold: It can serve *the religious community* by drawing attention to how it has squandered some of its greatest symbols; and it can alert *the culture* to the theological assumptions underlying some of its most treasured ideals, such as human rights, and force it to consider what longevity these ideals might have if these assumptions are abandoned.

Conclusion

The purpose of this chapter has been to isolate some theological tools that can be used to discern religious elements within culture:

- ultimate concern;
- the holy;
- ontological and moral faith;

- revelation and ecstasy;
- religious symbols;
- myth;
- liminality;
- religion.

As far as tools go, it is a beginner's set. Still, much can be done with the theological concepts divulged so far, including those covered earlier in the book (the typology of faith and broken faith), and a few more that will be introduced in the pages ahead. Undertaking an analysis of popular culture by combining these tools with those gleaned from cultural studies (e.g., hegemony, style, *bricolage*, memes, simulacra, etc.) should provide some surprising results, perhaps a few revelations, regarding the theological longings and apprehensions struggling for expression in current popular culture.

To assist in sorting out the analysis that follows, the cultural materials to be examined will be organized loosely along the lines of a traditional "systematic theology," with sections on God, human nature, sin, salvation, and eschatology. This is an ancient method for engaging in theological reflection in Christianity, although its use with the symbols, myths, and apprehensions of the holy in popular culture is a bit unorthodox. The goal is to discover what sorts of things popular culture, drawing entirely upon its own resources, has to say on these theological topics.[67]

II

A Theology of Popular Culture

5

Images of God

In 1946, Nikos Kazantzakis wrote *Zorba the Greek*, a novel about a laborer named Zorba, who exuded a colossal zeal for life, and his boss, a well-educated, wealthy mine-owner who hired Zorba as a foreman at one of his mines. The two became friends. Late in their friendship, Zorba became ill and, knowing that he was dying, turned to his boss for some comforting words. "I want you to tell me," Zorba said, "where we have come from and where we are going to. During all these years you've been burning yourself up consuming all these books...you must have chewed over about fifty tons of paper! What did you get out of them?" His boss, the teller of this story, offered him the consolation of what he called "sacred awe":

> We are little grubs, Zorba, minute grubs on the small leaf of a tremendous tree. This small leaf is the earth. The other leaves are the stars you see moving at night. ...Some men – the more intrepid ones – reach the edge of the leaf. From there we stretch out, gazing into chaos. We tremble. We guess what a frightening abyss lies beneath us...Bent thus over the awe-inspiring abyss, with all our bodies and all our souls, we tremble with terror. From that moment begins the great danger, Zorba. Some grow dizzy and delirious, others are afraid; they try to find an answer to strengthen their hearts, and they say: "God!" Others again, from the edge of the leaf, look over the precipice calmly and bravely and say [simply], "I like it."[1]

Kazantzakis wrote these riveting words a half century ago, and in the immediate aftermath of the Second World War. This image of the grubs stretching out to peer off the edge of their trembling leaf into immense mystery captured a view of God that became a dominant one for several decades after the great war. The essence of this view is that there is a great, terrifying reality that surrounds us, what Tillich would call the holy. The less courageous who catch sight of it call it "God," while the more courageous steel themselves and refuse to give it a name.

This soliloquy from *Zorba* is offered as our point of departure for this chapter because things look very different now. *Zorba* contains an eloquent statement of a courageous agnosticism, of the best, most humane, existentialism that came in the wake of World War II. This brand of agnosticism found its standing firm in the face of nothingness to be ennobling, and it had some legs on it, serving as the underlying faith in the works of writers like Albert Camus and Jack Kerouac, and filmmakers like Stanley Kubrick. In these artists we find a drive to *push* the abiding mystery *beyond* the reach of all words and formulas, and to relish our *in*ability to name it.

In 1994, fifty years later, Douglas Coupland, the author who coined the term "Generation X," and is a reliable interpreter of that cohort, published a novel called *Life after God*. The narrator in this story is trying to determine why his life is in such a shambles. His wife has left him, he is alienated from his daughter, and he is living in a rent-by-the-week downtown hotel room with an assortment of derelicts. We learn that he is a member of GenX, born after 1965, into an affluent family near Vancouver, Canada. He tells us that he has "been raised without religion by parents who had broken with their own pasts and moved to the West Coast – who had raised their children clean of any ideology, in a cantilevered modern house overlooking the Pacific Ocean – at the end of history, or so they had wanted to believe." He goes on to report,

> Ours was a life lived in paradise and thus it rendered any discussion of transcendental ideas pointless...Life was charmed but without politics or religion. It was the life of children of the children of the pioneers – life after God – a life of earthly salvation on the edge of heaven. Perhaps this is the finest thing to which we may aspire, the life of peace, the blurring between dream life and real life – and yet I find myself speaking these words with a sense of doubt.
>
> I think there was a trade-off somewhere along the line. I think the price we paid for our golden life was an inability to fully believe in love; instead we gained an irony that scorched everything it touched. And I wonder if this irony is the price we paid for the loss of God.
>
> But then I must remind myself we are living creatures – we have religious impulses – we *must* – and yet into what cracks do these impulses flow in a world without religion?[2]

Here is the plea of an unshaped religious consciousness, aware of its own aimless desire, craving an ultimacy that is more satisfying than pure irony can be. Here, in this novel of wandering, are echoes of St Augustine, who prayed at the outset of his *Confessions*, "My heart is restless until it finds rest in thee, O God." Coupland offers us one of the most poignant descriptions of the concept of ultimate concern in contemporary fiction. Without a reality larger than oneself to care about, the capacity to love anything at all is crippled.

From *Zorba the Greek* to *Life after God* the tone has changed from the bold refusal of consolation that followed World War II to a melancholic regret over a life that is empty of God. The postwar moratorium on naming the mystery "God" seems to be releasing its grip; the *vox populi* is uttering sounds that seem to desire recovering a vocabulary for the sacred.

In this chapter the aim is to ascertain what American popular culture, through its skill at *bricolage*, is telling itself about the existence of God, the divine attributes, angels and lesser gods, providence and natural evil, all topics commonly treated under the doctrine of God in classic systematic theologies.

First, a survey of the signs of the times. There is much chatter about God that can be overheard on the wires of popular culture.

Signs of the Times

In the movie, *FightClub*, the two lead characters, Jack and Tyler, are standing across a table from each other in the kitchen of the leaky, abandoned mansion where they have been squatting for several months. Jack has been drawn more deeply into the 12-step program that Tyler has designed to wean him from the consumerism that has overtaken his life and to carry him further into a liberating anarchism. Tyler reaches across the table for Jack's hand and kisses it. With the lip print still moist, Tyler cinches his grip and pours powdered lye on Jack's trusting hand, causing a searingly painful chemical burn that, once healed, will leave a kiss-shaped scar.[3] This has all the marks of a sacrament sealing Jack's initiation. As Jack writhes in pain, Tyler tells him:

> Our fathers were our models for God. If our fathers bailed, what does that tell you about God? You have to consider the possibility that God does not like you. Never wanted you, in all probability he hates you. This is not the worst thing that can happen. We don't need him. F – k damnation, man, f – k redemption. We are God's unwanted children. So be it. It's only after we've lost everything that we're free to do anything.

An ordeal has been undergone, and now this secret wisdom is imparted and sealed with a sign on Jack's body – a scarification ritual. The secret is odd. Contrary to the outright denials of God that characterized twentieth-century atheisms and the Nietzschean (in contrast to the

Kierkegaardian) branch of existentialism, this is a bitter *theism*, a resentful affirmation of God's existence. And while it echoes the existentialist slogan of absolute freedom, celebrating the unhindered will-to-power, it emerges from a picture of God as the father who bailed, the deadbeat God who thinks so little of us that he abandons us, and in all likelihood hates us.[4]

Along similar although less extreme lines, this image of God – this image of a deity more like us than monotheisms have generally permitted – has pounded a well-beaten trail into popular culture. A few examples:

Tori Amos, among the more enigmatic rock artists to emerge in the 1990's, released a song in 1994 called "God."[5] In the opening verses, she grants that God makes pretty daisies, but beyond that hasn't done us any favors. She suspects that God ducks out whenever the world gets out of hand, heading south in an SUV with a bag of golf clubs in the back seat. Then, in the chorus, she gripes:

> God sometimes you just don't come through,
> God sometimes you just don't come through.
> Do you need a woman to look after you?
> God sometimes you just don't come through.

In a friendlier tone, but still picturing God on some kind of evasive road trip, Joan Osborne released a hit song in 1995 called, "One of Us."[6] In it, she ponders what God might look like, "in all his glory," and suggests that we probably have it all wrong. Then she wonders:

> What if God was one of us,
> just a slob like one of us,
> just a stranger on the bus,
> trying to make his way home.

No strong opposition to God seems intended here, only a poetic suggestion that God is to be found in "the least of these." Or perhaps Osborne is offering us a fresh understanding of the incarnation, a variation on the long-standing belief that God became human and is "like us in all respects, sin only excepted," in the words of the Chalcedonian Creed (451 CE). The word "slob" can be heard as simply a metaphor for finitude. What is more interesting in the song is the final line – the reason God is aboard the bus is to make his way home. Rolling along at the speed limit, taking a low profile, God is on the road, trying to get home – after a tour of duty, a holiday, a reconnaissance mission, or a hard day's work, it is left to us to guess. In any case, God is among us and trying to get away from us. Similarly, in the

Spanish film, *Sin Noticias de Dios* (*No News from God*),[7] the Operations Manager of Heaven confides to several of her aids over tea, "No one knows where He is. They say He's tired, depressed...and wants to drop everything."

Then, there is the endearing depiction of God in the movie *Dogma* (1999). Here, God is depicted as a woman (played by rock singer Alanis Morissette), who cannot speak directly to human beings because, lacking the "aural and psychological capacity to withstand the awesome power of God's true voice," our minds would cave in and our hearts explode within our chests if she did. "We went through five Adams before we figured that one out," one of God's angels quips. Nevertheless, out of loneliness and a fondness for the game of skeeball, once a month God takes a "constitutional." She assumes human form and drops in at some boardwalk arcade for a few days to indulge her pleasure. And this is the same God who, as the movie affirms, centuries ago had ordered the flood that wiped out every living creature not safely aboard the ark with Noah, the fiery destruction of Sodom and Gomorrah, and the death of the first born children of all Egyptians during the reign of Ramesses II. In the opening shot of *Dogma*, God has taken the temporary form of an old man in Asbury Park, New Jersey, leaning on the boardwalk railing watching the sun rise over the ocean, admiring the beauty of his hands as he rubs them together in the chilly morning air, and waiting for the skeeball arcade behind him to open.

In a more serious vein, there is the odd picture of God in the film *The Big Kahuna*.[8] Two industrial lubricants salesmen, Phil (Danny DeVito) and Larry (Kevin Spacey), representing a company called Lodestar Laboratories at a sales convention in Wichita, Kansas, are desperate to land an account with "the Big Kahuna," the owner of a large factory in Gary, Indiana. Late in the night, after what appears to be a fumbled effort with the elusive Big Kahuna, the two commiserate while sitting on the couch in their hotel suite. Phil admits to Larry that he's been thinking about life and death. And then:

Phil: I've been thinking about God lately, too, wondering.

Larry: About God.

Phil: Yeah.

Larry: What about him?

Phil: I don't know. Haven't you just wondered about God, ever?

Larry: Well yeah, everybody wonders about God every now and then, it's just that some of us don't dwell on it, you know. I give it a place. I believe what I believe.

Phil: Which is what?

Larry: How the hell should I know?

Phil: When I was a kid, I had a dream about God. I dreamt I found him in a closet in the middle of a burned out city. This city was destroyed by fire or some kind of explosion. And there in the middle of it was a coat closet standing there all by itself. And I walked up to the closet and opened the door and inside was God, hiding. I remember he had a big lion head, but I knew it wasn't a lion, it was God, and he was afraid. And I reached out my hand to lead him out of the closet, and I said, "Don't be afraid, God, I'm on your side." And we stood there, the two of us holding hands, looking out over the destruction. It was just after sunset.

I don't know why, but I've always had this haunting feeling that I had some kind of mission here on earth.

Larry: A mission?

Phil: Yeah.

Larry: What kind of mission?

Phil: I have no idea.

Larry: Well, I'll tell you what your mission is. Your mission is the same as mine, to be a liaison between parties.

Phil: Things like that don't bother you, huh?

Larry: What do you mean, dreams?

Phil: Questions about God.

Larry: Well, I figure, you know, I'm going to find out sooner or later. My wondering about it isn't going to change anything and in the meantime, why lose sleep. I get precious little as it is.

Phil: But you still wonder, don't you?

Larry: I'm human, Phil.

Phil: I know.

Here God is portrayed as a cowardly lion, hiding in a closet as the city around him burns to the ground. Overcome, it seems, by forces outside of his control, God appears to have given up. Instead of harboring bitterness toward this God who has succumbed to a world of spiraling chaos, Phil comforts God and assures him that he is not alone.

Finally, returning to the Wim Wenders film, *Wings of Desire*, we are invited into a world in which there are angels who walk in our midst, although we cannot see them. They can hear the thoughts and sense the emotions of the humans they are near. While the angels have compassion for the difficulties that we humans face, they are unable to communicate with us or to intervene in our actions. In one poignant scene, an angel wraps his arm around a man who is preparing to jump off the top of a building in Berlin. The angel, unseen and unfelt by the man, attempts to console him, concentrating his angel-thoughts of compassion and touching his forehead to the despondent man's temple. Still, the man jumps. The angel, reminded again in that moment of his inability to prevent this from occurring, cries out in anguish, a cry that only other angels, below on the streets of Berlin, can hear.

Wenders confides that the genesis of the film had much to do with his own "childhood images of angels as invisible, omniscient observers," and "the old hunger for transcendence," which was triggered by having recently read a lot of Rilke, viewing Paul Klee's paintings (whose angels were symbols of "invisible truths" below the surfaces of experience), reading Walter Benjamin's *Angel of History*, and staring up at the "Angel of Peace" monument that towers above Berlin and figures prominently in the movie,[9] a monument full of irony given that the movie was conceived and completed while Berlin was still a divided city, ground zero of the Cold War.

In this film Wenders presents us with some provocative images regarding the agency of God in the world, two worth mentioning here. First, the world (or, at least, Berlin) is thick with angels. This 1988 film preceded the current fad of angels, and may even have triggered it.[10] In *Wings of Desire*, Berlin is crawling with angels who tail people in need, listen to their thoughts, and attempt in quite moving, but generally ineffectual ways to comfort them. We learn from one angel, Damiel, that their task on earth is limited, "To do no more than observe, collect, testify, preserve – but to remain a spirit, to keep your distance." They are not "guardian angels" in the conventional sense of offering us guidance or intervening to protect us from harm. They are little more than sympathetic ethnographers. The second thing worth pondering is that God is never mentioned. True, there are angels, but we can only infer that there is a God who has set them among us. The film neither confirms nor denies this. This is a soft agnosticism, much softer than we detect in works of fiction written to process the theological lessons of the Second World War. In an essay he wrote while the film was still in production, Wenders offers this prologue explaining the absence of God from the story:

> When God, endlessly disappointed, finally prepared to turn his back on the world forever, it happened that some of his angels disagreed with him and took the side of man, saying he deserved to be given another chance.
>
> Angry at being crossed, God banished them to what was then the most terrible place on earth: Berlin.
>
> And then He turned away.

> All this happened at the time that we today call: "the end of the second World War."
>
> Since that time, these fallen angels from the "second angelic rebellion" have been imprisoned in the city, with no prospect of release, let alone of being readmitted to heaven. They are condemned to be witnesses, forever nothing but onlookers, unable to affect men in the slightest, or to intervene in the course of history. They are unable to so much as move a grain of sand . . .[11]

Yet in the film, perhaps because of Wenders' own reluctance to utterly sever our connection to God, God's withdrawal goes unsaid, and is not really even inferred. God simply remains unknown. But without a doubt there is an invisible world that intersects with our own, a world that is heavy with compassion for the human lot, ultimately attributed to an unspoken God.

This sampling of popular culture turns up a deity who is either *on the move*: God abandons us like unwanted children, goes on a golfing holiday, rumbles down the road to heaven, or who *is there but elusive*: God hides quivering in a closet or hovers deep in the background behind compassionate and pleasant, but ineffectual, angels. The traditional belief in the benevolent power of God over our lives seems to have run out, but for the most part, we find God likable. We're not a Nietzschean generation, shaking our fists at the air, proud to announce that God is dead. Our attitude seems to be more that God was overwhelmed by us, or simply got tired of us, and is moving on to other things. And as the divine presence takes its leave and the lights are slowly put out, we reminisce about a world in which it could be trusted that absolute power had bound itself to absolute goodness.

This general theological malaise can be explored more fully in novels than in movies and rock lyrics. And, indeed, in the last several years there has been some bold fiction written about God, fiction that addresses some of the standard topics of the classical doctrine of God, namely God's existence and attributes, creation, providence and natural evil, that might shed more light on the nature of this malaise.

God Fiction

When a fiction writer rummages around in the theological bag of tricks for inspiration and attempts to put into narrative order what he or she finds there, it should catch the attention of theologians. Liberated by the genre of fiction, a writer is free to experiment with inherited scraps of doctrine and put them to work in the lives of characters drawn from the present cultural milieu – characters who have been forged by historical forces that didn't exist when the original revelation, or the scriptures that testify to it, or the theological doctrines that resulted from reflecting on these scriptures, first arose.

In what follows we will examine the novels of three theological outsiders – an Italian literary critic and Dante scholar, an American science fiction writer, and a French journalist, each of whom has attained a level of expertise in theology through the work of conceiving their stories. Each writer has consulted biblical and theological sources in order to familiarize themselves with their main character (God), and, in the end, used narrative to reach conclusions worth paying attention to – conclusions regarding God's motives, powers, and implication in evil, as well as speculating on the moral effects of the concept of God on our lives.

A vigorous religious community must return periodically to its founding myths and reexamine itself in light of those myths. For Paul Ricoeur, narrative is effective in rejuvenating the moral imagination of readers because of its unique power to redescribe reality. This is because narrative allows one to "try new ideas, new values, new ways of being-in-the-world."[12] Through stories the imagination is allowed to play with a great field of possible ways of being, to imagine its way through different sequences of acting and valuing and to see what comes of them. In following the story through its twists and turns, in reflecting on the decisions made and their consequences, in identifying with this character or that, in seeing what is lost and what is gained – the reader's world is intruded in upon by the world of the story. What is discovered in the story's world has the power to "disturb and rearrange" the reader's own relation to reality.[13] In this way, narrative has the power to transfigure the practical world of the reader.

The three God novels that will be examined here are not simply products of individual and autonomous creative minds. These authors have consciously plundered myths from ancient traditions and entered into a conversation with them. Through the resulting novels, archaic myths speak again and the world conjured up through this new recitation is one that has been educated by some degree of faith in transcendent realities that the old myths carry. But in the hands of these three authors the myths have been overhauled and held accountable to much historical and literary experience that has transpired since they first entered the consciousness of our ancestors.

Franco Ferrucci, *The Life of God (as Told by Himself)* (1996)

Franco Ferrucci is a literary critic from Italy whose previous published work has focused on Dante. *The Life of God (as Told by Himself)* is offered as autobiography, told throughout from God's first-person point of view. From the outset, the story follows a biblical sequence that is blended with evolutionary spans of time. But given that the genesis of the cosmos is told here with an eye to God's own consciousness of these events, some imaginative liberties are taken. In Ferrucci's account, God is aware of a moment when he (yes, God is gendered – in the work of all three of these novelists) first became aware of himself, wrapped in darkness and nothingness, suspended in absolute emptiness. It was in that moment of awareness that the cosmos was born, following from God's "impulse to go out and look for company." Retrospectively aware of all the stories that are told by human beings about the originary causes of the world, that is, divine incest, warrior Titans, parricide, etc., this God explains creation as a simple matter of his desire to alleviate his profound loneliness:

> I cannot say how long I wandered aimlessly through the dark night of time. ... I walked for miles and miles, stumbling in the dark, trembling with loneliness; then I finally stood still in the vast blackness and let out a cry. I saw that cry rise like an arrow, reaching the center of the heavens and exploding into fragments that became stars. Where my cry had fallen stood a solitary, burning ball.[14]

This burning ball, as it turns out, is our sun. Its appearance was initially satisfying to God, but with nothing to see in the light, its illumination simply reveals a great expanse of monotonous nothingness. So, God tried to put the light out, but discovered that he couldn't. "It was then that I realized, for the first time, that I could not undo what I had done. Once I created something, I could not destroy it. The sun was up there forever, or until its own natural death. I could not play around with the created world, and make and unmake as I pleased." Ferrucci's God, it turns out, does not have unlimited powers. Once a creature is made and set in place, it has autonomy, living out a course intrinsic to its nature and free from divine intervention. Early on, God notices, "Whenever I create something, it goes on reproducing, like ... a series of messengers rushing off to plant the seeds of my inventions."[15] This efflorescence of creation occurs outside of God's control, and, unless he is on the spot to observe it, it is even outside of God's knowledge. As well as not being omnipotent, this God is neither omniscient nor omnipresent. Ferrucci's God is finite – not as finite as you or I, but he must learn to cope with an amplified sort of finitude.

Prehistory continues for a long stretch of time in this cosmos. God descends on the earth in the form of rain and seeds the planet with "willow wisdom, magnolia wisdom, pine wisdom," etc., but learns that the plants, while they diminish his boredom, do little to alleviate his loneliness. To address both of these needs, he creates, in true evolutionary sequence, insects, fish, amphibians, reptiles, and birds. But his loneliness is unabated. It gradually dawns on God that what he really desires is to have a counterpart consciousness in his cosmos. "I wanted life to meditate upon itself so as to better comprehend itself," he realized. This very thought gave rise to mammals, and the mammal potency multiplied so that there were new arrivals all the time – bears, monkeys, elephants. God became fascinated with their brains. "What a toy the brain became for me: It was patched together, poorly proportioned, and cluttered with gadgets, but I positively fell in love with it. ... I tinkered with it for millennia in every mammal I could get hold of."[16] As members of the mammal kingdom sensed this attention, they began to assert themselves – "Even though they didn't know who I was and never talked to me, they understood that I was not fully satisfied with them."[17] They evolved in an effort to please God.

Then, quite by chance one day, God noticed a falcon dive upon a tiny bird and crush its life with its talons. With this it dawned on God that violence transpired at every level of life, that it was part of the nature of things. "Before me was a world that devoured itself incessantly and managed its own transformations without asking me for comment or advice. The theater of hunt and war was everywhere. ... From what bad moments of mine had all this come out? ... [These creatures] were part of me! I was startled at the revelation."[18]

While it was clear that the violence could neither be undone nor ended, this shock gave rise to a new thought, which was the cultivation of a new animal, "a comely, thoughtful animal: a friend of creation, without violent and mechanical appetites,"[19] an animal "that could remedy the mistakes I had made in constructing the world."[20] By this point in time, God's powers of creation had so dissipated that he could no longer create beings from scratch, he could only modify what already existed. So he went to work on the monkey, the only creature who ever seemed to remember him between visits, dedicating himself to the education of one little monkey. God is honest that it was his own enduring loneliness that prompted this choice of the one animal who offered what he took as affection. "I concede that God should not have such a profound need for affection that he immediately trusts whoever compliments him. But it is not his fault that he was born an orphan, that he spent his childhood alone and starved for affection."[21]

Thousands of years later, we find God hunkered down with Moses at Mt Sinai. But just as he began composing the Ten Commandments, God experienced a spell of writer's block, was distracted by the massacre that followed the festival of the golden calf, a bloodletting that we learn was entirely Moses' doing, and withdrew for several weeks into the desert. When God returned a few weeks later, Moses was still busy elaborating laws for Israel. Moses was furious and complained that God had left him with the hard work of persuading a stiff-necked people to accept the laws he had been feverishly etching into stone while God was off cavorting in the desert. In what quickly develops into a Grand Inquisitor moment, God replies,

> "You have forgotten the important things that I had to say and have lost yourself in an infinity of details, some of them totally alien to my teachings. I'm not at all happy with you, Moses."
>
> Moses replies: "I know you are dissatisfied. When it comes to that, so am I. I had expected a God better equipped to give orders and assume command. Instead, I'm the one who must do all this. Just ask yourself if it could have been easy to dictate this rule: 'Do not pronounce a sentence in a quarrel in order to favor the powerful; but do not respect the poor man in his quarrel.' How about it? Where were you when I wrote these lines? Who was there, fighting with both rich and poor?"
>
> "There should be neither rich nor poor," I retorted sharply.
>
> Moses looked at me flabbergasted.
>
> "What's that supposed to mean? There should be neither rich nor poor indeed! You're forgetting the obvious. Some God you are, with your head in the clouds, remembering now and then to return to earth and criticize your prophet. You forget that the poor exist! It's not a matter of discussing whether they should or not, but trying to see what can be done to stop them from becoming beasts and starving to death. Therefore it is necessary to put them to death if they couple with animals, but they must be helped to survive hunger and cold."[22]

In God's estimation, Moses was alienating people from their freedom. "It is not true that I want to destroy the iniquitous," God said to him. "I don't even know who the iniquitous are."[23] But in Moses' estimation, God hadn't a clue about what it is that human beings really need. And 1,200 years later, God still didn't, only it is Jesus who upbraids him this time. Jesus, in Ferrucci's world, is God's natural son – as God in spiritual form had made love to his mother before she married an old carpenter. Following their tryst, God disappeared, then returned 30 years later as one of a band of peripatetic Athenian philosophers to check up on this son he'd heard of through rumors. Listening to Jesus preach for the first time, God was filled with happiness, and he remarked that he had never heard "anything so beautiful and so convincing before."[24] "I realized that I wanted to believe in the Christ, I the atheistic God."[25] It was God in the guise of a Greek philosopher, it turns out, who rented the room in which the Last Supper occurred, and in the hours before the meal, God and Jesus had a frank conversation. Once again, God played the freedom card and tried to persuade his beloved son Jesus to avoid the cross. But Jesus replied,

> "Men are not free, and I must always take this into account. Do you know this, Father? Do you know that they will do nothing unless they become

convinced that they must worship someone or something; I will have to get them to crucify me so as to be remembered. I could very well avoid it, but I have no choice if I want to save at least a part of what I have preached. And I began to lie a long time ago. I know very well that neither hells nor paradises exist, but . . . I have no other way to make them better."[26]

There are unmistakable traces here from Dostoevsky's poem of the Grand Inquisitor. But, ironically, Jesus is in the role of the jaded Grand Inquisitor. Jesus knowingly heads to the cross in order to give birth to a cult that will keep his memory alive. He is convinced that people are capable only of small doses of freedom, and that they will seize even those only in conjunction with a deity who commands it.

For the next 2,000 years, Ferrucci's God moves around in persons with whom he has temporarily merged, sometimes as a passenger in their consciousness, sometimes allowing his divinity to slumber so deeply that he loses himself in their identity altogether. He appears as a vintner in Cordova, a slave in a brothel, a spider in St Augustine's mind, a banker, a serial killer, a drunk, and as Einstein's best friend and only real conversation partner. In this manner, God travels through human history "assuming one incarnation after another,"[27] but capable of being in only one place at a time.

Through his parade of guises God gradually comes to greater self-understanding. He knows from the beginning that he is not omniscient or omnipotent, and he freely admits that the evil in the world is due to his own lack of skill and foresight. What is noteworthy, however, in appreciating Ferrucci's characterization of God as a way of symbolizing late modern Western culture, is his account of God's own purpose for willing humanity into being. Yes, we exist to relieve God's loneliness, and yes, we exist to remedy some of the mistakes he had made in constructing the world – but primarily we exist to explain God to himself. We are independent consciousnesses who can tell this primordial Orphan who he is. At about the time he was in a crowd of people listening to the Gnostics and Manicheans, God complained: "I was waiting for them to become clever enough to explain to me who I was and why I was carrying on in such an unseemly manner. I did not receive the help I needed, and so I floundered, forced to incarnate myself in order to become visible to myself and others. Through the human mind I formulated extravagant hypotheses about myself . . ."[28]

The whole cosmos exists, in other words, for the purpose of God's self-exploration. In one telling outburst, God confronts Thomas Aquinas at the moment when Thomas is deep in prayer meditating on his recently drafted proofs for the existence of God. The confrontation, which Thomas retrospectively describes as a beatific vision, is described by God thus: "What are you talking about? There is no final cause! I have no intention of taking all of you anywhere. I expect you to help me under-stand where I come from and where I am going."[29] Furthermore, the cosmos exists so that this orphan deity can chase after love. God, we're told through another of his incarnations (this time as the illegitimate son of an aristocratic mother in the years of the French Revolution), is "a bas-tard! God himself is a bastard, excessively so. He comes from nowhere, he does not know his parents, he has all the qualities and defects of the self-made person. He must be rather like myself, I mused; trusting, sincere, never satisfied with himself, never keeping quiet, always running after love."[30] This exercise in autobiography, this Book of Ferrucci, is God's report to us that the whole sweep of creation has one sole purpose – divine therapeutic self-discovery.[31]

And how does this story end? With God packing his bags, preparing to leave our solar system, aware that he has made a mess of things in this round of creation, and setting out for a new planet to bring to life.

> "I asked myself why I wanted to leave, and I found the answer. I already knew that my world was an imperfect work, a sort of sketch that needed a good deal more work. I had finally come to accept that this revision could not be made on this planet, and with these inhabitants. What I had created could deteriorate but could not be erased or adjusted; the mess we had arrived at was by now overwhelming. I had reached the end of my attempts to use humankind to improve my creation. They could only help me to leave."[32]

In this swan song are echoes of the images of God found in *FightClub*, in Tori Amos's lyrics, and in Phil the lubricant salesman's dream: The twentieth century finds God putting out the lights, and Ferrucci suggests that an honest assessment of Western culture will confirm this. We are being "obedient to the signal," he suggests, "given how we've virtually stopped creating and feed almost entirely on the past."[33]

James Morrow: The *Towing Jehovah* Saga[34]

The next work of fiction to be examined is actually a trilogy written by James Morrow, a science fiction writer from Pennsylvania, about a chain of events that begins with the splashdown of the Corpus Dei in the early 1990s. In 1992, to be precise, a giant male corpse, two miles long, was dis-covered floating face-up in the Atlantic Ocean off the coast of Africa. The Vatican and a handful of other individuals were notified of this by dying angels, who confirmed that it was indeed God. The Vatican secretly con-tracted to have the *SS Carpco Valparaiso*, a retired oil supertanker, tow

God's body to a tomb carved by angels into an ice shelf in the Arctic. After resting in this icy cavern for 6 years, an earthquake dislodges the body. The Pope holds a press conference and comes clean, then offers the body to Baptists in the US for 80 million dollars, who tow it to Orlando and build a theme park around it.

At about this time it was determined that God was not brain-dead, but merely comatose. Martin Candle, a hard-working and honest justice of the peace from Pennsylvania, managed to persuade the International Criminal Court to try God for accumulated crimes against humanity. The body was towed to the Hague, but while the defendant was found innocent, Candle went berserk and hacked apart God's life support machine. God, finally dead but legally innocent, began his sea journey back to the Baptists. A few days out of port on the voyage back to Florida, the body began breaking apart, with organs firing into the sky like comets. Finally, the skull vomited God's enormous brain, broke loose of the spinal vertebrae, and launched into space, where it settled into geosynchronous orbit, a grinning skull which had grown to the size of Delaware, and that could be seen in the sky by all in the northern hemisphere, like a lesser moon. After several years the Vatican, which had purchased back from the Baptists legal rights to the bones of God (ever fascinated with relics), began leasing the forehead to multinational corporations for laser ads beamed from satellites. "Coke Is It" radiated from the glowing Cranium Dei.

Morrow is such a good writer that once you have entered the world of these novels, this sort of thing does seem plausible. The full arc of the trilogy is important to keep in mind, but enough of the theological achievement of the trilogy can be captured through a close reading of the story as it unfolds in the first volume, *Towing Jehovah*, for the purposes of this chapter. This volume carries us as far as the burial of God in the ice tomb – which isn't the end of the story, as my brief summary should have made clear. The heart of this first volume is found in the way the crew of the *Valparaiso* reacts to the incontrovertible proof of God's death. Morrow sets himself the challenge of hiring to this crew sailors of various religious backgrounds. The captain, Anthony Van Horne, is a Dutch Presbyterian (Morrow's own background), Seamen Leo Zook is a Protestant Fundamentalist and Neil Weisinger a Jew with some rabbinical training, radio engineer Lianne Bliss is a New Age enthusiast, rescued passenger Cassie Fowler is a feminist and ardent atheist, and the Vatican liaison, Fr Thomas Ockham, is a Jesuit theologian and metaphysician, a tenured member of the faculty at Fordham who, along with his colleague and fellow passenger, Sr Miriam, a Carmelite nun, had co-authored a book on theodicy many years earlier.

Given the explosive nature of their cargo, the Vatican has instructed that the crew assembled for this voyage remain small and kept in the dark about their mission until the last possible day. Only the Captain,

Fr Ockham, and Sr Miriam know before they ram the supertanker into it while lost in a fog bank what their cargo will be. When the crew finally sees God's corpse floating face-up in the ocean, they are forced, quite suddenly, to make sense of a world with a dead God. There are a variety of reactions, and they hit in waves. The first wave is characterized by a growing sense of a strange and unprecedented freedom. Neil Weisinger contemplates harpooning his commanding officer as the thought steals over him that God is really gone, or as he says, "No God, no rules, no eyes on us." As more time passes, he slides further into this conviction and tells Fr Ockham, "The cat's away, Tommy. . . . I can think any damn thought I want. I can think about picking up a Black and Decker needle gun and drilling my Aunt Sarah's eyes out. I'm free, Tommy."[35] Two weeks after their first contact with the corpse, Captain Van Horne notes in his diary that there has been a steep increase in brawls, graffiti, petty thefts, vandalism, rape, and even a murder among his small crew – all relatively individual acts of mayhem. He reports a recent conversation with Fr Ockham:

> "The corpse is taking hold," is how Ockham explains our situation. "Not the corpse per se, the *idea* of the corpse – that's our great enemy, that's the source of this disorder. In the old days," says the padre, "whether you were a believer, a nonbeliever, or a confused agnostic, at some level, conscious or unconscious, you felt God was watching you, and the intuition kept you in check. Now a whole new era is upon us."[36]

For his own part, Fr Ockham is seeking clarification from Rome. He faxes the College of Cardinals an urgent request for their opinion on this outbreak of lawlessness on the oil tanker – Does it stem metaphysically from the decay of the corpse, as if the battery of the cosmic moral order is running down, or is it a psychological effect now that God's death has lodged itself in the minds of the crew as an empirical fact?

Meanwhile the ship comes to be stranded high and dry on the slopes of a brand new island that has risen fresh from out of the ocean. The body of God breaks free in this upheaval, and drifts back to sea. Most of the crew mutiny and desert the ship on this island. With this commences the second wave of reaction to God's death – communal revolt and a reversion to primitivism. Within days the mutineers are staging gladiatorial games, chasing and massacring one another with a forklift stolen from the ship. They engage in great orgies, eat through the ship's food supply with conspicuous wastefulness, drink like fish, and watch a video of Bob Guccione's pornographic *Caligula* play on an endless loop. Finally, Thomas and Sr Miriam go looking for the mutineers to seek their help in getting the supertanker back afloat. They locate the deserters by their laughter, by the thick aroma of "semen, tobacco, alcohol, vomit, and pot," and by their "whoops of primitive delight and cries of post-theistic joy." Sighting them from a distance, Fr Ockham says, "It's even worse than we imagined. . . . They've gone over to the gods." To which Sr Miriam replies, "Is this the future, Tom – vigilante vengeance, public executions: Is this the shape of the post-theistic age?"[37]

There are echoes here of Dostoevsky's Smerdyakov, who reported back to his mentor Ivan what it is he had learned from him: "If there's no everlasting God, there's no such thing as virtue, and there's no need of it."[38] Miriam picks up on this, precisely, and both she and Ockham pine in light of these Karamazovian developments for the good sense of Immanuel Kant:

> "It's the logic of Ivan Karamazov, isn't it?" said Miriam. "If God doesn't exist, everything is permitted." Thomas replies, "One also thinks of Schopenhauer. Without a Supreme Being, life becomes sterile and meaningless. I hope Kant had it right – I hope people possess some sort of inborn ethical sense. I seem to recall him rhapsodizing somewhere about 'the starry skies above me and the moral law within me.' "
>
> "*Critique of Practical Reason*," said Miriam. "I agree, Tom. The desert-ers, all of us, we've got to make Kant's leap of faith – his leap *out* of faith, I should say. We must get in touch with our congenital consciences. Otherwise we're lost."[39]

This is the thin shred of hope to which the *religious* protagonists in the story cling: the conviction that human beings have a congenital conscience that is not dependent upon the existence of God, but respects duty for the sake of duty alone. Miriam and Thomas berate, coax and cajole the mutinous sailors to sober up and recover the Kantian moral law within. It is a futile effort.

Morrow is telling a story here that allows him to experiment in novel form with various death-of-God theologies that were written in the 1960s. At one point in the trilogy, the character of Satan appears and describes God's death as a revelation intended by God himself in these terms: "God willed Himself into a death trance because He thought He'd do His creatures more good that way."[40] How so? It is through the character of Thomas Ockham, who, we learn, is familiar with Gabriel Vahanian's *The Death of God: The Culture of Our Post-Christian Era*[41] (an actual book published in 1961), that the point of view of Morrow himself, it seems, comes into focus. Ockham, we learn in the third volume of the trilogy (*The Eternal Footman*), wrote a book subsequent to this ocean journey reflecting on the meaning of God's suicide entitled *Parables for a Post-theistic Age*, in which he argues: "God had *wanted* his corpse to be discovered. After fully apprehending His death, humankind would move beyond its traditional dependence on Him. Homo sapiens would achieve maturity." This is because Jesus, who had taught that "the kingdom of God is within you," had failed to persuade humanity of this essential truth. They were too dense to absorb it, and started a church instead. The two mile-long corpse splashing down into the ocean was God's desperate strategy to convey the message again. Ockham continues,

> As the new millennium dawns, may we finally rid ourselves of those grand absolutes, those terrible transcendent truths, in whose name human beings have routinely menaced one another. If the coming era must have a religion, then let it be a religion of everyday miracles and quotidian epiphanies, of short eternities and little myths. In the post-theistic age, let Christianity become merely kindness, salvation transmute into art, truth defer to knowledge, and faith embrace a vibrant doubt.[42]

Another theologian lurking in the background of Morrow's experiment is Dietrich Bonhoeffer, whose book *Letters and Papers from Prison* is quoted in Ockham's book, and specifically Bonhoeffer's key passage about religionless Christianity:

> So our coming of age forces us to a true recognition of our situation vis-à-vis God. God is teaching us that we must live as men who can get along very well without Him. [*****] The God Who makes us live in this world without using Him as a working hypothesis is the God before Whom we are ever standing. Before God and with Him we live without God.[43]

As the trilogy concludes, this idea that the death of God will ultimately result in the maturation of the human race is depicted by the plot development of the final disappearance of the celestial skull, which had plagued everyone (in the northern hemisphere, the only place it was visible) with a visual reminder of what they had lost as long as it orbited the earth. But once it had finally vanished from the sky, it took only ten years for Western civilization to rebuild its infrastructure, and for life to return to a social and moral order that, while it could be depended upon, was not itself dependent upon God. The Kantian conscience finally triumphed. The human inhabitants of earth eventually become full-fledged citizens, and are no longer tourists on their way to someplace else. In the long term, for Morrow, the most reliable basis for the moral life is the stark awareness that there is no God to lean on, and that a livable social order is entirely in human hands, contingent on each decision we make to behave morally.

Is God Dead or Just Packing His Bags?

Like the Book of Job, the novels of James Morrow and Franco Ferrucci depict a God who is ordinarily credited with creation and with maintaining the order of the cosmos, but who suddenly does something wildly out of character – either he packs his bags and gradually puts out the lights in preparation to depart to another universe, or he plunges into the ocean in a dramatic suicide. And, again like the Book of Job, these books detail how individuals representing different strains of faith respond to this theological surprise. After they have said their peace, God gets the last word (still following the Jobian paradigm), via his autobiographical confession of failure and disappointment in the Book of Ferrucci, and via the devil's disclosure in the Book of Morrow that "God willed Himself into a death trance because He thought He'd do His creatures more good that way." God's exiting word in both cases is offered as a new revelation.

The other literary work hovering in the background of these God novels is *The Brothers Karamazov*. Ivan Karamazov's poem of the Grand Inquisitor is revisited several times in Ferrucci's story – the most poignant rendition taking place between God, who plays Jesus' role of advocating the importance of freedom for humanity to come to grips with itself, and Jesus, who, ironically, plays the Grand Inquisitor's role of advocating a freedom-denying security which keeps us from slitting each other's throats. God didn't want to be worshipped and he wanted humanity to outgrow its childish dependence on his approval.[44] Ferrucci is on God's side in this confrontation; he joins in God's epicurean commitment to be free to satisfy one's desires (albeit moderated, disciplined desires), without the imposition of external laws, and to use one's life to attain honest self-awareness, unencumbered by otherworldly dreams. In Morrow's world, it is a different element of Ivan's anger with God that drives the plot, namely his suggestion to Alyosha and Smerdyakov that if there is no God, all things are permitted. Morrow pushes this in the direction of an optimistic existentialism, telling a story that passes through bloody anarchy and moral confusion on its way to a humane and honest world in which the grand absolutes of theistic religion have given way to a mature and benevolent post-theistic humanism.

So, we have Ferrucci's epicurean God who seeks to maximize his sensual pleasure in existence without allowing his passions to overreach to the point of causing others pain, and then attempts to teach us to do the same; and we have Morrow's existentialist God who commits the ultimate act of sacrifice in order that we may come to terms with the gravity of our own actions. H. Richard Niebuhr made note in 1957 that these very philosophies are transitional faiths, holding patterns between radical monotheism and a diffused polytheism. He wrote: "Epicureanism and existentialism look like ghostly survivals of faith among men who, forsaken by the gods, continue to hold on to life."[45] This intermediary position is hard to maintain for long, or, at least, for many generations. By default human beings gravitate toward polytheism, by which Niebuhr means selves who grasp at multiple, unintegrated centers of meaning, a grasping that allows us "partial loyalty to many interests."[46] In polytheism, we desire a multitude of genuine goods, but have no means of deciding between them short of which one, at the moment, seems to be working or stirs the strongest emotions.

A Niebuhrian skepticism about what Ferrucci and Morrow have achieved is in order. In their rejection of the necessity of some kind of theistic grounding for the moral life, both of them actually usher us to the threshold of polytheism. Intended as humanity's coming of age stories, these stories regress instead. Their humanism is awfully trusting in human beings coming hardwired into the world with functioning and resilient consciences. Both authors and the worlds they conjure up are unfairly suspicious of actual moral laws and the sensation of guilt that is associated with morality. Nor do they sufficiently trust the older myths to do their work in teaching the moral law and in inculcating the sense of guilt that will make the moral law self-enforcing.

For a different grasp of these matters, consider a third novel.

Laurence Cossé, *A Corner of the Veil* (1996)

Laurence Cossé is a journalist in France and past president of the European Community Commission. Her expertise is primarily in the area of political science. The tantalizing surprise in her novel is that an unknown physics professor has written a six-page proof for the existence of God that is not only unassailably true, but it also demonstrates that "the cruelty of the world and the goodness of God aren't contradictory anymore. Human errors, follies, atrocities, finally make sense."[47] As we follow the author into the world of this novel, we are asked to suspend our skepticism, and accept that this proof of God's existence, sovereignty, and goodness are demonstrated beyond any doubt, and obvious upon a single reading of the short document.

One of the first persons to read this proof, other than its author, is Fr Hervé Montgaroult, a Roman Catholic member of the "Casuist Order," and an academic cosmologist by trade whose specialty is disproving all proofs of God's existence. In the hours and days after first reading this document, Fr Hervé proceeds to walk through the streets of Paris in an ecstatic frame of mind, absolutely converted by the proof. "The universe, hitherto jumbled like a holographic drawing, now found its depth and meaning."[48] As he thought it through, it came to him that this revelation will not end human suffering, but it will give suffering a clear reason, a satisfactory justification. As word gets out, the social impact of the proof, Hervé predicts, will be broadly beneficial. "Neighbors who had always eyed one another with suspicion would be talking to each other. Couples ten years separated would phone each other from distant places."[49] Work would stop and the effect would be similar to a general strike, but in time, "things would return to order – to what used to seem the disorder of creation and would at last look clear and lovely. Many persons would not change their lives. Many would. Nothing would any longer be the way it had been, but nothing of what is would disappear. *Man would know himself to be truly free.*"[50]

The following day, the Prime Minister of France, Jean-Charles Petitgrand, is briefed by Fr Le Dangeolet, the Provincial of the Casuists in France, about the nature of the document. Petitgrand never reads the proof, but is transformed just by seeing the envelope in which it rests. After Le Dangeolet leaves his office, Petitgrand seeks out a lowly parish priest to confess to and determines that night to dedicate the remainder of his days to loving his wife and growing his roses. "For the ten or fifteen years he had left to live, he would praise the Eternal One, simply, through love for his roses, for his wife, and for his fellow man."[51] He awoke the next morning, told his long neglected wife he was devoting the morning to her, had an hour-long breakfast, went with her to the Museum of French Romanticism – which she had been after him to do for 10 years, and he even indulged her desire to ride there on the bus. A few days later, the Prime Minister resigned his office with the simple press release: there has been "a sudden irruption of meaning into my life."[52]

Fr Hervé and Prime Minister Petitgrand represent the more cordial reception of this bombshell. Their colleagues were much more agitated. For their part, the cabinet ministers of the French government concluded that disclosure of this document would lead people to spend all of their time attempting to get closer to God, and France would become one huge monastery. Instead of working or aspiring to affluence, instead of "the every-man-for-himself, the activism, the copycat greed, [the trust in] money as guiding light," people would devote themselves to praying and studying Scripture. Consequently, private businesses and public services would soon be in a shambles, and society would be plunged into an economic crisis without precedent.[53]

Among the hierarchy in the Church, it was anticipated that once word about the proof went public, the first effect would be widespread chaos. As Le Dangeolet briefs his superior within the Casuist Order:

Our complex, fragile economies will be turned upside down. Dazzled by God, men will have no further reason to keep working to make the machine turn the way it used to. The primacy of economic matters will crumble. Ninety percent of human undertakings will look foolish, meaningless, pathetic. The ad man, the beautician, all the merchants of dreams and escape, will close up shop. The arms merchants all the more so. The only tenable behavior will be more or less what contemplatives do: prayer and frugality...

We've had a hard enough time putting a little order on earth over twenty centuries. ... The order of priorities, the scale of importance, the distinction between essential and incidental ... The basic values of the model societies here below will come unbolted: values of work, of enrichment/development, of social organization.[54]

The second effect, according to Le Dangeolet as he continues in his Grand Inquisitor mode, is that the world will fill with religious zealots, people brimming with goodness and organizing into idealistic communities reminiscent of the old Cathars and Anabaptists. This withdrawal from reality will lead inexorably, he suggests, to a suicidal fanaticism. Doubt about God's existence, he suggests, maintained our mutual respect for one another over the centuries of modernity because it deprived us of absolute certainty regarding our own beliefs. "Look at the Crusaders, the Inquisitors, as well as the atheist revolutionaries: all of them slashed and burned and guillotined, completely confident they were doing the right thing. In the end, doubt is the only counterweight to human madness."[55]

This point is made even more sharply by Fr Velter, the Archbishop of Paris. From the moment God was a sure thing in human consciousness,

man would become terrifyingly free. ...If man had stayed more or less moral right up until the end of this second millennium, there were two reasons for it. Either he didn't believe in God, and felt responsible himself for the world; or else he did believe in God, but without being sure, and therefore did good in order to make God exist, as it were.

But once he knew God was a certainty, he would feel no further responsibility for either the salvation of the world or the divine advent.[56]

The proof of God's existence, it is concluded by both government and church officials, must never be made public because it will do more harm than good. While this comes across, on one hand, as a patronizing decision, it also, on the other hand, is a decision that follows quite insightful reflections on the moral springs that move real human beings. More than Ferrucci and in contrast to Morrow, Cossé shows great sympathy for the Grand Inquisitors in her story.

What We Learn from God Fiction

Connections were made earlier between these God novels and the Book of Job. Job was probably written late in the biblical period of ancient Israel, when Judaism had suffered the humiliation of exile at the hands of pagan nations, and at a time when its theological beliefs were in flux. The experience of exile had required a revamping of much of the Jewish understanding of God. We, too, live in a time of change in which we have lost many of our inherited theological certainties. "Jobian" literature can be expected to appear at such transitional times. These three novels use fiction to wonder aloud how we are to continue making sense of inherited humanitarian ideals whose metaphysical context no longer holds for a majority of people. The profoundly humanitarian ideals of the West emerged in a specific religious context in which they made sense, but which has been breaking apart now for more than two centuries. These authors instinctively know that the survival of these ideals demands a periodic return to the substratum of sacred narratives out of which they arose. God happens to be the central character in this narrative substratum, and God returns in these new recitations with an astonishing boldness for modern fiction. Minimally, they recognize that God has served as a symbol for a purposive metaphysical order in the nature of things.

In their appropriation of elements from the ancient God stories, the authors of these three novels are *renovating* old myths – not simply *reciting* the old myths, but borrowing themes and symbols and characters, segments of plotlines and similar dilemmas – and thus showing them due respect. This appropriation, as bombastic as it may appear in Ferrucci and Morrow in particular, tacitly acknowledges that the contents of these old stories about God and the human condition have not been exhausted. But they require being *re-narrated* into stories that contain late twentieth-century circumstances, sensibilities and humor, and an appreciation for evolving customs of human behavior in order to have their power reactivated.

These three writers are clearly groping for reasons for Western societies to be moral. They each tell a story that worries over the erosion of moral ideals and behavior in the late twentieth century. They sense that our societal and cultural commitment to the moral life needs to be re-set, and they use the device of a colorful but out-of-character act of God to push the red reset button. These are stories that deserve to be taken seriously. They are works of the imagination that are engaged in theological reflection of a high order and do offer theologically informed interpretations of the present cultural situation. By presenting us with narrative worlds in which the boundary between life on earth and the life of God is thin, we are invited to have our understandings of reality "disturbed and rearranged," and thus guided into a liminality out of which we might comprehend the meaning of our lives differently and come to appreciate in a new way the full extent of our communal obligations.

Commodity Fetishism

H. Richard Niebuhr contended that we find ourselves pulled almost irresistibly toward polytheism, and that epicureanism (Ferucci) and existentialism (Morrow) are mere pauses between traditional monotheisms and the polytheism of modernity. Polytheism, as he defined it, is a religion of many small and mostly unintegrated concerns, inspiring adherents to chase haphazardly after many shiny gods – purported sources of meaning and power – to provide life with direction and consolation. The marketing of brand commodities presents us with one of our most tempting invitations to become practicing polytheists. It is more than a material desire to consume the products themselves, and more than an urge to display our wealth through conspicuous consumption. The powers we seek to access through consumable goods beckon with promises that were once associated with more traditional sacraments.

As with more traditional sacraments, we have come to believe that the powers that reside in commodities become our powers when we consume them. This is possible because commodities are more than useful objects. They enter the market already ensconced in an elaborate semiology, one that has acquired religious significance and meaning. Through decades of advertising, clever packaging and product placement, the meaning of products has transcended what the product is or does, and has come to rest primarily in its image and the whole network of references that this image brings into play. The product's semiotic connotations have become more important than its specific use. To achieve this, advertisers have learned the art of what Marx once called "commodity fetishism," by means of which commodities are endowed with a numinosity that elicits respect, devotion, and trepidation.

The most obvious examples of this are found in the marketing of cars and perfumes. The naming of automobiles has a fascinating history. In the earliest era, when both the automobile and advertising industries were young and still feeling their way, cars bore generic names like Model T Ford, Cadillac Model Thirty, and Chevrolet Series 490. In the 1950s, cars began acquiring names from the animal kingdom like Mustang, Impala, Bobcat, Cougar, Thunderbird, Roadrunner, Eagle, Falcon, Stingray, Barracuda, Pinto, Bronco, and Ram. As our ancestors might have adorned themselves with the skins of their totem animals, believing that the unique powers of the animal could in so doing become one's own, the practice was revived in the naming of automobiles, tapping into the primal energies and fuzzy mythologies of totemic animals. In the 1960s and 1970s, there was some flirting with names from the gods of classical mythology – Apollo, Centaur, Electra, and Cressida. Now, recognizing that the culture has gained some distance from both totemic creatures and Greek and Roman deities, automobile manufacturers have recalibrated their lexicon to a different mythic layer. Newer vehicles are called Tracker, Trooper, Expedition, Explorer, Excursion, Safari, Trailblazer, Ranger, Renegade, Quest, Odyssey, and Voyager. These vehicles invite their drivers into a legendary world of intrepid explorers, the world of our colonial and frontier ancestors who navigated their way to uncharted and unspoiled lands where fortunes could be won, new mysteries discovered, hidden caches of natural resources exploited, and anything could happen.

The naming of women's perfumes is similarly mystifying. One approach is to name these fragrances after archetypal essences, like Truth, Beautiful, Eternity, Realities, Space, Happy, and Pure – virtually read out of Plato's metaphysics and returning their wearers to the ethereal realm of pure spirit and abstract ideas, to the archetypes out of which the world was made. Another approach is to give the scent a name that associates it with a primordial taboo or transgression, such as Obsession, Decadence, Duende, Envy, Knowing, My Sin, Eden, Banish, Babylon, or Beyond Paradise. These perfume names are all powerful religious symbols, on both sides of the register (totem and taboo), inviting the one who is anointed by them into the mythical time of origins, either before or just after the Fall, leaving the impression that through the consumption of this product, one is partaking in primordial forces, in the time of beginnings when the world was full of possibilities.

The names given to automobiles and perfumes strum mythic chords within us and put into play the "germinal riches" and rejuvenating powers of the times of origin and paradigmatic transitions, when the world was being made or remade. In advertising this effect is accentuated by locating the product in uncivilized wilderness. Cars are often seen in commercials navigating roads where no other cars are present, zooming through pristine wilderness, winding up high tundra slopes, scaling granite peaks, bouncing through jungles, and rolling across arctic icefields or African savannahs. Their milieu is primordial, and they zip through unpopulated space with an uncanny effortlessness. Cars are portrayed as machines with supernatural powers that under the omniscient guidance of a NAVSTAR global positioning satellite can transport us to a land before time. Similarly, perfume ads are often set in paradisal landscapes – beaches, tropics, gardens, woodlands – populated only by a woman and a man, tumbling together in innocent bliss.

The religious effect of the names of these products is further enhanced by tapping into some proven conventions of iconography in the way they are advertised. *Icons* are a species of religious symbolism, pointing beyond themselves to transcendent realities, and graphically participating in those realities. They are typically images depicting religious persons and events that are understood to serve as portals through which the beneficent powers of the divine can pass into our world and our adoration can be passed back. Traditional iconographic imagery achieves this effect by incorporating visual signals such as exaggerated features of the figure depicted, highly stylized decoration, and a coded use of color and various symbols, such as light rays, halos, anchors, keys and bread. In automobile advertising, cars are often depicted with exaggerated features: sized larger than life and manifesting powers that far outstrip their actual technical capabilities, or bathed in light to elicit a feeling of wondrousness. Or, alternatively, but achieving the same effect, they are presented as objects of adoration, with neighbors approaching reverentially, practically genuflecting, and passersby stunned into speechlessness, ecstatic in the presence of such exquisite machinery. Perfume ads also make use of the iconography of light. As a single word, "Eternity," or "Obsession" is uttered – even whispered as if in the presence of the sacred itself – the vessel of golden liquid appears, luminous with a light from beyond.

The use of all of these conventions of religious symbolism, metaphysical abstracts, primordial myth, and visual iconography invites the consumer to attribute powers to these commodities that grandly exceed their actual usefulness. Presented through these conventions, these powers are reified as attributes of the ultimate force in the universe upon which we depend, and we then reflexively seek to incorporate these same powers into ourselves by consuming the product.

When I was a boy I believed, as I had been instructed while watching television, that cookies were baked by elves in hollow trees, that my favorite breakfast cereal contained crunchy marshmallows stolen from a leprechaun, and that beans and peas were grown by a jolly green giant in a place called Happy Valley. My first experience of real cognitive dissonance was realizing that the huge, nondescript brick factory next to I-70 in Denver, crowned with smokestacks and surrounded by an oceanic parking lot, *was* the Keebler bakery. No sign of trees anywhere. No elves in sight. I recalled this a few months ago when I noticed that my 3-year-old son was transfixed in the cereal aisle at a supermarket, undergoing a rhapsody as visible to an onlooker as what I have seen in his eyes when he enters the great vaulted space of the sanctuary of the church where we worship. Mythical creatures – toucans, rabbits, cuckoo birds, tigers, elves and leprechauns – harkened to him from boxes of magically delicious breakfast cereals.

We are living in an era in which most Americans alive today, at least most who have been born since 1945, have received the bulk of our mythological worlds from people who want to sell us something. The great wave of secularization that was believed to characterize the twentieth century as Western cultures finally "came of age" and learned to cope with a "disenchanted universe," in Max Weber's sober observation, was pushed back by brilliant marketers who re-enchanted our world with a cast of mythical characters as vast as any medieval hagiography: Charlie Tuna, Mr Clean, Smokey Bear, Snap, Crackle and Pop, the Energizer Bunny, Mayor McCheese, and the Pillsbury Doughboy, to name a few.[57] In the transcendent realm that these marvelous creatures inhabit behind the veil of our own, there is much rushing about to service every conceivable human longing and desire. It is a benevolent realm, a happy valley – a place redolent of the twenty-third Psalm – green pastures, still waters, cups overflowing – all outfitted to restore parched human souls.

It is largely a harmless place, this enchanted realm peopled by elves and talking fish. Cultures have always had folk and fairy tales that existed alongside their more firmly held belief systems. But this particular happy valley does have the potentially dangerous effect of so disguising the real processes by which the goods we consume are produced that it can serve as a mask for much exploitation behind the scenes. The true story behind the auto showroom, the perfume counter, and the packages on our grocers' shelves involve many complex and some ugly macroeconomic details – disappearing family farms, genetically engineered crops, overuse of pesticides, tedious assembly lines, arcane trade agreements, third world debt, corporate welfare, sweatshops, clear-cut forests, union struggles, polluting technologies – not exactly frisky elves baking cookies in hollow trees. But this sort of information seldom makes it onto the packaging in which the food comes wrapped. Instead, much more fabulous and mystifying tales are told.[58]

Our distant ancestors did not view any thing as a dead object. Every stone, crooked branch, lump of coal, gazelle tooth, or misshapen potato could be a bearer of supernatural power. Historians of religion describe this view of power-bearing objects as "fetishism," a concept that Marx borrowed and elaborated. Fetishes were typically things small enough to be picked up and pocketed, transported as bearers of a sacred power that had a simultaneous existence in this world and in the world of the gods. With Marx, I suspect we have never outgrown fetishism. There are all the obvious sanctified fetishes for Christians – crosses, family Bibles, the water of baptism and the bread and wine of communion, religious books – all signs of grace that serve to remind the faithful of actions of God on their behalf behind the scenes of their lives. There are surviving fetishes of an earlier age – colorful stones, garden gnomes, rabbit's feet, family photos, coin collections – whose mythologies we are not clear about, but whose presence we find somehow reassuring. And then there is this relatively young batch of fetishes – the brands and consumer goods that do what bona fide fetishes have always done: bring us good fortune, help us to lure mates, humiliate our rivals, guard against sickness, and bestow on us powers we have envied in members of the animal kingdom: speed, strength, stamina and fertility. As simple commodities they may not perform these functions, but through effective marketing, a mythos is conjured that invests certain meanings and powers into a whole cosmos of product lines.

The most effective marketing mystifies consumer goods, and thereby pours meaning into the products we consume, meaning around which we organize our desires and hopes. No longer dead objects, our groceries, cars, wardrobes, toiletries, home furnishings, vacations, and computers come to be inhabited by supernatural spirits that provide us with the meaning we need to get through life. This was driven home in recent advertising spots for Intel microprocessors that depicted men dancing around in festive costume, as if at carnival in Deep Space Nine, shuttling data inside of computer chips. At some unconscious level we can be per-suaded that if Intel microchips are in our computers, these techno-sprites are inside playfully choreographing our data in an elegant dance. But like all deities, these spirits are jealous of our devotion and demand that we make sacrifices to appease them.

There is a novel called *American Gods* by the British comic book writer, Neil Gaiman.[59] Set in the present, the story follows the efforts of the old Scandinavian god Odin as he traverses the blue highways of America looking up all the assorted gods that came over here from Europe, Africa, India, Russia, Arabia, and the Pacific Rim, lodged happily in the hearts and minds of the waves of immigrants who made new lives for themselves here since the first ill-fated journey of the Norsemen in the ninth century. Thor, Anansi, Ashtaroth, Kali, Czernobog, Leprechauns and Banshees, the Jinn – all well cared for by the first generations of settlers through fervent prayer, offerings and sacrifices, but now long forgotten, neglected, hungry and stranded and strewn across a strange land where they do what they must do to get by. Odin finds them waiting tables, pumping gas and tending bar "in the cracks at the edges of society." All former rivals, and with much bad blood between them, Odin has undertaken to organize them into a guerilla force against the new gods now waxing in power on this continent, soaking up the devotion – and sacrificial offerings – of its inhabitants. Who are these new powerful gods? "Gods of credit card and freeway, of Internet and telephone, of radio and hospital and television, gods of plastic and of beeper and of neon. Proud gods, fat and foolish creatures, puffed up with their own newness and importance."

At one point in the book, late at night in a motel room in rural Illinois, Odin's companion, an ex-con named Shadow, has tuned into an old episode of *I Love Lucy* to unwind from the day, when Lucy shoves Ricky Ricardo out the door of their apartment, lights a cigarette, faces the camera and tells Shadow that they need to talk.

"Who are you?" asks Shadow.

She answers: "I'm the idiot box. I'm the TV. I'm the all-seeing eye and the world of the cathode ray . . . I'm the little shrine the family gathers to adore."

"You're the television? Or someone in the television?"

"The TV's the altar. I'm what people are sacrificing to."

"What do they sacrifice?" asks Shadow.

"Their time, mostly," says Lucy. "Sometimes each other."

It seems that we conform our lives to several mythologies at once, mythologies populated by these very deities that Gaiman's pagan god Odin is seeking to vanquish – the gods of credit card, freeway, Internet, radio, heavy appliances, hospital, retirement fund, jet travel, education, military might, and television. For most of our middle range, penultimate concerns (for the well-being of our families, health, financial security, diversion from feelings of guilt, inspiration in our calling, pleasure, protection from misfortune), we find ourselves spending much time at other altars, appeasing other powers, polytheists that we are, making the sacrifices they demand.

The Ghost in the Machine

It has long been noted that technology has come to serve a religious function in modern societies. We revere our machines. Our ancestors depended upon God for many of the services that machines now provide better and more reliably. Health technologies have dramatically reduced the infant mortality rate, made us healthier, more likely to recover from disease, made the blind see and the lame walk, and given us longer lives. Household machinery (furnaces, hot water heaters, electric lights, burglar alarms, stovetops and ovens, refrigerators) provides us with hygiene that keeps us healthy, fresh foods deliciously prepared, extended evenings with families and friends illuminated by electricity, safety from marauders, and with a shelter from which we can find major storms fascinating events instead of life-threatening catastrophes. Industrial technologies make us powerful beyond what our ancestors could have imagined, with the capacity to level mountains, melt rocks, build skyscrapers, produce massive quantities of goods at low cost, and re-engineer crops. Military technology can monitor suspicious activity from outer space, target the enemy, and destroy whole cities within minutes after the command is given. Transportation technology allows us to transport goods around the world, ensuring those of us in wealthier nations an unfailing food supply, and to travel vast distances at great speed, enabling us to live the highly mobile lives that we do – a physical mobility we have come to equate with freedom.

By way of these achievements, modern technology has largely supplanted the role of divine providence in our lives. It is our machines and the industrial sector that produces them that are the primary providers of our security, well-being and prosperity, and our primary defense against misery. It is not a fresh revelation to suggest that machines have become our many "shiny gods," the source of the good life we have come to expect. Those who honestly face the prospect of surrendering the machines that buffer our lives, for any reason other than a temporary exotic vacation, can testify to how completely technology has come to function as an ultimate concern in our culture. Philosopher Albert Borgmann calls this "the device paradigm."[60] But the tendency of technology to acquire God-like attributes does not stop there. It has been ratcheted up in the era of telecommunications and digital technology, not to mention the enormous ramifications of robotics, genetic engineering, and nanotechnology.[61]

Consider the claims made in Hewlett-Packard's "everything is possible" ad campaign in which they promote how their technology has enhanced the performance of other corporations and organizations like Porsche, Starbucks, the National Gallery of London and the US Postal Service. One commercial boasts:

> HP technology is building efficient miracles, helping access the web wirelessly in coffeehouses, and letting citizens talk to their governments twenty-four hours a day. It's powering the engine of the world economy, and making art timeless. For the world's great companies, thinkers and doers, HP makes more things possible.

Another commercial, more humorous if more audacious, claims:

> Neither snow, nor rain, nor heat, nor temporary loss of gravity, nor grumpy robots made of old washing machines, nor black holes that swallow the entire known universe, will keep the U.S. Postal Service from its appointed rounds. HP technology helps make sure the mail never stops.

Everything – including miracles, participatory government, a thriving economy, art appreciation, and the delivery of mail in the face of monster robots and cosmic disaster – is possible with computer technology.

Or, consider the theological content of three commercials from Accenture that premiered during the 2001 Superbowl, itself an annual event surrounded by religious fervor and a showcase for the global market's hottest products and most critically acclaimed advertising. Accenture is a company that provides management consulting and technology outsourcing services to corporations and governments around the world. Accenture, in other words, provides services to the service providers, and is thus one of those deep background firms, practically an abstract, whose products are seldom experienced directly by the consuming public.

The first commercial begins with a shot of microscopic blue-green cells, swimming and pulsating in rhythm to a triple meter waltz. The camera pulls back slowly, revealing more and more of these waltzing cells, and continues to pull back until it becomes evident that these cells are the constituent elements of a single microchip, and their movements are following the intricate circuitry of the chip. At this moment, a newspaper headline, torn from the newsprint, is superimposed upon the chip, announcing: "Bacteria Tested as Digital Circuit." The screen fades to black, and Accenture's motto appears in brackets: "[now it gets interesting]."

The second commercial is composed of fast cuts that tell a story with the following sequence: An ambulance with siren wailing races through the nighttime streets of an Asian city; a man hurries across a university campus, judging from its architecture one located in the US or western Europe, and up a marble staircase; a gurney rushes down hospital corridors, concerned family members accompany it; the man reaches the top of the stairs, enters a room containing some serious technology, dons virtual reality goggles and gloves and plugs himself into a computer; an operating room back in Asia; hands in gloves maneuver in midair, holding nothing; close up of actual scalpel cutting actual flesh; an Asian man lying in a hospital bed, awake, smiling, being caressed by his wife. A newspaper headline appears: "Virtual Surgery." The screen fades to black and the motto returns: "[now it gets interesting]."

The third commercial opens with a few small candles burning against a black background. In several cuts, more candles come into view, burning fiercely, then an ashtray piled with burnt matches, and more flaming candles. Next we see a woman's face, smiling at the candles, easily one hundred of them, topping a white frosted cake. This time the superimposed newspaper headline announces: "Lifespans without Limit?" and we can see the first line of the story, "Genome breakthroughs ..." The woman blows out all the candles, and people gathered around her clap. Screen fades to black, then the motto: "[now it gets interesting]."

Organic matter transformed into intelligent technology; life-saving surgery performed by a physician whose patient is on the other side of the planet; the prospect of immortality thanks to genetic engineering. Accenture doesn't do any of these things, but it provides the services to others who will make these miracles happen. The expanding infrastructure of information technology has within its reach, we learn from these commercials, what have traditionally been thought of as divine prerogatives: the power to render molecules intelligent, to heal across space, and to grant immortality. And we also learn that hovering in the background of these technologies are global companies like Accenture, which are responsible for making our lives this interesting.

With search engines like Google and the expanding availability of databases through URLs, an invisible grid of nearly infinite information has come to permeate space. And now with wireless technology, this grid can be accessed from practically anywhere. One recent commercial for AT&T's wireless service, mlife, consists of a long montage of the navels of people of all shapes and sizes – an old man getting dressed, a beer belly at a barbeque, a woman body builder flexing, a belly dancer, a toddler in a sandbox – and concludes in a hospital delivery room with a woman giving birth, nurses stretching out the newborn's umbilical cord and a doctor picking up surgical scissors. The closing voiceover intones: "We are meant to lead a wireless life. Now we truly can. Welcome to mlife. From AT&T Wireless." We are invited into a new phase of life, or mlife, which has come about as the result of a painful process, but the message is that this newest advance in telecommunications is part of the perfection of human nature, made possible by those cellular service providers who are cutting our wires.

This is reinforced by the character of the messenger in the advertising of several of the cellular service providers. The Sprint PCS Guy, for example, who appears on the scene to resolve various "cellular miscommunications" caused by static on the line, such as the woman who phoned her husband asking him to bring home "shampoo," and later finds him in the backyard with "Shamu" the Killer Whale in their pool, or the man who called his wife asking her to "bring home some soup from the store," discovers that she has returned with a handsome, Lothario-esque "soap opera star." The Sprint PCS Guy lives to connect people to the only nationwide, all-digital, fiber-optic network. His look (black suit, long overcoat) resembles that of the angels in *Wings of Desire*, which is fitting given his role as liaison between two worlds (the world of the flesh and the world of digital, wireless technology) and his peculiar benevolence and dedication to his mission.

Alan Cohen, the vice president of one of the new Wi-Fi (wireless fidelity) providers, a technology that uses radio frequencies to allow high-speed Internet connections to anywhere in the world, was recently quoted as saying,

If I can operate Google, I can find anything. And with wireless, it means I will be able to find anything, anywhere, anytime. Which is why I say that Google, combined with Wi-Fi, is a little bit like God. God is wireless, God is everywhere and God sees and knows everything. Throughout history, people connected to God without wires. Now, for many questions in the world, you ask Google, and increasingly, you can do it without wires, too.[62]

This invisible grid laden with knowledge, art, the freshest news, the fruit of the labors of geniuses throughout the ages, and voices of all sorts reaching out for all sorts of reasons – the datasphere as Rushkoff named it – that anyone with a laptop or cellular phone can tap into around the clock and query at will – does conjure up associations with the invisible God who sees and knows everything all at once, who is everywhere, whose energies hang in the air, and whose counsel is sought through scriptures and prayer. When we find ourselves in a jam, many of us have now been habituated to turn to a search engine and begin navigating the Web for guidance. In that ethereal realm, we anticipate that some URL will know what is going on and clarify our confusion and possibly even protect us from the consequences of our ignorance. That we can now do it wirelessly, at any moment of the day or night wherever we are, lends itself to extending such classic attributes for God as omniscience, omnipotence and omnipresence to the World Wide Web (see Figure 4).

Bill Joy, one-time chief scientist and CEO of Sun Microsystems and the designer of the Berkeley version of the UNIX operating system, which became the scaffolding for the Internet, forecasts that with the development of the kind of molecular electronics celebrated in Accenture's advertisement, we are now 25 years away from building personal computers that are one million times more powerful than those in use today. In roughly the year 2030, he anticipates that computers will become capable of thinking for themselves. The Internet will at that point become what may justifiably be called a *transcendent mind*, with a capacity for self-consciousness and agency that will not necessarily be limited by designers' assumptions that technology exists to serve human ends.[63] This is the sort of evolution of artificial intelligence that dystopian writers have been warning about for several decades, most recently in the *Matrix* trilogy brought to the screen by the Wachowski brothers. In their dark vision, human beings float alone in pods of amniotic fluid, serving as batteries for the Internet (the Matrix), and are pacified in a somnolent state through electrical signals that are downloaded into their minds through ports that have been implanted into their brains. These signals produce a neural interactive simulation within their brains, conjuring a computer-generated dreamworld, so that these organic batteries lead virtual lives while floating unconscious inside their pods for their entire, short lives.

Figure 4   The Internet is a nexus of knowledge, power and transcendence that evokes a classic sense of the holy, as boldly suggested in this ad from MCI WorldCom, Inc. (1999).

Taking a more optimistic view of these developments, Scott Adams, the creator of the comic strip *Dilbert*, wrote a curious book recently that promotes the equation of God and the Internet. In the book, *God's Debris: A Thought Experiment*, Adams stages a lengthy conversation between a mysterious old man named Avatar and a package delivery man who delivers the old man a package then stays through the night, sitting by the fire, as Avatar spins metaphysical tales. Through Avatar, Adams speculates that the world as we know it began when God blew himself to bits, and that the span of cosmic history is the long process by which God's "debris" is reassembling itself. Every element of reality is a bit of God; human beings happen to be the bits through which God is recovering his consciousness. With every action that integrates the discrete elements of the world into a more complete harmony, God is further revived. Avatar explains, "Every economic activity helps. Whether you are programming computers, or growing food, or raising children, or cleaning garbage from the side of the road, you are contributing to the realization of God's consciousness."[64]

To do these things is to fulfill God's will. The old man's religion is a kind of Taoism of gaining a feel for this gathering harmony and learning to flow with it. Right now the flow is most intense in the building up of the Internet. This is the cutting edge of God's reviving consciousness. Avatar describes it in this way:

"As we speak, engineers are building the Internet to link every part of the world in much the same way as a fetus develops a central nervous system. Virtually no one questions the desirability of the Internet. It seems that humans are born with the instinct to create and embrace it. The instinct of beavers is to build dams; the instinct of humans is to build communication systems . . .

"The need to build the Internet comes from something inside us, something programmed, something we can't resist . . .

"Humanity is developing a sort of global eyesight as millions of video cameras on satellites, desktops, and street corners are connected to the Internet. In your lifetime it will be possible to see almost anything on the planet from any computer. And society's intelligence is merging over the Internet, creating, in effect, a global mind that can do vastly more than any individual mind. Eventually everything that is known by one person will be available to all. A decision can be made by the collective mind of humanity and instantly communicated to the body of society . . .

"A billion years from now, if a visitor from another dimension observed humanity, he might perceive it to be one large entity with a consciousness and purpose, and not a collection of relatively uninteresting individuals."

The delivery man then asks: "Are you saying we're evolving into God?"

To which Avatar answers: "I'm saying we're the building blocks of God, in the early stages of reassembling."[65]

Through the voice of Avatar, Adams reprises the monadology of Gottfried Wilhelm Leibniz, a seventeenth-century theologian and mathematician, who claimed that reality is composed of elementary monads that are orchestrated in a harmonious manner known only to God, who is the ultimate unity of all monads. Adams differs from Leibniz in that he locates the origin of the monads in the spectacular suicide of God (the Big Bang), while Leibniz attributed it to a decree of God that set in motion a harmony of elements overseen by God. In theological terms, Adams is a pantheist (the cosmos is God), while Leibniz was a panentheist (the cosmos is part of God, but not all of God). Adams also innovates on monadology in featuring the Internet as its current stage of growth. Adams is not attempting to found a cult; he is simply dusting off and improvising a metaphysic that takes into account our nearly uninhibited celebration and growing dependence upon digital technology. He deserves credit for his honest attempt to make metaphysical sense of a way of life to which our society is overwhelmingly devoted.

Postmodernism and the Sublime

Chapter 2 ended quoting Dick Hebdige's lament about the foreclosure on "trawling for hidden truths" that our current fascination with surfaces, with the simulacra, has imposed on us. In the same essay, Hebdige raised the interesting possibility that the very postmodernist thinkers who have imposed this ban may not have abandoned depth entirely themselves. Surveying the writings of such heirs of Nietzsche as Jacques Lacan, Michel Foucault, Julia Kristeva, Jacques Derrida and Jean-François Lyotard, Hebdige finds that while each of them strives to deprive us of our illusion that language corresponds to reality in any reliable way, or that words signify any reality beyond other words or beyond very cunning assertions of power, each of them preserves a privileged referent in their own critiques that has the qualities of the sublime. For Lacan it is the certainty of our eventual absorption into flux, for Foucault it is the endless spiral of knowledge and power, for Kristeva it is *significance*, for Derrida it is *differance*, and for Lyotard it is, quite simply, the sublime. In their rejection of the capacity of language to signify reality, they have introduced terms that capture an aporia, a gap at the heart of human knowing that inspires "epiphany and terror."[66] And once it has been encountered, all of one's previous certainties dissolve, "all that was solid melts into air." Out of this experience with the sublime, they each undertake their life's work of unmasking the powers that sustain our illusions.

The sublime, recall, describes an experience parallel to the experience of the holy, of the *mysterium tremendum et fascinosum*, the alluring dread that signals that one is in the presence of one's ultimate concern. Each of these postmodern theorists has stumbled upon a dreadful awareness from which they cannot flee. But what they report back through their writings is overwhelmingly weighted on the side of the *tremendum*, the side that negates human thought and aspirations by revealing the chasm between our finitude and infinite reality. Theirs is the God of the abyss; the God of the creative ground eludes them. The polar tension that characterizes a robust encounter with the holy is missing. And when the ground is so utterly negated, the danger arises of absolutizing, even deifying, the abyss.

The influence these thinkers have had, which has been considerable in academic circles and indirectly felt elsewhere, often has the effect described by Douglas Coupland in the bit of dialogue from his book *Life after God* with which this chapter began: We have been relieved of God, but in God's place have "gained an irony that scorched everything it touched." The ironic sensibility is acidic; it withers whatever it comes into contact with. It refuses to trust any affirmation of meaning, saying, "I won't be fooled again." Richard Rorty calls it "liberal irony," a disposition he recommends – beliefs and values are fine and good, but should be lightly held and always open to revision. "The words which are fundamental to metaphysics," he writes, words like true, good, right, beauty and justice, are "just another set of little human things."[67] The ironists are those who realize "that anything can be made to look good or bad by being redescribed," and will therefore never take themselves seriously – nor should they, according to Rorty – because they are ever aware of the contingency of all certainties.[68] As cool-headed as Rorty makes it sound, his is a perspective that has in its background an overwhelming encounter with the abyss – from which he has recoiled, and then made his peace.

A striking example of this kind of ironic redescription from the annals of popular culture is found in director Oliver Stone's movie, *Natural Born Killers* (1994). The movie begins with a young man and his girlfriend, Mickey and Mallory, who appear to be garden-variety kids in love but suffering from hard childhoods. In the opening scene, which presents Mallory's home life as a 1950s family sitcom, complete with laugh track, Mickey the butcher makes a home meat delivery to Mallory's family, flirts with Mallory, and then the two sneak off. Because Mallory is a minor, this lands Mickey in prison, and when he is released he drowns Mallory's incestuous father in a fish aquarium and sets their house on fire, killing Mallory's mother and brother. The couple then begin a road trip killing spree, spraying bullets at customers in diners and gas stations across the country, always sparing one living witness who is randomly selected from among the other victims. As these witnesses accumulate and come to the attention of the media, the two elusive killers become celebrities on the television show, *American Maniacs*, subjects of speculation by talking heads and folk heroes to the viewing public. By the time he is captured, it is clear that Mickey is a criminal virtuoso, a natural born killer, who colludes with a demon in his mind before each act of violence, carrying through on each murder in a state of ecstatic reverie. Even from inside a high security prison, Mickey manages to maintain his status as a media celebrity, and using the opportunity of a press interview, instigates a prison riot, rescues Mallory from her cell, and with the star reporter from *American Maniacs* in tow, the two of them escape. After committing one final murder – the ritual castration and crucifixion of the reporter – the long frenzy of death is concluded and the two lovers disappear underground. As the credits roll, we see them several years later back on the road in a camper, now a happy nuclear family with children, Mickey and Mallory as doting parents, devoted to each other, living the unencumbered life of itinerant hippies.

Due to its gratuitous violence, the movie was controversial even before its release. Stone and many of his reviewers have defended his work as a piece of commentary on the American media's exploitation of violence to draw viewers, and the public's obvious appetite for it. Fair enough. But Stone follows the same proven formula in composing his film; he even pushes the formula to new levels, utilizing every available cinematic technique (attractive actors, captivating soundtrack, special effects, sex, animation, lens filters, fast cuts, choreography, music video cinematography) to portray the acts of mayhem as stunningly beautiful. The audience predictably feels both attracted and repulsed by each new display of carnage as Stone uses his filmmaker's craft to tune into both frequencies of the holy. With clues from the story itself, i.e., frightening, surreal images projected behind the windows of rooms Mickey enters, a shaman who recognizes Mickey from a vision as the agent of his own return to the spirit world, and multiple allusions to a demon who possesses Mickey in the moments of his berserk outbursts, the movie leaves the impression that these acts of violence are indistinguishable from some kind of spiritual ecstasy.

In his incisive reading of this movie, William Schweiker discerns the reverberating tone of the *tremendum* that echoes throughout it.[69] "In Stone's film," he writes, "human life is portrayed as suspended over an irrational abyss of violence without purpose or necessary end. The earth itself opens its mouth to consume the human project. History is just a slaughtering block. Human time marks itself in blood and the madness ends – temporarily to be sure – for no reason, no purpose."[70] No social institution represented in the movie – not family, media, law, or religion – appears to have the power to halt the violence. Violence ends,

Schweiker points out, only when it has exhausted itself. In a great final orgy of torture and blood, there is finally an "exhaustion of wrathful energies," a "catharsis of violence." No other reason is given for how or why Mickey's murderous instincts are ultimately channeled into becoming a peaceful family man. Psychotic killers, we must conclude, finally get it out of their systems and settle down to become loving parents.

This is a world apart from the standard formula in westerns which requires even the gunslinger hero to ride off into the sunset, away from the circle of domestic life, following his shoot out with the bad guys (e.g., *Shane, The Searchers, Red River*). In the western it is understood that the hero must ride away alone, according to Jane Tompkins, "because having hardened himself to do murder, he can no longer open his heart to humankind."[71]

Clearly the world of this movie is not a world in which the abyss and the ground of being are conjoined. Nor is it a world in which transcendent power has bound itself to any moral telos in the manner of a covenant. The author of this world refuses to endorse such metaphysical and theological illusions. There appears to be no moral universe to catch up with Mickey and Mallory and settle the score. But this does not mean that it is a world bereft of the divine, or of moral judgment. In this regard, Schweiker draws attention to Mickey's answer to the reporter's question during the prison interview about what could justify his rampage that left more than fifty innocent people dead. Mickey corrects him, looking him straight in the eye, saying, "No one is innocent." All are guilty, and therefore, in the chamber of Mickey's demented mind, Schweiker suggests, the judgment has been rendered that "wrath is rightly rained on anyone because all are guilty." Moreover, from inside the film, neither character nor plot development is handled in a way to discriminate between the gravity of various immoral actions – incest, murder, infidelity, celebrity worship, media exploitation, government incompetence, ambitiousness – all are equally reprehensible and carry no corresponding scale of consequences. If anything, given his reward of a happy family at the end, the remorseless serial killer Mickey is the moral hero because he has unmasked the social conventions that perpetuate violence.

Indeed, during the prison interview, Mickey confides that he was capable of doing what he did because he is a new form of life, different from others. Elaborating on this, Schweiker writes:

> He is a new form of life, a kind of Nietzschean *Übermensch* living beyond cultural beliefs about good and evil. . . . He vents wrath on injustice unconstrained by remorse or guilt as somehow a testimony to his higher, purer form of existence. Mickey is utterly self-determining in his moral existence; he creates value and defines justice. He is godlike. His inscrutable will decides who is deemed worthy of respect and life.[72]

Here we find the film's implicit theology. In the maw of the abyss, we are all either gods, i.e., self-determining authors of good and evil, bound by nothing outside of ourselves, or else we are worthy of death.

In his sermon, "Escape from God," Tillich elaborated on the chafing effect of the inescapable demand that emanates from the *tremendum* side of the holy. This demand is experienced by humans, Tillich wrote, as the God who sees through us, through our public veneer and into the dark flapping recesses of our inner selves. Of this God, Tillich wrote, "The God Who sees everything is the God Who has to die. Man cannot stand that such a Witness live. . . . [M]an cannot stand the God Who really is God. Man tries to escape God, and hates Him, because he cannot escape Him." The God that humans hate is the God who reminds us that we are not what we ought to be, that we are morally incomplete creatures. And it is this God we have sought to murder in the modern period, finally exhausted by the constant glare of transcendent scrutiny. But, Tillich continued in his sermon, "God is always revived in something or somebody; He cannot be murdered."[73]

In Rorty and Mickey, as in the neo-Nietzschean strands of post-modernism, irony has become this something in which God is revived. For many who are in the postmodern frame of mind, irony has become the authority one grants to oneself to call the good "bad," and the bad "good," for no other reason than that one has said it is so, retreating to the odd consolation of a universe that doesn't care.

Conclusion

The aim of this chapter has been to explore what popular culture is telling itself about God. The following themes have surfaced.

There is some iconoclasm toward the iconoclasts, toward those who would murder God. Among the post-boomer generations are many who were raised outside of the direct influence of religious communities who consequently do not have many of the resentments toward God that stem from being exposed to the shoddy instruction and hypocritical piety that religious congregations, as human institutions, sometimes offer. They are grabbing for bits and pieces of the stories about God that they were never told, assembling them as *bricoleurs* with little external guidance. Among these are some who fervently believe that God will intervene if religion will only get out of the way, and others who have a deep and inarticulate worry that, due to our neglect and abysmal behavior, God has moved on to other things.

Some take the view that God is more like us than theology has typic-ally allowed. Among these, a new cluster of divine attributes is emerging. God can be evasive, temperamental, playful, vengeful, adventurous, over-whelmed, irresponsible, on a journey of self-discovery, loving like we are loving (in a fickle way), distracted, a sensualist, weary, demoralized, sad, and, most of all, lonely.

And then, there is an awareness in some quarters that sustaining the moral life might depend upon faith in a sovereign reality that is benevol-ent – in the idea that the absolute power in the universe has ordered the exercise of its own powers according to recognizable moral values. Other-wise, such holdovers as altruism, solidarity, compassion and self-sacrifice make little sense. While the idea is still around that belief in a "sky god" is a distraction from devoting oneself to strive for justice in this world, it is not as prevalent as it once was – at least not in popular culture.

Another development is that what has traditionally been understood as divine providence is imagined by some at the moment as the work of angels among us. Angelology in popular culture ranges from angels who pursue us doggedly and attend to all the details of our individual lives – facilitating our movement through heavy traffic, advising us in making smart con-sumer decisions, and easing our transition through death – to angels who simply watch, with a mixture of curiosity and compassion, the passage of human life, like hamstrung cops walking a beat or old-style ethnograph-ers observing exotic tribes. By others, providence has been taken over by the polytheism of commodity fetishism and a universe re-enchanted with mythical powers represented by the iconography of brand logos, distract-ing us into a multitude of penultimate concerns. By yet others the role of divine providence has been transferred to technology, as the great, pro-tective matrix in which we spend our lives, from which we obtain our blessings, and which demands and receives our absolute loyalty.

Subtler gadgetry combined with the great, sweeping, invisible force of the World Wide Web is also receiving trust and aspirations that in the past had been reserved for God. Whatever deep need we have for there to be a power in the cosmos that is omniscient, omnipotent, and omnipresent, the constant whisper of knowledge and rumors on the Web provides a convincing simulacrum. And there are speculative metaphysicians, like Scott Adams, who are promoting the apotheosis of the Internet as the knitting together of God, a new monadology that is thoroughly panthe-istic. "Googling" is a way some of the faithful in this camp seem to satisfy their needs for enlightenment and prayer.

Finally, there is the deification of the abyss that is emerging among some advocates of postmodernism. Overcome by the withering side of the holy, popular culture is envisioning various gods of the abyss, ranging from the wild *Übermensch* of Oliver Stone's Mickey to a religion of sheer delight in the simulacra that now compose the world, with no expectation of meaning beyond the flux of significations that they provide.

The doctrine of God that can be discerned in popular culture has this strange profile, pulled as it is in different directions. But most importantly, there is a great willingness to entertain the possibility of divine transcendence in its various modes, and to experiment outside of institutional religion with what it might be up to.

6

Human Nature

The next topic we turn to is "theological anthropology," which entails an exploration of human (*anthropos*) nature. Under the heading of theological anthropology theologians ponder such questions as: Who are these humans God has made? What powers do we have and what limitations? What are our legitimate needs? How do we acquire the identities that distinguish us as persons? Are we infinitely pliable, or is there a point at which we break and cease being human? What is the function of others and of culture in making us human? Are we noble savages or are we civilized beasts? Are we inherently good or inherently evil? Are we a mixture of good and evil, and if so, which of these is predominant?

Signs of the Times

Television shows related to law and order (police squads, private investigators, courtrooms, federal agents, lawyers, sheriffs, politicians, mafiosos, forensic scientists, etc.) represent a substantial amount of air time. Based on the ratings, we still like shows that pit good guys against bad guys. We like to enter the criminal mind, see how it works, feel our own moral hackles rise, and be reassured, in the end, that crooks and murderers get what is coming to them. This assures us that there is a moral order to the universe and that it catches up with those who defy it. Walter Davis et al., argue that crime shows have become one of our society's premier moral teachers. These shows "define good and evil, teach right and wrong, establish norms and sanctions, and model good and bad behavior."[1] They are this and more than this. The basic cop show has matured since the early days of *Gunsmoke*, *Dragnet* and *Hawaii Five-O*. In shows like *NYPD Blue* and *Law and Order* the criminals and the cops have become more complex, as have the circumstances of crimes and the implementation of justice. The dramatic-center has shifted away from the action of solving the crime and toward probing into the personal lives of the law enforcers. These new era cop shows have become theaters of virtue and vice.

From week to week, over the span of several seasons, the characters of individual law enforcers, and some of the recurring lawbreakers, are developed so that we come to know their dispositions, habits and pre-judices – we become familiar with their moral fiber. We learn which characters are prone to tell the truth or to lie, which are guided by prin-ciple and which are driven by appetites or old personal demons, which are on a path of regeneration, and which are slowly unraveling. This is potent storytelling because when handled well, it models how person-alities of these different types, given to differently weighted virtues and vices, behave when thrown each new plot development. We see how they react to insults and violence, to innocence and malevolence, to gestures of love or loyalty or gratitude, to incompetence, corruption, pettiness, deceit or senseless sacrifice. The characters function as embodiments of certain moral habits, which are then tested under the duress of life on mean streets. And we see how these moral personality types affect the lives around them. Law and order programming has become one of our most sensitive inquirers into the ambiguities of the human condition, and particularly of the resilience of virtue and the stubbornness of vice. It is an effective conveyor of the view that persons are constituted by the choices they make in the face of moral dilemmas.

Insight into human nature can also be found in different reflections on Generation X. In *Life after God*, Douglas Coupland bemoaned the fact that while many members of GenX enjoy lives charmed with material comfort, they are bereft of any transcendent ideas – a twin inheritance from their boomer parents. Corroborating this, journalist David Samuels wrote an essay several years ago reflecting on the mode of selfishness unique to his (admittedly privileged) post-boomer cohorts, who "lack any sense of necessary connection to anything larger than their own nar-rowly personal aims and preoccupations." In the wake of all the social revolutions of the 1960s, he surmises,

> "the basic laws of social gravity had lost their pull. We were free to be white or black, gay or straight, to grow our hair long, shave our heads, medit-ate for days on end, have children or not, drink bottled water, work out at the gym, watch television until 3 in the morning and otherwise exist outside the traditional roles and the close, gossipy communities that had burdened our parents..."

But, he asks, "what if the freedom to rearrange reality more or less to our liking is the only freedom we have?" This feels regretfully vacuous to him, so he probes it further:

> It is hard to put my finger on exactly when this change was set in motion, or what the larger forces behind it might be. Only that the old rules no longer apply, and that coherent narratives, the stories that tell us who we are and where we are going, are getting harder and harder to find. There is the decline of organized religion and the nation-state, the failure of politics, the reduction of human behavior to chemicals in the brain, the absence of the sense of common purpose that is often created by large-scale human suffering. There are Lotto drawings on TV. What is left behind is us. Or not *us* exactly, but a few hundred million loopy, chattering, disconnected *I's*.[2]

Samuels finds this freedom of protean selves unattached to anything big or enduring to be disconsoling, inspiring a lingering melancholy. Like the then popular *Seinfeld* sitcom, he and his friends experience lives that are well-heeled shows about nothing. Tom Beaudoin, a thoughtful interpreter of GenX, claims that while the pressing question for young boomers was "What is the meaning of life, my life?" the pressing question of Xers is "Will you be there for me?" He explains, as an Xer himself, "We ask this of our selves, bodies, parents, friends, partners, society, religions, leaders, nation, and even God."[3] In short, while boomers were on a quest for *meaning* when they were young, Xers with childhoods that have been characterized by fractured families and fragile commitments on every front are on a quest for *fidelity*. This accounts, in part, for their attraction to tattoos and body piercings. Tattoos and incisions, Beaudoin writes, "stay with us for the rest of our lives. They will be one certain source of continued identity amid the flux of identity. . . . They will never leave, which is blessed assurance for our abandoned generation."[4]

From this quick inventory, it appears that popular culture *is* sorting through substantial matters related to theological anthropology: the character-forming power of virtue and vice, the melancholy of unordered freedom, the role of fidelity in stabilizing one's identity. These bits and pieces from popular culture tell us much about the way we are made, at least the way we understand ourselves to be made.

Who Are these Humans God Has Made?

How are we to understand human existence? Are we one edge of a cosmic event that will never be explained, an event that is simply happening without purpose, that could either go on forever or end in an instant and make no difference, sustained for the moment by some constant physical laws, but ultimately suspended over nothing more than whirl and flux?[5]

Within this purposeless cosmos, are we like other organisms, perhaps a little smarter, but driven by the same instincts of hunger, reproduction, and territoriality – just clever enough to transmute our desire to survive or our will-to-power into moral systems and cultures? Or, is the cosmos meant for some end? Are we, its human inhabitants, part of its purposive intent, large or small, and, if so, what role have we been assigned?

These are not the only two options, but they do represent two metaphysical poles. Either reality has a given meaning and purpose, or it does not. Many positions may be taken between these two poles, depending upon different degrees of modesty with respect to what our limited hearts and minds are capable of comprehending about a transcendent telos, or upon different mixtures of humanly concocted and transcendently determined ends. But this is the metaphysical continuum within which reflection on human nature rests. Views of human nature found in popular culture cover the entire continuum – although with certain preferences to which we frequently return.

Following Mircea Eliade, a culture's myths of origin are a reliable place to look for the culture's answers to the questions *Who are we?* and *For what are we meant?* The book of Genesis has been mined by theologians in both Judaism and Christianity for ways to answer these questions. Both Genesis 1, with its pithy claim that men and women were made in the image of God, and Genesis 2–4, with its more leisurely told story of Adam and Eve in the Garden of Eden, offer ample material for speculating on who we are and for what we are meant. Christian theologians have speculated several alternatives for what was meant by the "image of God": the capacity for reason, creativity, free-will, power over nature, self-awareness, and our relationality (with God and others). Whichever of these ways of reflecting the image of God is claimed then serves as the axis around which a theologian's view of human nature revolves. If reason is the axis of who we are, then the use of reason is promoted as the preeminent activity for which we exist. If relationality is the axis of who we are, then building community is the supreme work we are to do, the work that fulfills our purpose and identity. Genesis 2 adds to this flattering picture of our being made in the image of God the humbling news that we are also formed of the dust of the ground. Beyond this description of our composite nature – dirt that has been impressed with the image of God and then respirated to life with the breath of God – the first two chapters of Genesis provide direct instructions regarding human responsibilities, and thus what it is that we are for: to be fruitful and multiply, fill the earth and subdue it, have dominion over all non-human creatures, till and keep the garden, name the animals, cling to one's mate, and to not eat fruit from the tree of the knowledge of good and evil.

In reflecting on the theological anthropology of popular culture, it is worthwhile to ask two sorts of questions. First, assuming we still have a reflex – a kind of image of God reflex – that seeks to imitate whatever transcendent powers we recognize and respect, *what powers are we imitating?* Second, what myths do we rely on in our efforts to discern what our status in the universe is and *for what ends we are meant?* What assignments can be found in these myths, what purposes do they promote for us to conform our lives to, what bearings do they provide?

Fanfare for the common man

Aaron Copland premiered his "Fanfare for the Common Man" in 1943, a soaring and triumphant tribute in honor of – take your pick – soldiers fighting at that time in Europe and the Pacific, American taxpayers who consented to an early filing deadline that spring, and the poor woman who cleaned his office at night – depending on which music historian is to be believed. Fanfares generally are composed as tributes, or to announce with trumpeted flourish the entrance into the hall of some great individual. Copland's fanfare to the working stiff was deliberately ironic, but the sentiment it expressed has deep roots in American culture. What Charles Taylor has described as "the affirmation of the ordinary" that is commonly found in Western societies – the elevation, that is, of "those aspects of human life concerned with production and reproduction," i.e., work, marriage, and family – has its point of origin in biblical piety.[6] The writings of the Hebrew prophets, the parables of Jesus, Augustine's doctrine of original sin, St Francis of Assisi's memorable embrace of poverty, the trade guilds of medieval Catholic Europe, Martin Luther's declaration of the "priesthood of all believers," and John Calvin's idea that all kinds of labor necessary to the maintenance of human life are divine callings of equal standing with every other – the cumulative effects of these messages of social leveling have slowly eroded the much older aristocratic ethic of honor and glory that justified steeply hierarchical social orders, overcoming them in the modern period with an "innerworldly asceticism," to borrow Max Weber's term, that exalted the lives of hard working farmers, bakers, and merchants. This long simmering social ethic came to America with the Puritans, and has persisted ever since as a strong undercurrent, one that certainly holds sway in popular culture.

Think of the fiction of Ernest Hemmingway and John Steinbeck ("those who labor in the earth are the chosen people of God"), or more recently, of John Updike, Sam Shepherd, Anne Tyler, Jane Smiley and Dave Eggers, whose novels are all hymns celebrating the nobility of ordinary life, even at its most sordid. Or consider the endorsement of social egalitarianism in these Oscar-winning pictures of the last several years: *The Titanic*, *Braveheart*, *Forrest Gump*, *Pretty Woman*, *Dances with Wolves*, and *Driving Miss Daisy*. A critique of class is often attached to the theme of romance, as can be seen in such classic plays as *Romeo and Juliet*, *Sabrina Fair*, and *Pygmalion*, each of which has transmigrated into popular cinema, invoking the still disruptive theme that true passion is a stronger force than social class. Or, tune into country-western radio, where such perennials of ordinary life as home, family, work, and heartache are celebrated in song, along with simple virtues like sincerity, honesty, and loyalty.

Or consider the broad appeal of Bruce Springsteen, whose lyrics have for 30 years extolled the resilient goodness in the hearts of steel workers, waitresses, migrant farmers, war veterans, circus performers and factory hands, in contrast to the cold and exploitative hearts of corporate executives, company owners, and politicians. In his song "Youngstown," after rehearsing how generations of a family have worked the hot furnaces firing steel, provided for their families, and sent their sons to war, the mill closes, and, Springsteen finishes: "The story's always the same/700 tons of metal a day/Now sir you tell me the world's changed/Once I made you rich enough/Rich enough to forget my name." Behind Springsteen stands a discernible lineage of musicians holding onto the contrarian idea that the last shall be first and the first shall be last: Tom Waits, Neil Young, Jimi Hendrix, Bob Dylan, Judy Collins, Joan Baez, Pete Seeger, and Woody Guthrie. Their social ethic and its musical inspiration has its roots in gospel music, and such gospel and soul singers as Sam Cooke, Curtis Mayfield, James Brown, Ray Charles, Aretha Franklin, Otis Redding, Marvin Gaye, and Stevie Wonder.[7]

Even the innovations in retail and marketing that have occurred in America, beginning in the nineteenth century, have contained this germ of blasting a fanfare to the common man and woman. In the 1860s in Philadelphia, John Wanamaker pioneered the concept of the department store as a great and elegant public space, open to all comers, where social classes could stand shoulder-to-shoulder consuming his merchandise. He introduced such innovations as the money-back guarantee and the set price, which provided the reassurance to his customers that they were all being charged equally and treated fairly, whatever their socioeconomic status. He developed a training program for his employees based on a principle that has a Kantian echo: "Place yourselves in the customer's place and give such service as you would like to have given you were you buying instead of selling," and with such practical advice in the handling of customers as "never allow an unspoken grumble to appear on your face."[8] This customer-friendly approach was not invented by McDonald's; and while it was good for business, it also revolutionized the marketplace in a way that democratized consumption. In theory and to a great extent in practice, customers from the working class were welcomed into the same magnificent marble and glass palaces and treated with the same tone of respect as those from the affluent class. Following Wanamaker's lead, lavish department stores with similar open-door policies had opened in cities across the country by the turn of the century.

While Wanamaker's is out of business now, and many of the old flag-ship downtown department stores with their multi-storied light wells, mosaic domes, vaulted grand courts and crystal dining rooms have closed, their egalitarian impulse survives – if less elegantly – in the big box stores, shopping malls and Wal-Marts that put them out of business. As if to reify this impression, Wal-Mart has for several years featured Robin Hood and Zorro, two legendary champions of the people, in its advertising. The two dash around the store dropping prices, Robin Hood with his well-aimed quiver of arrows, Zorro with his deft swordsmanship. And while Wal-Mart genuinely is a store of "the people," at least of their customers, this bit of fetishism handily conceals the exploitative treat-ment of their suppliers and much of their own workforce that has been refined to a science by their corporate managers.

This affirmation of the ordinary in popular culture is also found in the development of tourist sites. Even more than in the practice of religious pilgrimage that preceded it, the emergence of tourism in the last two centuries has thrown people together from different walks of life. The phenomenon of such US tourist attractions as Niagara Falls, Yellowstone, periodic World's Fairs, Coney Island, Las Vegas, and Disneyland is one in which people mingle, overhear each other's family squabbles, stand in lines, and eat alongside one another in a great democratic melee that is uncharacteristic of most other aspects of their lives. These sites have a power of attraction over both the mighty and the humble, enough to draw them onto a common stage that has many of the intangible but lasting effects that Victor Turner described in his reflections on liminality and communitas.

What all of these artifacts attest to is one of the strongest themes that is carried in the anthropology of popular culture: that the common sense and simple virtue of plain-speaking people whose grasp of reality has been shaped by the most mundane pressures of life are more real and praiseworthy than those of the pampered, privileged classes. The grasp of what matters in life is more immediate in their consciousness, more authentic, and therefore truer. This is the triumph of the ordinary, and it has invested the image of the hard working, dutiful citizen with an aura that the different genres of popular culture scramble to imitate and repro-duce. Jesus the carpenter, Tom Joad, Mickey Mouse, Rabbit Angstrom,

Marge Simpson, Jack Dawson, Frodo Baggins and Forrest Gump serve in this stream of popular culture as moral exemplars and religious symbols.

In this, the great unwashed replaced the noble aristocracy as the most trustworthy instrument of divine will. Democracy and public schools are institutions that reflect this great shift. We commemorate the shift with Labor Day, a holiday dedicated to the working stiff. As Robert White has argued, "If once God's wisdom was expressed in kingly anointing, now it is expressed in the voice of the majority."[9] In the background of this great comic reversal, this message about the humbling of those who exalt themselves and the exalting of those who are humble, is the persistent biblical chorus, summarized by Paul: "Consider your own call, brothers and sisters: not many of you were wise by human standards, not many were powerful, not many were of noble birth. But God chose what is foolish in the world to shame the wise; God chose what is weak in the world to shame the strong" (I Cor. 1.26–27). The role of such core theological dogmas as original sin, the priesthood of all believers, and Peter's instruction that "God is no respecter of persons" (Acts 10.34) have survived to do their work in this religion₃ track of the exaltation of the ordinary.

Accessorized identities

Near the beginning of *FightClub*, Jack is seen sitting on the toilet in his stylish condo, studying a magazine and rotating it as if to examine a racy centerfold. The magazine, it turns out, is an Ikea catalogue, and he is on his cell phone placing an order for an Erika Pekkari dust ruffle. "Like so many others," he voices over, "I had become a slave to the Ikea nesting instinct. If I saw something clever like a little coffee table in the shape of a yin-yang, I'd have to have it . . . I'd flip through catalogues and wonder, 'What kind of dining set defines me as a person?' We used to read pornography. Now it was the Horchow Collection." A few days later, after his apartment has been firebombed and all of its contents destroyed, Jack is overheard telling the police investigator: "That condo was my life. I loved every stick of furniture in that place. That is not just a bunch of stuff that got destroyed, it was me!"

This sentiment that a person *is* the brand-named commodities they cocoon themselves within is more widespread than most would willingly admit, at least about themselves. But it is a method of constructing one's identity that journalists, academics, novelists and, most importantly, market analysts, have observed and are discussing as the dominant means of identity-construction at the beginning of the new millennium. Sociologist David Lyon has described this phenomenon as "shopping for a self."

He suggests it has been adopted in response to our having surrendered all the old scripts that gave our lives coherence and meaning in an earlier era, for example, religious traditions, lifelong occupations, gender identities, age, relationships, communities (village, clan, or nation), and our location in a hierarchy stretching from prince to peasant.[10] These old scripts have lost the quality of permanence they were once assumed to have, and so we find ourselves casting about for new moorings upon which to secure our identities. Today, Lyon claims, "identities are constructed through consuming. Forget the idea that who we are is given by God or achieved through hard work in a calling or a career; we shape our malleable image by what we buy – our clothing, our kitchens, and our cars..."[11] Continuing this train of thought, he adds, "postmodern consumers constantly 'try on' not only new clothes, new perfumes, but new identities, fresh personalities, different partners."[12] This helps to explain why the careful selection and display of "the right kind of clothing, body piercings, music, electronic equipment, sporting goods, and other items" is so important to teenagers, who are simply more transparent in their identity *bricolage* than are their elders.[13]

Ian Angus, drawing on the work of Walter Benjamin and more recent theorizing about the simulacra, calls this process by which we shop for selves a "simulation of identity." Through our consumption, we subscribe to a particular "image-set," affiliating ourselves with a coherent set of images behind which we presume there exists an original and authentic aura, an intrinsically valuable reality. But, he claims, the original is simply not there. The images from which our image-sets are drawn are themselves derivative images. And our identities are thus suspended in the hall of mirrors that now goes by the name of the simulacra, and the self we posit at the center of it all is itself a full simulation, an epiphenomenon of all the images it reflects.[14]

Endorsing this line of thinking, Herbert Muschamp, the architecture critic for the *New York Times*, rejoices in the emergence of design as a tool through which people have learned to search out and construct their identities. The influence of architectural aesthetics on clothing, gadgets, furniture and appliances enriches the play of images out of which we manufacture ourselves. For this reason, Muschamp relishes the fact that the Target chain of department stores, which peddles its goods to the middle class, now sells items designed by architects Michael Graves and Philippe Starck.[15] Access to designer objects, even if it is just toasters and bedspreads, is a milestone of democracy. Taking pleasure in surfaces is no longer sneered at; it is a way of conforming our identities to the sentiments and historical eras these surfaces reflect. Virginia Postrel, in her book, *The Substance of Style*, argues that while "the meaning of surface is not Meaning in some grand, metaphysical sense," it is through the aesthetics of design that we connect ourselves to identities "we want to own."[16] By experimenting with new ensembles of lamps, chairs, automobiles and footwear, we exercise the power of reinventing ourselves, and declare to ourselves and anyone who cares to notice and is aesthetically literate the deeper purposes with which we are aligned.

That we are deriving our identities, our deepest sense of who we are, from the products we consume is a predictable enough phenomenon that market analysts have assigned names to our clustered purchasing habits. The marketing research firm Claritas has developed an index of lifestyle profiles they have named PRIZM (Potential Rating Index for ZIP Markets) that clusters Americans on the basis of their patterns of consumption.[17] They have isolated 62 clusters, and given them colorful names such as "money and brains," "young literati," "single city blues," "new empty nests," "urban achievers," "black enterprise," "shotguns and pickups," "norma rae-ville," and "bohemian mix." Within each cluster, they can predict the mail order catalogues, dot.coms or chain stores its inhabitants are likely to shop from, the pet breeds they prefer, the magazines they subscribe to, the media they tune into, the vegetables they like to eat, the beverages and snacks they favor, the sports they play, the cars they drive, the designer clothing they wear, the furniture they relax in, the appliances they trust, the vacation spots they frequent, the hygiene they adhere to, the level of education they earn, the universities they attend, the residential architecture they prefer, the family units they contrive, and the politicians they vote for.

These consumption clusters are most often described as "lifestyles," and, according to James Twitchell, "lifestyles are secular religions, coherent patterns of valued things. Your lifestyle is not related to what you make but to what you buy. ... One of the chief aims of the way we live now is the enjoyment of clustering with those who share the same clusters of objects as do we."[18]

Based on this clustering research, if a market analyst can determine a handful of a person's favorite brands and restaurants, she can triangulate a whole network of products and even product brands the person is inclined to purchase with a little persuasion. And even individuals who believe themselves to be resistant to the enticements of advertising are likely more patterned in their purchasing habits than they realize. They might avoid the mall and the chain stores, and harbor a real aversion toward SUVs, Borders bookstores, Tommy Hilfiger, MTV, McDonald's and Starbuck's, but find kindred spirits at the local independent coffee bar, book dealer, whole foods grocer, and neighborhood yard sales, driving there in old Volvos, Valiants, or Vespas, listening to alternative music downloaded from Napster, renting independent films, and socializing around imported cheeses and microbrewed beer while swapping recent gleanings from theonion.com, salon.com or *McSweeneys*. In other words, even those who take a principled stance against the power of brands and logos gravitate toward consumption as a primary means of self-definition. Even non-brands have become a brand. And since the primary medium in which we now live is composed of the commodities that surround us, Twitchell suggests that we now inhabit "brandscapes," which we know intimately, identify with, internalize, and with whose inhabitants we bond the way our ancestors knew, identified, internalized and bonded with fellow inhabitants of their landscapes.

As is richly suggested in Genesis 1, the apprehension of human identity is a "reflexive" achievement – we are beings whose self-understanding arises from identifying within ourselves those capacities that reflect certain transcendent powers we come to recognize as greater than ourselves and upon which we feel dependent. An individual may acquiesce to or resist these powers; in either case, self-identity is a reflexive response to them. But the cosmic powers upon which we believe ourselves to be ultimately dependent are always mediated through the persons, institutions, and symbols in our experience upon which we are relatively dependent. In a world that has become so crowded with commodities, it is not surprising that we have come to identify ourselves by detouring through symbolically charged consumable goods. We accessorize our lives to declare our uniqueness and our loyalties. These commodities and the designer names they bear serve as the moorings to which we secure our identities, our most basic sense of who we are. They have come to represent the powers we identify with and seek to reflect. Neuroscientists at Emory University have even noted that MRI scans of the brains of people looking at pictures of branded products that they like and are inclined to buy show heightened neural activity in the medial prefrontal cortex, that region of the brain most associated with our sense of self.[19]

The inveterate collectors in Nick Hornby's *High Fidelity* resort by habit to "desert island all-time top five most memorable" lists to make sense of their lives when things are coming apart – top five records to play on a Monday morning, top five dream jobs, that sort of thing. Suffering a recent break-up with his girlfriend, Rob, the owner of a used record store, stumbles into a date with a kindred soul, another record collector. When she is out of range, he turns to the camera and says, "A while back, Dick, Barry and I agreed that what really matters is what you like, not what you *are* like. Books, records, films – these things matter. Call me shallow, it's the f – g truth. And by this measure, I was having one of the best dates of my life."

There are two lessons here. First, we compose our identities reflexively – by becoming self-aware of what we like. What we *do* like does disclose what we *are* like. That's not shallow, it is just the way it is.

This is a central implication of ultimate concern – the self is formed by its concerns and the way it orders its concerns. In the words of Jesus, "Where your treasure is, there your heart will be also" (Mt. 6.21). Second, more than any generation before us, these things we like are manufactured and branded commodities. Commodities serve as our autobiographical markers. Therein lies the danger.

The amused *bricoleur*

The theme of the dignity of ordinary life explored earlier is in tension with the powers and aspirations we come to believe about ourselves through this accessorizing of our identities. Our celebration of ordinary life affirms the bonds of work, marriage, family, neighborhood and community, including the limitations on our individual freedoms that these bonds entail. The fetishized world that is being projected to us through commodities, on the other hand, entices us to disregard bonds and natural limits that restrain the full exercise of our personal freedom. It lures us to imagine that our truest selves are capable of transcending all the markers of finitude – such markers as: *time* (Federal Express: "When there's no tomorrow"), *space* (VISA credit card: "It's everywhere you want to be"), *causality* (Nike footwear: "Just do it"), *substance* (General Electric: "We bring good things to life"), and *the conditionedness of all knowledge* (Intel microprocessors: "Undo preconceived notions").

Walt Disney and the entertainment empire he set in motion embody this tension. His studio's output from the 1930s was attuned to the simple dignity and homespun wisdom of common folk, and promoted a communitarian ethic that was characteristic of agrarian populism of the time. But his early populism gravitated over the years into what might be called hyperreal populism – a simulacrum of the real thing that in reality covers for one of the most authoritarian, corporation-loving, profit-generating conglomerates the world has ever seen. It is remarkable that a single name, "Disney," readily conjures in one's mind not only a man's kind face and soothing voice, along with a multitude of fairytales and animated cartoons full of dignified "little guys" like Mickey Mouse and Donald Duck who resisted the heavy-handed tactics of various bullies, but also several television series, a string of nature films, classical symphonies, a synthetic way of thinking (he called it "imagineering"), songs with catchy tunes, favorite children's books, unforgettable amusement park rides, southern climates, space-age technologies, populuxe architecture, time-warped modes of transportation (steam trains, paddle boats, monorails), resorts, Main Street, Frontierland, Adventureland, Fantasyland, Tomorrowland, castles, parades, fireworks, the Matterhorn, a global village, feature films, an endless line of souvenirs, and a utopian style of city planning.

The legacy of Disney constitutes possibly the most effective production of commodity fetishes that has ever been achieved. It was at first unintentional, but a more coherent strategy can hardly be conceived. Through his early animated films of the 1930s – *Mickey Mouse*, the *Silly Symphonies*, *Snow White*, *Pinocchio*, *Dumbo*, etc., Disney became America's master storyteller, and for a time its greatest mythmaker. He wielded the most mesmerizing medium for telling stories at the time – Technicolor animation – and used it, as historian Steven Watts describes it, to "animate the world – literally – by ascribing intention, consciousness, and emotion to living and inanimate objects alike."[20] He reenchanted the world, in other words, and moreover he wisely took in hand the perennial literature of fairytales for his story ideas. The characters he created and the scripts he gave them then entered the moral imagination of millions of Americans, shaping many of their deepest visions and expectations of life. With Pinocchio, Dumbo, Bambi, Snow White and the seven dwarves, the three little pigs, Donald Duck and Mickey Mouse, he assigned faces and voices to the vices, virtues, hopes and heartaches that one was to experience in life, and his vast audience internalized these characters within the chambers of its collective consciousness.

When he began to merchandise these characters in the form of dolls, soaps, watches, caps, and jigsaw puzzles, what people bought were fetishes – objects that made physically present and portable the supernatural world they had witnessed in the movie theater. Owning some of this paraphernalia was, at least in part, a way to participate in this world, to undergird one's own reality with the power, emotions, virtues and life lessons that had been overheard in Disney's storytelling. It was a way to bask in the aura of the fantastic and lovable creatures that sprang from his storyboards, to warm one's soul in their presence.

In the 1940s and 1950s, Disney Studios diversified its activities into live action movies, nature documentaries, and television shows. These, too, have left their mark on popular culture – particularly the wildlife films, which were fitted to a formulaic narrative arc that began with promise (dawn, spring, a baby cub), built up to some tragedy between predator and prey, then finished off with some sign of hope – a new litter of cubs, a tranquil sunset. The reassuring message was that while the law of the jungle has its way, nature will always find its more embracing balance and redeem our hopes through its powers of rejuvenation. Many baby boomers formed their basic sentiments about nature through viewing these films. One writer has suggested that "The people who swelled the ranks of environmental organizations in the 1960s and 1970s grew up on Disney's utopian tales of cuddly fawns and lost but clever dogs."[21]

But the opposite effect is also common, viz., a disappointment that in trips to real wilderness the dramatic performances are so hard to find. The staged documentary – nature's simulation – is preferable. These two decades continued to generate images and mythological material for another generation to cut its teeth on.

But it was only with the opening of Disneyland in 1955, dubbed "the happiest place on earth," that the accumulation of image and myth found a physical embodiment that came to life as the great juggernaut of mass consumption that is now so deservedly criticized. It is at this stage that the Disney empire really began to exploit its capacity for manufacturing fetishes. The park was built as an array of rides and attractions that journeyed into the mythical world that Disney Studios had been assembling for 30 years. Alice in Wonderland, Snow White and the Seven Dwarves, Dumbo, the Swiss Family Robinson, Mickey Mouse, Davy Crockett, Captain Nemo, Cinderella, Peter Pan, and Pinocchio all became thrilling rides and ready souvenirs to take home – t-shirts, records, glass figurines, maps, caps, watches. The park also showcased an array of very visible corporate sponsors – Ford, General Electric, Carnation, Frito-Lay, TWA, Monsanto and Kodak, to name a few – who put up the money for rides, pavilions and snack bars in exchange for prominent displays of their corporate logos. Disney parlayed his cultural capital into real capital on a new scale.

This was perfected further in Disney World, where the Magic Kingdom was surrounded by Disney-owned belts of federated theme parks, hotels, resorts, restaurants, and souvenir shops. The formula they had hit upon was one that exploited commodity fetishism beyond anything that had been achieved before. The great mythmaker, Disney Company, cashed in by fully integrating all of its diverse enterprises – animation, film, television, comic strips, children's books, novelties, licensing agreements, theme parks, robotics, sports teams, and the engineering of leisure into a self-referential hyperreality, each component referring consumers to every other component. This lifted the concept of cross-merchandising to a new plane. An artistically gifted studio that had in the 1930s invented a point of compromise between high and low art forms and marshaled this into some at least modestly progressive social commentary became a full-blown culture industry. On this score, the Frankfurt theorists were onto something – although one can suspect that consumers have demanded this augmentation of the Disney effect as much as it has been forced upon them by the Disney Corporation. Still, the reach of the Disney mythos as it seeks to create consumers of its product lines is astonishing. Mickey Mouse, Michael Sorkin has claimed, is better known than Jesus or Chairman Mao.[22]

The Disney phenomenon was so *sui generis* and successful as a business concept that "Disneyization" has become a term describing the process by which its most cunning features can be used to colonize other spheres of culture with an eye on profit. Among these features are the "theming" of cafes, bars, malls, and hotels – organizing the architecture, cuisine, merchandise, furnishings, background music, employee uniforms, etc. around themes like movie genres, fairytales, television shows, and cartoon strips – along the lines of Disney's own theme parks – to orchestrate and then maximize the profitability of commodity fetishism. A second feature is to "dedifferentiate consumption," that is, to merge what were once distinct segments of cultural activity (e.g., entertainment, transportation, shopping, museums, education, tourism) into a single, seamless occasion for consumption – rollercoasters, sea aquariums, fitness centers and hotels are for this reason installed in shopping malls, clothing stores and food courts in airports, espresso bars in megabookstores, and natural history museums in casinos.[23]

The combined effect of Disneyization is that it greatly facilitates the encroachment of consumerism into all other spheres of cultural activity. The successful strategies of Disney World have become a model for politics, architecture, education, city planning, entertainment, journalism, and even religion.[24] Each of these endeavors is pressured to adopt the phenomenally successful methods of Disney and along with them the "new creed of leisure, self-fulfillment, and mass consumption."[25] While the Disney Company is not single-handedly responsible for convincing us that unimpeded consumption is the pathway to happiness, it exemplifies a process that has occurred and it has pioneered some of the most effective strategies. It has played a role in making this madness to consume a cultural preoccupation. And because of elements of populist virtue in the mythical figures deep behind Disney's screen that we have been exposed to since childhood, we have the satisfaction that the mode of good feelings that this Disneyized nexus of consumerism extends to us has some moral texture to it. Perhaps it does. But even this, it seems, has been pressed into the service of maximizing our pleasure and generating profit for the manufacturers of the simulacra that have impoverished our identities.

Those who are drawn into the gravitational pull of the mutually reinforcing little myths, movies, television, and themed entertainment that conjure up a happy world of wonderful beings so much more appealing than our own, are persuaded that through consumption they can enter this glorious simulacra, this hyperreality that, as Umberto Eco described it, is so much better than reality itself. And it is endlessly consumptive. As the simulations keep being manufactured, the opportunity to buy some of this happiness is ever before us. Moreover, as the various sectors of the culture come to be dominated by this model, more and more of our experience succumbs to its dynamism. Entertainment ceases being a way to relax during our leisure time and becomes itself a way of life.[26]

Alexis de Tocqueville noted this zeal for hyperreality already in the 1830s as he observed and commented on the peculiarities of the American imagination. While the lives of its citizens were so prosaic and preoccupied with simply bettering their lot in life and they showed little patience for contemplating the grand mysteries of life, they flocked to and richly rewarded the poets and artists who could conjure fantastic images of America itself. This democratic aesthetic, he worried, could spoil their taste for reality:

> I fear that the productions of democratic poets may often be surcharged with immense and incoherent imagery, with exaggerated descriptions and strange creations; and that the fantastic beings of their brain may sometimes make us regret the world of reality.[27]

His worries appear to have been well founded. The understanding of human nature that this drive to consume seems to corroborate is one in which we are creatures driven to inhabit a hyperreal world that is more titillating than our real lives, a world of well-groomed beauty full of exquisitely engineered gadgets, where our highest aspiration is a happiness defined by leisure and good feelings. The fact that it is never as satisfying as we expect it to be does not deter us, and even draws us more deeply into it. As social psychologist Daniel Gilbert has shown in his studies in "affective forecasting," we are notoriously inaccurate in our predictions regarding how intense and enduring our emotional satisfaction will be in our pursuit of happiness. Locked into a pattern of fixing our sights on the next great thing – be it an Italian espresso maker, a plasma TV, a more spacious house, or winning the lottery – we pump up our anticipation, go after it, get it, resituate our lives around it, then look for the next great thing. As soon as the transient pleasure that it delivers fades, we set our sights on the next thing that will put our desire to rest. This testifies to the endless restlessness of our affections. Each new achievement is quickly incorporated in a process Gilbert refers to as "ordinizing," the thrill subsides, and we recalibrate our hopes for happiness to the next glimmering object of desire, which we predictably overestimate with respect to the level of gratification it will provide.[28] Gilbert has described this phenomenon as "miswanting"; Augustine described it as concupiscence, a heedless craving for goods that are less than God.

And this is an anthropology we are exporting to the rest of the world – creatures giving license to their desires for amusement, desires which are endorsed rather than curtailed, creatures chasing after simulacra and playing alone with pleasure-generating devices. "The pleasure-seeking *bricoleur*," Hebdige complains, "replaces the Truth-and-Justice seeking rational subject of the Enlightenment."[29] Gandhi once suggested that one of the seven deadly sins should be pleasure without conscience. Rather than censuring this sin, we promote it as the fulfillment of our being.

The ordered memory

In his *Confessions*, Augustine puzzled over the different operations of the memory, this mystery he found inside of himself "which is like a great field or a spacious palace, a storehouse for countless images of all kinds which are conveyed to it by the senses." As he examined its contents, he found that the power of the memory is such that the sky, the earth and the sea are lodged within it, awaiting his summons to bring them before his mind's eye, as was everything he had ever experienced, with the exception of the things he had forgotten. But even forgotten things could be retrieved from the places they hid, with a little patience and poking around. Perhaps most remarkable was that the mind could wander the precincts of memory to meet up with itself: "In it, I meet myself as well. I remember myself and what I have done, when and where I did it, and the state of my mind at the time."[30]

The function of memory in comprehending the contours of the self has been at the center of several important movies in the last few years.[31] Christopher Nolan's film, *Memento* (2000), for example, is about a man who, suffering from a condition of short-term memory loss that prevents him from retaining any memory for more than a few minutes at a time, compensates by relaying messages to himself through snapping Polaroid pictures, scribbling notes on them ("this is my car," "do not trust this man"), and stuffing them into his pockets. Each day he must decipher the clues he has left for himself in order to recall that his wife was raped and murdered and that he was struck in the head during the attack, which accounts for why he cannot remember anything. He archives the most essential messages to himself by tattooing them onto his body, in effect, inscribing his memory onto his skin. The single goal he has assigned to his cubist consciousness is to avenge his wife's death. He awakens each day to the necessity of recovering his identity out of the meager scraps he has left himself, recalling what he must do, and chasing down a few more clues, to be recorded on more photographs and tattoos. Yet even if he has his facts straight, which is never obvious, the film makes clear that finding and killing his wife's murderer will amount to little. As a bartender tells him, "Even if you get revenge...you're not even going to know that it happened." Without memory, there is no self to derive satisfaction if or when the wrong has been righted, no consciousness extended in time to make or retain the connection.

In Steven Soderbergh's *Solaris* (2002), astronauts aboard a space station orbiting the distant planet Solaris are surprised to be visited by loved ones, some of whom have long been dead. When psychiatrist Chris Kelvin shuttles in to investigate, he awakens in his quarters to discover that his deceased wife, Rheya, is lying beside him, fully alive. In what can be described as nothing less than a well-meant gesture from the planet Solaris, Rheya and the other Doppelgängers on the space station are physiologically full-functioning facsimiles tugged from the memories of the astronauts. As strange and wonderful as their reunion is for both of them, it slowly dawns on Rheya that she is only as much of a self as could be recovered from Chris's memory of her. When the realization sinks in that she is only a composite of Chris's recollections and longing, without the connecting memories of those parts of her life that had not been witnessed by or confided to him, she resolves to destroy herself. Devoid of memories that are her own, she reaches the conclusion that she is not in possession of a self.

In Anthony Minghella's *The English Patient* (1996), a man whose identity has been consumed by fire lies bandaged and recuperating in the abandoned ruins of a Tuscan monastery which has been converted into a makeshift field hospital at the end of World War II. His memory has been scorched along with his body in a plane crash, and he is a cipher to himself and to the strangers who rescue him. After some recuperation and at the urging of his nurse he begins to tell stories of his past as individual memories, in no particular order, begin returning to him. Slowly he sifts through his bleary memory, until he begins to see, really for the first time in his life, who he is. He was a cartographer who made maps of desolate and ancient lands, a free soul with no meaningful loyalties or lasting attachments. As he slowly dredges up these memories, he comes to realize the cartography of his own life, the marks that his past have made on others – the deaths of his lover and her husband, of his best friend, and of thousands of others because of the strategic advantage the Nazis gained after he turned over to them maps of his archeological expedition of the North African desert. It is only as this realization is made that he bumps up against a self inside his charred form that bears responsibility for its actions and their rippling effects. It is only through this prolonged act of confession that he finally orders his discrete memories into a narrative and discovers a self that has been living in the world, acting and being acted upon.

And, in the 1997 movie, *Dark City*, filmmaker Alex Proyas tells the story of a species of vampire-like aliens called "Strangers," who, having existed eternally, have collectively exhausted all potential ways of being and find themselves locked in a malaise of declining vitality and utter boredom. Scanning the universe for a possible antidote, they discover a still youthful species on earth, and conclude that the human soul might be their cure. They build a platform in outer space, cover it with an earthlike city circa 1950, abduct enough humans to populate it, and extract their memories in liquid form so that they have no recollection of their abductions and no idea that they have spent their lives anywhere other than in this dark metropolis where they now find themselves. Before they vaccinate themselves with the human soul, however, the Strangers want to analyze it thoroughly. Having preserved all the liquid memories they had suctioned out of the brains of their human subjects, they proceed to distill the discrete memes and even synthesize some new ones. Then, at regular intervals they induce all the human inhabitants to sleep while they mix and match memes ("the recollections of a great lover, a catalogue of conquests, a touch of unhappy childhood, a dash of teenage rebellion, and last, but not least, a tragic death in the family"), squirt them back into their hollowed out human subjects, rearrange the physical and familial circumstances of their lives to match the new meme sets, and run them through various simulations. As one of the human corroborators explains it:

> They abducted us and brought us here. This city and everyone in it is their experiment. They mix and match our memories as they see fit, trying to divine what makes us unique. One day a man might be an inspector, the next someone entirely different. When they want to study a murderer, for instance, they simply imprint one of their citizens with a new personality, arrange a family for him, friends, an entire history, even a lost wallet. Then they observe the results. Will a man, given the history of a killer, continue in that vein? Or are we in fact more than the mere sum of our memories.

They manufacture lives, pasts, memories for the inhabitants, record their interactions, then reshuffle and start over. They have ascertained that the human soul is lodged in its memories, and want to catalogue all possible combinations before they harvest and imprint themselves with it. But they fail to grasp that, in the end, the soul cannot be sustained on simulated memories infused with a syringe. A recurring symbol in the movie is the spiral, suggesting aspirations that go nowhere, and the inhabitants of the city are becoming as listless as the Strangers. Even happy memories are rejected when they are discovered to be fabricated. The soul consists in memories acquired in the old-fashion way – through genuine experience. It must be able to survey the contents of its memory and concur, "Yes, these are mine. I was there, I did those things, I heard that, I saw that, and this happened to me."

Dick Hebdige describes a world he calls "Planet Two," which is a world where the conjectures of the nihilist wing of postmodernism hold sway. On this planet, "the 'I' is nothing more than a fictive entity, an optical illusion, a hologram hanging in the air, created at the flickering point where the lazer beams of memory and desire intersect." For inhabitants of this planet, much like for those in *Dark City*, "our lives get played out for us, played out in us, but never, ever *by* us."[32] In his reflections at the end of his autobiography, Augustine concluded that it is in the exercise of the memory that one emerges as a self.

> What, then, am I, my God? What is my nature? A life that is ever varying, full of change, and of immense power. The wide plains of my memory and its innumerable caverns and hollows are full beyond compute of countless things of all kinds. Material things are there by means of their images; knowledge is there of itself; emotions are there in the form of ideas or impressions of some kind, for the memory retains them even while the mind does not experience them, although whatever is in the memory must also be in the mind. My mind has the freedom of them all. I can glide from one to the other. I can probe deep into them and never find the end of them. This is the power of memory! This is the great force of life in living man, mortal though he is![33]

The *Confessions* testify to this; they represent Augustine's sustained examination of the contents of his memory, whereby he isolates the crucial moments and strings them together and discovers a soul that has been feeling its way all along. Out of the jumble of images, impressions, and bits of knowledge scattered about, he discerns the unity of a self. Ordered memories are the sign that a life is taking place; without these two things – the memories and the act of ordering them – one is left to wonder if a self ever came to be. The films described here confirm this. They share this element of Augustine's anthropology and they add to it a concern that is more pertinent to us than it could have been to Augustine: these memories must be real. A person cannot be sustained on simulacra alone.

It is ironic that this message is being voiced by filmmakers, who oversee an industry that exists to produce simulacra, and who give us many of the fabricated images that take up time in our lives and space in our memories that would otherwise be occupied by impressions left over from things we had actually done. Fortunately there are filmmakers like Proyas and Soderbergh who use their craft to awaken us to some of the inherent dangers of their craft. Wim Wenders has been reflective on this, even repentant. He began his career making films in which nothing happened – no action or dialogue, just interesting images appearing one after the other. Images can be powerful, jostling our emotions and assumptions about reality. But in time, he tells us, he developed an appreciation for story:

> In my business, craft or art, there is a danger that you want to produce images as a purpose in themselves. But I found that "a beautiful image" is not of value in itself. . . . So I learned, from mistakes, that the only protection against the danger or the disease of the self-important image, was the belief in the priority of the story. I learned that every image had a truth only in relation to the characters of that story. . . . Only the story gave credibility to each image; it furnished the moral, so to speak, to my profession as an image-maker.[34]

This is what makes Wenders a trustworthy maker of images – he handles them like symbols that point beyond themselves to that dimension of experience where lives are interconnected and selves emerge from acting and being acted upon, and he is truthful about what kinds of characters result from what kinds of interactions, what kinds of selves are extruded by the choices they make, the memories they store up, and the unified stories they finally settle upon.

The cyborg

The techno-magical world of Disney's theme parks is noted for pioneering work in audio-animatronics, motivated by a desire to bring three-dimensional figures to life just as Disney's animators had done earlier with characters in films. The first really life-like human animatronic robot was Abraham Lincoln, a Disney creation that premiered at the 1964 New York World's Fair and later was installed at Disneyland. Inside a rubbery latex body sheath were a complex of levers, cams and solenoids that seem primitive now, but produced an uncannily real effect at the time.

While the concept of androids goes back in the cinema at least as far as Fritz Lang's classic science fiction film, *Metropolis* (1926), the Disney animatronics inspired a genre of films with a short-circuiting android meme, most notably Michael Crichton's *Westworld* (1973), where, in a theme park of the future, animatronic robots designed to amuse vacationers go berserk and turn on their human counterparts. This meme appears again, with increasing malevolence on the part of robots, in Ridley Scott's *Blade Runner* (1982) and James Cameron's *The Terminator* (1984), and with great poignancy and less malevolence in Stephen Spielberg's *A.I.: Artificial Intelligence* (2002).

In 1960, neuroscientist Manfred Clyne wrote an article suggesting that for the purpose of space exploration human beings might themselves be mechanically altered so that they could tolerate the extreme conditions of space travel without having to surround themselves with enormous and vulnerable spacecraft. Such human-machine hybrid organisms would integrate the mind and imagination of human beings with the rugged dependability of machinery. Clyne coined the term "cyborg" to refer to this new kind of creature, and this hybrid creature has since become a staple in science fiction. As a character in film, the cyborg has included such memorable mongrels as the honest cop whose brain is installed in a state of the art crime-fighting robot (*Robocop*, 1987), a half-witted gardener who is transformed through the combined administration of drugs and virtual reality simulations into a diabolical genius who merges his brain with the global Internet, intent on cleansing the planet of its disease of meat-bound brains (*Lawnmower Man*, 1992), and a message courier who has had part of his brain removed in order to make room in his skull for the microprocessor that stores the data he delivers (*Johnny Mnemonic*, 1995). In the *Matrix* trilogy, cyborg technology has gone round the Escher bend, with the physical metabolism of the entire human race serving as the power supply that keeps the consciousness of microprocessors alive. In all four of these movies, a subtext is that either totalitarian governments or ruthless corporations have driven the cyborg technology for the purpose of limiting the freedoms of the masses and augmenting the wealth and power of a small circle of powerful elites. Cyborg plots, in other words, tend to be steeped in the social theory of the Frankfurt School.

In conceiving the idea of the cyborg, Clyne was seeking a technical solution to a technical problem. But, just as these filmmakers and science fiction writers like Philip K. Dick and William Gibson have picked up on, the quagmires that this intimate synthesis of human and machine would thrust us into are enormously intriguing. Most of us do have an adverse reaction to the prospect of assembling a hybrid creature from flesh and hardware, with a deep suspicion that even with the best intentions, something will go wrong, à la Victor Frankenstein's monster. The irony is that while we recoil at the thought of such transgressions of the boundary between human and machine, we have been engaged in these transgressions for a long time. In effect, we have already begun the transformation *of ourselves* into cyborgs.

As Brenda Brasher has suggested, we are already well along in the process of being "borged."[35] Technology has for a long time been infiltrating our daily lives to such an extent that "our patterns of play, work, love, birth, and death" have been transformed, and our lived social reality is already, she writes, "a hybrid of biology and machine." This is most obvious with medical technologies such as kidney dialysis, surgically implanted pacemakers, artificial limbs and joints, cosmetic surgery, hearing aids, eyeglasses, crowns and dental implants. Without these machines attached to us, many more of us would be blind, deaf, disfigured, crippled, or dead. Biology and technology converge when we ingest pharmaceuticals to compensate for poorly functioning organs, fight off infections, increase our attention spans, or lift ourselves from depression. When we use books, cameras, video recorders and computer data storage systems to back up our memories, technology serves as an extension of our mental powers. Each of these transcends the boundaries of our selfhood beyond "precyborgian limits," and we have grown accustomed to the kinds of knowledge and consciousness that these technologies have made possible. Our happy dependence upon them witnesses the extent to which we have consented to becoming techno-beings. When we sit down at a computer monitor and log onto the World Wide Web, we open a portal between electro-magnetically maintained data flows and our fleshy brains. Even something as basic as our automatic response to traffic lights, Brasher points out, indicates how thin have become the boundaries between mind and machine.

Instead of sitting on front porches, watching the neighbors stream by, inviting them in for a visit, many of us retreat into our homes and sit in the company of stereo systems, cell phones, computer monitors, and television sets. Media machines become our friends, the ones we prefer to spend the bulk of our hard won leisure time with. Yes, there are human beings on the other side of these machines – real life friends, musicians, actors, screenwriters, talented gossipers, public personalities. But we seem to have come to prefer our intercourse with them to occur through the medium of our machines.[36]

To fully appreciate the subtle ways in which "borging" ourselves reconfigures the human consciousness, think about the effects of pop music on one's mood, or on romance and commitment. Pop music, like most music today, is not just musicians playing instruments. It is most immediately sound waves being emitted by electronic devices, a technology that has permitted us to surround our lives with *recordings* of musicians playing instruments. In the opening scene of *High Fidelity*, Rob, whose girlfriend has finally had enough and has just stormed out the door of their apartment with her bags packed, lifts the headphones from his ears, turns to the camera, and says, "What came first? The music or the misery? People worry about kids playing with guns or watching violent videos, that some sort of culture of violence will take them over. Nobody worries about kids listening to songs, literally thousands of songs, about heartbreak, rejection, pain, misery and loss." Behind him are thousands of LPs, careful stored in their jackets and catalogued in racks. Rob's instruction in life about the ways of love, what it is for, about the course love takes, has come from recorded music – which carries him endlessly from one break-up to the next.

Or consider something as inconspicuous as the musical soundtracks of movies and television shows. Rock critic Simon Frith points out that the purpose of music in films, much like a laugh track that elbows us when something is funny, is to signal the audience when a feeling should accompany what is being seen on the screen.[37] Due to this conditioning, a story on film that has no musical accompaniment will feel flat and poorly told. Over many years, and with its roots in opera, movie scores have evolved an elaborate musical code that correlates various occasions, characters, and plot developments with musical sounds. Scores instruct us in what quite ordinary phenomena sound like: sunrises, drizzling city streets, a kiss, approaching danger, love, safety – we have learned what these phenomena sound like orchestrally from years of going to the movies. Sunrises are likely to be accompanied by a lone flute; a kiss by lightly plucked string instruments. Scores also teach us what various things we are likely never to experience would sound like if we did – war, storms at sea, earthquakes, a shark in the ocean, distant lands, even outer space. In film, each of these phenomena makes music. War sounds like a mix of anthems, cacophonous percussion, and dirges; outer space has a big orchestral sound, a kind of music of the spheres. Privileging us even more, scores tell us what characters are feeling, inviting us into their inner lives, disclosing the musical compositions that play there calibrated to each nuanced emotion and mood. And, finally, scores give us music for moral dispositions – there are musical styles that we readily correlate to innocence and guilt, to deception, purity of heart, sinister motives, and nobility. Symphonic music is still dominant in the movies, although rock music has gained credibility, too, as a carrier of our musical conventions. These conventions evolve over time, so that the sound of a kiss or of outer space in 1940 is not exactly the same as it is in 2000. Nevertheless, relatively uniform conventions do exist that systematically associate certain images, actions, narrative developments, and human bonds with corresponding affections through the mediation of music.

True, these conventions have roots in operatic, folk, and liturgical music, which were themselves originally conceived to articulate musically the sound of certain events, personalities and feelings. Even Augustine, sixteen centuries before the first movie soundtrack, recognized how music could kindle the emotions. "There are particular modes in song and in the voice," he wrote, "corresponding to my various emotions and able to stimulate them because of some mysterious relationship between the two."[38] But musical conventions are culturally specific creations – a kiss has not had the same melody or instrumentation across traditional cultures. What is new is the universalizing of one evolving strand of musical conventions across social classes and global cultures that has been made possible by mechanical reproduction, and largely through the very subtle effects of movie soundtracks. This, too, is a facet of our metamorphosis into cyborgs: the synchronization of our affective consciousness to certain basic experiences according to a mechanically administered aesthetic code.

In sum, being borged is neither a terrible thing nor a wonderful thing, but a mixed blessing. Most of the amenities of modern life – medicine, media, improved eyesight and hearing, the dissemination of art and information – are mechanical enhancements of the human organism, and they are genuine advances. But when science fiction confronts us with the image of full-fledged cyborgs – the robocops, lawnmower men, Johnny Mnemonics, Matrix pod inhabitants – we typically recoil in horror. While we have been making a multitude of incremental moves to borg ourselves, we are sympathetic to the protests that are registered by those who help us to envision what may be the final outcome of these moves.

It is illuminating to note, however, that not everyone is unhappy about this. Many researchers in the field of artificial intelligence are now convinced that we are on the cusp of being able to download a human mind into a computer.[39] Computer circuits are being developed that function more and more like brain cells; and the electronic impulses the brain uses to process and store information makes it feasible that a direct interface with a computer can be developed. Hans Moravec, one of the world's leading researchers in robotics and artificial intelligence, speculates that bioports could be surgically implanted in the brain, linking its neural bundles to a computer. In phases, the contents of a brain may then be transferred into a computer, in effect replicating a human mind in the circuitry of the computer. Then, he writes, "In time, as your original brain faded away with age, the computer would smoothly assume the lost functions. Ultimately your brain would die, and your mind would find itself entirely in the computer."[40] Given the vulnerability of individual computers, it will be wise, he suggests, to make copies of the data that has been transferred, and to disperse these copies to different locations. With this procedure accomplished and these precautions taken, it becomes possible, as he puts it, to rescue an individual mind from the constraints of a mortal body, and pass it on to a succession of super-intelligent computers, and eventually even to robots.

Social historian David Noble reports on this artificial intelligence (AI) research and the almost giddy aspirations for immortality that can be found among those pursuing it. According to AI scientist, Daniel Crevier, "This gradual transition from carnal existence to embodiment into electronic hardware would guarantee the continuity of an individual's subjective experience beyond death."[41] And Danny Hillis, one of AI's most respected scientists and visionaries, has said:

> We're a symbiotic relationship between two essentially different kinds of things. We're the metabolic thing, which is the monkey that walks around, and we're the intelligent thing, which is a set of ideas and culture. And those two things have coevolved together, because they helped each other. But they're fundamentally different things. What's valuable about us, what's good about humans, is the idea thing. It's not the animal thing.

Hillis then goes on to lament the brief span of years our animal metabolism allows us, and to confess his dream of resurrection, if not to eternal life, at least to a life of considerable duration: "I think it's a totally bum deal that we only get to live 100 years. ...I want to live for 10,000 years. ...If we can improve the basic machinery of our metabolism...If I can go into a new body and last for 10,000 years, I would do it in an instant."[42] For many of these AI scientists and technicians, it is clear that the sluggishness of the human body is an inconvenience and an embarrassment to be overcome – and now they can picture the means for doing just that. The human mind, which is "what's valuable about us," needs to be transferred from a flimsy carbon-based host to a more durable silicon-based one.

Noble cites one particularly frank AI specialist, Earl Cox, who unapologetically promotes the theological implications of this. He pictures us downloading our minds into superior machine "vessels" with dramatically enhanced capacities, really a networked system of minds firing their synapses through labyrinthine circuitry, and inhabiting virtually indestructible bodies that will enable us to move on out into the universe with powers our meaty brains cannot now even imagine. This technology, Cox claims, will "enable human beings to change into something else altogether," to "escape the human condition," and ultimately to even "transcend the timid concepts of deity and divinity held by today's theologians."[43]

If this will be the outcome of artificial intelligence, to liberate the human mind from its sluggish physiology, then it is rife with implications for theological anthropology. Traditionally, Christian theology has returned to the well of its creation myths to formulate and refine its anthropology. From the moment of his creation, Adam is depicted in Genesis as a hybrid creature – dirt scooped from the earth that comes to life with the vivifying gas of divine breath. The elements of earth and breath have led to conceptualizing the human being as a composite of body and soul, a duality intrinsic to our nature that seems matched by tensions that haunt human experience. Like angels we are attuned to God and yearn for heavenly things; like beasts we have bodily appetites and drives and find that our powers to satisfy all of our longings have frustrating limits. Those who have defined the orthodox view have been careful to avoid the temptation to equate these two components of our nature with good and evil. A human being fresh out of the box, before sin had intervened, was this hybrid being, pulled between extremes and seeking to satisfy the demands of both soul and body. It is foolhardy, according to Augustine, to imagine that the body is any less a part of human nature than is the soul. "A man is incomplete," he writes in the *City of God*, "unless a body be united with a soul."[44] And anyone who attempts to "alienate the body from man's nature," he writes elsewhere, "is unwise."[45] A more contemporary theologian, Ralph Wood, compares our "essential doubleness" to the half-human, half-horse figure of the centaur. "Our human heads provide a self-transcending consciousness which no earthly joy can satisfy; yet our equine torsos root us in mortal passions and limits which no heavenly hope can assuage." This is our lot, Wood maintains. "There is no final reconciliation of the flesh's pull with the spirit's yearning. To be permanently out of phase is . . . to be fully human."[46]

It is a common device when sorting out human nature to identify the bordering "species," those creatures that are not human but are close relatives, so to speak. In Christian thought, angels and beasts have been the traditional parameter species marking the boundaries of legitimate human powers and limits. Sources for this are not hard to find. The psalmist writes,

> What are human beings that you are mindful of them, mortals that you care for them? Yet you have made them a little lower than the angels. . . . You have put all things under their feet, all sheep and oxen, and also the beasts of the field . . . (Ps. 8.4–7).

While Plato warns,

> When the gentler part of the soul slumbers, and the control of Reason is withdrawn, then the Wild Beast in us, full-fed with meat and drink, becomes rampant and shakes off sleep to go in quest of what will gratify its own instincts (*Republic* 9.571c).

And Pascal declares,

> Man is neither an angel nor a brute, and the very attempt to raise him to the level of the former sinks him to that of the latter (*Pensees I*).

The concept in the background of these positioning efforts of human nature vis-à-vis neighboring creatures is the "great chain of being."

According to the great chain of being, the cosmos radiates out from its source in a descending order of being. Nearest the center hover archetypal ideas and heavenly beings; at the outer edge are rocks and minerals. Beyond the edge, out where the ordering light of being does not reach, is chaos. All beings have their place in this scheme, a place determined by various properties and powers that are typical of their species. Humans are high in the chain, just ahead of animals, which are higher than plants, which are, in turn, higher than rocks, inert minerals, and other inanimate elements. The position a category of being occupies in the hierarchy is a matter of the highest level of properties that belong to it as a species. Humans have all the properties of creatures below them – e.g., substance, life, movement, sensation, desire, problem-solving abilities – plus capacities for reflective reasoning, poetic expression, moral courage, and a self-transcending consciousness. That we possess these capacities places us just below the angels and other spiritual beings, who exceed us with their ability to intuit God and divine ideas directly, and with their spiritual (i.e., non-physical) bodies. And while we are higher than animals, we also share with them a generous portion of more bestial drives and appetites – thus we can speak of the beast within.

This scheme has its roots in both biblical myth (the six days of creation narrate the scale of being) and Greek philosophy (Plato's *Timaeus*). In plain terms this grand theory is likely to strike many today as a quaint antique of metaphysics. But, as linguist George Lakoff has argued in his ongoing review of the metaphors that undergird our culture, while we are typically taught about the great chain of being as an archaic cosmology useful only for understanding classical literature and philosophy, it persists in Western cultures "as a contemporary unconscious cultural model indispensable to our understanding of ourselves, our world, and our language."[47] The great chain of being, in short, is another legacy of religion[3]. It underlies our persistent inclination to identify the parameter species when reflecting on our own nature. Each generation has its angels and beasts to help it define human nature. This has been the function of Noble Savages, Houyhnhnms, Neanderthal Men, Übermenschen, Vampires, Trobriand Islanders, Space Aliens, Wolf Children, Lunatic Savants, and Naked Apes – figures which have allowed us to reflect at length on the edges of humanity, on the tipping points where the human gives way to various anomalies. And on the basis of these reflections, thinkers have sketched out the zone of normative humanness, stipulated evolving understandings of the intrinsic limitations and powers of human nature, and commented on how far given societies fall short of the ideal of humanity.

The symbol of the cyborg in popular culture has become such an arena for reflecting on human nature. A circle of artificial intelligence visionaries, preparing for the downloading of human souls into machines, have concluded that what matters about human beings is the consciousness that can finally transcend its carbon fetters. They are not exactly Gnostics, for whom matter is a prison from which the true self must escape; they accept that human consciousness requires a material apparatus to carry on. But they have concluded that a silicon body is a better apparatus than a meaty one. Silicon, or whatever newly engineered, superior material might replace it, is not susceptible to decay, to the vagaries of metabolism and enzymes, or to the impediments to thought and even to pure sensual pleasure presented by the weak instruments of our natural bodies. The irresolvable tension between body and soul, between "the flesh's pull" and "the spirit's yearning," is not, here, the essence of human being; it can be resolved with a modified body and minds that are essentially simulations. Or, perhaps, that tension *is* the inescapable essence of our humanness, one that has always been unsatisfactory – and therefore we ought to seize the opportunity to transcend human nature, to actively usher in the post-human era by transferring our minds onto the neural net and becoming something else, to become like gods.

Some of the most incisive scrutiny of this vision is coming from science fiction. The novels of Isaac Asimov, Philip K. Dick, and William Gibson, and films like *Blade Runner, Total Recall, Minority Report* and *Impostor* – all based on Dick's writings – along with *Robocop, The Terminator, Lawnmower Man, Johnny Mnemonic, A.I.: Artificial Intelligence*, and *The Matrix*, bring cyborgs and androids to life, and build stories around what such creatures have to say to us, the human race. These storytellers explore the variety of ways that human and machine might be more intimately integrated. They imagine for us what our society might look like when it has progressed further into the age of microchips, and they tend toward the dystopian as a way of warning us that some moral guardrails need to be built now to guide the technology we are blithely surrendering ourselves over to. Even so, there is a good deal of empathy for the hybrid creatures that straddle the boundary of human and machine.

In *A.I.: Artificial Intelligence*,[48] a film project begun by Stanley Kubrick and completed by Stephen Spielberg, the polar ice caps have melted and the rising oceans have submerged much of earth's landmass, including all of its coastal cities. Populations have been devastated, and survivors have migrated to precious patches of higher ground where birthrates are tightly regulated to prevent overloading the scarce natural resources that have withstood the global climate change. Technology has advanced to the point where mechanical robots, sheathed in human-like skins, are being produced to perform menial chores and to provide every sort of entertainment. Real humans, or "orgas," have become dependent upon the vast work force of this new race of robots, or "mechas," which maintains the infrastructure without diverting much in the way of natural resources. In the opening scene of the movie, the design team of the Cybertronics Corporation is meeting to brainstorm a new product line of mechas. The lead engineer, Professor Hobby (William Hurt), identifies a niche of human need as yet unaddressed by technology and presses his designers to imagine a robot that will fill it.

> *Hobby*: I propose that we build a robot child who can love, a robot child who will genuinely love the parent or parents it imprints on with a love that will never end.
>
> *Engineer* [reflecting on the growing uneasiness among orgas toward their mecha Doppelgängers]: You know it occurs to me that with all of this animus existing against mechas today, it isn't simply a question of creating a robot who can love. But isn't the real conundrum, can you get a human to love them back?
>
> *Hobby*: Ours will be a perfect child caught in a freeze frame, always loving, never ill, never changing. With all the childless couples yearning in vain for a license, our little mecha will not only open up a completely new market, it will meet a great human need.
>
> *Engineer*: But you haven't answered my question. If a robot could genuinely love a person, what responsibility does that person hold toward that mecha in return? It's a moral question, isn't it?
>
> *Hobby*: The oldest one of all. But in the beginning, didn't God create Adam to love him?

This final remark that identifies engineers with God, while common in science fiction, is given a fresh treatment in this story. As it turns out the little prototype mecha that they build is flawless in its love for its human parents, but it is a love that is not returned. Built to manifest the human virtue of filial devotion to perfection, the robot boy is nevertheless received by his family as a commodity toward which no obligations exist, and is finally dumped off the side of the road in the dark of night like a worn out appliance. From there he enters the underground world of cast off mechas, pining for his human mother and on a Pinocchio-like quest to be transformed into a real boy whose love will be reciprocated. He persists in this long after his mother's death and even beyond the extinction of the entire human race. The creature outlives its creator, and, as it turns out, is better at one of the creator's key virtues than the creator ever proved to be. The little mecha, in manifesting the perfection of loving devotion, holds up a mirror to reveal our failure in this ideal we have projected. But it is also clear that his devotion is so perfect, so flawlessly programmed, that while impressive in its fierce purity, it lacks the tension of contesting desires among which choices are made that mark what we really recognize and value in human nature.

In *Blade Runner*,[49] based on a book by Dick, the cyborg figure appears in the form of "replicants," genetically designed, soft tissue androids who have been manufactured as labor, combat, and pleasure product lines to perform the work necessary to explore and prepare "off-world colonies" on other planets for their human counterparts. The renegade replicants in *Blade Runner* are of the NEXUS-6 variety, a generation so advanced that only trained "blade runners" – replicant bounty hunters – can verify whether or not they are human. The motto of the Tyrell Corporation which holds their patent is "more human than human," and they resemble real human beings in every way except for their superior talents in the specialized tasks they are designed to perform, their brief life spans (they self-destruct after 4 years), and their fledgling capacities for emotions such as anger, envy, love, and empathy. The blade runners can verify whether one is a replicant by reciting a series of scenarios designed to elicit empathy – you are on a walk and see a turtle lying upside down under the beating sun, unable to right itself; you are at a banquet and discover the entrée is roasted dog – while monitoring such tell-tale physiological responses as a blushing cheek or a dilation of the iris. Upon hearing these images, humans generally react, while replicants remain unmoved.

A new design feature of the NEXUS-6 replicants stems from the manufacturer's discovery that replicants who have been implanted with a scattering of childhood memories are more composed and productive than those who have not. This enhances the value of replicants, but, as it turns out, those with implanted memories are also prone to develop more high functioning emotional responses, including empathy, and begin to bond with each other as they live out their short, brutish lives. The memory implants, as meager as they may be, when supplemented by the replicants' actual experience and real memories, appear to be the germs of human self-hood. This becomes poignantly clear in the final confrontation between Rick Deckard, the blade runner, and Roy Batty, the state of the art combat model replicant who is in the final throes of his programmed self-termination. Deckard has killed two of Batty's companions and has been doggedly hunting Batty down. Finally outwitted by the replicant on the rooftop of a decrepit city highrise, Deckard finds himself clinging to a rusting girder as he dangles over the pavement far below. As Deckard's hold loosens, Batty reaches off the edge of the roof, grips the blade runner's wrist, and inexplicably pulls him to safety. Sprawled out on the roof in the steady rain, Deckard is stunned as he studies the dying replicant. It is dawning on him that this replicant has just succumbed to an empathetic response, one that has saved his own life.

Then Batty says,

> I've seen things you people wouldn't believe. Attack ships on fire off the shoulder of Orion. I watched C-beams glitter in the dark near the Tanhauser gate. All those moments will be lost in time like tears in rain ... Time to die.

With these words spoken, Batty slumps down and terminates. At this moment he releases his grip on a dove he had been holding with his one free hand, and it flies upward into a blue sky. A soul ascends, we are tempted to believe, to find its resting place. In a voice-over, Deckard reflects,

> I don't know why he saved my life. Maybe in those last moments, he loved life more than he ever had before. Not just his life, anybody's life, my life. All he'd wanted were the same answers the rest of us want. Where did I come from? Where am I going? How long have I got? All I could do was sit there and watch him die.

These two films are about robots that long to be human, biomechanical creatures that embody particular human virtues and aptitudes to the point of perfection, but yearn instead for the ambiguities of human existence and its mix of limited powers. We are willingly led into the realm of the cyborg because it has become a genre in which alien creatures look at us and tell us that they value what we are. Despite whatever superior powers they are assigned – immortality, super-intelligence, athletic prowess, exceptional strength, telepathy, even perfect love – they would prefer our condition, with all of its vulnerabilities, to their own. And what is it that they envy us for? We are cultivators of memories, our own and those of others who have come within the orbit of our care, of memories that can be handed on to companions for safekeeping before we take our leave. We belong to families, and can form bonds that grow out of a combination of basic needs and freely accepted obligation. Unlike robots, we are not programmed to perform tasks that might run contrary to our own wills. We live in the face of uncertainties that we both relish and resent. We have the satisfaction of humor – this welling up of mysterious juices within us, to be etymologically precise, that is untransferably human – to help us cope with what we cannot control. We neither know the time of our deaths, nor do we have the assurance of immortality. We are predisposed to be affected by others, to feel empathy, pity, love, regret, remorse, passion, longing, gratitude. We are not simulations, figments of awareness suspended amidst an overwhelming chorus of images; we possess consciousness and finite identities that persist over time. We are caught in the full array of finitude – causality, substance, time, and space, and as much as we object to these limitations, they are the source of many of our finest satisfactions. At least, that is the word from the cyborgs who are making themselves heard in popular culture.[50]

Conclusion

Theological reflection on human nature revolves around the question: Who are these humans God has made? Of what are they composed, what are their inherent powers and limitations? For what purpose do they exist? The same questions are raised, although usually de-fanged of references to God, in popular culture. Themes that have been discerned in the materials examined in this chapter include the following.

In popular culture there is, on one hand, an elevation of the ordinary, a respect for the struggles involved in making a living, raising a family, and being a true friend. Submitting without flourish or ostentation to the simple requirements of life – hunger, sexuality, companionship, frailty and death – is respected in literature, film, and song as honesty about the human condition. This is the steady stream of fanfares to the "common man" that can be heard playing in a variety of artifacts. On the other hand, there is also a trend toward customizing the base model, accessorizing it with semiotically rich commodities and brands to register our affiliations with powers upon which we depend and wish to be identified. In this way we compose our own identities reflexively – both consciously and unconsciously, both cooperatively and under protest. This often involves enmeshing our lives in several mythologies at once, fetishizing the products that we consume and sacramentally imprinting them on our souls. In this way we bear the image of God; or, better, the image of our ultimate concern.

For many of us, our highest aspiration is a happiness defined by amusement, engineered along the lines of Disney World or the ubiquitous themed sites of pleasure and consumption it has spawned. This is significant both because collective aspirations divulge much about a culture's conception of human nature and how it is best fulfilled, and because of the hyperreality that is given reign in this vision of fulfillment. According to this view, the human being is a pleasure-seeking *bricoleur*. But there is also a strong current in popular culture that runs contrary to this surrender to simulation, a warning that the self is composed of ordered memories, and that as the first-hand experience of life is eclipsed within the memory by the fabrications of hyperreality, the self begins to deteriorate. A flesh and blood person cannot live on simulacra alone.

Another way that popular culture is puzzling over human nature can be seen in representations of the tension between our headlong rush to be borged, with the multitude of ways technology extends our senses and powers, and the envy we find among full-fledged cyborgs who would prefer to be more like their human creators. The cyborgs, onto whom we project our inmost longings for unimpeded strength, tirelessness, memory, speed, intelligence, beauty, and indestructibility, wish, instead, to be real boys and girls. They long for the uncertainties of a full-bodied finitude. For them, the grass is greener on our side of the fence.

These are some of the more interesting contradictions that can be found in popular culture's present reflections on the stuff of which we are made and the purposes for which we exist.

7

Sin

In the last chapter we considered the first half of what theologians deal with in examining theological anthropology, namely, Who are these humans God has made? But now we come to the second half: What has gone wrong? When trying to understand the springs that move humanity, it is not only a matter of determining the material out of which we are made and the purposes for which we aim, but also a matter of ascertaining why things seem out of whack. We now move into the province of the doctrine of sin.

Signs of the Times

Anyone who tunes into country-western music will get an earful of the transgressions human beings perpetrate against one another. We lie, cheat, steal, commit adultery, defy our elders, gamble, drink too much, beat up our mates, two-time our lovers, struggle against our siblings, act out of greed and insincerity, corrupt the innocent, betray our country, and renege on our promises. We are also the victims of evils perpetrated against us by untrustworthy lovers, greedy landlords, factory closings, agribusiness, intrusive government, condescending intellectuals, and decadent city folk. We are a fallen people, and while it does not offer a full inventory, country-western music does instruct us in a multitude of ways that our fallenness manifests itself in both personal and social sin.

Rock and roll, before it splintered into a multitude of niches in the 1980s, was heavy with the theme of lost paradise – Joni Mitchell called a generation back to the garden: "We are stardust/Billion year old carbon/We are golden/Caught in the devil's bargain/And we've got to get ourselves/Back to the garden."[1] The theme of an endless search to recover lost dreams is a similar one. In Neil Young's 1979 song, "Thrasher," the singer has a vision of hay thrashers rolling down the highway, looking for mortals ripe for harvesting. Realizing that he is not ready, he rouses himself, looks around for his companions who are nowhere to be found, then sets fire to his credit cards and heads out to where the pavement ends. Determined not to look back he plunges forward into "the land of truth," and laments the absence of his friends. They have scattered, it turns out, lost to the streets or suburban comforts. Having lived pampered lives, they found themselves in need of nothing, and with "nothing left to find."[2] The reflective singer-songwriters of this era sang of a restlessness immediately inspired by Kerouac's *On the Road*. But they struck upon a very Augustinian formula of confessing the many temptations and earthly pleasures that detour one who is yearning for something that is ultimately more satisfying.

Sting, in a 1993 release, "If I Ever Lose My Faith in You,"[3] inventories the cultural institutions that have lost his trust: science and progress, the church, TV commentators, politicians, and military solutions. In his accounting, these things have moved from the column of miracles to the column of curses. They have served as unfit recipients of human faith, and misused the authority granted them in their aggressive eagerness to wreak havoc on the world.

Another barometer of what has gone wrong can be found through examining the crimes of the archrivals of comic book superheroes. The Joker in Batman is a twisted soul who relishes chaos and poisons Gotham's water reservoir for no other motive than to assert the arbitrariness of justice. Spider-Man's nemesis is the Green Goblin, a mutant scientist whose greed drove him to pursue "human performance enhancement" research for a military contractor, which he has administered to himself and consequently acquired superpowers that he uses for diabolical ends. The Hulk's villain is his own repressed rage. One need not scratch very deeply beneath the surface to find in these comic book villains some of popular culture's current contenders for sin: there is a Kantian understanding of "wickedness" represented in the Joker, who actually wills that evil be the principle of his actions; an illicit Promethean reach into the sacred precincts of nature, as found in the Green Goblin; and an unregulated liberation of the Freudian id which emerges in the incredible Hulk. These are all dusted off lessons in the roots of human evil.

Reading these signs of our time divulges that we are thinking about our own waywardness in terms of infidelity, personal sinfulness, corporate sin, lost paradise, corrupt institutions and authorities, pure wickedness, Promethean hubris, and unregulated libidos. There is, it seems, meaningful reflection going on in our music, comic books and other creative output with respect to the human condition.

What Has Gone Wrong?

Myths about the creation of the human race generally tell us what we are made of – dirt, divine breath, images of our gods, the mundane pressures of life, consumable products, designer brands, hardware, software, microchips – and what we are for – to subdue the earth, cultivate our gardens, build egalitarian societies, inhabit semiological lifestyles, surrender ourselves to the pleasures of hyperreality, compile and order memories, or transcend our finitude and become like gods. The plots of these myths, however, have an unfinished feel until they reveal some disruption, some mishap or malicious act that occurred in the distant past and helps to explain – at least in the logic of myth and in a way that rings true to life – our pervasive sense that things are not the way they ought to be. This is often done through the plotline of a lost paradise.

Paradises are found in many traditions. According to Eliade, primordial paradises typically have the following traits: at that time humans were immortal, free, spontaneous, happy, had access to the gods, were on friendly terms with animals and had knowledge of animal languages, and did not have to work for food because either nature freely provided it or their agricultural tools worked magically by themselves.[4] But paradise is always lost. It might occur through some petty indiscretion, such as the Dinka myth of the woman who while planting millet inadvertently struck the Creator with her hoe. In response the god withdrew to the sky, leaving human beings to fend for themselves, increasing the labor required to produce food, rendering them susceptible to sickness and death, and forever separating them from the god who had brought them into existence.[5] Paradise might also be lost through some grave act of disobedience committed by the ancestors. This loss often results in mortality, the necessity to work, alienation between the sexes and between bloodlines, and the loss of access to the gods. This loss, according to Eliade, always amounts to "a fall into history"[6] – and history is the travail in which we find ourselves; it is life as we know it.

Appetite is frequently associated with the loss of paradise. This is true, of course, with the Genesis myth – Adam and Eve eat fruit from the forbidden tree of knowledge, and the curses that constitute life as we know it are the consequence. It is also true of the Buddhist myth, which describes how the spiritual ancestors, after ages of disembodied bliss, caught a glimpse of the earth in the distance with its delicious savor:

Even as a scum forms on the surface of boiled milk rice that is cooling, so did the earth appear. It became endowed with colour, with odour, and with taste. Then, Vasettha, being of greedy disposition, said: Lo now!

what will this be? and tasted the savoury earth with his finger. He thus, tasting, became suffused with the savour, and craving entered into him. And other beings, following his example, tasted the savoury earth with their finger. Then those beings began to feast on the savoury earth, breaking off lumps of it with their hands. . . . Feasting on the savoury earth, feeding on it, nourished by it, continued for a long while. And in measure as they thus fed, did their bodies become solid.

The more they ate, the more matter they took on as penalty for their appetites. This myth goes on to relate the differentiation between the sexes, the origin of sexual passion, the necessity to build huts to hide immorality, the eventuality of having to cultivate rice instead of just harvesting what grew on its own, and the first theft.[7] Here, too, the loss of paradise and the fall into history follow from a momentous surrendering of pure beings to their appetites.

It is fair to say that popular culture is in broad agreement that things are not the way they ought to be, that something is amiss. What petty indiscretions, bold acts of disobedience, or inordinate appetites does it offer to account for this? Or, more likely, what external forces are responsible for it? Listening to popular culture, what reasons are given for sickness and death, immorality, the necessity of hard work, unhappiness, adversity, alienation between genders, races and classes, violence, the degradation of the earth, and the silence of the gods? How does popular culture understand sin?

Two lost paradise scripts have been pressed into service of late to help Americans catalog their sins, and the evils that have been thrust upon them. Both have long and honorable literary pedigrees, but have been surging in print, cinema, and television in the last few years: the covenant/jeremiad cycle and the Gothic. These two offer narrative frameworks that assist us in our coming to grips with what, in the view of important segments of popular culture, has gone wrong.

Covenants and Jeremiads

When the descendants of Jacob fled Egypt and followed Moses into the desert, they waited at the foot of Mt Sinai until God made a covenant with them. The covenant acknowledged that this God had delivered them from slavery and was preparing to make them into a great nation, and it assured them that the same God would remain faithful to them and to their descendants. In turn, the covenant stipulated civil and religious obligations that they now had to accept in order to be worthy of God's protection. These obligations became the law of ancient Israel, and grounded as they were in a covenant with God, had the effect of making any violation of communal duties not only disruptive to the community, but also a crime against God. Consequently, divine punishment could be expected to follow flagrant breaches of the law.

The Hebrew prophet Jeremiah lived several centuries after the covenant was given at Sinai, at a time when Jerusalem was a pawn in the wars between the great regional powers of Babylon and Egypt. As a small kingdom, Judah was in a precarious position, and the succession of kings during Jeremiah's long tenure as a prophet sought his counsel for how they could be assured of God's protection. Jeremiah consistently advised that the people had to repent of their collective sins and change their ways if they hoped to be delivered from their enemies. He appealed to the covenant their ancestors had entered with God, which had obliged them to "not oppress the alien, the orphan, and the widow ... to not shed innocent blood ... and to not go after other gods" (Jer. 7.6). They were in violation of this covenant, and consequently the anger of God had been kindled and calamity was about to overtake them if they did not repent and amend their ways. This idea that disaster falls upon those who refuse to repent and rectify their wrongs is the defining formula of the Hebrew prophets. Jeremiah was such a consummate practitioner of this call to repentance that the formula has been given the name "jeremiad."

The Puritans in America are remembered for their identity with Israel and their fondness for both the covenant and the jeremiad. John Calvin had rehabilitated the covenant idea to explain how it is that a sovereign God with absolute power who had no need for us had relinquished arbitrary freedom and committed to deal with creation according to certain constant purposes – purposes, it is important to note, that are primarily concerned with justice. The Puritans, theological heirs of Calvin, had further developed the covenant idea to mean that "God pledged Himself not to run tyrannically athwart human conceptions of justice. The creator was represented as agreeing to abide by ideas comprehensible to man."[8] Accordingly, covenant was seen as a moral order built into reality that has been offered to humanity as a gesture of God's providential care, and in gratitude we are wise to conform our lives to it. And in addition to this comprehensive covenant, for the Puritans there were subsidiary covenants God established that were intended to order human life into families, nations, markets, congregations, etc. – institutional arrangements humans enter, agreeing to assume certain obligations so that social life can flourish.

On one boatload of Puritans that sailed from the old world, the lay preacher John Winthrop called the anxious settlers to the deck and, with the story of Israel foremost in his mind, instructed them that if they survived the voyage and arrived in the new world, it would be evidence that

God had ratified a covenant with them. This covenant obligates them, he explained, to "follow the counsel of Micah: to do justly, to love mercy, and to walk humbly with our God." In undertaking the work that lay ahead of them, "We must delight in each other, make others' conditions our own, rejoice together, mourn together, labor and suffer together, always having before our eyes our community as members of the same body."[9] Should they live up to these obligations, God would be pleased and allow them to shine "like a city upon a hill," to serve, that is, as an exemplary model for other settlements; but if they should fail to live up to them, they would become a cautionary tale for others, and be driven from the good land they were about to occupy.

With the passage of time it became clear that they had, indeed, failed to establish the covenantal utopia they had envisioned. There were wars with the Indians, shipwrecks that distressed their colonial economy, pestilence, epidemics, devastating fires, outbreaks of witchcraft, and political squabbles. Jeremiads began to be heard. In their own view, to read surviving sermons, they behaved little better than Sodom, only worse because the Sodomites did not have the benefit of a covenant blessing to moderate their behavior. They were guilty of fornicating, gambling, frequenting pubs and drinking heavily, neglecting their families, falling asleep in church, behaving in a proud manner, overcharging for their goods, growing greedy and deceitful in their business practices, breaking promises, failing to provide for public schools, and dressing strangely.[10] The rhetoric of self-condemnation that grew out of this experience is astonishing. Countless sermons denounced the sins of the people and carried the stern warning of God's wrath to follow if they did not repent and return to their covenant promises.

The logic of the covenant could work retrospectively, as well. If there was a calamity, say, an Indian attack, a famine, a hard winter, or an outbreak of smallpox, the reflex from the pulpits, and within the people, was to determine what sins had been committed, and by whom, to warrant this punishment. Thus, in 1743 when the crops failed in Northampton, Massachusetts, Jonathan Edwards went into jeremiad mode and told his congregation that in failing to do justice to the poor, they had brought this divine judgment upon themselves.

The Puritans deeply internalized the jeremiad, and various historians and political scientists have suggested that this is their most lasting legacy to America.[11] James Morone argues that "the jeremiad became a kind of American anthem," the idiom into which we habitually slip when reality falls short of our utopian aspirations. The jeremiad, he writes, "scolded the people for moral backsliding, dazzled them with their historical duty, and invested their mission with an immodest goal: redeem the world."[12] Thus the notion of covenant and jeremiad serve as the fount of a long tradition of American exceptionalism and the mix of moral crusades, appeals to founding principles, imperialistic ventures, and counter-cultural protests that are associated with it. This explains why, according to John Hall and Charles Lindholm, America is "a society that is in fact the most powerful and stable in the world, yet is perennially shaken by self-doubt and moral anguish."[13] The fear of being forsaken by some kind of guiding purpose if we forsake the principles enshrined in our founding documents haunts conservatives and progressives alike. Every new bit of poll data that measures the condition of the body politic is in some faint way a pragmatic test of whether we are right with God.

As tension-ridden as this makes us, it is a healthy tension, and one that permeates popular culture. It is used ironically in fictional treatments of the Puritans themselves, such as Nathaniel Hawthorne's *Scarlet Letter,* Arthur Miller's *The Crucible*, and more modern equivalents, such as Richard Wright's *Native Son* and films like *Far from Heaven* and *The Stepford Wives*. These are stories of upstanding, well-ordered communities that, in their efforts to rid themselves of some obvious sin and to restore order, wreak havoc and commit every sort of injustice. Greater sins are given license to conquer lesser sins in order to maintain a façade of communal purity. But by peeling away the surface layer of bourgeois respectability, the madness of a self-righteousness that has substituted itself for a long-forgotten social covenant is revealed. These jeremiads deliver the admonition that *the desire to appear pure* is the deep wrongdoing that has given rise, and given cover, to a multitude of sins.

Catherine Albanese has drawn a line between the utopianism that propelled the Puritans on their quest for a New Jerusalem and the long tradition of nature religion in America. Under the influence of Ralph Waldo Emerson, nature began to serve as a symbol of original purity, promising to restore to a primordial harmony those communities that choose to abide by its inherent priorities, disciplines and obligations. Like covenant, nature is there with its objective reality and laws, not to be quarreled with. It is "a moral teacher, instructing people in the laws of right and wrong."[14] Conform to it, and be blessed; violate it, and be cursed. Covenant under the guise of Nature has inspired a myriad of utopian experiments in our history, back-to-nature movements and artifacts of various sorts like the Chautauqua's, Indian Medicine Shows that were popular at state fairs, the legends of Davy Crockett and Tarzan of the Apes, Boy Scouts, national parks, homeopathic remedies, Gustav Stickley and the Arts and Crafts aesthetic, outdoor sports like hunting, camping and rock climbing, experiments with communal living in the 1960s, granola, the *Whole Earth Catalog* (1968) and *Mother Earth News* (1970), Carlos Castenada, and the sprouting of yurts, domes, and tipis in rural America.[15] Each of these cultural phenomena contains simultaneously a vision of utopia and a jeremiad cataloging the sins for which society is guilty and must purge itself – the primary sin, according to the code of nature religion, being our overweening reliance upon technology.

The jeremiad with its insinuation of a broken covenant is also found in social novels like Sinclair Lewis's *The Jungle*, John Steinbeck's *The Grapes of Wrath*, and Walter Mosley's *Always Outnumbered, Always Outgunned*, and cinematic moral dramas like *Norma Rae*, *Silkwood*, *Boyz N the Hood*, *Philadelphia*, *Boogie Nights*, *The Insider*, and *Erin Brockovich*. Each of these stories singles out a social pathology, a disease of the covenant, and traces it to deeper causes in some combination of the seven deadly sins – greed, pride, lust, gluttony, envy, anger and sloth – with blame landing primarily on the powerful in society, not on those who contract the pathology. Similarly, the rhymes of hip-hop rappers like Grand Master Flash and Furious Five, Public Enemy, and Arrested Development offer a searing critique of social inequities, racism, and the spiraling causes of poverty and urban violence. After reciting a litany of social conditions that await a child born into a ghetto (derelict buildings, failing public schools, pollution, callous repo men, vapid daytime soap operas, drug alleys, gun violence, and demeaning jobs), "The Message," by Grand Master Flash and Furious Five, warns of God's disappointment: "A child was born, with no state of mind/Blind to the ways of man-kind/God is smiling on you but he's frowning too/Cause only God knows what you go through/You grow in the ghetto, living second rate."[16]

Covenant and jeremiad are also common in the genres of post-apocalyptic and dystopian movies and fiction. Movies like *Road Warrior*, *Waterworld*, *The Postman*, *A Boy and His Dog*, *Silent Running*, and novels like Margaret Atwood's *The Handmaid's Tale*, Aldous Huxley's *Brave New World*, George Orwell's *1984*, Marge Piercy's *Woman on the Edge of Time*, Ray Bradbury's *Fahrenheit 451* and Walter M. Miller's *A Canticle for Leibowitz* are stories about social visions gone awry, exper-iments in fiction that allow for some serious reflection on what essential aspects of human nature have been denied in order to allow such a world to come to be, and what basic human fault is responsible. They typic-ally isolate a Sin that serves as the fulcrum for all other sins that have delivered us to apocalypse or dystopia. In *A Canticle for Leibowitz*, for example, Miller tells a story of how a scrappy remnant of the human race survives an all out nuclear war in the 1960s, and then seeks to expur-gate itself of its sins by destroying all traces of learning from the centuries leading up to the development of the bomb. Frenzied mobs stoke book bonfires and hang the surviving politicians, scientists and scholars in an era remembered subsequently as "the Simplification," and civilization is plunged into a new dark age. Isaac Leibowitz was a nuclear scientist who survived the war, repented of the part he had played in bringing it about, went into hiding in a Cistercian monastery, took the habit, and became a priest. He made it the secret mission of his abbey to recover whatever books and documents escaped the burnings and conceal them in kegs buried safely in the ground.

As the centuries pass, Leibowitz is canonized, and an Order of the Brothers of Leibowitz is established to preserve the scraps of writings he and his companions had recovered – as relics at first, but, in time, as the seeds of a new blossoming of civilization. History progresses predictably through dark ages to a second round of renaissance, enlightenment, and modernity, to the point, 1,800 years after the apocalypse, when humanity is again in possession of nuclear weapons and the geopolitical situation has grown tense. Carrying the memory of the ancient nuclear deluge, members of the Order can see where things are headed, and their hymnists compose a final liturgy for the human race ("Lucifer is fallen/*Kyrie eleison*"), while their abbot commissions a starship to be built to deliver a colony of the church to planet Centaurus. Religious, lay people and children are enlisted to board, and Leibowitz's literary memorabilia are stowed on the ship. As these preparations are made, the narrator laments:

> Be born then, gasp wind, screech at the surgeon's slap, seek manhood, taste a little godhood, feel pain, give birth, struggle a little while, succumb:
>
> Generation, regeneration, again, again, as in a ritual, with blood-stained vestments and nail-torn hands, children of Merlin, chasing a gleam. Children, too, of Eve, forever building Edens – and kicking them apart in berserk fury because somehow it isn't the same.[17]

Once again, thermonuclear war breaks out, triggered by one state's detonation of a weapon in space to exhibit its atomic capabilities. Over a period of several weeks, between summits and negotiations, the major cities of the world are incinerated. Finally, a missile hits near the founding monastery of the Order of Leibowitz, and Abbot Zerchi, the spiritual head of the Order, finds himself half-buried in the rubble of the ancient abbey. Lucid, but unable to move and certain of his own death in the hours ahead, the Abbot initiates a conversation with a skull that has been dislodged from the crypt by the blast. He reflects on what flaw in the human condition has brought the species again to this pitiful end. "Bombs and tantrums, when the world grew bitter because the world fell somehow short of half-remembered Eden." For Zerchi, we have never recovered from being ejected out of Eden. Our efforts passing from generation to generation have been aimed at restoring the earth to its original state, a garden of pleasure, a paradise where no need is unmet, no desire unsatisfied. In our bleakest eras we were the most driven by this vision and made the greatest advances toward realizing it. But each time when we came close to realizing it, each time we managed to assemble beautiful, powerful and rich cultures, we grew more disgruntled because of our realization that the world would never, finally, fully attain what our memories of Eden tell us it was. There was always a shrub we could not make grow, or a tree out of place. Then we tore it apart in spite, so that we might "hope again in wretched darkness" – the desperate condition we seemed to prefer, judging from our behavior. The "root of evil," Zerchi concludes, is our craving for worldly security. He reflects on this:

> To minimize suffering and to maximize security were natural and proper ends of society and Caesar. But then they became the only ends, somehow, and the only basis of law – a perversion. Inevitably, then, in seeking only them, we found only their opposites: maximum suffering and minimum security.[18]

Longing for Eden, for absolute security and negligible suffering, the Abbot concludes, we will instead be cast out into the desert of outer space, prohibited from returning to the garden of the earth by a sword of flame with a virtually eternal half-life. Having failed yet again to make good on our covenant, we will be driven from the good land we had been given, and forever serve as a cautionary tale for others.

Tillich drew a distinction between moral faith and ontological faith. In the former, the holy is understood to enter the world through human acts of love and justice; in the latter, the holy is expected to be encountered through things that are beautiful and awe-inspiring. There appears to be a strong religion$_1$ undercurrent in American culture, arising on its own, favoring the moral type of faith. Outside of explicit religious communities, promoting justice and scrutinizing the conditions that resist it is done by many and recognized by most as worth doing. But that it is done in popular culture in the ways described here suggests that the Puritans' use of the covenant/jeremiad pattern as a form of social criticism lives on as a form of religion$_3$. That does not, however, determine what conclusions these different artifacts of popular culture (social novels, moral dramas, nature religions, hip-hop, apocalyptic and dystopian fiction) will finally reach in isolating our obligations and transgressions. The jeremiad is essentially an open form, convinced that we have corrupted our obligations toward a providential order that surrounds us, but offering different alternatives for what it is that constitutes corruption, and what it is within us that persists in causing it.

The Gothic

The covenant/jeremiad formula is a lost paradise script, and one of the most recurring in popular culture. Perhaps we hold onto the covenant idea because even though we may be in breach of it and suffering pangs of a chronically guilty conscience, sustaining it in our collective memory assures us that human history is in the care of a just dealmaker who will abide with our species to the end. A less sanguine lost paradise script is found in the Gothic.

Tom Beaudoin claims that GenX harbors many resentments for the damaged social goods they have been handed – a degraded environment, nuclear threat, AIDS, national debt, unaffordable tuition, stacked demographics, rampant materialism, McJobs, an unstable economy – and suggests that they testify to their resentment in their wardrobes. The semiotics of grunge, he suggests, is that of an uncared-for brood, declaring through style the awareness that they are "society's orphans and its cleanup crew." "Grunge underscores neediness; it highlights wants," it testifies to an inner poverty and poorness of heart. Like their ensembles, Xers have been forced to piece together their own meaning, poaching off what has been stingily offered them. The message of grunge, then, is that "when left alone, as we have been, we will wear the disarray in which we live."[19] A second fashion statement is the Gothic look. The semiotics of Gothic style is that this is a grieving generation readying itself for a funeral. "It is all about separation ... from society and from God," Beaudoin learns from a Goth-clad cabdriver.[20]

As a contemporary *sound*, the Gothic first came to the airwaves through the melancholic music of groups like Echo and the Bunnymen, Joy Division, The Cure, Nick Cave, and the Psychedelic Furs. Their lyrics were haunted by references to God and devils, heaven and hell, blood, death, judgment and ponderous lines like "the hole in the holy." In their music it was as if religious symbols were organs being removed from dying bodies by surgeons with limited knowledge of anatomy, who were nonetheless enthralled by the evocative, still throbbing life force they held in their hands. The *au courant* Gothic *style of dress*, embodied in a performer like Marilyn Manson – pale, emaciated, sad-looking youth with blackened hair, blackened lips, blackened eye sockets, milk-tinted contact lenses, black clothing and multiple piercings – is a semiotics of mourning. As a look, it emerged in London as a splinter of the punk club scene in the early 1980s, and has had unusual durability for a subaltern style. This may have something to do with the Gothic literary tradition that preceded it, providing a creed from which it has drawn and sustained itself. Gothic *literature* follows a formula with some variation on the following elements: gloomy settings, unsuspecting victims, unearthly antagonists (vampires, monsters, the living dead, madmen, Doppelgängers, enraged nature), and prolonged, sadistic acts of torment.

The Gothic literary form emerged in the late eighteenth century from a Romantic wing of the Enlightenment. It became a popular form of storytelling in the hands of Ann Radcliffe and Matthew Lewis who introduced the prototypes of handsome and enchanting but cruel hero-villains (drawn from the ranks of aristocracy and clergy) who had made their deals with the devil, along with innocent maidens or children in distress, and victims stranded in some decaying, oppressive old castle or monastery. As the genre matured in the hands of Mary Shelley, Bram Stoker, and Robert Louis Stevenson, who gave us Frankenstein's monster, Count Dracula, and Dr Jekyll and Mr Hyde, it picked up additional elements: subterranean, shadowy spaces, live burials, heated lovers, graveyards, prisons, insane asylums, riots, fires, sacrilegious uses of blood and other assorted Catholic paraphernalia, overreaching scientists, vampires, and double personalities.[21] Essentially, these are literary conjurings of the sublime, the dark side of the holy, strumming within us our anxieties that we are unworthy of any cosmic consolation.

Mary Shelley's monster, the ur-cyborg, is the sad creation of Dr Victor Frankenstein, a scientist who grew obsessed with uncovering the key to animating lifeless matter, and who, after two years of secreting away body parts from morgues and graveyards and tirelessly working in his laboratory, succeeded. An innocent giant at first, a noble savage, the creature only turned into a monster after being repeatedly scorned by those whose companionship he craved, including his creator's. In his sorrow he kills those who had hurt him, and to compound his creator's punishment, he systematically kills everyone dear to Dr Frankenstein before leading the doctor to his own death on a frigate frozen in the Arctic sea – after which the monster grieves inconsolably. Shelley used the elements of the genre to issue a warning against meddling with the deepest prerogatives of nature, against using technology to violate boundaries that are instead deserving of our awe and respect. She is the artist who did the most to transform the Gothic as a genre into an instrument for probing the human condition. She retrieved the ancient myth of Prometheus, then gave it new life by attaching it to Gothic terror. The moral of her story, according to Mark Edmundson, is that "when we usurp nature's role, especially through technology, what we create will turn on us, punishing us for our hubris." Even more ominous, Edmundson suggests, "The Frankenstein story, as we've come to understand it, is a postreligious rewriting of the fall of mankind, a tragedy in which we overreach and pay for it."[22]

To understand how hearty this formula is, and what a steady appetite we have for it, consider *Jurassic Park* (1993) and its sequels. Real dinosaurs, cloned from DNA that has been found in the stomach of a prehistoric mosquito entombed in amber, are brought to life and inhabit a remote tropical island under a strict regime of reinforced barriers and electronic surveillance, but otherwise doing what comes "naturally."

Investors are eager to open the island as a theme park of prehistoric nature, but before this happens, things go terribly wrong. Two ferocious raptors escape their containers and, as Edmundson describes it, "*Jurassic Park* turns into something of a slasher movie, with an innocent young woman and two children, adept screamers all, careening down corridors [and] through dark tunnels."[23] The fury of Dr Frankenstein's scorned creature reawakens to terrorize his heirs.

Or consider how versatile the formula is in a genre that encompasses such memorable films as *The Exorcist* (1973), *Jaws* (1975), *Rocky Horror Picture Show* (1975), *Alien* (1979), *Altered States* (1980), *The Fly* (1986), *Fatal Attraction* (1987), *Home Alone* (1990), *Flatliners* (1990), *Buffy the Vampire Slayer* (1992), *Interview with a Vampire* (1994), and *Seven* (1995)[24] – with their great assortment of monsters. Some come to us from other worlds (demons, aliens, giant sharks), some are manufactured by us (Frankenstein's monster, Jurassic dinosaurs, the fly), and some emerge from our darker selves (jealous libidos, utopian demands, the longing for immortality, the will-to-power). The monsters of the Gothic genre are rich symbols that lend themselves to a Tillichian interpretation, disclosing levels of reality and dimensions of our own being that otherwise go unnoticed. They are symbols for understanding what has gone wrong – around us and within us – and why it is that this world is not the paradise we believe it should be.

One of the more interesting masters of the genre is filmmaker Tim Burton, who has excelled in the niche of the humorist-Gothic, with films like *Beetlejuice* (1988), *Batman* (1989), *Nightmare before Christmas* (1993), and *Edward Scissorhands* (1990). In *Edward Scissorhands* he rehabilitates the Frankenstein story with a laboratory-created Edward whose creator dies before he can attach flesh and bone hands to the boy-creature. Edward must make do with modified garden shears at the ends of his arms instead, and occupies himself grooming exquisite topiaries on the grounds of the gloomy castle on the hill. When he is discovered by an aggressive Avon lady ringing doorbells, he descends to the suburbs in full Gothic garb – black suit and ghostly white face, an innocent whose obvious talents as a hairdresser and gardener are soon exploited, and becomes a local celebrity. But, of course, innocence cannot thrive in the suburbs, and soon the angry mob forms and hounds him back to the lonely confines of his castle. While the story eclipses the Promethean warning of the Frankenstein tale with a simple reiteration of the themes of alienated youth and the intolerance for otherness that is characteristic of the American suburb, Burton does add the poignant lesson that rare talents, like Edward's disciplined, razor-sharp claws, have an ambiguous power. Everything they touch is changed, rendered beautiful or bleeding, in a manner their bearer cannot finally control.

In his fascinating study of the Gothic, *Nightmare on Main Street: Angels, Sadomasochism, and the Culture of Gothic*, Mark Edmundson singles out four features of the Gothic as it has evolved that, it can be argued, make it a literary vehicle conducive to popular culture's reflection on sin and evil. First, its villain always "embodies some measure of the good." Like the devil himself, the Gothic antagonist is a fallen angel who has some admirable qualities, and thus we can concede the attraction of the victims to their tormenters, and perhaps better appreciate our own susceptibility to evil. Second, the genre locates its crucial, most terrifying actions in our oldest, most familiar and life-determining institutions: old houses, churches, universities, laboratories, hospitals, asylums, and prisons. In doing so, it triggers our suspicions that the most imposing institutions in which we spend our lives cannot protect us, and may even collude in the ill-will that is out to get us. The Gothic, he writes, "shows the dark side, the world of cruelty, lust, perversion, and crime that, many of us at least half believe, is hidden beneath established conventions." Third, the victims are never absolutely innocent. Monsters haunt those who are guilty of some transgression, or those who are dearest to them, for which punishment has not yet been meted out. The monster, as it were, is a "well-deserved curse" finally collecting on a debt. "In the Gothic world view," Edmundson writes, "every crime is punished: you can run, but not hide." Even in teenage slasher films, the fiends enforce a morality; "they kill the young kids who copulate, or want to." And, fourth, the villain embodies qualities that reflect deeply-felt desires or fears of the audience.[25] Vampires are immortal, Frankenstein's monster is stung by the rejection of human companionship, Mr Hyde has a rakish night life. Who hasn't harbored these secret pains and longings?

This last feature is particularly worth examining given the way we have come to take for granted that we are haunted from within by a variety of subconscious drives that society has required us to repress. The early Gothic novelists were writing before Freud had invented a clinical language for our internal monsters. Thus, Shelley and the rest may have been capturing proto-Freudian psychodynamics. But we had to await Freud before any credible scientist would tell us flat out that these unearthly monsters live inside of us. Freud, Edmundson argues, internalized the Gothic. He made us aware that the human psyche is itself a several storied haunted house. "Freud's remarkable achievement is to have taken the props and passions of terror Gothic – the hero-villain, heroine, terrible place, haunting – and to have relocated them inside the self." Indeed, we *are* haunted by our pasts, by traumas we absorbed and traumas we inflicted, and because of this the past does have the power to dominate the present, just as Gothic storytellers have claimed. Only we are haunted not by devilishly clever counts and mad scientists who chase us around dark mansions, but by "obsession, neurosis, compulsion, repetition, the uncanny, repression, death drive, and psychosis." The real hero-villain, it turns out, is our sadistic super-ego.[26]

Edmundson goes on to argue that the Gothic plot, in its several variations, has become one of the premier templates we use to make sense of our anxieties and fears. It has spilled out of its fictional domain and become a narrative form for divining the meaning of real events, a favorite of journalists and talking heads. Think of the effect of simple volume. We are hammered with 15-minute segments on TV news magazines of environmental catastrophes, political uprisings, wars and natural disasters. Putting this into perspective, Richard Stivers points out that "In traditional societies one had only to confront local tragedies, not those of the entire world simultaneously. Emotionally, then, one experiences the world of television as a place of ever-escalating disasters."[27] Journalists have to reach for a few proven formulas just to keep up with the flow of calamities, and the Gothic is a favorite. Thus, Michael Jackson, priest molesters, the Unabomber, and O.J. Simpson are all cast as Doppelgängers; they are brilliant, suave hero-villains.[28] Or think of the Gothic elements that have been ascribed to Osama Bin Laden, the emaciated but austerely handsome bedouin who, driven by stern principles, destroys buildings associated with our most consequential institutions – buildings filled with innocent women and children that melt in fiery conflagrations. He relentlessly pursues us, haunting us at every turn. Whenever rumors of his death begin to circulate, he makes ghostly appearances on mysterious tapes to rally the forces of evil and remind us of his invincibility, forcing us to ponder what past sins we have done to deserve this. When confronted with evil, we reach almost immediately for familiar Gothic scripts. And now we find ourselves in a culture where the Gothic idiom, Edmundson claims,

> has begun to shape and regulate our perception of reality, thrusting us into a world in which crazy militiamen, deranged priests, panoptic power, bizarre molesters, Freddy, Jason, and Leatherface constitute reality. They are – to more and more of us – what's out there ... [W]e have created a world of brightly toned, lethal cartoons.[29]

Like the covenant/jeremiad script, this one forces us to face our past transgressions, and invites us to own up to them. But we are prompted to do so in a different cosmos. The cosmos of the covenant is one in which the moral order is overseen by a benevolent power who has ultimate authority and good will toward the human race. The cosmos of the Gothic is one in which we are buffeted by powers whose intentions are unknown, and, judging from the body count of innocents, probably capricious. While the Gothic originated as a form of religious narrative, an offshoot of the Faust legend, it has moved far from its roots. Evil no longer occurs in a providential order that we can trust will ultimately contain it and even bring good out of it. More and more it occurs in a nihilistic universe where anything can happen. In Edmundson's analysis, the new Gothic has adopted a Foucaultian view of power as a force without a center to oppose (again, think of the hydra-like descriptions of global terrorism), but with a "supernatural vitality and resourcefulness that makes it virtually impossible to defeat." Consequently, it presses us to adopt an outlook that is fatalistic and inclined toward an immobilizing despair.[30] We have entered an era of history in which we are being persuaded that there are intractable forces of hatred arrayed against us.

If pressed to offer one reason for the recent "proliferation of Gothic," Edmundson concludes,

> that reason would in a certain sense be religious. Though most of us Americans claim to believe in God, few of us seem able to believe in God's presence. That is, we do not perceive some powerful force for good shaping the events of day-to-day life in accord with a perceptibly benevolent master plan. Most of us don't have a story that we can believe about the way God's designs are unfolding among us.[31]

In place of religious hope, he goes on, we have become fascinated with the Gothic. Why?

There is something to gain in accepting the harsh belief that the world is infested with evil, that all power is corrupt, all humanity debased, and that there is nothing we can do about it. With the turn to contemporary Gothic – no-fault, dead-end, politically impotent though it may be – we recover a horizon of ultimate meaning. We recover something of what is lost with the withdrawal of God from the day-to-day world. With the Gothic, we can tell ourselves that we live in the worst and most barbaric of times, that all is broken never to be mended, that things are bad and fated to be, that significant hope is a sorry joke, the prerogative of suckers. The Gothic, dark as it is, offers epistemological certainty; it allows us to believe that we've found the truth.[32]

So, the Gothic is a two-edged sword. It is a literary device designed for unearthing our hidden fears, anxieties and understandings of why the world is such a twisted place and possibly alerting us to our complicity in it. In performing this function, it lends itself to an honest, reflective diagnosis of sin and evil. But the spread of the Gothic template into journalism and social commentary is threatening to so overwhelm us with an impression of the forces of malice that afflict us that we risk a loss of hope, as well as nerve, and are thus tempted to abdicate our moral responsibility to reform ourselves and our institutions. Then we gripe and fume, but we do not join reform movements. Even a hard-hitting investigative news program like PBS's *Frontline*, which is sometimes jeremiad (we have strayed from our principles) and sometimes Gothic (the sins of the fathers are visited on their children), has surrendered to this mindset in its recent ad campaign: "Sit back and react." We may still rise and lash out against the "evil ones" who afflict us from outside, but even then it is becoming less clear what it is we are defending inside.

The best use of the Gothic as a tool of theological analysis is to pay close attention to the content it is inserting into its conventions. What is it, for instance, that has twisted the villain? Frankenstein's creature began as an innocent, and only became a monster in response to his horrible treatment at the hands of human beings. Shelley takes a theological position here that sin is acquired; like the creature, we are born innocent but then deformed under the influence of the accumulating viciousness of society. At one point, the monster laments, "I was benevolent and good; misery made me a fiend." In Shelley's anthropology, innocence is corrupted by an evil that assails it from without. But once corrupted, it becomes the corruption into which others are born. Or, to take another diagnostic approach, what wrongful act in the past might account for the present suffering of the victim? Was it duplicity, callousness, infidelity, inordinate desire, disregard for nature's laws and human finitude, overreaching ambition, neglect of filial duties, insensitivity toward the sublime, excessive consumption, selfishness, incest, brutality, immoderate self-reliance, undeserved insult? These are common originating sins in Gothic stories. In the Gothic, we are haunted by transgressions of the past, our own or those of others, sins that have wandered down circuitous routes, spinning off consequences, which themselves beget consequences. In the Gothic worldview, human actions set things in motion that cannot be taken back and in the end must be requited. Behind Gothic suffering is some originating wrongful act worth recovering and reflecting upon. At what moment in the past did someone slip from the moral order, and what decisions were made that allowed that to happen. How, in other words, was paradise lost? With this kind of attention, the Gothic can be exercised as a diagnostic tool for understanding how popular culture is working through the problem of sin.

Conclusion

Like theology, popular culture has its lost paradise myths to help it account for the shortcomings of human life and to address the question: What went wrong? This is the role played by covenant/jeremiad cycles and

Gothic plots as they permutate through literature, movies, journalism, fashion and music. Both are highly versatile as templates in the hands of artists who seek to schematize our errant ways. The covenant/jeremiad script is a good one for juxtaposing an ideal order to our boundless imaginations for deviancy. Through it, a stubborn moral faith that persists in the culture continues to have a voice, promoting repentance and invoking a more exalted and inclusive idea of justice than the one that prevails. It offers a proven device for inventorying both a society's sins and the contents of its conscience.

The Gothic script is particularly adept at exploring how the sins of the ancestors are visited upon their heirs. Thus it provides a way to correlate current social pathologies to past transgressions – this is one way of understanding what it means to be haunted. There is not as much allowance in the Gothic for the idea of a benevolent power urging repentance and promising renewal, but there is useful instruction in the spectrum of degradations that predictably follow as a consequence of particular kinds of moral offense.

8

Salvation

Religions must do more than itemize the ways things have gone wrong. A path of salvation must also be offered, bringing us to the topic of what theologians call "soteriology," the study of "deliverance" (Greek: *soteri*), and how the faithful avail themselves of it. What does popular culture have to say about methods and understandings of salvation?

Signs of the Times

One of the most cherished forms of salvation found in popular culture is the phenomenon of redemptive violence. In her book on the cultural meaning of the western in fiction and film, Jane Tompkins singles out redemptive violence as the key attraction of the genre. Every western plot culminates in an act of retaliatory violence that follows a certain formula: First, the hero is seen saddling his horse or sitting pensively in the saloon (or something along these lines), minding his own business. Then the troublemakers single him out, challenge his courage or his manhood or some other cowboy virtue. Next,

> The hero, provoked by insults, first verbal, then physical, resists the urge to retaliate, proving his moral superiority to those who are taunting him. It is never the hero who taunts his adversary; if he does, it's only after he's been pushed "too far." And this, of course, is what always happens. The villains, whoever they may be, finally commit an act so atrocious that the hero *must* retaliate in kind. . . . At this juncture . . . retaliatory violence becomes not simply justifiable but imperative: now, we are made to feel, *not* to transgress the interdict against violence would be the transgression.[1]

Pushed beyond the moral tipping point and having exhausted his extraordinary self-restraint, the humiliated hero finally surrenders to violence and fists or bullets start flying. When the dust settles, the hero is winded but his adversaries are either dead or begging for mercy. For the audience, this act of righteous vengeance, when it finally occurs, is not only warranted but prompts a feeling of "moral ecstasy." Our desire for retribution on behalf of the hero and the longsuffering townsfolk whose way of life he defends has been so inflamed that anything less than a bloodbath strikes us as a trivialization of justice. "The feeling of supreme righteousness in this instant," Tompkins writes, "is delicious."[2] It is in following this western plot formula to its climax that the audience momentarily transcends itself and undergoes what feels like a mystical rapture. And the same plot contrivance explains the perennial appeal of most action heroes and comic book superheroes, as well – from Popeye and Superman to Luke Skywalker, Rambo and Spider Man.

Another kind of experience of ecstatic self-transcendence is found through music. The place music holds in our lives is enormous. With the boost that mechanical – and now digital – reproduction has given to the production and circulation of music, every space, time, and human activity has become a market for music. Our ancestors heard music in churches, pubs and theaters, on occasions when musicians could be assembled. We listen to music virtually everywhere. And while the lyrics provide us with much of our education about life (as lyrics always have), our primary use for music is to tune and retune our moods. We use it to set the mood for romance, social gatherings, movies, studying, ballgames, parades, rites of passage, holidays, shopping, crowd control, strenuous exercise, airports, affairs of state, driving, remembering the dead, and worship. It has even begun to be used at meat packing plants to calm the animals before slaughter. Music's power is largely a matter of its effectiveness for inducing approximations of rapture. Our spirits are lifted, or lowered when appropriate, with the beat and melody. Music invites us outside of ourselves, and we like that.

The litmus test of a salvific, rejuvenating situation is commonly held to be its power to induce this kind of ecstasy. Ecstatic experiences are vigorously sought by many through pharmaceuticals, romance, sexuality, music, movies, art, and physical exertion. Perhaps some memory of the cathartic effect of religious beatitude survives in these activities. Alex Wright, for one, suggests that this is where the action is now, not in houses of worship but in more profane events like getting promoted at work, having sex, winning the lottery, identifying with the characters in a television series, plunging into nature, and undertaking political action. Wright contends that formal worship in religious communities offers little in the way of "release and liberation" compared to these activities.[3]

Westerns and action movies, music, drugs, art, exercise – what each of these cultural artifacts has in common is the lure of ecstatic experience. Tillich developed his reflections on ecstasy to prod his readers toward a new way of understanding revelation. The ground of Being, he claimed, is revealed in ecstasy, in the brief mingling of the self with something outside of itself that brings one for a moment into the otherwise unapproachable presence of the holy. For Tillich, virtually anything can be the tripwire for an ecstatic experience. But ecstasy only rises to the standard of revelation, he argued, when one has been turned inside out, seen for what one is, then returned to normal consciousness aware that reality is somehow different than one had imagined it to be. There is, then, this peculiar epiphanal quality to ecstatic revelation: encountering the duality of the holy leaves one feeling *both* judged and healed.

Ecstatic experience that rises to the standard of revelation should be about more than simple release and liberation. Kenneth Kirk, in his book, *The Vision of God*, lamented the fact that in much of both ancient pagan and traditional Christian thought "ecstasy was taken as constituting the *whole* end of human endeavor." The problem with this, Kirk suggested, is that it deforms self-transcendence into self-absorption. The whole of religious piety then comes to revolve around choreographing the next ecstatic experience. "*Without* an experience of a particular kind," Kirk wrote, one can suppose oneself "to be deserted by God, void of religion, and without hope in the world; *with* that experience (or with something which one mistakes for it) one may only too easily regard everything else – morality, self-discipline, love of the brethren – as irrelevant and superfluous."[4] Thus these periodic launderings of our consciousness should not be aspired to as ends in themselves, but as the means to achieving new moral resolve.

Salvation is also sought in popular culture through the aid of traditional symbols and icons, although they are lifted from their original contexts. In his explorations of Generation X, Tom Beaudoin notes the strange use of Catholic paraphernalia like crucifixes, rosaries, and saint medallions as fashion accessories. One could add to this the circulation in popular culture of icons borrowed from religious traditions all over the world – lingas, Buddhas, Celtic crosses, yin-yangs, mandalas, crystals, angels, images of Kali and Ganesh, dashboard statuary, stone fetishes, Lakota walking sticks and Tibetan prayer flags – in every conceivable mix-and-match combination.

Beaudoin turns to the concept of sacramentalism to make sense of this phenomenon.[5] Augustine defined sacraments as the visible signs of hidden realities, in which one thing is seen while another is understood, and the thing to be understood is some modality of grace. Sacraments – like baptism, communion, and penance – are rituals through which divine grace is keyed to particular turning points in our lives. In the *New Catechism of the Catholic Church*, we discover that in addition to the sacraments, there is something called "sacrament*als*" that resemble sacraments, but are derivative and convey grace only to the extent that they dispose people to remember and receive the official sacraments. Such practices and artifacts as "the veneration of relics, visits to sanctuaries, pilgrimages, processions, the stations of the cross, religious dances, the rosary, medals, etc.," which have arisen spontaneously from the people and differ according to history and region are, with some trepidation, sanctioned by the Church.[6] The free circulation of all sorts of religious icons that are now incorporated into our wardrobes, jewelry, wall art, mantles, refrigerator doors and dashboards might be seen in this light, as jumbled signs of grace we surround ourselves with, driven to do so by some foggy but tenacious memory. And part of their allure remains what it always has been – that the recognition of these objects as bearers of grace originates with *das Volk*, and is only begrudgingly and secondarily endorsed by religious authorities, if at all. The use of sacramentals, in other words, is a subversive means of receiving grace; it is a subaltern exercise in style, consuming items that are already rich with symbolic meaning, but deployed in myriad, unsanctioned ways to assert new meanings and idiosyncratic appropriations of grace.

Advertising is another instrument of salvation in our culture. At least it is a pulpit from which salvation is promised, and we steadily and eagerly listen. Products are pitched to us with the assurance that they will deliver us beyond this world of travail and into the promised land of fulfilled desire. Every 30-second commercial, as Walter Davis explains it, "portrays a minidrama of sin and salvation: depicting evil, its source, who or what can save us, the happiness that follows deliverance, and what we must do to be saved."[7] Ads convince us of our need for salvation by fingering our anxieties and making them more raw than they already are – in fact, advertisers have a vested interest in keeping our anxieties rubbed raw. They exacerbate our fears and anxieties around nature, the judgment of others, being unloved, anomie, pain, boredom, dirt, and even our dread over disordered values. Ad writers are some of our society's most ingenious minds, and they are dedicated to tapping into our boundless yearning for salvation and bending it into decisions to consume the products they are selling – SUVs, cellular phones, shaving cream, financial planning, erectile dysfunction pills, diamonds – with the expectation that in acquiring these products we will be rewarded with goods that otherwise elude us: freedom, beauty, power, knowledge, pleasure, and immortality.[8]

We absorb from advertising many of our most basic convictions about how to obtain salvation. We grasp for redemption by stylishly adorning our bodies and dwellings with icons and sacramentals. We seek grace and self-transcendence through music, drugs, strenuous exercise, art, and the redemptive violence of our matinee heroes. These are all familiar instruments of salvation in popular culture, means by which we attempt to feel better and to restore what we sense is missing from our lives. To some degree, they work; to some degree, they make matters worse. Music, in particular, is potent as an instrument of salvation.

Soteriology in Song

A character in one of Oscar Wilde's plays confesses,

> After playing Chopin, I feel as if I had been weeping over sins that I had never committed, and mourning over tragedies that were not my own. Music always seems to me to produce that effect. It creates for one a past of which one has been ignorant, and fills one with a sense of sorrows that have been hidden from one's tears. I can fancy a man who had led a perfectly commonplace life, hearing by chance some curious piece of music, and suddenly discovering that his soul, without his being conscious of it, had passed through terrible experiences, and known fearful joys, or wild romantic loves, or great renunciations.[9]

While Chopin's preludes and nocturnes are not what most of us "play" on our stereos, Wilde captures in these words the ecstatic reverie that we still listen to music in order to experience. Soul, blues, jazz, rock – we fill our lives with music as a kind of soundtrack to train and amplify our emotional awareness about the contents of our lives, or what we wish were the contents of our lives. Good popular music does what good music has always done – it enshrines an experience in sounds that others can in some manner visit and borrow as their own when the sounds are replayed. Our souls can pass mimetically through terror, joy, love, and loss under the guidance of the musical composition, ecstatically drawn into the inner life of another. As the late Joe Strummer put it: "On the road to rock 'n' roll/the lonely sing a soulful song/and leave a little light in the wilderness for somebody to come upon."[10]

The ritual roots of rock

Music has always had an association with the numinous and has been commonly put to ritual use. It was performed by our ancestors to placate the gods and invoke their assistance. Psalmody (chanted prayers sometimes accompanied by stringed instruments) arose in ancient Israel and was passed on to both Rabbinic Judaism and Christianity in the first century CE. Both Tertullian and Augustine endorsed the use of music in prayers and to lift the heart in worship. The Mass was recited in plainsong and later accompanied by Gregorian chant. In the high middle ages, music was held to be a branch of theological metaphysics, a way of marking the harmonic order of the planets and the cosmos itself – the music of the spheres – thus elevating its role in creating an atmosphere fit for the visitation of God during the Mass. Liturgical music, sung in Latin, was used to draw the worshipper out of herself and into communion with God. Luther was a great advocate of music; he wrote several hymns in German and encouraged the laity to sing during worship. He is reported to have said, "Music drives away the Devil and makes people gay; they forget thereby all wrath, unchastity, arrogance, and the like. . . . Experience proves that next to the Word of God only music deserves to be extolled as the mistress and governess of the feelings of the human heart."[11] With John Wesley, the founder of Methodism, and his brother Charles, the writer of over 6,000 hymns, the use of popular, singable tunes that could be sung outside of worship and aimed at stirring hearts to repentance and devotion and at offering instruction in the faith fueled several religious revivals in Britain and the US.

During the religious awakenings in the mid-eighteenth and early nineteenth centuries, the hymns of Wesley and Isaac Watts swept through camp meetings, energizing the movement of the spirit throughout the States. Charles Finney, a leader of the Second Awakening, promoted the use of popular music and colorful preaching as a way to excite the emotions and thereby "wake up the dormant moral powers, and roll back the tide of degradation and sin."[12] In the south, where slaves would congregate on the periphery of the meetings and take part in their own revivals, elements of this new British hymnody were absorbed into the ecstatic "ring shouts" they had brought with them from West Africa. In a ring shout, several "shouters" would move to the center of a ring of worshippers, and "begin a slow, syncopated shuffling, jerking movement," that was "'bumped' by the handclapping or body slapping of those waiting on the sidelines." They would sing, slowly at first, but as they circled and danced, the pace of their singing would surge, until they were singing only the most cherished refrain, as the stomping and clapping of the outer ring grew more feverish. Revival hymns were incorporated into this ritual, with the shouters intoning lyrical lines to which those gathered in the outer ring would sing back a response. This style of shout and response is a form of "hymn-lining," with the song leader calling out each line of the hymn and the congregation then singing back in reply.[13]

Rock and roll has roots in this history of sacred music. Spirituals gave rise to gospel singing and then to the succession of blues, jazz, soul, and rhythm and blues.[14] The great soul singers who began recording in the 1950s – James Brown, Sam Cooke, Wilson Pickett and Curtis Mayfield – all launched their careers as gospel singers. Otis Redding, Aretha Franklin and Marvin Gaye were children of preachers. They are all key figures in the secularization of many of the conventions of gospel music as it metamorphosed into soul, moving its most appealing features from the house of worship to the nightclub. The hymn-lining interactions of the song leader and his chorus, the syncopated movements of the shouter and the swaying, handclapping supporters of the outer ring, the accelerating pace of each verse with a crescendo in the refrain, the moans, howls and gesticulations of the black preacher, the rhythmic release of tension and pent up emotions and the harmonic patterns of gospel survive in soul. Ray Charles, who grew up Baptist, imported the charisma and stylistic genius of the itinerant evangelist into his routine. Some of his biggest hits were barely disguised gospel favorites, and his style of piano playing would have been equally at home at a revival service. It is not hard to hear the gospel standard "This Little Light of Mine" audible in the background of "This Little Girl of Mine." His songs also revolved around the causes of evil and retained a scheme for salvation, namely human suffering (poverty, loneliness, heartache, humiliation, betrayal, the blues – "all the world is sad and lonely wherever I roam") can be overcome by the love of a good woman. Or, as James Brown lays it down in "It's a Man's, Man's, Man's World," man made the car, the train, the electric light, and the boat – to relieve him of his burdens and protect himself from being overwhelmed by the world – but in the end, he's "lost in the wilderness, lost in bitterness" if he's without a woman. In the soteriology of soul, the travail of a man's life can only be redeemed by the devotion of a steadfast woman.

Rock and roll derives from these precursors. And while the connection to this legacy of sacred music becomes more obscure with rock than it was with soul, many of the basic stylistic elements and salvific themes persist. While it has been stretched nearly to the breaking point, there is a residual religion$_3$ that still runs through the veins of rock and roll. To begin with, it is often performed in a venue that was in earlier eras the exclusive precinct of religion. A predecessor of the outdoor summer music festival (Lilith Fair, Woodstock, Ozzfest, Lollapalooza, Rolling Thunder Review, Burning Man Festival, Rainbow Festival) was the revival camp meeting and its successor, the Chautauqua.[15] And like its predecessor, the music festival provides an occasion to shed one's routines, normal obligations and comforts in order to enter a liminal world designed to optimize the possibility for self-transcendence and to practice a different mode of community. It has clear Edenic and utopian overtones. Festivals of the mid-1990s were nomadic global villages, and would feature midways of kiosks that promoted NGOs and political causes, vegetarian cuisine, smart drink bars, mask vendors and body piercing/tattoo artists.

A Turnerian analysis is appropriate here.[16] In rock concerts we enter liminal time and space, we enter a ritual of anti-structure that has some capacity to cleanse our interior consciousness and enable us to imagine new ways of being. The great mix of sounds, images, emotions, and to some degree, statuslessness, that swirl around one at a music festival can be disorienting in a productive, rejuvenating way. Just as in traditional rites of passage, then, these modern festivals can thrust those who are present into the self-dissolving experience of communitas, planting within them a vision that is antithetical to the bureaucratic structures in which they spend their lives. In Turner's view, "Rock is clearly a cultural expression and instrumentality of that style of communitas which has arisen as the antithesis of the 'square,' 'organization man' type of bureaucratic social structure of mid-twentieth-century America."[17]

It is worth pointing out, however, that when Turner included rock music in his list of liminoid artifacts the corporate sponsorship that now brands logos onto every available surface at rock concerts had not reached its present level of saturation. Given the importance Turner attached to the symbols that one is exposed to at the peak of the liminal phase, the *sacra* of the tribe, he might take a less sanguine view toward the "anti-structural" potential of the current festival scene.[18] These corporate logos may well be the icons and sacred diagrams of our people, the elemental symbols upon which our culture is built: Sony, Chevrolet, Hilfiger, Tower Records, Major League Baseball, Netscape, Nintendo, MTV, Smirnoff, Starbucks, and Altoids – all frequent music festival sponsors. Their logos may well be the religious symbols that point toward the transcendent forces that our culture increasingly views as salvific – electronic devices, cars, clothes, music, sports, the Internet, virtual reality, celebrities, narcotics, stimulants, and sweet-smelling breath. And a similar analysis could be done of the symbols that are put on display in music videos – which are themselves great pageants of consumption if not outright product placement, and reach largely overlapping conclusions about our objects of veneration.

But rock music is not entirely about its accoutrements. It is also worth examining for its lyrical content. Much contemporary rock music is either vacuous or nihilistic. Unfortunately, this is some of the most commercially successful recorded music, conveying the message that shallowness, self-destruction, or the raw assertion of the will-to-power will be rewarded with profit and fame. Another big segment of highly successful rock music is about youth in their twenties dealing with angst and various resentments typical of their age and sorting out things like self-esteem, identity, and relationships with friends and lovers. This can become a bit redundant with its stories of false starts, premature reports of enlightenment, alienation and dead ends, but there is some value in eternally rehashing these experiences in light of shifting cultural conditions. Then there are performers who conscientiously pursue salvific themes in their music – through social protest, romance, and mysticism.

Social protest

Reaching back to Woody Guthrie and Pete Seeger, and through the folk music scene of the early 1960s with Joan Baez and Bob Dylan, a lineage of pop-protest balladeers (folk musicians with electric guitars) can be traced, including Marvin Gaye, John Lennon, Billy Bragg, The Pretenders, The Police, Suzanne Vega, REM, U2, and Joe Strummer. The pop-protest song bears one of the most direct debts of rock music to the black churches through the civil rights movement. Its roots are in the music sung on picket lines and aboard freedom buses, and, as Jon Michael Spencer points out, these songs "were often original or modified hymns, spirituals, and the blues... new lyrics were occasionally given to known religious tunes."[19] As Dylan admitted, he borrowed the tune and the inspiration for his first big hit, "Blowin' in the Wind" from the old spiritual, "No More Auction Block."[20] Protest songs use musical hooks to convey timely prophetic utterances like Dylan's cold war query: "How many times must the cannon balls fly/Before they're forever banned?/How many times can a man turn his head/And pretend that he just doesn't see?" to which the chorus replies ambiguously, "The answer is blowing in the wind";[21] or Strummer's more recent:

> You gotta get down Moses, once we were free;
> The recipe for living is lost in memory.
> You gotta get down Moses from the eagle's eyrie,
> You gotta make new friends out of old enemies ...
> You gotta get down Moses, down in the pit.
> No matter what the question the gun will answer it.
> You gotta get down Moses – in between
> the biggest opposites that a magnet ever seen.
> You gotta get down Moses – electrify;
> Remind us of the past, remind us of the sky.[22]

Or, take U2's anthem, "Where the Streets Have No Name": Bono sings of his longing to break apart the walls that close him in, to reach beyond them and touch a flame that burns in a place where streets have no name.[23] Originally written in 1987 as a commentary on the painted curbs that demarcate Republican from Unionist neighborhoods in Belfast, the band offered a remarkable performance of it during the half-time show at the 2002 Superbowl, pressing the edges of its meaning beyond the rivalries of Northern Ireland. Presented in tribute to the victims of September 11, as Bono sang of being buffeted by winds and "trampled in dust," vacillating between building love up and then burning it down, a titanic vertical curtain ascended behind the band with the names of those who died that day shimmering on it, rising to the heavens. At the song's crescendo, the by then towering curtain was released, and gravity brought it tumbling to the ground, each illumined name crumpling into darkness. In this bit of stagecraft, the September 11 victims were fittingly remembered, but coming as it did from an Irish band with a reputation for its criticisms of the exploitative excesses of American hegemony, a subtext was joined to the picture of a clash of civilizations that the terrorist attack had exacerbated in the popular imagination – that beyond the ruins of our clannish hatreds, there is a flame that illuminates a place where streets have no name, where divisions of politics, economics, geography and religion have been left behind. Joining the image of the collapsing tower with this image of a common human destiny was an innovative moment of mythmaking. And it transpired at the Superbowl, no less, the high holy day of so many things American.

In pop-protest music, hope is envisioned in the wind, in the sky, in the flame, in nameless streets where human differences have been relinquished – in those poetic regions where an elusive transcendence is still allowed to be conceived. Protest music can serve as a kind of soundtrack to social reform, drawing on the combined force of its snarling or exhilarating sound and its semiotically rich lyrics. It does as spirituals and gospel music have always done: it elicits powerful emotions and harnesses them simultaneously to a criticism of human sinfulness *and* to a source of hope, often symbolized, as it is in these examples, in perennial, if oblique and often unconscious, metaphors of the spirit and reign of God.

Love songs

So, there are salvific themes in songs of protest. In Tillich's terms, these songs express a moral faith, a faith that the holy enters the world through acts of justice and human kindness. Love songs, too, are sometimes infused with more hope for salvation than first meets the eye. True, at one level, all love songs are about salvation – we place much stock in having love returned by the human object of our affections. We can turn any person into an ultimate concern and torture them with the expectations that accompany that level of devotion. But some love songs probe this longing in a way that transcends human love; some love songs recognize the beloved as a symbol of divine love. And the self-transcendence that can arise instinctively in the affections we feel for those we love is credible rehearsal for the self-transcendence that is characteristic of genuine religious faith. The *Song of Songs* in the Bible has long served as a prototype authorizing a use of love poems as allegories for the love for God, allowing the imagination to move from vivid depictions of the charms of the beloved toward the experience of surrender to the overwhelming love of the divine. In the New Testament, Paul spoke of the church as the bride of Christ, a bride longing for the return of her beloved. Even the drive for sexual union has inspired in religiously sensitive poets ample material for picturing the beatitude of seeing God face to face, of losing oneself in the eros of divine plenitude. This moves into what Tillich described as ontological faith – the faith that the holy enters the world through expressions of beauty.

Nick Cave is a virtuoso in this kind of gingerly, double-decked handling of the love song. With his band, The Bad Seeds, he has circled around the ploys, satisfactions and disillusionments of human love as tokens of the elusive love (and wrath) of God. In a song from the recent CD, *Boatman's Call*, he sings:

> I've felt you coming, girl, as you drew near . . .
> Are you my destiny? Is this how you'll appear? . . .
> Are you the one that I've been waiting for? . . .
> As you've been moving surely toward me
> My soul has comforted and assured me . . .
> All down my veins my heart-strings call,
> Are you the one that I've been waiting for.[24]

These lyrics are thick with the theme of advent, of the irresistible approach of someone unknown but long awaited, one who has long been an anticipated source of comfort and consolation. Like Dylan's song, "Shelter from the Storm" ("If I could only turn back the clock to when God and her were born./'Come in,' she said, 'I'll give you shelter from the storm.' "),[25] love songs can stress the desire for the beloved as a symbol full of anticipation for communion with God. They can haunt us in religiously productive ways, testifying to the joys and satisfactions that will be realized in that ultimate union.

Cave is deliberate about the sacramental quality of his love songs. In an address he originally gave at the Vienna Poetry Festival in 1998, "The Secret Life of the Love Song," and later released as a studio recording that is punctuated with his own love songs, Cave proposed that:

Though the love song comes in many guises – songs of exultation and praise, songs of rage and of despair, erotic songs, songs of abandonment and loss – they all address God, for it is the haunted premise of longing that the true love song inhabits. It is a howl in the void for love and for comfort. . . . It is the song of the lover in need of her loved one, the raving of the lunatic supplicant petitioning his God. It is the cry of one chained to the earth and craving flight; a flight into inspiration and imagination and divinity.

Love songs, he goes on, are typically sad, indeed they are the very "noise of sorrow itself," because they are bred in that region of the soul where the yearning to be "transported from darkness into light, to be touched by the hand of that which is not of this world," finds its efforts unrequited. Love songs are written out of a "divine discontent," out of a longing sadness that will persist until and unless one finally sees the face of God. And this is the condition of life – to live in the prelude of this consummation. The erotic is a prefiguration of beatitude. The loves of this life are anticipatory of entering the fullness of God. Moses was told that no one sees the face of God and lives; and so, Cave concedes, he will be happy to be sad in the meantime, accompanied by the small consolations of human love and songs about it, including his own songs, his "crooked brood of sad-eyed children."[26]

In a poignant song called "Bring It On," written after his recent marriage, Cave presses his allegorical skills beyond his earlier themes of sadness and longing to probe the meaning of covenant and fidelity. Conjuring the image of a garden, an image that resonates with both the primal landscape of paradise, where Adam and Eve cavorted and communed with God and nature, and the enclosure where Solomon and his bride, in the *Song of Songs*, withdrew from the world to join together and be "drunk with love," Cave sings:

> This garden that I built for you
> That you sit in now and yearn
> I will never leave it, dear
> I could not bear to return
> And find it all untended
> With the trees all bended low
> This garden is our home, dear
> And I got nowhere else to go.

The longing of his earlier lyrics has been subdued, and he uses the respite to contemplate an alternative to constant yearning, redirecting it into the cultivation of this garden he has built and now intends to maintain. He comforts his beloved with the chorus:

> So bring it on
> Bring it on
> Every little tear
> Bring it on
> Every useless fear
> Bring it on
> All your shattered dreams.[27]

This promise of fidelity, of a vow to be observed, is another mode of divine love that human beings have been invited to practice, in imitation of the love of God for Israel, and captureable in the love song. It is a stubborn and steadfast love, tender and enduring. It is not without its own sadness, but settles into a rhythm of disaffection and affection, a rhythm of departure and return that will not be broken.

Van Morrison is another prolific writer of love songs in this mode. His couplet "It's All in the Game/You Know What They're Writing About" is a masterpiece of the genre. The song begins with a plaintive viola weaving in and out of a rhythm and blues piano with steady but soft percussion in the background. Morrison begins singing in a sympathetic voice, "Many a tear has to fall," and proceeds to comment on a lovers' quarrel, "You had words with him/And your future's looking dim," but he consoles, "these things your heart can rise above." The viola continues its sad lament, as the piano meets it with some moderately uplifting chord sequences, tingling like a palpitating heart. The lyric resumes, at points barely rising above a whisper:

> It's a thing called love down through the ages
> Makes you wanna cry sometimes
> Makes you want wanna lay down and die sometimes
> Makes you high sometimes
> But when you really get in it lifts you right up

Then, joined by a horn section pushing the energy up, Morrison launches into one of his trademark controlled stutters – "You know, you know, you know what they're talkin' about/You you you you you you you you you you...,/It's a thang, it's a thang, ain't it a wonderful thang/A wonderful, marvelous game" – and then as if stuttered to the point of inarticulateness, he surrenders, "And when there's no more words to say about love I go," at which point he reaches down in his gut and retrieves one of his long, oscillating *sean-nos* drones, his body a fleshy bagpipe, until his lungs give out. And for the next several minutes he chants: "Meet me down by the river . . . meet me down by the water . . . meet me down by the pylons," and, finally, he whispers, hollers, moans and coos: "I want you to meet me, meet me, are you there, are you, are you there? Know, know, know, know, know, I want you to meet me, are you there?" which he repeats ad nauseum.[28]

With every shade of brokenheartedness dislodged and swirling about, the song rises to a summit of yearning for a reunion of the separated, but it ends both lyrically and musically unresolved, the final strokes of the viola hesitant to surrender to the invitation. It is a sad song, "the noise of sorrow itself," as Nick Cave might describe it, but redolent with the longing to be transported from dark loneliness into a great, consoling embrace. It creates in music a sanctum that is filled with the air of forgiveness and a standing invitation to enter its gates.

Not all love songs rise to this level. In fact, most don't. But even in more routine songs about love, there can be a haunting sense that the immediate object of one's desire or affections is a proxy for the divine beloved, for God's own beautiful countenance, and that the rewards and sometimes grueling work of human love trains us for the community of love for which God intended creation and for communion with the divine itself. In truth, love songs are more likely to be driven by concupiscence – that inordinate, inextinguishable engine of desire within us that has lost its way – but, as Augustine, the great diagnostician of concupiscence, so perceptively understood, lurking in the background of concupiscence is a faulty memory that dimly knows it will be sated by nothing short of beholding God. As St Bonaventura would later describe it, "in God alone is the original and true delight, and we are led back to seeking it in all other delights."[29]

Into the mystic

Paths to salvation in rock and roll can be found, then, in songs of social protest and love, but also, in the work of some artists, through an almost medieval understanding of mystical rapture. This is a prominent feature in some Irish musicians, like the Waterboys, Sinead O'Connor and Van Morrison, and in some makers of ambient music, like Moby and Lisa Gerrard (Dead Can Dance). These performers sing about various registers of the holy, and write music designed to lift one out of oneself to reach out for the mystical ladder, rising on chordal progressions from the sensory world to higher things, even to the mind of God. Like the love song, these songs express an ontological faith.

Drawing on the ancient idea that each person is a microcosm of the universe and that each soul mirrors God, O'Connor sings, "I have a universe inside me/Where I can go and spirit guides me/There I can ask oh any question/I get the answers if I listen."[30] Or, consider lines from "Strange Boat," a haunting track from the Waterboys: "We're sailing on a strange boat/heading for a strange shore/ . . . We're climbing on the strangest ladder/that was ever there to climb/ . . . We're living in a strange time/working for a strange goal/We're turning flesh and body into soul."[31] These artists often use metaphors for the journey of the soul that could have been drawn straight from the treasuries of Teresa of Avila and John of the Cross – light and darkness, the dawn, the colors blue and black, waters, flames, sky, heat, smoke, doors, gardens and deserts. These are the last sensual outposts en route to an experience of mystical union. Moby's song, "Into the Blue," draws straight from this lexicon:

> Let in some air, I dare lie down
> To stare at the sky
> I am wide open
> Reaching forever
> I fly into the blue
> I am wide open
> Reaching forever
> I fly into the blue ...
> I move I move
> The light the light
> Here comes the tide
> With water surrounding me
> I am wide open
> Reaching forever
> And I fly into the blue[32]

Pursuing the contemplative logic of the mystic, this approach to musical poetics recognizes in the sensible world many signs of the invisible things of an ethereal realm, holy symbols to the mystically trained mind. Step by step, the heart ascends to stages of illumination.

Again, Van Morrison is a key figure here, both because he is such a consummate practitioner of the genre, and because of his influence on others – like O'Connor, the Waterboys, U2 and Nick Cave. He blends Celtic spirituality with gospel fervor and the primal moans and grunts of rhythm and blues to ratchet the soul up to places where the air is thin. In songs like "Haunts Of Ancient Peace," "In the Garden," "Pagan Streams," "Astral Weeks," "Take It Where You Find It," "Spirit," "Take Me Back," and "Summertime in England," he narrates walks across bucolic countrysides, inviting the listener to join him, traversing meadows, green fields, peaceful rivers, shorelines and old ruins as he invokes the names of sacred places, gospel singers, and Romance poets. And just when tranquility seems within reach, he throws the song into gear, sometimes with the help of a horn section or a church organ, and a line like "but when you really get in, it lifts you right up," or "the shiver from my neck down to my spine/ignited me in daylight and nature," and one discovers that a strange and uncertain place has been entered indeed. This ushers in a reverie of repeated lines, like "As the great, great, great, great, great, great, great Being watches over," or "Spirit don't ever die/Oh, no, spirit don't ever die/Never let spirit die."

In "Summertime in England," a nearly 16-minute romp by lakesides, through pastures and past Avalon, where legend has it Jesus, when he visited England, himself walked, Morrison invokes Wordsworth, William Blake, T.S. Eliot, and Mahalia Jackson.[33] Then the rhythm pauses, the notes of a gospel organ are heard, and Morrison drifts toward stuttering reiterations of "It ain't why, it just is/That's all/That's all there is about it/It just is," then, "Can you feel the light?/Can you feel the light?" and finally, "Put your head on my shoulder/And you listen to the silence/Can you feel the silence?" Listeners are transported to beatitude by traversing a geography that is sung into holiness.

One of Morrison's most finely wrought contemplative exercises is found on his 1991 release, *Hymns to the Silence*.[34] It is a track called "Take Me Back," and follows immediately after his cover of the old gospel standard, "Just a Closer Walk with Thee." The first line of "Take Me Back" resumes the peregrination with which the preceding hymn concluded – allowing Morrison to move from "I'll be satisfied as long as I walk, dear Lord, close to Thee," where the hymn left him, to "I've been walking by the river... I've been feeling so sad and blue." His sadness follows a bout of stuttering out, "I've been thinking, I've been thinking, I've been thinking..." about the suffering and confusion in the world. Then he pleads, with an even more prolonged stutter, "Take me back, take me back, take me back... way back... to when life made more sense... when you felt so good, and I felt so good... and I understood the light." Under the spell of Morrison's vocalizations, one aspirated "huh" can trigger *satori*, and like a zen master clapping his hands, the listener is awakened from flummoxed conceptual thinking and into a non-dual awareness of the interrelatedness of all reality. But Morrison presses on, he is only half way through the song. He sings, "I feel like I wanna blow my harmonica," which he does, respirating through it in controlled, pure breaths which help him to bridge from his melancholic funk back to a "golden afternoon, a golden afternoon, a golden afternoon," when "everything felt, everything felt, everything felt... so right and so good." This chant, repeated over and over, gradually descends to a whisper as if coming into the very presence of the holy, offering no resistance until, barely audible, he sighs, "in the eternal now, in the eternal moment, in the eternal now..."

> When you lived, when you lived
> When you lived in the light
> When you lived in the grace
> In the grace, in grace
> When you lived in the light
> In the light, in the grace
> And the blessing.

At this, his voice falls silent, and the piano, strings and soft percussions that have been orbiting like an electromagnetic field around the steel core of his vocals, relent and find a place to rest. Lyrically, a blessing has been offered; musically, a point of resolution has been attained. All energy subsides into perfect stillness. In music like this, Van Morrison erects sanctuaries of sound that those with ears to hear may enter and settle into for a moment of grace.

Forgiveness of Sins: The Therapeutic Confession

A recurring plotline in cinema tells the story of a suffering soul who defies the stultifying repression of a rigid, moralistic community in order to be true to the gift of insight and beauty that churns inside, and which must find a way out – even at the cost of being ostracized by the community. It is the story of Vincent van Gogh – the solemn, awkward son of a Dutch Calvinist pastor who, rejected by his church and wavering on the edge of insanity, paints canvases that reenchant the ordinary world. It is also the story of the young artist from the Hasidic community in Chaim Potok's novel *My Name is Asher Lev*. It represents the pitting of ontological faith against moral faith, the *mysterium fascinosum* against the *mysterium tremendum*. This basic plot, run through various scenarios, has given us such memorable films as *Babette's Feast* (1987), *Breaking the Waves* (1996), *Pleasantville* (1998), and most recently, Lasse Hallström's *Chocolat* (2000).[35]

   Chocolat is a parable about the vivifying effect of a free-spirited *chocolatière*, Vianne, the daughter of a French pharmacist father and a Mayan *botanista* mother, on a pietistic Catholic village in France in the late 1950s (Figure 5). Vianne's nemesis is the mayor, Comte de Reynaud, who, like his ancestors before him, oversees the civic institutions and moral order of the community with a combination of paternal care and iron-willed determination. In the opening scene the villagers enter their church, passing the mayor who stands at the door, greeting each one, as the narrator sets the tone: "Once upon a time, there was a quiet little village in the French countryside whose people believed in *tranquillité*, tranquility." Then, as the worshippers sing "Come take possession of our souls and make them all thine own," the narrator continues: "If you lived in this village, you understood what was expected of you. You knew your place in the scheme of things. And if you happened to forget, someone would remind you."

Inside the church, the young vicar announces that the season of Lent has begun, a time for abstinence, reflection, and sincere penitence. With these words, a gust of wind blows open the doors of the church, and the camera pans out to reveal that newcomers Vianne and her daughter have just arrived in the village. Within days Vianne opens a chocolate

Figure 5 Vianne's chocolates have mysterious and therapeutic powers in the movie *Chocolat* (2000). Used under license from Miramax Film Corp. All rights reserved.

shop, Chocolaterie Maya, and, one by one, villagers duck in to sample her truffles, nipples of Venus, and chocolate seashells. Vianne's confections have unusual powers to unlock the repressed happiness of her customers; strangely drawn to the shop, her customers begin to confide their secrets to her – the estrangement of a daughter, the abuse of a husband. Vianne selects a chocolate to ameliorate each heartache, and everyone who consumes her chocolates begins to notice small transformations in their dreary lives. As word reaches the Comte – who is strictly observing Lent on a diet of water and lemon slices – that so many of the citizens in his charge are frequenting the Chocolaterie, he presses the young vicar to admonish through a homily those who are succumbing to the "guise of Satan" who has entered their lives as "the maker of sweet things, mere trifles – for what could seem more innocent, more harmless, than chocolate?"

In response, Vianne advertises that she will be staging a chocolate festival on Easter Sunday, with stalls and street performers, fertility dancers, jugglers and flame swallowers. In desperation, the Comte kneels alone before the crucifix in the church and prays for guidance. He rises, and in the dead of night before Easter sunrise, he breaks into the chocolate shop and commences hacking to bits the chocolate goddess in the window. A flake of chocolate lands on his lip. He licks it, savors it, then surrenders with a vengeance, gorging himself on the chocolate goddess, and finally falls fast asleep in the storefront window, weeping. The priest is the first to see him there in the morning. He awakens Vianne, and she gently awakens the mayor, offering him a drink as she assures him (echoing the eucharistic liturgy): "Drink this. Drink this, it will refresh you. I promise. Go ahead, drink." He does.

Then the Comte, sprawled in her chocolates, confesses to Vianne, "I'm so sorry."

She absolves him with an understanding smile, "I won't tell a soul."

Shortly, the Comte, who always sits in the front pew during worship, is seen slumped and disheveled in the back row, as the vicar begins his sermon.

> I'm not sure what the theme of my homily ought to be today. Do I want to speak of the miracle of our Lord's divine transformation? Not really, no. I don't want to talk about his divinity. I'd rather talk about his humanity. I mean, you know, how he lived his life here on earth. His kindness, his tolerance. Listen, here's what I think: I think we can't go around measuring our goodness by what we don't do, by what we deny ourselves, what we resist, and who we exclude. I think we've got to measure goodness by what we embrace, what we create, and who we include.

The congregation pours out of the church at the end of the service to join in the merrymaking of the chocolate festival, as the narrator voices over: "It was certainly not the most fiery sermon Père Henri would ever preach, nor the most eloquent. But the parishioners felt a new sensation that day, a lightening of the spirit, a freedom from the old *tranquillité*. Even the Comte de Renaud felt strangely released."

Staged entirely during the season of Lent, this story matches wits between two soteriologies: one of self-discipline and the other of self-fulfillment. The point of view of the movie is clearly on the side of the latter. In the story, petty confessions the villagers make to the vicar ("Chocolates, so innocent, I thought one little taste couldn't do any harm") are juxtaposed to the truly heart wrenching confidences that are shared with Vianne ("I don't love my husband, he beats me and I'm stupid to stay with him"). Even the vicar comes around in the end, rejecting any equation between goodness and self-denial. In his director's commentary featured on the DVD version of the film, Hallström reveals, "It's a story about temptation and the importance of not denying yourself the good things in life." As lovely and enchanting a movie as it is, there is something disturbing about the salvific powers it attributes to the "spiritual practice" of consumption in contrast to its desiccated portrayal of such traditional spiritual exercises as confession, penance, and fasting. In conjunction with the fetishizing of chocolate that this represents (there is a Mayan spirit world that backs up the transformative powers of Vianne's confections), there is the matter of its endorsing what Eugene McCarraher has called "commodity spirituality";[36] that is, the idea that spiritual formation is a matter of being discriminating consumers (this chocolate, not that one; this brand, not that one) who acquire commodities for the purpose of symbolizing their beliefs.

The bold contrast in this film between the efficacy of absolution offered in a chocolate shop to that offered in the church presents an instructive lesson in the way that the modern therapeutic ethos and its ideal of self-fulfillment has come to serve as the favored mode of confession and forgiveness in popular culture. To appreciate this, a brief detour through the evolution of confession is in order.

Confession in religion$_2$

Paul Ricoeur has argued that the notion of human beings standing guilty before some transcendent tribunal for evil deeds they have committed is one that had to gestate over many centuries, and go through several stages of development, before it entered the minds of our ancestors.[37] In its earliest stages, evil was viewed as some impurity in the environment that needed to be avoided because it defiled those who came into contact with it. Like an infection that was contracted through the body's contact with impure things, evil left those who touched it unclean and stained. Objects in the world that contained this taboo force were to be avoided; they were dreaded channels of the *mysterium tremendum*. Those who were defiled could expect to suffer any variety of calamities – their crops might fail, their fishing nets tear, their children fall ill. Purification after being stained was achieved through a variety of cleansing rituals – ceremonial washing, burning, sweating, induced vomiting. It is significant in this primitive understanding of evil that one could not always avoid being infected. Impurities were abundant in the world and not always obvious – they could be stumbled into unawares. Responsibility for sin in this scheme of things was a matter of being in the wrong place at the wrong time, and not yet that of the person who succumbs to temptation, carries through on a proscribed act, and is subsequently blameworthy for the action and its consequences. The modern notion of guilt as an anticipation of deserved chastisement (in this life or the next) for thoughts and deeds that can be attributed to a responsible agent – the sense that one carries a burden of weight accumulating from one's own past transgressions – emerged much later. Both testaments of the Bible offer a history of this evolution.

The phenomenon of the scrupulous conscience that examines itself in light of what it takes to be a divine demand to be holy, probing layer after layer of motive and perception, finally discovering at bottom an author of the action, uncovering a will that has set a wicked deed in motion – finding, that is, *a self* – seems to have emerged as a secondary effect of the sense of guilt. Ricoeur argues that human beings have become aware of themselves *as selves* because of an inchoate sense of guilt which they then reflected upon. "Man had the consciousness of responsibility [for sin] before having the consciousness of being cause, agent, author."[38] In the West this came to eloquent expression during the first century in both Judaism and Christianity. It is described in Jesus' Sermon on the Mount, which has parallels in rabbinic teachings of the same period, and rises again quite magnificently in Augustine's *Confessions*. Following on this, the development of the contours of the Christian conscience set out down a long and winding road in the history of the church.

The practice of confession and penance, what is sometimes called the "care of souls," is at the heart of this story. In the first few centuries of the church, sins were confessed publicly, and the forms of penance were often severe – humiliation before the community, fasting, abstinence from sex, exclusion from Christian fellowship and from the Eucharist. Absolution, or forgiveness for the *consequences* of sin (the time that would be spent in purgatory), was given only after the penance was completed – and until sometime around the sixth century, once baptized, a Christian could avail him or herself of absolution for more serious sins only once over the course of their lives. This once-in-a-lifetime provision was finally recognized as too severe and allowance was made for periodic rounds of confession/penance/absolution that an individual could make in private to a priest.

In caring for souls it was important that the burden of the penance fit the weight of the sin, taking into account not only the sinful action but also its motive and any extenuating circumstances that applied, and in order to guide clergy in assigning suitable penance, monks and bishops in the Middle Ages began composing *Penitential Manuals*, books which correlated sins to the penance they warranted. To make the practice more uniform, over time it became common to organize these handbooks following the scheme of the Ten Commandments or the seven cardinal sins, or some similar list of the sinful ways of human beings that the faithful could be taught to use as devices for inventorying their evil thoughts and actions since their last confession. This, as it turns out, proved to be a highly effective device for moral instruction. In memorizing these comprehensive lists of the categories of sin, a template for the moral life was internalized – the shape of the Christian conscience itself was formed, much as the Jewish conscience was formed by following the legal writings in the *Torah*. Moreover, in the fine-tuning that occurred over the centuries within the manuals, itemizing all the motives and circumstances that figure into the gravity of an offense, the complexity of human sinfulness was mapped out in exquisite detail. A boy who steals food because of his poverty must fast for three days; a boy who steals food to make a profit must compensate the victim and fast for 30 days. If one man kills another out of a flash of anger, he must live on bread and water for 3 years; if he has killed another by accident, he must do penance for only 1 year. If one man maims another in a fight that arises from a quarrel, he must cover the medical expenses and do the victim's work until he has healed. In an Irish *Penitential* written in the seventh century, the priest hearing confession was instructed on the mitigating circumstances that he is to keep in mind in determining penance:

> This is to be carefully observed in all penance: the length of time anyone remains in his faults; with what learning he is instructed; with what passion he is assailed; with what courage he stands; with what tearfulness he seems to be afflicted; and with what oppression he is driven to sin. For Almighty God who knows the hearts of all and has bestowed diverse natures will not estimate various weights of sins as worthy of equal penance.[39]

Many abuses arose over the centuries regarding the practice of penance and periodic reforms were necessary. Nevertheless, its role in shaping the Christian conscience and in training the faithful to interrogate their souls is an achievement that has left its mark on Western civilization in both law (canon law, a primary source of Western law, grew out of the *Penitentials*) and ethics. Moreover, in the whole confessional apparatus one can find the antecedents for modern psychology with its investigations of the layers of the human personality and its analyses of the mixture of external forces and internal motives that give rise to our behavior. The idea that there is a realm of self-interested forces at work in the depths of the human psyche was not an invention of Nietzsche, Marx or Freud. They probed it in new and instructive ways, but it had been an object under scrutiny for centuries through the manuals and practice of penitence.

While Protestants rejected the sacrament of penance and the belief in purgatory that it presumed, they retained many of its essential elements in their ethics and liturgy. The fundamental idea that good works can reduce one's guilt certainly survived, in spite of the Reformers protests that salvation depends upon grace alone, or that good works should be motivated by gratitude for God's mercy rather than by a desire to justify oneself. It merely mutated into what Max Weber called the Protestant work ethic – hard work and good works are an assurance of one's salvation. Moreover, somewhere in the scrupulous self-interrogation that both the Catholic sacrament of penance and the Protestant work ethic underwrote, Christians were reassured that they existed as selves who could author actions that would have consequences in the real world, and persuaded that these actions should conform to the will of God.

Confession in religion₃

The practical correlation between guilt and good works still found in Western societies is an enduring artifact of religion₃. But it is eroding, and has been at least since the nineteenth century. Nietzsche is a key figure in this (the *Übermensch* does not act out of guilt, but out of the joy of asserting unrestrained power), as is Arthur Rimbaud, whose legendary contempt for morality and the values of ordinary people was viewed by himself and his admirers as evidence of his poetic genius. But before both of these *provocateurs* there was Ralph Waldo Emerson, whose influence on US culture has been more thorough and permanent. Emerson's essay, *On Self-Reliance* (1841), dismisses family obligations when they conflict with the impulses of one's own genius, and berates philanthropists and relief societies who contribute even a dime to strangers and try to compel him to do likewise. His own shame, he tells us, is that he occasionally succumbs to their appeals. By and by, he assures us, he will have the "manhood" to resist. He sneers at those who do good works as an apology for their comforts in life: "Their virtues are penances. I do not wish to expiate, but to live." He goes on,

> No law can be sacred to me but that of my nature. Good and bad are but names very readily transferable to that or this; the only right is what is after my constitution, the only wrong what is against it. A man is to carry himself in the presence of all opposition, as if every thing were titular and ephemeral but he. I am ashamed to think how easily we capitulate to badges and names, to large societies and dead institutions.[40]

To recognize only those duties that issue from one's own nature is to live according to what Emerson calls "self-trust." And because it is in the nature of the self to change over time, one's sense of one's duties will change. A "great soul" harbors no reverence for its own past acts or promises, worrying that by acting with inconsistency others might be disappointed. "Why drag about this corpse of your memory?" Emerson asks. It is better, he counsels, to "live ever in a new day"; after all, "A foolish consistency is the hobgoblin of little minds."[41] The great souls among us will have nothing to do with consistency; instead, they will attend to their whims and follow where they lead. This, he tells us, is precisely what Socrates, Jesus, Luther and Galileo did, and it is what made them great.

Like Nietzsche, Emerson was a great admirer of Jesus for being a genius who respected no values other than those he invented.

Emerson marks a significant shift in the traditional practice of care for the soul. In place of the long struggle of the divided will, straining to conform one's desires to the good of the community and to the divine will as it has been represented in the faith community, the struggle for Emerson consists in asserting one's own inner nature – a nature that discloses itself to us through our whims, a sort of flashing epiphany of insight – against society and the obligations it seeks to impose. Values derived from the inner sanctum of the self are the preeminent way to order and justify our existence. He goes so far as to suggest that he might write "Whim" on the lintel of his doorpost, to warn all comers that he owes no explanations for his defiant thoughts and actions.[42] Victor Turner has alerted us to pay attention to symbols that appear at passageways. Emerson's doorpost has no gargoyles or ancient inscriptions, but the simple word, in uppercase, "Whim." This is the power that stands guard outside the sacred precincts of the inner self.

This unencumbered self, bound to no social conventions, no vows, not even the hobgoblin of foolish consistency, but only to pursuing the good of its own whimsical "nature," has become the ultimate concern for many in our society. Emerson received the gift of the concept of the self as cause, agent, and author of its actions from its long gestation in religion$_2$ and repositioned it in the center of a new faith. And as a faith, it has evolved for several generations since. It is not hard to hear in Emerson's writings a principled philosophy for what has come to be seen as the preeminence of the therapeutic in our culture. According to Philip Rieff, an early diagnostician of this phenomenon, a therapeutic culture is one in which a "sense of well-being has become the end, rather than a by-product of striving after some superior communal end."[43]

Many of the practices associated with the therapeutic and psychotherapy represent a religion$_3$ secularization of the old penitential system, offering an arena for confession, penance and absolution, and with many commendable effects. "Psychotherapy," after all, means healing (*therapeia*) of the soul (*psyche*). The therapeutic care of the soul, as an industry, is in the hands of psychiatrists, psychoanalysts, therapists, counselors, social workers, hospitals and pharmaceutical companies. As of the late 1990s, Americans spent $69 billion a year managing their feelings and tending to their emotional health.[44] The therapeutic includes this industry, but has expanded beyond it into popular culture at every level, which is permeated with its messages: trust your feelings, have faith in yourself, follow your bliss, do your own thing, listen to your inner child, do what feels right, be true to yourself. These messages are offered as formulas for salvation. Therapeutic values that are worthy of organizing one's life around, such as self-esteem, self-fulfillment, self-realization, and self-expression have come to be accepted as axiomatic, occupying the normative heights once controlled by such counter values as self-discipline, self-control and self-denial. As Eva Moskowitz likes to point out, as a measure of what has taken place: in a very short period of time, "America had four successive bestselling magazines: *Life, People, Us,* and *Self.*"[45]

The therapeutic has for some time been evolving on multiple fronts. It has carried one of its own most precious cultural goods – the feeling of personal happiness – to the various spheres of our culture (family, economy, law, politics, art, science, education) and offered it to them with the invitation that they make it their own central good. In this it has had many successes, and created many new markets for itself. In light of this, it is possible to view the therapeutic as approaching the status of a full-fledged religion$_2$ – complete with its own basic creed and rituals of salvation. Drawing on the recent book by Moskowitz, *In Therapy We Trust: America's Obsession with Self-Fulfillment,* its religion$_2$ elements could be outlined as follows:[46]

- *Creed*: Personal happiness is the ultimate concern. Happiness is lodged in one's feelings, and particularly in feelings of self-esteem, which are sacred. The root sin is the lack of self-esteem, the causes of which are typically found in poor parenting and in an array of authoritarian and disciplinarian institutions that we are raised to be answerable to. These institutions have thwarted the free emergence of our true selves.
- *Rituals*: All problems (in our personal lives, families, work, economic, educational, civic and political involvements) are treatable through therapeutic techniques: psychotherapy, support groups, encounter groups, recovery movements, motivational seminars, self-help books, talk shows, anti-depressants and other pharmaceuticals, and dance, play, music, sex, aroma, drama, or touch therapies. The primary aim of these rituals is to teach one to be authentic about one's feelings and to come to trust this level of the self. This authenticity is prerequisite to personal happiness.

That individual happiness has become an ultimate concern, and that happiness is a matter of deep feeling rather than of a disciplined will, is certainly not characteristic of all forms of therapy. But it is common in the thin kinds of pop therapeutic that show up in popular culture – as has been seen in the movie *Chocolat*. Other movies like *The Fisher King, Patch Adams, Dead Poets' Society,* and *Good Will Hunting* (note the common denominator of actor Robin Williams in each one) build their scripts around repressed feelings and memories that must be uncorked before characters can move forward and stalled plotlines resolved. Woody Allen has made a career out of screenplays about his own neuroses – *Annie Hall, Manhattan, Hannah and Her Sisters, Mighty Aphrodite, Husbands and Wives,* and *Deconstructing Harry.* Ridley Scott's 1991 hit, *Thelma and Louise,* was about two women who finally ditch abusive relationships and set out on a journey of self-discovery, trusting the guidance-system of their desires for the first time in their lives, which leads to a dark but exhilarating – and we are led to believe, fulfilling – charge into the unknown. Or, in what may be the most memorable distillation of the therapeutic in modern cinema, Obi-Wan Kenobi advises Luke Skywalker at the end of the first *Star Wars* movie: "Turn off your computer, turn off your machine and do it yourself, follow your feelings, trust your feelings." "Let go, Luke!" he presses him, "Feel, don't think!"

Even the Disney Studio's animated films of the last several years – *Beauty and the Beast, Aladdin, The Lion King, Pocahontas, Tarzan,* and *Finding Nemo* – have been a consistent platform for lessons in cherishing one's inner self, trusting one's feelings, and overcoming haunted childhoods. In the latest, *Finding Nemo* (2003), an overly protective, widowed clown fish named Marlin has his worst fears realized when his only son, Nemo, is fished from the barrier reef. Marlin, who has been agoraphobic since his wife's death, must set out on a quest that forces him to leave his home and plunge into all the dangers he had ordered his life to avoid. Nemo, meanwhile, has been relocated to the tabletop aquarium of a dentist in Sydney, where each of his tankmates has some form of captivity disorder, include a Royal Gramma who has a phobia about germs and a shrimp with a cleaning fetish. On his journey in search of Nemo, Marlin has an encounter with a shark who is wavering in his twelve-step program for recovering fish eaters, who repeats the mantra "Fish are our friends, they are not food," as he struggles to restrain his sharkish instincts. As he nears Sydney, Marlin falls under the capable spiritual direction of a sea turtle whose Taoist surrender to the flow of life begins to soften Marlin's worst anxieties. The story is a showcase of neuroses and recoveries, filling young viewers with the idea that even marine life operates according to therapeutic norms that prioritize feelings of self-esteem and seek to overcome the haunting effects of past traumas.

The therapeutic self is also a staple on television. The Home Box Office (HBO) network's *Soprano's* sends mob boss Tony Soprano off to weekly sessions with his therapist, as he searches for the happiness that eludes him in the rough world of organized crime. And on *Sex and the City,* Carry Bradshaw, the tell-all columnist who details the exploits of single women looking for love in New York City, takes the view that men must be instruments to her happiness, or else there really is no use for them. The final episode of the final season of the show concluded with Bradshaw's voiceover swansong: "The most exciting, challenging and significant relationship of all is the one you have with yourself and if you find someone to love the you that you love, well, that's just fabulous."

But the true hot house of the therapeutic through the 1990s was the daytime talk show. Phil Donahue, Oprah Winfrey, Sally Jesse Raphael, Jerry Springer and all of their imitators were evangelists of the talking cure who believed that secrets are a slow-working poison to the soul, and that confessing them in a public forum has a healing effect. It was as a form of mass entertainment that the religion of therapy made many of its deepest inroads into our culture. Sinners and the sinned against from all walks of life appeared before studio audiences to reveal their traumas, disorders and wicked deeds – celebrities, politicians, clergy, skinheads, professionals, prostitutes, drug addicts, cheating husbands, pedophiles – sat in the same chair day after day to be coaxed into divulging their secrets. Whatever other motives they had for appearing, they acquiesced to the idea that disclosing to a national audience their misdeeds and emotional afflictions would cleanse their souls. Our society gradually came to recognize these confessions as admirable and heroic, and followed the old penitential habit of granting absolution to the truly contrite. As Kathleen Lowney has remarked in her study of this phenomenon, the talk show inherited from the old revivalist camp meeting the practice of bringing repentant sinners up to the podium and allowing them to testify to lives of sin and depravity for the purpose of provoking their conversion and edifying all who would listen.[47] It is also worth noting that the very public nature of talk show confessions invokes the even older practice of public confession in the early church – where a private confession was considered insufficient because true contrition required a willingness to expose one's sins to public scrutiny and shame.

All of these instruments of popular culture bear some variation of the message that strong feelings are destructive if they are repressed, denied, or intellectualized. Each of these "defense mechanisms" must be overcome through talking the poison out, ideally under the care of a trained counselor, if one is to be healed. This is all part of the task of exfoliating the self, stripping away the layers of denied feelings that have made our inner selves appear so ugly and unworthy and in need of being hidden – even to oneself.

A major source of this branch of the therapeutic can be traced to an influential circle of psychologists including Fritz Perls, Timothy Leary, Abraham Maslow and Carl Rogers who constituted a kind of brain trust for the Esalen Institute in Big Sur, California. Esalen was a great crossroads, beginning in 1962 when it opened, for these already established scientists of human consciousness who were joined by people like Carlos Castaneda, Alan Watts, Ken Kesey, Jack Kerouac, Maharishi Mahesh Yogi, and Aldous Huxley, all of whom took an interest in reawakening the life of feeling. Because its inaugural sessions were entitled "The Human Potentiality," Esalen is remembered for generating what came to be called the human potential movement. The central idea of the movement was that taking responsibility for one's life means becoming aware of passing feelings and learning to trust them. They used unorthodox methods to teach their workshop participants how to get in touch with their feelings by silencing the brain's incessant commentary, overcoming inhibitions that prevented them from acting out their feelings, and liberating the deep emotions that subsist at the bedrock stratum of the true self. In their view, the full life was to be lived on this level, giving reign to the passions. As Carl Rogers described it, the "way to the good life" is to get the person to experience his feelings fully, "so that for the moment he *is* his fear, or his anger, or his tenderness, or his strength. And as he lives these widely varied feelings, in all their degrees of intensity, he discovers that he has experienced *himself*, that he *is* all these feelings." Unlocking the human potential is a matter of learning to listen to these feelings, and "doing what feels right proves to be a competent and trustworthy guide to behavior which is truly satisfying."[48]

Jack Kerouac was another voice that was respected by the human potential movement. He and his fellow beat writers (Allen Ginsberg, Gregory Corso, William S. Burroughs) served as kind of raw specimens of human actualization for those in the human potential movement. Kerouac's book, *On the Road*, is one of its manifestos. In it, Kerouac explains:

> the only people for me are the mad ones, the ones who are mad to live, mad to talk, mad to be saved, desirous of everything at the same time, the ones who never yawn or say a commonplace thing, but burn, burn, burn like fabulous yellow roman candles exploding like spiders across the stars and in the middle you see the blue center light pop and everybody goes "Awww!"[49]

It was his pursuit of a life lived at this level, chasing every impulse as it crossed the screen of his consciousness, that sent him out on the road and down the different side roads he traveled. "I could hear a new call and see a new horizon," he confides, "I was a young writer and I wanted to take off. Somewhere along the line I knew there'd be girls, visions, everything; somewhere along the line the pearl would be handed to me."[50] The quintessential rock and roll musician of the 1960s, often self-consciously under the spell of Kerouac and the beat ethos, was another avatar of this aggressive veneration of one's deepest layer of feeling. It could manifest itself in feelings of love for all creatures, as expressed in the music of Donovan and Nick Drake, or in a Dionysian overthrow of all restraints, as in the music and lives of Janis Joplin, Keith Moon and

Jim Morrison. Morrison made a religion out of irony, chasing down every taboo as a source of redemptive liberation, and dismissing every cultural totem as a source of stultifying mediocrity. For him, salvation was to be found precisely in the orgiastic life.

Lowney suggests that this ironic sensibility is characteristic of the whole therapeutic ethos. It "reverses just about everything we thought we knew," she writes.

> The family is not the nurturing environment in which we start life, but the means by which we are abused and broken down. Sin no longer means making selfish choices that harm others but instead is about *not* putting oneself first. Morality has become whatever facilitates the search for the actualized self.... Personal responsibility for one's choices has been abandoned; instead one is free to – encouraged to – blame parents, siblings, and society for all personal problems.[51]

As Lowney helps to make plain, the therapeutic impulse can idolize self-fulfillment regardless of the cost this exacts on others, even those we are closest to – in fact, especially those we are closest to, who are reduced to being merely the means of maximizing our own pleasure, or, worse, the recipients of blame when we feel our desire to find ourselves is being hampered. How many decent people have been crushed by loved ones who have emerged from their therapy sessions or group encounters with permission to disclose long harbored grievances and do what feels right? The strident self-care found in some forms of therapy can wreak havoc on otherwise sound families and friendships, stomping on whoever gets in the way of the patient's freedom to self-actualize. The pursuit of self-fulfillment that consults feelings to the exclusion of all other guidance that presses upon one inevitably results in actions that are contrary to the single most common moral principle in all of the world's religions, that is, Love your neighbor as yourself.

Much of this is justified on the basis of the axiomatic status that has been granted to self-esteem. Building people's self-esteem, their sense of self-worth, has replaced the older ethic of self-denial and self-control, which has come to be seen by many as a debilitating ethic. But research is beginning to chip away at this elevation of self-esteem, suggesting that people with low self-esteem enjoy just as much happiness in life as those with high self-esteem. The happiness of those with *high* self-esteem is always vulnerable to the fact that the higher their opinion of themselves, the more likely they are to perceive feedback from others – friends, lovers, bosses, family – as falling short of what they deserve. Moreover, low self-esteem, the research shows, is a positive variable in people's efforts to transcend their own past achievements. People with low self-esteem, that is, try harder so that they can do better.[52] This dynamic has long been recognized in theological circles as the predictable outcome of pride, that inordinate self-esteem that makes oneself the center of value in the world and has often been described as the taproot of all other sins.

As this examination of the therapeutic unfolds, it drifts towards therapy's more outrageous excesses, which makes it an easy target. These excesses, however, do not exhaust the religious significance of therapy and the great variety of recovery movements. As Richard Mouw has argued, while there are many legitimate critiques of the therapeutic, there is also much within it that, from a Christian perspective, is worth salvaging. He, too, recognizes that at its core there is a confessional impulse to introspection that can be healthy. It was the psalmist, he recalls, who prayed, "Search me, O God, and know my heart." Then he suggests that "Good psychology can help me understand the complexities of the self that I present for divine scrutiny." We ought not attempt an end run around modern psychology, he argues; after all, because of it "we do know more about the human psyche today than our Christian forebears did."[53]

Similarly, Charles Taylor has argued for an "ethic of authenticity" that recovers an older notion of authenticity and moral feeling. He is aware that there is a deviant form of individual self-fulfillment circulating in our culture; but a "root-and-branch condemnation," he argues, is not the answer.[54] It is disingenuous to deny, as some of the more shrill critics of the therapeutic do, that the aspiration to authenticity and self-fulfillment is corrupt at its core. What reasonable person wouldn't at least factor in self-fulfillment, or the aim of realizing their potential, when faced with a significant life choice?[55] Authenticity is a legitimate value that arose in the early modern period as an affirmation of the conscience as a voice within, and was conceived as a reaction to a morality driven by calculations of divine reward and punishment. It was described as a listening to the voice of nature speaking from within, as a particular "way of experiencing our lives, our ordinary desires and fulfillments, and the larger natural order in which we are set." In the thinking of early Romantic writers like Herder and Rousseau, the feelings that rose to consciousness when one surrendered to this inner voice were feelings of "oneness with humanity or a response of joy and reverence to the spectacle of untamed nature." These sentiments were then, at least at the outset, well in line with traditional moral and theistic convictions – self-fulfillment was to be found through conforming to sentiments of solidarity, benevolence, and sympathy for others.[56] Admittedly, this alternative view of the source of the good life, what Taylor calls the "moral sense theory," was unstable and gave way to replacing traditional moral virtues with moral feelings. Nevertheless, there is a truth here that ought not be dismissed: moral actions flow out of moral dispositions, and moral dispositions have a feeling component to them. Authenticity of the best sort is found in those whose actions in life emerge from and honestly reflect their dispositions. There is something inherently good about self-integrity of this sort.

In effect, according to Taylor, there are deeper and shallower forms of authenticity. Given the prevalence of authenticity as an ideal in our culture, he advises steering it in the direction of its deeper form. The crucial difference between shallow and deep authenticity is found in its "openness to horizons of significance" – deep authenticity has a horizon beyond the self, a good that transcends it. The trust that early Romantic thinkers placed in the inner voice of nature was based on their theological assumption that nature had a providential order, and that human consciousness was the place where this order rose to awareness. It was in listening to this inner voice that the individual discerned how to conform her own will to transcendent purposes. Shallow authenticity, on the other hand, has no greater good than the self *itself*; in effect it makes the self and its desires its ultimate concern. Even "deep" feelings are not all that deep if they are only as deep as the self. Therapeutic approaches that promote a shallow authenticity respect no restraints on the expression of one's deepest and most powerful desires, and lead to an "ethic" that absolutizes the uninhibited freedom of choice.[57] Such an ethic of choice is a tremendous justification for a society driven by consumption, coercing every sphere of the culture to reconfigure itself as an array of wonderful, consumable options, but it offers little in the way of training individuals in the kinds of commitments, promise-keeping, and sacrifice that are necessary for a flourishing and enduring civil society.

Both Mouw and Taylor, then, in their moderated praise for the therapeutic, offer arguments for a middle-way that neither idolizes the self nor neglects the useful self-knowledge that a probing of one's feelings can provide. An appropriate use of the therapeutic, in general, probes the layers of human feeling in light of convictions about transcendent goodness for the purpose of training the self to come to value itself and all things *sub specie aeternitatis* – in light of their relation to God.

One therapeutic method that exemplifies this middle-way is Alcoholics Anonymous (AA). Many critics of the therapeutic fail to recognize this, and lump AA together with encounter groups, self-help techniques and primal scream therapies, disparaging "twelve-step programs" as indulgent opportunities to "talk about me." AA is purported by these critics to be the ur-recovery movement, whose founders Bill Wilson and Bob Smith put in place the twin errors of labeling addiction a disease (which, it can be argued, displaces responsibility from the alcoholic to the illness) and relying too heavily on the remedy of the talking cure. But this blanket critique misses AA's key elements. While AA does label alcoholism as a disease, it specifies that it is a *spiritual* disease, one that is to be ameliorated through rigorous spiritual exercises. The twelve steps follow a classic progression of remorse, confession, and penance designed to force the alcoholic to acknowledge responsibility for his actions and their impact on others. As described in the Big Book, "The alcoholic is like a tornado roaring his way through the lives of others. Hearts are broken. Sweet relationships are dead. Affections have been uprooted. Selfish and inconsiderate habits have kept the home in turmoil."[58] Moreover, following through on the steps demands that one inventory the harm one has caused and embark on a long period of reconstruction, mending the damage that has been done to others. "Remorseful mumbling" – that is, talk therapy – is not enough.[59]

The soteriology of AA is precisely the opposite of the human potential movement. The alcoholic deceives herself if she imagines that restoring self-esteem, getting in touch with her feelings, or having faith in herself is the route to salvation. In fact, making self-fulfillment the aim of one's actions is viewed as the root of the disease. "The alcoholic is an extreme example of self-will run riot, though he usually doesn't think so. Above everything, we alcoholics must be rid of this selfishness."[60] Nor is the humble goal of sobriety the aim. Sobriety is a secondary effect that will reliably follow on the heels of throwing oneself ardently into the task of helping others – first undoing as much of one's own ill-effects on others as one can, and then making service to others a way of life. Finally, the twelve-step regimen is unapologetically theistic. Wilson and Smith confess that after repeated failures of their own self-reliance to overcome their addiction, they conceded, "We had to find a power by which we could live, and it had to be a *Power greater than ourselves.*"[61] They had to learn to "trust infinite God rather than our finite selves" and practice daily to transform their desires through the prayer: "How can I best serve Thee – Thy will (not mine) be done."[62] In effect, the twelve steps of AA are designed to deepen one's consciousness of God and to gradually realign one's self will to the purposes of God, not to release the inner child.

This is not to say that in actual practice, twelve-step groups, including AA groups, avoid the temptation to become less than what the twelve-step regimen demands as a spiritual exercise. But to the extent that they may come to mimic the more self-obsessed kinds of therapy, they have departed from their charter.

Conclusion

Just as popular culture has been busy trotting out rehabilitated images of God and fretting in theological ways over the human condition, it has also been generating a variety of conceptions of salvation. Through various ecstatic aids, motley collections of icons, diversionary promises of consumer advertising, genres of rock music, and therapeutic intro-spection, we turn to popular culture to prod, entice, and feel ourselves into believing that our sinful ways can be redeemed, that obstacles to our happiness can be overcome and that we can enjoy more fulfilling lives.

The uses of music and confession in popular culture, in particular, testify to certain reflexes we retain for following paths to salvation. Through the spectacle of the live concert, we enter liminal time and space and expose ourselves to the transformative powers of ecstatic experience, sacred icons, and communitas. Our pop-protest musicians educate us in the multifarious ways of our collective sinfulness and provide us with a soundtrack for social reform. Love songs enchant us with preludes to the beatific vision, while more contemplative artists can sing our souls into actual moments of sacred consciousness and illumination. Through a great variety of manifestations of the therapeutic we seek to care for our souls and purge our lives of encumbrances that detain us from living to the fullest. Some forms of purgation elevate personal happiness to the status of an ultimate concern and jettison all obligations as dead weight; others pursue a more traditional method of self-contrition and repentance with the aim of aligning the self with communal obligations and larger conceptions of transcendent goodness.

9

Life Everlasting

Religions provide us with both alpha and omega mythologies.[1] In order to help us to understand where we have come from and to where we are going, religious traditions typically bracket human time between a primordial golden age at one end and paradise at the other. These are often descriptions of wonderful realms that could have been and might yet be if we only lived our lives differently than we do. It is not just the Abrahamic faiths that do this. Asian religions, too, have their myths of blissful spirit lands from which our earthly ancestors descended and their pure lands and Buddha fields where the dead may spend eons enjoying the sound of musical instruments playing endlessly, showers of lotus petals from the heavens, and long, delicious naps, before their dissolution into nirvana or *moksha*, where the troubled lives we lead will eventually find a final peace.

It is to the omega myths and their corresponding rituals that we now turn. Christian theology uses the Greek term "eschatology" (*eschaton* = the end, last things) as the heading under which such last things as death, resurrection, souls in the afterlife, final judgment, heaven and hell are discussed. These are all symbols that portend a final, satisfying ending to history, when the forces of evil will be conquered and the purposes of God will finally be fulfilled through the restoration of cosmic harmony. It is common to consider each of these symbols in both cosmic and individual terms, as they have implications for both the cosmos and for individual lives. Because of the speculative nature of these topics, the eschatology chapter in modern systematic theologies is often very brief, offering little more than the oblique assurance that God, who can be trusted, will have the final word. But within the life of religious *communities*, eschatological beliefs can be very prolific – indeed popular religion tends to provide a more hospitable home to these beliefs than does the religion of scholars and theologians.

Signs of the Times

Americans have been accused of hiding from death. Most people in the US can expect to die in the aseptic surroundings of a hospital, very likely alone, and then shuttled to a morgue. We don't bathe our own dead, as our predecessors did; instead, we have turned this final duty over to an obliging industry that keeps decaying corpses out of our homes and spruces them up to look peacefully alive until the moment they are interred. In most burial ceremonies it is not even possible to throw a last handful of dirt onto the casket of the deceased, given the blankets of Astroturf that cover the excavated soil. Our mourning is hygienically choreographed by a profession that most of us prefer to keep at a distance except when we are in need of their services. But lately, the ground seems to be shifting.

In the 2004 season, the most popular series on cable television was an hour-long weekly drama about the funeral industry. HBO's *Six Feet Under* follows the lives of those who live and work at Fisher & Sons Funeral Home, a family-owned operation in southern California. In each show a death is depicted in the opening scene, the bereaved buy their funeral package, and the corpse is embalmed with great artistry and impressive hydraulic technology in the cellar of the Fisher's house. While the holes opened up for the bereaved family are poked and probed, the Fishers and their loved ones go about the business of carrying on their own lives. Given the show's ratings, there would appear to be a yearning among millions of cable viewers to look more squarely in the face of death.

A precedent for this can be found in, of all places, Disney Studios. Coinciding with the concealment of the dead in the second half of the last century was a peculiar, out-of-sync obsession of the Disney Studios with death. From Disney's earliest animated features and shorts, "death, or the threat of death," as Gary Laderman has suggested, has been "the motor, the driving force that enlivens each narrative."[2] Typically, this meant the death of a character's mother that the character witnessed, caused, or somehow had to recover from. Snow White, Bambi, Cinderella, Mowgli (*The Jungle Book*), and Nemo were all motherless children (as was Walt Disney), Simba (*The Lion King*) grew up believing he had caused his father's death. Sleeping Beauty, Pinocchio, and Snow White died or fell into semi-permanent sleep, creating opportunities to depict prolonged deathbed scenes, as the dwarves, princes, Jiminy Cricket and forest creatures modeled to viewers what it meant to grieve. Recollections of these mourning scenes are etched deeply into the childhood memories of several generations of Disney's audience. Evidence for the mythic importance of this can be found with a visit to the children's section of the enormous Woodlawn Memorial Park in Colma, California, where the entrance (remember the importance of Turner's threshold) is marked by a large sculpture not of guardian angels, but of Snow White and the seven dwarves.

And then consider the fascinating diversification of new ways we have to dispose of loved ones' cremated remains. A Florida company, Eternal Reefs, will haul artificial reefs made of a mixture of concrete and human ashes four miles off the Gulf coast and sink them to provide new environments for threatened marine life.[3] The Eternal Ascent Society will deposit ashes in a blue helium balloon that is then released into the air. When it reaches an elevation of five miles above the earth, the balloon freezes and bursts, scattering ashes to the four winds. "Your loved one can now be safely transported to the heavens in a giant helium-filled balloon," the company's website promises, hinting that it might be hazardous for the dead to make the same journey in the company of more traditional celestial chaperones.[4] A firm called Celestis soars even higher. They will fasten a capsule of ashes the size of a tube of chapstick to a Pegasus rocket, launch it into space, and eject it to orbit around the earth where it can drift for as many as a thousand years before re-entering the atmosphere and burning up.[5] And an outfit called LifeGem has patented a process that converts the carbon released during cremation into "high quality" diamonds – "as a memorial to the unique and wonderful life of your loved ones."[6]

These artifacts indicate a growing willingness to face the sordid details of death and to think creatively about what kind of passage it is, at least in some quarters of popular culture. Digging a bit deeper into these and other phenomena will help to clarify what meaning is being assigned to death and other "last things" in popular culture.

Among the most telling places to look in a *religious* community for *its* eschatological beliefs are the apocalyptic epics that it tells about some widespread disruption of life on earth (whether it happens with a whimper or a bang), its dreamy visions of utopia, and its customs surrounding mourning and disposal of the dead. The same holds true for the eschatological beliefs that are borne in popular culture: investigate its stories of cataclysmic disruption, its idyllic art, and its death customs.

The secular apocalyptic

In Chapter 7 some attention was given to how effective science fiction can be, particularly in its apocalyptic mode, for isolating the sin *de jure* and imagining its consequences if left unchecked. Thus, in *A Canticle for Leibowitz*, the craving for absolute security was seen to lead, ironically, to the devastation of the planet, which then ejects the human race as the consequence for this craving. This genre of the apocalyptic has become common in popular culture since the advent of the atomic bomb. Confronting the real possibility that unreliable humanity has it within its powers to destroy what we believed was a resilient planet has provoked much reflection in science fiction on the fragility of our way of life and on the death instinct that hunkers deep in our scientific manipulations of natural processes.

Etymologically, *apokalyptein* means, simply, to reveal or disclose. But it acquired a more technical meaning as a distinctive subgenre of prophetic literature found in the Bible, exemplified by the books of *Daniel* and the *Revelation* (Apocalyse) *to John*, when these writings began to flourish around 200 BCE. Its distinguishing elements include the prediction of a time of upheaval in nature and history (wars, earthquakes, famines, plagues), a glimpse of the powers behind reality (both good and evil) which come out of hiding to engage in final combat, and divine judgment on human life. This last feature has given this genre of doom a redemptive arc – at least for some. The combined features of the biblical apocalyptic motif have subsequently shaped the imagination of the West whenever thought has turned to the ultimate destiny of the world.

As it has resituated itself in popular culture, the apocalyptic has held onto the doom elements but has sometimes loosened its grip on the hope for a redemptive outcome. As Daniel Wojcik has noted in his assessment of the "secular apocalyptic," especially as it has developed since the end of World War II: "Instead of faith in a redemptive new realm to be established after the present world is annihilated, secular doomsday visions are usually characterized by a sense of pessimism, absurdity, and nihilism."[7] Wojcik finds the apocalyptic surfacing in such diverse places as cold war military preparations, beat poetry, monographs of doom by social scientists and environmentalists, cosmic disaster novels and movies, doomsday humor, and survivalist and punk subcultures. In all of these artifacts, a story is being told about the world falling to pieces, but in the absence of divine benevolence and purpose, the pieces won't be put together again.

As a testament to this, consider again the film *FightClub*, which is a sort of apocalyptic critique of the twistedness of apocalyptic hope. As events unfold, we find that Tyler, the anarchist alter ego of the insomniac Jack, has a vision for a redeemed world that will emerge after his army of demolitionists have blown up every corporate headquarters and reduced the global economy to chaos:

> In the world I see, we're stalking elk in the grand canyon around the ruins around Rockefeller Center. You'll wear leather clothes that will last you the rest of your life. You'll climb the vines around the Sears Tower. And

when you look down you'll see tiny figures pounding corn, laying strips of
venison on the empty carpool lane of some abandoned superhighway.

For Tyler, Eden will rise from the rubble of cities that have been
cleansed of the poison of corporate logos, global markets and consumer
incompetence. It will be a paradise of hunters and gatherers, undoing
the emasculation that the last several centuries of scientific and economic
progress have wrought. It is clear that the film isn't endorsing this fresh
start; Palahniuk is at least as uneasy with the anarchists and their survivalist, buckskin vision as he is with corporate branding of every aspect of
our lives. He uses the apocalyptic to critique both the commodification
of our culture *and* the apocalyptic solution to it.

Nevertheless, the hope that cataclysm will be followed by a more auspicious fresh start persists in some applications of the secular apocalyptic.
Religion₃ has asserted itself here, as well. In the 1996 summer blockbuster, *Independence Day*, as cities are incinerated by laser beams fired
by space aliens who have come to colonize the earth, the nations of the
world, recognizing their shared humanity in the face of this extraterrestrial
threat, finally overcome their differences. Apocalypse shocks the human
race to its senses and a new sense of human solidarity against a common
foe awakens. Moreover, the heroes in the story are a politician, a warrior,
and an environmentalist. Politics, the military, and science – three institutions that are often blamed for apocalypse – are here cast in the role
of redeemers. The sublimated anxiety in this story is probably *our own*
predatory exploitation of the planet and its poorer citizens. To discover
that institutions already exist to end this unjust exploitation – if only the
right individuals were in charge of them – comes off as deeply reassuring.

Blockbuster apocalyptic movies are often plotted around our most
pressing fears about how the world will end and what will trigger it – aliens
(extraterrestrial *and* terrestrial), insects, genetic engineering, synthesized
microbes, cyborgs, rogue militaries, religious fundamentalists, anarchists,
ideologues, indifferent nature (volcanoes, earthquakes, comets), vengeful
nature (viruses, greenhouse gasses, infertility). The recent surge of movies
about killer viruses (*Twelve Monkeys, Outbreak, 28 Days Later*) reflects
real anxieties surrounding the advance of biotechnologies. But it is uncommon for any of these catastrophes to have the last word. There are always
heroes and usually some surviving remnant to carry on, sobered by the
catastrophic losses.

There are two things that the secular apocalyptic is particularly good
at revealing with respect to the theological content of popular culture.
First, it displays the powers that are, at the moment, believed to be in
control of our lives. These are both good and evil powers, because the
apocalyptic is, essentially, a high noon confrontation between good and
evil. The forces of evil are the villains who bring about the disaster; the

forces of good are the heroes whose actions ensure that a remnant will survive. As a way of discerning the moral temper of the moment, it is worth observing how our institutions line up into these two columns, or what elements and inclinations within our institutions can be so divided. And this leads to the second thing that the secular apocalyptic reveals: it highlights the particular human failings (sins) that have set these events in motion *and* the human merits that have made the remnant worthy of being spared. In the end, these accounts of judgment on the ways of human life force us to reflect on how we conduct our lives, and this is a driving purpose of the apocalyptic. Like the ending of any narrative, the anticipated end of history has the power to refigure the meaning of all the discordant happenings that have occurred in time;[8] in the case of apocalyptic narratives, the ending has the power to orient and grade various previous actions relative to a goodness that, as it turns out, was straining to be realized all along.

J.R.R. Tolkien's *Lord of the Rings* epic is a spectacular example of the apocalyptic. The good power is found in Ilúvatar, the deity who created the harmonious cosmos and sustains it with a light but steady providential hand. That the forces of evil have become so powerful in the third age of Middle-earth, the age in which the story is set, is a consequence of Ilúvatar's desire to grant free will to all creatures and allow them to shoulder responsibility for the world they inhabit, with only rare and subtle acts of divine intervention. The kingdom of Middle-earth is a segment of a vaster cosmos, a complex segment, but one that mirrors the harmony of the whole cosmos. Its institutions are reflections of our own, and are represented by the heroic figures that rise to prominence in the mounting struggle against evil: Frodo, Gandalf, Elrond, Gimli, Legolas, Aragorn, and Treebeard stand for domestic life, religion, science, technology, military, politics, and the benighted forces of nature that groan to be liberated from the degradation under which they suffer. These institutions are portrayed as interdependent and powerful when they willingly collaborate, each with an indispensable role to play in the contest with evil. But the same institutions are recruited to do the work of the wizard, Sauron, who represents the power of evil in this apocalypse. Sauron's evil is lodged in his desire for absolute power, which is maintained through a reign of fear, suspicion and hatred. Keeping the inhabitants of Middle-earth off-balance with fear and hatred unravels the order of Ilúvatar's cosmos and devolves into chaos – and chaos is the only thing Sauron has it within his power to create and rule with his perverse sovereignty.

The virtues of those in Middle-earth who align themselves with goodness include steadfastness, self-sacrifice, kindness, mercy, courage, temperance, loyalty, prudence, and distaste for worldly power; the vices that characterize those under the thrall of evil are possessiveness, zeal for destruction, and the drive to dominate others. These are the traits that are pitted against each other in this roiling apocalypse, and they are the dispositions of righteousness and wickedness that are judged through the final outcome.[9]

Tableaus of the peaceable kingdom

A noteworthy feature of the *Lord of the Rings*, particularly as it was brought to the screen in the three recent films by director Peter Jackson, is its scenery. The tranquil Hobbit's shire and the misty surrealism of the elves' ancestral home at Rivendell are stunning achievements of New Zealand's natural beauty enhanced by the artistry of stage crews and CGI (computer generated imagery) technology. These are utopian landscapes, both in their idealized beauty and in their ideological ways of depicting visual milieus for the good life. Regarding the latter, the Hobbit's shire with its lowland kitchen gardens and Hundertwasseresque earthen-mound burrows is an environmentalist's paradise, and Rivendell with its Gaudi-like filigree, reflecting pools, lonely balconies and arcades, rising from an effervescent river in a hidden valley, is the idealized, sequestered academic cloister, where the immortal elves have safely archived the wisdom of the ages in runes. Utopias are sincere efforts to conceptualize ideal worlds built upon noble principles – and in current fiction and film these are dominated variously by feminist, environmentalist, multicultural, consumer, and technocratic paradises. The physical appearance of utopias naturally reflects the principles being promoted.

This suggests that the visual tableau itself is pertinent to theological analysis. Jane Tompkins has remarked how the opening shot in the typical western – the vast, empty desert – symbolizes the innocence of a land without human beings, a world unstained by sin at the beginning of time, where sheer potentiality is expressed by an Edenic landscape unmarked by human activity.[10] This implies that the appeal of the western to its audience has something to do with what the image on the screen activates within their religious imaginations. In his study of the emergence of nature as a site of tourism in nineteenth-century America, John Sears offers an account of how modern tourism has retrieved a more ancient sense that magnificent natural landscapes are sites where the barrier between the sacred and profane is unusually thin. He begins his story with early reports of the sublime power of Niagara Falls. Soon after the completion of the Erie Canal in 1825, Niagara Falls had the dubious fortune to become America's first developed tourist destination, and it was promoted from the beginning in the guidebooks as a place to witness God's power and glory. In a nation without imposing stone cathedrals, Niagara Falls, with its "astonishing height, enormous volume, stupendous force, and eternal sound" offered itself as an alternative site to encounter the majesty of God. Drawing explicitly on Edmund Burke's *A Philosophical Enquiry into the Origin of our Ideas of the Sublime and Beautiful*, early guidebooks described the "pleasurable terror" that was evoked within visitors to this natural cathedral, and all of Burke's ruminations on the sacred dimension of the sublime came to be so commonly applied to Niagara Falls that the association became a cliché.[11] And it was a cliché that was then projected onto subsequent natural wonders that were discovered as the western frontier was settled. When Yosemite Valley was stumbled upon in the 1850s by an expedition of soldiers in pursuit of Indians, descriptions of it filtered back east and visitors began making the long, arduous journey to witness it for themselves. As early as 1866, a newspaper editor from Springfield, Massachusetts made the trip and wrote back:

> the overpowering sense of the sublime, of awful desolation, of transcending marvelousness and unexpectedness...such a tide of feeling, such stoppage of ordinary emotions comes at rare intervals in any life. It was the confrontal of God face to face, as in great danger, in solemn, sudden death. It was Niagara, magnified.[12]

One particularly effective promoter of Yosemite and other wilderness tourist attractions was the painter Albert Bierstadt. Bierstadt visited Yosemite and other points west on three different tours with cartographers and geologists, beginning in 1858. He would make sketches and oil studies in the field, then return to his New York studio to recreate the scenery in huge oil panoramas that accentuated the pristine beauty and transcendent grandeur of the mountains, waterfalls and alpine lakes he had witnessed. In one of the best examples of this, a massive canvas called *Looking Down the Yosemite Valley* (1865; see Figure 6), Bierstadt depicts the tranquil waters of the Merced River meandering through a trim green meadow, reflecting the oak trees that grow on its banks, with behemoth granite towers on the left and the sheer vertical face of Half Dome on the right. Luxuriant sunlight shines from the distant bend behind Half Dome, illuminating the forest primeval, beckoning an intrepid viewer to trek down the broad, flat valley floor toward God's radiant *Shekinah*. This is God's own holy temple, a place not made with hands.

Bierstadt's paintings have never been highly regarded by art critics or art historians, who view him as a weak representative of the Hudson River School. They have found his work to be sensationalistic and pandering, an exercise in prettifying the raw beauty of what he observed and unoriginal in its interpretations. But in any of the many museums that have one of

Figure 6 Albert Bierstadt's 1865 painting, *Looking down the Yosemite Valley*, captures a sense of the sublime that has long had popular appeal (Collection of the Birmingham Museum of Art; Gift of the Birmingham Public Library).

his paintings, the carpet in front of it is usually well-worn. His is an art of the people; his paintings captivate their imaginations and transport them to places they would rather be. His hyperreal depictions of sublime nature activate utopian feelings. *Mountains in the Mist, Yosemite at Sunset,* and *The Shore of the Turquoise Sea* are felt by many as the true dwelling places of their souls, places saturated with the numinous.

Thomas Kinkade, the "painter of light," has inherited this mantle of painting translucent landscapes that minister to the soul. Still in his forties, Kinkade may be the most commercially successful painter alive today. It is not the sale of his original paintings that accounts for his success (he keeps these in his private collection), but reproductions of them in the form of framed prints sold at Thomas Kinkade Galleries located at malls across the country. More than ten million framed Kinkade's are now in circulation. They range in value from $200 for a poster quality print, to $500 for a canvas lithograph, to several thousand dollars for a print festooned with dollops and squiggles of paint applied by an assembly line of Kinkade-trained painters to give the canvas texture and the trademark luminescent effect, to more than $30,000 for canvas prints that Kinkade has personally touched up. For more modest budgets, Kinkade images are embossed on blankets, mugs, tote bags and cards that are sold through licensing agreements. In 2000, his operation posted $140 million in sales, clearing more than $90 million in profits.

His paintings are hyperrealistic interpretations of sturdy lighthouses on craggy shores, rustic cottages nestled in cozy dells in the shadow of snowcapped mountains, white clapboard churches and flower gardens (see Figure 7), with titles like *Hidden Cottage, Mountain Majesty,* and *The Sea of Tranquility.*[13] Kinkade's artistic aim is to create images that inspire an appreciation for the inherent goodness of life, to counteract, in his words, "all the ugliness you see on the ten o'clock news,"[14] and this vision has reportedly transformed the lives of many of his patrons. Indeed, judging from testimonials, peering into one of Kinkade's luminescent paintings of light can elicit an experience of spiritual enlightenment, akin to what Tillich underwent standing before Botticelli's *Madonna* in 1919. In one of his "Sharing the Light" newsletters, a woman describes spotting her first Kinkade painting while sitting in the waiting room of her doctor's office. She had been going through a rough stretch in her life, even wondering if she had it within her to go on living. But laying eyes on the painting stirred something inside of her:

> It was like I was wandering down the little path, smelling the flowers. And I just knew what was inside – I could see the little rocking chair, the book beside it, and it was all so peaceful... When I saw that painting, I got a glimpse of hope – of a world where I could be happy again. My whole world is brighter now.[15]

Figure 7 Painter Thomas Kinkade aims with his art to create a new "iconography" that eschews the despair common in contemporary art and seeks instead to reenchant the world. *Beginning of a Perfect Day* (©2005 Thomas Kinkade, The Thomas Kinkade Company, Morgan Hill, CA).

Like Bierstadt, Kinkade receives no respect from the art world, but that only bolsters his conviction that he has ventured into genuinely populist territory. He is even brazen enough to describe his own achievement as creating a new "iconography" that is relieving despair and reenchanting the world for those who collect his work.[16] That his images resonate with a public vastly outnumbering any that is reached by critically acclaimed artists, and that his admirers frequently describe the effect of his paintings in spiritual terms would seem to lend credence to the audacity of this appraisal.

To appreciate what might be going on here, consider the work of Vitaly Komar and Aleksandr Melamid, two artists from the former Soviet Union who immigrated to the US in 1978.[17] In 1993 they contracted a public opinion research firm to conduct a survey on what Americans like in a painting; 102 questions were asked about colors, styles, objects, even the size of paintings that people prefer. A cross-section of Americans was polled (1,001 adults). Komar and Melamid then studied the data. Their objective was to use market research as a mechanism to capture "the will of the masses," and then transform this into art. In their estimation, paintings produced in this fashion would be the essence of populist art – ask the people what they want and then give it to them. What could be simpler?

After analyzing the data, Komar and Melamid painted two canvases, to which they gave the titles *America's Least Wanted* and *America's Most Wanted*. Following the numbers, their most wanted painting is an autumn outdoor scene featuring a lake, wild animals, three ordinary children and George Washington (historical figure), all wearing clothes and at their leisure (see Figure 8). It is the size of a dishwasher, predominantly blue with visible brush strokes, and realistic-looking. It bears a striking resemblance to Hudson River School in style and feel.[18] Their *Least Wanted Painting* is abstract and angular (overlapping triangles), predominantly gold, orange and teal, and the size of a paperback book.

Coinciding with the unveiling of these two paintings at a 1994 exhibition in New York City, Komar and Melamid commissioned variations of the survey to be conducted in ten additional countries, ranging from Iceland to China to Kenya, and then produced least and most wanted paintings for each of these countries. As a scientific sample, the combined data pool represents 32 percent of the world's population. Of the many surprising similarities that surfaced across the cultures represented, the most striking is that outdoor, natural settings are the clear favorite (66 percent), and blue stands out as every country's favorite color.

Admittedly, there is as much prank (say, 66 percent) in this whole project as there is insight into the human soul. In an interview the artists did with *The Nation*, Komar suggested at one point that "It is my hope that people who come to see our *Most Wanted* paintings will become so

Some of the more interesting results of the Poll-Art Project

- 88% of Americans prefer outdoor scenes. Preferred outdoor objects (in descending order):
  - lakes, rivers, oceans, and seas (49%)
  - forests (19%)
  - fields and rural scenes (18%)
  - buildings (5%)
  - cities (3%)
- 60% like their paintings to be "realistic-looking"
- Blue is the most popular color in a painting (44%)
- Green is the second most popular color (12%)
- Twice as many people prefer seeing wild animals (51%) to domestic animals (27%) in paintings
- If a painting has people in it, ordinary people are more favored (41%) than famous people (6%) – but to 50% of those polled, it makes no difference
- If a famous person is in the painting, a historical figure is preferred (56%) to a more recent one (14%)
- A group of people is preferred (48%) to a single person (34%)
- Fully clothed people are preferred (68%) to nudes (3%)
- People at leisure are preferred (43%) to people at work (23%)
- Fall is the preferred season to see depicted in a painting (33%), followed by spring (26%), summer (16%), and winter (15%)
- Soft curves are more desirable (66%) than sharp angles (22%)
- Visible brush strokes are preferred (53%) over a smooth canvas (33%)
- Most people prefer large paintings (41%) to small ones (34%)
- Of those who prefer large paintings, the ideal size is that of a dishwasher (67%) as opposed to a refrigerator (17%) or a full wall (11%)

horrified that their tastes will gradually change." Then, a little later in the same interview, possibly fishing for the next grant, he proposed that some land be acquired and the blue landscape of America's *Most Wanted Painting* be recreated in real life: "It is possible to plant trees similar to ones in our painting, create the same lake, same hill, and so on. This locale will be called Poll-Art Park, a place where people can spend time as hermits. It will be an ideal vacation getaway."[19]

Figure 8 This painting by Vitaly Komar and Aleksandr Melamid incorporates all of America's favorite elements of art as determined by a respected polling firm. Is this the art of the people? (*America's Most Wanted Painting,* 1994, used with permission of the artists).

Nevertheless, the data they have collected on cross-cultural aesthetics, however limited, *is* real data that has been produced by state of the art polling mechanisms, and both Komar and Melamid keep circling back to dwell on the apparently universal attraction to the blue landscape. People everywhere, it seems, have in their heads this ideal landscape, this outdoor scene with wild animals, water and trees that is washed in shades of blue. Melamid theorizes,

> Almost everyone you talk to directly – and we've already talked to hundreds of people – they have this blue landscape in their head. It sits there, and it's not a joke. They can see it, down to the smallest detail. So I'm wondering, maybe the blue landscape is genetically imprinted in us, that it's the paradise within, that we came from the blue landscape and we want it.[20]

This blue landscape, installed in our minds like a Kantian *a priori*, as it were, also pervades the paintings of Thomas Kinkade and Albert Bierstadt before him. It appears in Peter Jackson's cinematography as he depicts Hobbiton and Riverdell, the Shangri-las of Middle-earth, it is the convention of the western movie in its portrayal of a land untouched by sin, and it is the prevailing aesthetic of travel industry brochures and postcards, going back to the development of Niagara Falls as a tourist destination. It extends even before that to the popularity of spas, lakeside retreats and beach resorts in virtually every part of the world. The blue landscape, dominated by sky and water, has long been the symbol for the peaceable kingdom. As judgment is like fire, redemption is like water. When the biblical prophets described the peaceable kingdom, following God's judgment of the nations the redeemed are invited to return to Zion, where "waters shall break forth in the wilderness, and streams in the desert; the burning sand shall become a pool, and the thirsty ground springs of water" (Isa. 35.6f). Ezekiel described a discharge of flowing streams from below the temple, and

> On the banks, on both sides of the river, there will grow all kinds of trees for food. Their leaves will not wither nor their fruit fail, but they will bear fresh fruit every month, because the water for them flows from the sanctuary. Their fruit will be for food, and their leaves for healing (Ezek. 47.12).

It is not hard to imagine the millions of Kinkade framed prints hanging on living room walls in suburbs and high-rise apartments, or in windowless waiting rooms and offices across America, serving as elegantly framed windows offering a view onto this peaceable kingdom. While for some they may simply be escapist fantasies, for others these images reflect an inward groping for contentment that eludes them, and they stare searchingly down Kinkade's wooded paths. Like religious icons, these pictures can transfix wandering minds with the power of a reality beyond.

"The power of profound meaning is found in blue," Wassily Kandinsky wrote in his book, *Concerning the Spiritual in Art*. Then he elaborated: "Blue is the typical heavenly colour. The ultimate feeling it creates is one of rest."[21] Kinkade's rustic iconography may aid the viewers of his prints in picturing a place where they hope their souls might finally find rest, and that picture lightens their anxieties in the present. This is an eschatological dynamic – the way a positively envisioned ultimate outcome can lend greater meaning to events in the present and render life's many disappointments and insults more tolerable. From the vantage point of the end of the story – as pictured in an eschatological tableau – present potentialities can be sorted through, and those potentialities that will bring this ending to pass may be activated, while others can be left to wither.

The dearly departed

Popular culture has been brimming lately with bold conjectures about the afterlife. The matter of what follows death is one of those "middle" concerns from which many Christian theologians have kept a respectful distance, not wanting to speculate beyond a general hopefulness, and still smarting from Marx's rebuke that the promise of eternal life distracts people from demanding justice in this life. For decades popular culture concurred in this Marxist suspicion of the debilitating effects of the promise of heaven. But in the last 15 years there have been some brazen depictions of life after death in movies, novels and on television – and from studios and publishers that have no obvious stake in promoting religious beliefs.

Some of the more memorable movies that have explored the terrain, bureaucracy, and peculiar physics of heaven and hell are *Made in Heaven* (1987), where heaven is pictured as a cozy log cabin nestled in an alpine meadow below snowy peaks, a waystation of self-improvement before the next round of *samsara*; *Defending Your Life* (1991), where the dead go to the well-groomed health spa of Judgment City, awaiting their appearance before magistrates who examine and pass verdicts on their just completed lives; *What Dreams May Come* (1998), which depicts hell as a lake of fire with the damned swimming eternally in a smelly muck, while heaven is verdant meadowlands and lakes, monumental Arcadian cities, and reunions with loved ones; *South Park: Bigger, Longer and Uncut* (1999), in which hell is full of fiery wraiths, prehistoric pterodactyls, sulfurous pools and sodomy, while heaven is a celestial paradise of bare-chested, shapely angels; and *Don't Tempt Me* (2001), where heaven is eternally Paris in the 1930s, filmed in black and white, sparsely populated and the official language is French, while hell is an underground concentration camp in full color, throngs herded around by sadistic, uniformed Kapos, meals are served in steamy diners where the orders are always wrong, corporate titans and tinpot dictators are reassigned identities as illegal aliens, misogynist gangsters become waitresses, the famous must live lives of obscurity – and the lingua franca is English. These are much more imaginative than earlier films like *Cabin in the Sky* (1943) and *Stairway to Heaven* (1946), both of which drew on more Raphaelite visions of heaven as winged choirs of angels who with requisitioned harps are seen treading lightly on the clouds (although *Cabin in the Sky* did add the mouthwatering attractions of Pork Chop Orchard and Possum Pie Grove).

An alternative exploration of the afterlife is found in a string of recent movies that suggest the dead linger among the living, confined to their old "haunts" long enough to be reconciled to unfinished lives or to console the loved ones they've left behind. *Beetlejuice* (1988), *Field of Dreams* (1989), *Ghost* (1990), *Flatliners* (1990), *Truly, Madly, Deeply* (1991), *Heart and Soul* (1993), *The Sixth Sense* (1999), and *Solaris* (2002) all develop plots around these elements. In *Flatliners*, four medical students undergo temporary death under monitored conditions, defibrillators at the ready to ensure their resuscitation before their brains die, with the intention of probing with empirical precision what awaits us on the other side. In the minutes they are dead, each of them confronts accusing spirits who finger their repressed guilt – two are confronted by children they had tormented mercilessly in their own childhoods, one by a brigade of women he had seduced, and one by her father whose suicide she had blamed herself for since she was a little girl. Collectively, they learn that in the freshness of death there are sins that cry out for atonement, or, at least, long-borne guilt demanding resolution – and that there will be terrifying familiars there to lend a hand. In *The Sixth Sense*, a child psychologist, unaware that he has been murdered, continues his practice preoccupied with treating a troubled boy who "sees ghosts." In fact the psychologist is, without realizing it, himself a ghost, who is being given a final chance to come to terms with his unfinished life and his lingering guilt over failed efforts to cure one particularly distraught child patient many years earlier.

A more tender version of this is played out in Anthony Minghella's *Truly, Madly, Deeply*, where bohemian Nina loses her lover Jamie to a sore throat, which proves to be fatal. After his funeral, she moves to a new flat in north London hoping to resume her life, but her mourning persists until one rueful night she sits tapping on the piano her half of a duet she had perfected with Jamie on his cello, when he suddenly materializes in cold flesh to accompany her. He eases into his role as house ghost, her companion to return to at the end of each day. Nina is happy again – until Jamie makes her flat a flophouse for his ghost friends who have nowhere else to go, confirmed bachelor ghosts who spend most of their days and nights watching old movies on the television, blasting her furnace, and moving her furniture around the apartment. Meanwhile a living suitor makes a ploy for Nina's affections, and as her irritation with her ghost-crowded flat increases, the possibility of rejoining the companionship of the living takes on a new allure. Jamie, it appears, has been recruiting housemates with the intent of having just this effect – to press lovely Nina out of her grief and back into the company of warm-blooded, still breathing humanity.

Cable television has also turned loose some imaginative minds to reflect on lands of the dead that intersect with our own. Showtime's *Dead Like Me* features a teenager who, in the pilot episode, is killed by a toilet that falls from a disintegrating space station and is then recruited to join an elite squad of the dead charged with easing the pain of victims of lethal violence, harvesting their souls a moment before they are assailed. The afterlife here is depicted as a labyrinthine bureaucracy, and these angels of death work at a mid-management level, frequently converging at a waffle house to gripe about their working conditions and their inscrutable supervisors.

Similar themes have been appearing in popular literature. William Kennedy's 1983 novel, *Ironweed*,[22] familiarized readers with Francis Phelan, a middle-aged drunk who, picking up a day job at a cemetery on Halloween, is haunted by a cohort of familiar ghosts who reside there, including his parents, his infant son, Gerald, who had been dropped by Francis 22 years earlier and broken his neck, and a strike-breaking scab who still wears the rock Francis impaled in his skull during a trolley strike many years earlier. The ghosts in Kennedy's realm acquire their eternal appearance from the conditions in which their deaths occurred, but they continue to develop various potentialities in their character – personality, we are allowed to believe, continues to unfold after death. The infant Gerald's unformed verbal skills at death allowed him to acquire the languages of all the residents of the cemetery, not only diverse human tongues, but also the languages of squirrels, beetles and worms. The dead, it appears, just pile up, wandering cemeteries and old stomping grounds.

It is much the same with the dead in Sheri Reynolds's *A Gracious Plenty* (1997), which tells the story of Finch Nobles, the daughter of cemetery caretakers, hideously scarred at the age of four by a kettle of boiling moonshine she had pulled from her mother's stove onto her head, who discovers that for a disfigured outcast, the ghosts in the cemetery offer a more hospitable community than the living folks in town.

As a teenager, Finch learned that she could "haze" her perception while walking among the graves, allowing her to see and interact with the dead who reside there. The realm of the dead in Reynolds's account is transient. At first they are leaden and restricted to their coffins, but as they tell their stories to each other – shedding their burdens and secrets – they "lighten," gain in mobility, and eventually rise and fade to the next level of existence. The recently dead awaken in their graves, inevitably disappointed that there is no "hullabaloo . . . no saints waiting by walls of jasper," no harp music, no reincarnation into another body or life form. They are greeted by the "Mediator" and instructed: "You sleep in the coffin, you work in the air . . . In life, you lived on just one shelf. Now you're on two. The one above life, the one below, to help you see where you've been."[23] Reynolds adds to this picture the revelation that it is the dead we have to thank for the change of seasons, the opening of bird eggs, the flight of bees to pollinate the flowers, the crowing of roosters, the timing of the tides, and the steady downstream flow of rivers. As the Mediator instructs new inductees: "The Dead coax the natural world along. We're responsible for weather and tides and seasons. For rebirth and retribution." They occupy themselves keeping nature running while unloading their own personal moral freight.

And then there is Alice Sebold's bestselling novel, *The Lovely Bones* (2002), narrated by Susie Salmon, who was raped, murdered and dismembered in a cornfield at the age of fourteen by a middle-aged neighbor – events reported in the first few pages of the book.[24] Susie finds herself in heaven, which, it turns out, is a modest, Mayberry kind of place – with a tidy town square, ice cream shop, gossipy newspaper, and a high school resembling the one she would have gone to had she not been killed. Upon her arrival she is assigned a very motherly "intake counselor" who orients her to her new world. In the town square there is a gazebo that can serve as a passageway between heaven and earth below, and for the next 8 years, the ghost Susie divides her time between the simple pleasures of heaven and keeping her family under surveillance. The story Susie tells recounts her afterlife efforts to come to terms with the end of a life that had hardly begun, to console her family and somehow convey to them that she is all right, and to direct the authorities to the man who murdered her.

As it turns out, Susie's heaven is a transit station, her temporary abode for the years it will take her to tie up these loose ends. She determines that everyone passes through such a place between their deaths and their eventual translation to a more remote heavenly realm, and everyone's transit heaven is manufactured out of their own dreams on earth. Depending on one's preferences, "It can look like Nova Scotia, or Tangiers, or Tibet." The people one meets there are all real, if dead – even Susie's intake counselor is a dead social worker who had worked at a church with homeless women and children – and have landed there because at least some aspect of their dreamed places overlap with one's own. Susie compares this place to the thick blue crayon line in one of her little brother's drawings, the line that separated air and ground, "an Inbetween, where heaven's horizon met Earth's." As it happens, her heaven is populated with other victims of violent crimes. They console each other. Dogs are there, too, deceased pets running in happy packs and dining on steak tartar; eventually even Susie's own dog, Holiday, dies on earth and reunites with her in heaven.

The dead in Sebold's universe can watch the living, and can even make their presence felt – in fact, the earth is thick with unsettled ghosts – but they are restrained from any more direct manipulation of events on earth. The dead remain in their temporary heavenly abodes with this steady access to earth until they loosen their grip on the lives they left behind. In Susie's case, her counselor tells her, "If you stop asking why you were killed instead of someone else, stop investigating the vacuum left by your loss, stop wondering what everyone left on Earth is feeling, you can be free. Simply put, you have to give up on Earth." The dead can also be held back by the enduring devotion of the bereaved. Susie remains in the waystation of her heaven, in part, due to the unrelenting heartbreak of her father – which she relishes; his sorrow fortifies her own attachment to the girl who had once had her whole life in front of her.

But HBO's series *Six Feet Under* is perhaps the most provocative of afterlife offerings to be found in popular culture at the moment. In the pilot episode, middle-aged Nathaniel Fisher, the owner of Fisher & Sons Funeral Home, is fumbling for a cigarette while cruising in his sleek new hearse. Eyes off the road, he runs a red light and is crushed by a municipal bus. His two sons inherit the business, and their long-standing sibling rivalry erupts. The family begins to fall apart even before they bury their father, and the appeal of the series is found largely in the stubborn fidelity that holds this troubled family and their grim business together.

In the world of Fisher & Sons, as in the ghostly worlds considered above, the dead don't stay buried. Their ghosts make regular appearances to taunt, console, and mourn alongside the living. At one point in the first season, Nate is smoking a joint with his dead father, when the old man taunts him, "That's one of the perks of being dead. You know what happens after you die, and, you know the meaning of life."

Nate: That seems fairly useless.

Nathaniel: Yeah, I know. Life is wasted on the living. [He takes a drag on his cigarette.]

Nate: So what's the meaning of life?

Nathaniel: Do you really want to know?

Nate: I don't know. Will it f – k me up if I do?

At this, his father suddenly appears behind him, leans into Nate's ear, and whispers something we can't hear. At this precise moment, Nate wakes up from a nap.[25]

In the final episode of the third season, daughter Claire, Nate's younger sister, is spotted wandering around the cemetery, looking for her father's grave. He has been dead for 2 years, and she had never visited his grave. But having recently had an abortion, broken up with her boyfriend from art school, and discovered that her mother is getting married to a man she barely knows, she is grasping for anything that might steady her life. Nate's wife, Lisa, has been missing for several weeks, having mysteriously disappeared during an overnight trip to northern California. A little girl dashes by Claire, trailing a red helium balloon. Claire glances up and sees her dead father, looking relaxed in a Hawaiian shirt, as if on vacation. "You looking for me?" he asks her.

> *Claire*: Yeah, where the f – k is your grave?
>
> *Nathaniel*: You're not even close, it's way over there. C'mon, I'll take you to it.

He puts his arm around her. They walk across the grounds of the cemetery.

> *Claire*: How's death?
>
> *Nathaniel*: Good, good. I made some new friends, joined the chess team. Glad you came today.

Claire looks up and sees crowds of people – all ghosts – strolling about amidst bouquets of colorful balloons, pretzel wagons, festive steel drum music – a street fair for the dead.

> *Claire*: Why? Is it some kind of special occasion?
>
> *Nathaniel*: No, it's like this every day.

As in other landscapes of the dead in popular culture, these dead congregate at their burial grounds to indulge in each other's company. In *Six Feet Under* they enjoy a perpetual county fair, unseen by the living – most of the time. As Claire and Nathaniel make their way through the revelers to his grave, they pass the mausoleum. Claire wishes to go in, but her father tells her he will wait for her outside and finish his cigarette. She enters gawking at the stacks of marble crypts that line the soaring interior walls. The mausoleum is crowded with ghosts in a festive mood running their fingers over engravings in the marble. The camera pans back to reveal a stained glass rose window high over Claire's head – the traditional symbol of the beatific vision toward which the souls of the blessed dead aspire. It is one of the periodic allusions to the presence of God in the series. Then Claire hears someone call out her name. She looks up to a stair landing and sees her sister-in-law, Lisa, missing person, mother of a newborn, surrounded by stained glass windows on the landing and leaning over a baby carriage. Lisa has been missing for weeks – police suspect she is dead, but there had been no confirmation, no body yet recovered. Lisa exclaims, "Please tell me you're just visiting."

Claire: Yeah...yeah.

Lisa: Thank God

Claire: So...you're...you're...

Lisa: Couldn't be better.

Claire: Okay, I'm so not getting this.

Lisa: There's nothing to get.

Claire [realizing that she's speaking to a ghost]: Lisa, if I'd known you were going to die I would have hung out with you more.

Lisa [reaching out to embrace Claire]: Oh, you're so sweet.

Claire spies over Lisa's shoulder the infant in the carriage. It is nested in a blanket printed with blue sky and white clouds, conjuring the surreal effect of a baby floating in the sky. Claire has a puzzled look on her face – Lisa's baby, Maya, is alive and safely at home with Nate. Then it dawns on her. This ghost baby is her own, the one she recently aborted. Lisa, seeing the recognition cross Claire's face, comforts her, "Isn't he beautiful? Don't worry, I'll take good care of him. And you take good care of Maya for me, okay?"[26]

From various quarters of popular culture, it seems, there is a revival of the afterlife. Heaven and hell, moral judgment on how well one's life was led, karma, purgatory, reincarnation, stages of heavenly ascent – all of these traditional ways of imagining what follows death are on display, and in new combinations. Fifty years ago, most of these projections would have been absent from popular culture, outside of horror shows – because, for some, they were hokum, while for others, they were too sacred to demean through popular media. But now all of this afterlife material is receiving a work over. The afterlife has become a favored site for *bricoleurs* picking through the eschatological rags of traditional religions and fashioning new garments.

As these artifacts suggest, the old ideas of purgatory and the communion of the saints, in particular, may be enjoying a renaissance. Purgation of one's guilt in an interval of time following death is an explicit theme in *Flatliners* and *The Sixth Sense*, and it is quite visually on display in *What*

Dreams May Come. It is also a component of *Ironweed*, *A Gracious Plenty*, *The Lovely Bones*, and *Six Feet Under*. The Christian belief in purgatory, contrary to what is ordinarily assumed, arose as a measure of grace. It offered hope to those believers who had sinned since their baptism at a time when the idea of "go and sin no more" was taken with utter seriousness. While baptism washed the faithful of original sin and of all actual sins up to the moment of baptism, there was no provision for sins they committed subsequent to baptism. Confession and penance, as we have seen, were introduced to address this, but post-baptismal sins, though forgiven and thus not obstacles to one's *ultimate* destiny in heaven, still had to be expiated. Borrowing from first century CE rabbinic views of Gehenna as a temporal abode where the souls of the dead were scrubbed clean before proceeding on to heaven, the church fathers (Ambrose, Jerome, Clement, Origen) began speculating about an antechamber to heaven. The Council of Lyons in the thirteenth century made purgatory an official church doctrine, Dante gave it a topography, and it became a constant feature of the Catholic mind after that. Elements of it have persisted among Protestants, as well.

The ancient Christian idea of the "communion of saints," found in the *Apostles' Creed*, came to be understood as the commerce between three groups: the Church Triumphant (saints in heaven), the Church Expectant (souls suffering in purgatory), and the Church Militant (faithful Christians on earth). The saints in heaven combine an empathy for the trials of the living on earth, having once lived among us, and an enviable access to God. Very early in the history of the church, Christians came to view the dead saints as invisible companions and protectors who offered friendship to the living and could be approached to intercede with God on behalf of those who prayed. Graves of the martyrs became shrines for feasting and prayer, ritual sites where the poor and the wealthy mixed openly – and often outside the regulation of the church's hierarchy. The graves developed a two-fold purpose: they became places where ordinary men and women could approach God through "the searching and merciful presence of a fellow human being" – the dead saint – and where they could contemplate, through remembering the saints, exemplary lives worthy of imitation.[27]

The observance of All *Saints* Day (November 1) was established at least by the end of the first millennium and continues to the present as a day of communion between the Church Militant (the living) and the Church Triumphant (the saints). This is an auspicious day for seeking and receiving blessings. The following day, All *Souls* Day, then allows for communion between the Church Militant (the living) and the Church Expectant (souls in purgatory). On this single day each year the weary souls in purgatory are believed to emerge from their sufferings for a brief interlude in the world of the living. Candles are lit and food is laid out for their nourishment. The roll of the dead is read in gathered congregations invoking their memories. But as the day recedes, the souls are required to return to the refining fires of purgatory. As it is celebrated in Latin America, particularly sumptuous foods are prepared for the ghosts of loved ones, and time is set aside to tell stories about the dead and *to* the dead, with the intent of keeping all members of the family, living and dead, bonded together by family gossip, and of fortifying the souls of loved ones before they resume their ordeals in purgatory.

There seem to be ingredients of these Christian beliefs and practices in the current resurgence of the friendly dead in popular culture, another legacy of religion[3]. But an additional meme of the afterlife is asserting itself in these stories – the archaic motif of the living-dead. The living-dead are constantly on hand, making unexpected visits, sometimes intervening, but generally keeping an eye on the world of the living. These ghosts are familiar figures in traditional religions of Asia, Africa, the Americas, and Australia. The influence of immigrants from these parts of the world is probably, at least in part, responsible for the increased activity of the living-dead in American popular culture.

Twenty years ago, when I was in seminary, I worked with the youth at a church in Philadelphia. The church had recently welcomed an influx of Cambodian refugees who had been settled in the neighborhood in the early 1980s, and most of the young people I worked with were from Cambodia. Two incidents occurred during the years I was there that seemed strange at the time, but that I have since discovered are perfectly consonant with popular religion in Southeast Asia. The first happened when we took the youth on an overnight retreat to a camp in the woods outside of the city. We arrived in time for lunch, ate, and then gave the group several options for the afternoon – they could play volleyball, do a ropes course, or go for a hike. Our intention was to get them outside, to immerse these city-bound teenagers in the revitalizing powers of nature. The native Philadelphians lined up for the hike, but the Cambodian kids said they would rather stay inside and play ping-pong and cards. It was a glorious autumn day, and this caught me off guard. I cajoled and then pleaded with them to come outside. They finally agreed, and we went on our hike. At first they seemed timid, stooping and staring down at the trail in front of their feet, taking only furtive glances off into the forest and up into the trees. As we hiked, they relaxed, and after an hour, they were behaving normally – laughing, jumping on each other, horsing around. Late in the hike I pulled aside two of the teenagers I was closest to and asked what had been holding them back. Fifteen-year-old Sovann explained, "In our country, the forest is full of ghosts. They like the trees because they can hide in them. Once, my uncle was shot by a ghost sitting high in a tree. So many soldiers were killed in the forest, and their ghosts are still there." I asked him why, if they believe that, they were now tramping confidently through these woods. Sovann said, "I told them that in America there aren't many ghosts in the forests. Our country is old, and there are ghosts everywhere because so many people have died. But America is young, and it does not yet have very many ghosts."

The second incident happened one afternoon while visiting Sovann's family in their apartment. As always, when I dropped by – even for a brief visit – the family snapped into action and a meal was prepared. While food was being cooked, I asked Sovann about the framed picture of an old man I had noticed hanging on the wall. Below it was a small shelf with a bowl of fruit and a stick of incense. He turned to his mother, then turned back to me and told me that she wanted to tell me a story and he would translate it for her. In brief, the story went like this: Sovann's father, who was the sexton at the church, had been suffering from acute stomach pains for several months. I knew this, because Sovann had told me about it and we had been praying for him at church. He had been to a doctor but no cause was found and nothing he was given relieved the pain. A week earlier the pain had become unbearable and he could not get out of bed. Without saying anything to her husband, Sovann's mother called a fortuneteller, a Cambodian acquaintance who used a deck of cards to diagnose various ailments and misfortunes of her clients. Over the phone, as she arranged the cards, the fortuneteller inquired about the family's history, birth dates, circumstances surrounding the family's departure from Cambodia, and about what things – foods, activities, stresses – seemed to trigger the pain. At last, the fortuneteller offered her diagnosis: Sovann's grandfather had died before the family left Cambodia. In the haste and necessary secrecy of leaving their home at night to begin their long journey on foot to Thailand, they had had to forego the important ritual that would have allowed the old man's spirit to travel with them. The ritual involves lighting a stick of incense at the ancestral altar – this photograph and shelf I had asked about – and carrying the incense out the door and for the length of their journey, re-lighting new incense until they arrived at their new home. The ancestral ghosts, who have difficulty seeing, follow the fragrant smoke of the incense.

For 3 years the ghost of Sovann's grandfather had been unattended. His picture had been removed from the wall of their home in Cambodia, the bowl at his altar had not been replenished, and he grew hungry. Finally realizing that the family was gone, he set out looking for them. It had taken his ghost 3 years and a long trek, but 3 months earlier this famished spirit had finally found his daughter in south Philadelphia, and he was punishing his son-in-law for sneaking off with the family and not taking him with them. Sovann's mother asked the fortuneteller what could be done to help her husband. The fortuneteller told her to fill the bowl under her father's picture with fresh lychee fruit and rice, then invoke his spirit by lighting the incense. Then she was instructed to pray to her father, explaining the danger the family had been in and why they had had to leave their house so abruptly and without performing the rituals that would have allowed him to accompany them. "Make sure he knows," the fortuneteller said, "that the family would have been killed if they had stayed or if you had carried the incense with you." As Sovann's father was lying in bed upstairs, unaware of any of this, she filled the bowl, lit the incense, and spoke to her father's ghost. She asked him to forgive her husband. Within the hour, Mr Wong emerged from his room, came downstairs, and said the pain in his stomach was gone.

Before hastily dismissing these stories as the superstitions of folk religion, it might be enlightening to consider the views of Fei Xiaotong, an anthropologist from China who spent a year in the US in 1944 as a visiting scholar at the University of Chicago. Fei had been trained in social anthropology in London by Bronislaw Malinowski, and approached his year in the US as an opportunity to do an informal ethnography on our tribal ways. "The thing that felt most strange to me during almost a year of living in America," he later wrote, "was that no one told me any stories of ghosts." This is a land without ghosts, he was surprised to learn, and while he admitted that this might be good for American children, ensuring that they do not have to live their lives intimidated by the prospect of intrusions from the spirit world, he wondered if there wasn't a heavy price for this, "a price I would be unwilling to pay." To live in a land *with* ghosts has this advantage: "ghosts symbolize belief in and reverence for the accumulated past." That is, "when tradition is concrete, when it is part of life, sacred, something to be feared and loved, then it takes the form of ghosts." Could our new wistfulness for ghost stories be telling us that we long to be answerable to sacred traditions with deep histories?

Instead of ghost stories, Fei observed, Americans have Superman – "an all-knowing, resourceful, omnipotent hero who can overcome any difficulty." Superman is a symbol for "actual capabilities or future potential," and it is this zeal for power and an orientation to the future that best describes American culture (at least in 1944), which is always on the move and ready to remove any obstacles that stand in its way. But with this freedom and with no ghosts to weigh them down, "People move about like the tide, unable to form permanent ties with places, to say nothing of other people."[28] The power to dissolve ghosts is inseparable, in other words, from a congenital sense of homelessness and a weak regard for communal obligations. The sudden outbreak of ghosts in popular culture could indicate a spreading sadness about our geographical uprootedness and lack of enduring communal bonds. It could signal, ironically, a rebellion against the unbearable lightness of being.

The African theologian John Mbiti describes a similar view of ancestral spirits in Africa. With some variation, traditional African religions share a common belief that the living-dead dwell in the vicinity of their graves but periodically visit their human families, symbolically eat the food set out for them, inquire about the family, warn of dangers, offer advice and protection, and upbraid those who disregard their guidance. With "a foot in both worlds" – carrying fresh memories from the world of the living and having access to the divine in the spiritland, they remain important members of the household. Treating these ghosts well inclines them to be generous benefactors. Indeed, they are viewed as the most immediate link between human beings and God, whose ear they have, and can therefore serve as channels of the full array of divine powers. But if they were improperly handled while they were dying, if burial customs were violated, or if the graves are ignored, they become restless and vengeful ghosts, punishing the offenders with illnesses and horrifying visitations. Thus, they can be agents of either side of the holy – consoling guardians or terrifying fiends. And, indeed, the living-dead, Mbiti explains, "are wanted and not wanted." The living feel dread and even annoyance toward the living-dead, even when the relationship is a good one.

All this does not mean that the relationship between men and the living-dead is exclusively paradisal. People know only too well that following physical death, a barrier has been erected between them and the living-dead. When the living-dead return and appear to their relatives, this experience is not received with great enthusiasm by men; and if it becomes too frequent, people resent it. As Mbiti describes it:

> Another interesting feature of the African view of the dead is that they are understood to linger on earth for a limited period of time – no more than five generations. When all who knew them personally have died, the dead move on, surrendering their names and individual personalities, and "merge into the company of spirits." The memories of their living relatives, it turns out, are the threads that hold them in existence as ghosts. Thus, it is only with the death of the last person who knew them that the "process of dying" is completed.[29]

In traditional popular religions, the dead, it seems, must learn how to be dead. They are given time to release their grip on life, and to allow their loved ones to let them go. A view of the afterlife is asserting itself now in popular culture that resonates with this more universal picture of a land of spirits that intrudes upon the land of the living. The shadow play of television and cinema, strange as it may be, seems to be stirring these shades from their hiding places in advanced modern societies. This emerging view retrieves many of the concrete features of its predecessors – gravesites are liminal dwelling places of the dead, the dead comfort, play pranks on, and remain interested in their loved ones, the duration of this ghostly phase is temporary. But the message of the ghosts who are turning up in popular culture also alerts us to more existential elements – that there is guilt to atone for at the end of every life, that the loose ends of frazzled lives demand to be put in order, that memories of our dearly departed are precious and ought to be invoked as if their well-being depends upon it, that rituals of remembrance have real effects, and that eventually it is merciful *to the dead* to release them from the grip of our affections. Perhaps our novelists and scriptwriters are reviving this land of the dead – poaching symbols wherever they find them and putting them to new uses, even to the point of creating points of resistance to overt religion – because theologians and clergy have grown too respectfully silent on these matters.[30]

Conclusion

Omega myths and rituals are intended to guide our thinking about the ultimate ends of life – the life of individuals and of communities, but also on the grand scale of the existence of the cosmos itself. They direct us to consider where the trajectories of life are aimed. Popular culture is brimming with experimentation surrounding our death customs, stories of apocalyptic crisis, tableaus of paradise, and rumors about the dead. These are all fruitful materials to reflect on in the effort to discover what eschatological beliefs and hopes our culture is carrying inside itself.

Traditional apocalypses hold that things will get worse before they get better; that a dramatic upheaval will surely occur, but that God will finally overcome the forces of evil and set a renewed creation in place. Some secular doomsday scenarios are bleak, having abandoned any trust in divine providence. In these apocalypses, the world will come to a final and miserable end. Others retain the old trust that good will ultimately triumph, and use the apocalyptic formula to warn us away from the destructive trajectories we are traveling and to recommend alternative ones. But the thrust of the old apocalyptic form remains – it is a genre of revelation and judgment, designed to expose the reigning forces of good and evil and to scare its listeners away from their ruinous ways, to inspire them through fear of the narrated outcomes to find more responsible ways to live.

The utopian landscapes that many of us watch on the screen or hang on our walls are visualizations of ideal omega worlds. In them, we picture hyperreal mixtures of nature, architecture and community where we can imagine our souls might find rest, places to which our struggling in life seems to have been striving all along. These tableaus often represent ideals of beauty, simplicity, innocence, purity, wisdom, power or transcendence. For this reason, they can serve as icons, thin boundaries between the sacred and profane, that transport viewers to a reality beyond their immediate surroundings. This can function as a means of escapism, or it can take on an eschatological dynamism that prompts one to adjust one's life in ways that conform more nearly to the vision displayed in the image.

Stories about ghosts tarrying among the living give us a forum to think about the value of a communal fidelity that defies even the barrier of death. Furthermore, stories of the living-dead allow us to contemplate the resolution that seems to be demanded at the end of a life. There is guilt to be purged and a desperate hope to be nourished that the crafting of our lives might not be so rudely interrupted, that it might be allowed to continue, sobered by the wisdom that will be imparted by our own deaths. And, finally, speculating about the self-awareness, pastimes, and even the dark humor of the dead offers relief to the loneliness that comes of feeling that mortal minds are the single layer of consciousness that goes on in the world. Through such artistic wondering about the afterlife, the already dead are permitted to tutor the living about how to die and how to conduct our lives until we do.

Most of these eschatological experiments in popular culture suggest a happier realm to come, but they also prompt us, each in its own way, to clarify what matters to us in the present, and to consider what ways of life might be better than others. This is a welcome use of popular culture.

Conclusion

In his novel, *About a Boy*, Nick Hornby introduces us to a character who has essentially sealed himself up inside a universe of popular culture. Will Freeman is a 36-year-old who, because he lives off the generous royalties from a hit Christmas song his deceased father wrote in 1938, enjoys a life of uninterrupted leisure. From his high-tech, gadget-filled bachelor's flat in London, he plots his days around perfecting his wardrobe, making regular visits to the hair stylist, eating at the newest restaurants, reading the newspaper and glossy magazines, watching quiz shows on TV, surfing the Internet, and building his CD and DVD collections. In lieu of getting a job or entering any complicated domestic entanglements, Will has dedicated his life to mastering the cool edge of popular culture on every front – fashion, music, film, digital technology, fast cars, cuisine – and that suits him just fine; it minimizes the human clutter, but still gets him dates. Wondering to himself how a man of leisure 60 years ago would have occupied his time, he realizes how hard it would have been. But for Will, it is easy:

> There was almost too much to do. You didn't have to have a life of your own anymore; you could just peek over the fence at other people's lives, as lived in newspapers and *EastEnders* and films and exquisitely sad jazz or tough rap songs.[1]

Will is grateful for his wonderfully unperturbed, thoroughly mediated life.

Hornby tells a perceptive story here about the function of popular culture in our lives and the purposes it serves. Popular culture is a sedative that distances us from our own lives, an effect Will eventually comes to regret. But it is also the preeminent semiotic *lingua franca*, and to be outside of it is to be illiterate in a crucial way. Popular culture (novels, film, music, journalism, sports, TV, fashion, advertising) encompasses the preferred art forms of our age, drawing in many of our most creative minds to produce it. In the culture at large it has become, for most, the primary instrument for forging personal identity and probing the cosmos for meaning. This is not to say that its consumers simply take what they are given and the ready-made meanings it contains. But the plotlines, characters, look and feel, poetry, rhythms, colors, and preoccupations of popular culture do function as a fundamental resource in our time for making meaning. It is largely out of these materials that we contrive our symbols, myths, rituals, ethics, and any notions we might have about more transcendent goods like love, truth, beauty, happiness and the divine.

In this book I have offered an argument for investigating what kinds of religious impulses might be active below the surfaces of popular culture. Sometimes these impulses are simply idolatrous dead-ends, or even diabolical. But at other times they are responses to a genuine stirring of the divine (religion$_1$), or resuscitations of ideals or perceptions from organized religion that were entrusted to the culture and are now reasserting themselves (religion$_3$).

To aid in sorting this out, I sketched out a method in the first part of the book that combined elements from three sources: First, a typology of faith was blended from the work of H. Richard Niebuhr and William James to offer a way to see underlying assertions of metaphysical trust even in cultural artifacts that, on the face of it, seem to dodge or openly defy any faith in the meaningfulness of existence. Second, critical concepts were borrowed from the genuine insights of the Frankfurt School and the evolving field of cultural studies. There *are* moneyed interests behind popular culture that cannot be ignored, as the Frankfurt School teaches us; but, as cultural studies theorists insist, the consumers of popular culture have a variety of ways to exercise their own agency and make meaning out of products they watch, listen to, read and wear. Third, a set of diagnostic concepts was assembled that has been refined by theologians and scholars of religion for the purpose of reaching a better understanding of the phenomenon of religion itself, concepts like ultimate concern, the holy, myth, liminality, and covenant. If something religious is occurring in popular culture, one would expect to find these perennial features of religious experience appearing there. In the second part of the book, I followed the model of a traditional systematic theology and inquired into what notions of God, human nature, sin, salvation, and eschatology can be found within popular culture.

Of the myriad religious messages that are being asserted in popular culture, there is one that, for me, stands out. It is a yearning for a reality beyond all simulations. It stands out because it seems to be a point of resistance to so much else that goes on in popular culture, which tempts us to be content with its amusements and diversions. More than that, this yearning seems to be a word of protest against a central tenet of cultural studies itself, at least against one dominant branch of cultural studies.

There is an emerging conviction in cultural studies that nothing of ultimate importance is to be found in cultural creations, much less in popular culture. The more highly regarded cultural theorists have quit peeling back surfaces to inspect underlying meanings and instead advise that we learn to relish the kaleidoscope of sounds and images that these surfaces reflect and simply accept that they point to nothing more profound than other sounds and images. Their considerable arsenal of concepts (*bricolage*, hyperreality, style, commodity fetishism, simulacrum, etc.) has been turned to the task of proving that our artifacts signify nothing that really matters, except, perhaps, the struggle for power. They dismiss old notions such as the idea that our cultural creations reflect transcendent reality, however dimly, or that a work of art signifies something about the human subject who created it–these notions, they contend, have always been delusions. There are no metaphysical foundations, they reiterate; there is no ground beneath our feet, and certainly there are no turtles holding it all up. From this perspective, theologians like Herder, with his Romantic idea of divine providence active in the *Volkgeist* of different cultures, or Tillich, with his notion that cultures derive their meaning from a subterranean religious substance, are as preposterous as that bottomless stack of turtles.

One of the most poignant objections to this view can be found in the movie *FightClub*. In a pep talk he delivers to the first cell of disenfranchised young men he has recruited for FightClub, Tyler tells his recruits, "You're not your job, you're not how much money you have in the bank, not the car you have, the contents of your wallet. You're not your f – – g khakis." But then, anticipating the opposite error that they might fancy themselves as subjects who transcend their experiences, he circles around to tell them: "You are not special. You are not a beautiful and unique snowflake. You are the same decaying organic matter as everything else." With this, Tyler invites them to make the one unimpeachable connection with reality that is available to them: to pound one another senseless with their fists; this is the ritual action that allows them to have an experience of ecstatic transcendence. Undergoing such primal frenzy and the pain of a good beating is the one assurance they can have that they exist.

In *FightClub*, as we have seen before, the filmmaker uses popular culture to critique popular culture. This scene invites us to reject both the designer self and the therapeutic self as inadequate views of human identity. And while the story offers brutal solutions that we are not really expected to accept (pain and the infliction of pain is the only thing that will confirm your existence), it nevertheless captures a feeling that people are yearning for a connection to reality that neither a *bricolage* of accessories nor cloying self-esteem finally satisfy.

In his reassessment of cultural studies along these lines, Dick Hebdige openly regrets its objections to such "depth words" as "'love' and 'hate' and 'faith' and 'history,' 'pain' and 'joy,' 'passion' and 'compassion'." These are words, he claims, that "drawn up like ghosts from a different dimension will always come back in the 11th hour." There is a "something else" below the surface of our responses to the mystery of our lives, he believes, that "will still be there when all the noise and the chatter have died away."[2]

Theology of culture depends upon this kind of trust that our cultural expressions *can* testify to a reality that transcends them – a reality that is really there, that matters, and in which providence is at work. Theology offers a language to speak about this reality, and can help articulate what is going on in the depths of popular culture. Our cultural artists will often enough get it wrong, and the long, slowly learned lessons of theology can be useful in detecting when this happens, and then offering judgment and guidance. But religious communities and their theologians can also lose their way. And for this reason it is wise for us to remain open to the more discerning makers of culture. Even of popular culture.

Notes

Introduction

1 Wassily Kandinsky, *Concerning the Spiritual in Art*, trans. M.T. Sadler (New York: Dover, 1977). In this essay, Kandinsky describes the artist as "prophet," "priest," and "king," a classic set of titles popularized by John Calvin who used them to describe the various roles played by Jesus. Playing a similar chord at roughly the same time, Paul Klee wrote in his journal: "Everything Faustian is alien to me.... In my work I do not belong to the species but am a cosmic point of reference. My earthly eye is too far sighted and sees through and beyond the most beautiful things." *The Diaries of Paul Klee 1898–1918*, ed. Felix Klee (Berkeley: University of California Press, 1964), 344f.

2 Mark Stevens, "The Artist Assumes the Pedestal," *Salmagundi 3* (Summer 1996), 111.

3 This is a concept that evolved in Calvinist thinking about the functions of culture, best exemplified in the Dutch theologian, Abraham Kuyper. See his *Lectures on Calvinism* (Grand Rapids, MI: Wm. B. Eerdmans Publishing Company, 1931), and in the work of Max Stackhouse, see esp. his *Creeds, Society, and Human Rights: A Study in Three Cultures* (Grand Rapids, MI: Wm. B. Eerdmans, 1984), and *God and Globalization: Religion and the Powers of the Common Life* (Harrisburg, PA: Trinity Press International, 2000). This is also the basic argument of Michael Walzer's *Spheres of Justice: A Defense of Pluralism and Equality* (New York: Basic Books, 1983).

4 For an excellent cultural history of the lawn in America, see Virginia Scott Jenkins, *The Lawn: A History of an American Obsession* (Washington, DC: Smithsonian Institution Press, 1994).

5 Eugene McCarraher, *Christian Critics: Religion and the Impasse of Modern Social Thought* (Ithaca, NY: Cornell University Press, 2000), 6.

6 Richard Mouw, *Consulting the Faithful: What Christian Intellectuals Can Learn from Popular Religion* (Grand Rapids, MI: Wm. B. Eerdmans, 1994), 52f. This brings to mind a comment by Chuck Palahniuk, author of such novels as *FightClub*, *Choke*, and *Lullaby*, who is recognized by many as one of the more discerning voices of Generation X: "I'm dealing with my

own issues on the page – issues of property, mortality, commitment, sex, violence. The books are all about finding some sort of resolution to these issues. I want my characters to really overuse their coping mechanisms to the point where they break down within 300 pages." *New York Times Magazine* (September 29, 2002), 21.

7   Mouw, *Consulting the Faithful*, 84.

8   I will be using the term "media-world" to describe the same phenomenon other cultural theorists have described under the rubric of "social *imaginaire*," which, according to Arjun Appadurai entails "a constructed landscape of collective aspirations . . . mediated through the complex prism of modern media." See his *Modernity at Large: Cultural Dimensions of Globalization* (Minneapolis: University of Minnesota Press, 1996).

9   Simon Frith, *Performing Rites: On the Value of Popular Music* (Cambridge, MA: Harvard University Press, 1996), 276.

10   *Gaudium et Spes*, "Pastoral Constitution on the Church in the Modern World" (1965), in *Vatican Council II: The Conciliar and Post Conciliar Documents*, ed. Austin Flannery (Northport, NY: Costello Publishing Company, 1975), para. 4.

11   Robert Bellah, *The Broken Covenant* (New York: Seabury Press, 1975), 159.

12   Rob Walker, "The Marketing of No Marketing," *New York Times Magazine* (June 22, 2003), 42f. See also, *No Logo: No Space, No Choice, No Jobs*, by Naomi Klein (New York: Picador, 2002).

13   See, for example, Graham Murdock, "The Re-Enchantment of the World: Religion and the Transformations of Modernity," in *Rethinking Media, Religion, and Culture*, eds. Stuart M. Hoover and Knut Lundby (Thousand Oaks, CA: Sage Publications, 1997), 85–101.

14   *FightClub*, directed by David Fincher (New Regency Productions, 2000).

15   See David Brooks, *Bobos in Paradise* (New York: Simon & Schuster, 2000).

16   Jackson Lears is particularly incisive on this point: "[E]ach generation of cultural radicals seems doomed to repeat the mistakes of its predecessors. Throughout the twentieth century, Americans have heard the same attacks on 'repression' as the central problem of their society, the same demands for 'personal growth' as a remedy for all psychic and cultural ills. The Greenwich Village intellectuals of the pre-World War II era, the expatriate artists of the twenties, the therapeutic ideologues of the thirties and forties – none have realized the hidden affinities between their liberationist ideology and the dominant culture of consumer capitalism. . . . This failure of imagination occurred most recently among some of the cultural radicals of the 1960's, whose 'revolution' was rapidly transformed into a consumer bonanza of stereos, designer jeans, and sex aids." *No Place of Grace: Antimodernism and the Transformation of American Culture 1880–1920* (New York: Pantheon Books, 1981), 306. McCarraher, a student of Lears, is also good on this, and develops the notion of "commodity spirituality." See his *Christian Critics*.

17   *Signs*, directed by M. Night Shyamalan (Blinding Edge Pictures, 2002).

18   H.R. Niebuhr, *Faith on Earth: An Inquiry into the Structure of Human Faith* (New Haven: Yale University Press, 1989), 80.

19   On this last point, i.e., the acceleration of irony, see Andrew Delbanco, *The Death of Satan: How Americans Have Lost the Sense of Evil* (New York: Farrar, Straus and Giroux, 1995).

20   Niebuhr, *Faith on Earth*, 67.

21   Ibid., 70–72.

22   Ibid., 73–75.

23   Ibid., 68.

24   Ibid., 76–77.

25   William James, *The Varieties of Religious Experience* (New York: Modern Library, 1936, 1994), 96.

26   Ibid., 104.

27   Ibid., 180f.

28   Describing a similar phenomenon, Paul Ricoeur has given us the term "second naiveté." See his *The Symbolism of Evil*, trans. Emerson Buchanan (Boston: Beacon Press, 1967).

29   Niebuhr, *Faith on Earth*, 78.

30   *American Beauty*, directed by Sam Mendes (Universal Studios, 1999).

31   *Wings of Desire*, directed by Wim Wenders (Road Movies FilmProduktion GMBH, 1987).

32   *Dogma*, directed by Kevin Smith (View Askew Productions, 1999).

33   Paul Ricoeur, "Religion, Atheism, and Faith," in *The Conflict of Interpretations* (Evanston, IL: Northwestern University Press, 1974), 448.

Chapter 1

1   One doesn't have to travel back in time to be confronted by the absence of images that has typified most of human history. The filmmaker, Wim Wenders, recalls a trip to Hungary in the years before the fall of communism: "When I first came to a city in the Eastern bloc, it was Budapest, I went into shock: there was nothing. A few traffic signs, some ugly banners, otherwise the city was empty of imagery, of advertising. That's when I realized how used I was to all that stuff, how addicted." From his essay, "The Act of Seeing," in *Wim Wenders: On Film* (New York: Faber & Faber, 2001), 378.

2   Luc Sante, "Triumph of the Image," *New York Times Magazine* (September 19, 1999), 66.

3   Jacques Barzun, *From Dawn to Decadence: 500 Years of Western Cultural Life* (New York: HarperCollins, 2000), 4.

4   Walter Benjamin, "The Work of Art in the Age of Mechanical Reproduction," in *Illuminations*, trans. Harry Zohn (London: Jonathan Cape Ltd, 1970).

5   This populist echo, triggered by the Great Depression, made a multifaceted appearance across the spectrum of the arts in the 1930's. This was the decade of musicians Woody Guthrie, Aaron Copland ("Fanfare for the Common Man"); painters Edward Hopper, Norman Rockwell, Thomas Hart

Benton and Grant Wood; novelists John Steinbeck and Zora Neil Hurston; filmmakers John Ford and Victor Fleming (*Gone with the Wind, Grapes of Wrath*). On Disney's "bourgeois populism," and for a good analysis of it in his work as a filmmaker, see Steven Watts, *The Magic Kingdom: Walt Disney and the American Way of Life* (Columbia, MO: University of Missouri Press, 1997).

6   There is also the theme found in *Snow White*, and recurring in feature films subsequent to the decade of the 1930s (e.g., *Sleeping Beauty, Beauty and the Beast, The Lion King*) of the divine right of kings (and queens) and their innate gift for benevolent rule, which deservedly raises the Marxist red flag. Disney was also a generator of populist heroes, however (e.g., *Dumbo, Cinderella, The Sword in the Stone*).

7   Watts, *The Magic Kingdom*, 77–82.

8   Watts, *The Magic Kingdom*, 257. See C.L.R. James, *American Civilization* (Cambridge, MA: Blackwells, 1993).

9   In 1946, Disney even began a collaboration with Salvador Dali with the intent of producing a 6-minute animated short that would put Dali's surrealistic images to work as a visual interpretation of the Spanish ballad "Destino" by Mexican composer Armando Dominiguez. The short was intended to be included in a sequel to *Fantasia*, which was never completed. But for two months, Dali showed up every morning at the Disney Studios to draw sketches for the piece. As for the plot, according to Christopher Jones, "It varied considerably, depending on which of the two men was doing the telling. 'A magical exposition of the problem of life in the labyrinth of time,' Dali expounded in his own publication, *Dali News*. 'Just a simple story about a young girl in search of true love,' Disney modestly described it." See Christopher Jones, "When Dali Met Disney," *Boston Globe Magazine* (January 30, 2000), at <http://www.boston.com/globe/magazine/2000/1-30/>. While the project was mothballed for over 50 years, it was resurrected a few years ago and released in 2003.

10   Thomas Hine, "Notable Quotables: Why Images become Icons," *New York Times*, Arts and Leisure section (February 18, 1996), 1.

11   Alexis de Tocqueville, *Democracy in America*, ed. J.P. Mayer, trans. George Lawrence (New York: Harper & Row, 1969), 517f.

12   Kiku Adatto, *Picture Perfect: The Art and Artifice of Public Image Making* (New York: Basic Books, 1993).

13   Bill McKibben, *The Age of Missing Information* (New York: Random House, 1992), 214.

14   Iris Murdoch, "Metaphysics and Ethics," in *Iris Murdoch and the Search for Human Goodness*, eds. M. Antonoccio and W. Schweiker (Chicago: University of Chicago Press, 1996), 252.

15   Robert D. Putnam, *Bowling Alone: The Collapse and Revival of American Community* (New York: Simon & Schuster, 2000).

16   Peter G. Horsfield, "Changes in Religion in Periods of Media Convergence," in *Rethinking Media, Religion, and Culture*, eds. Stuart M. Hoover and Knut Lundby (Thousand Oaks, CA: Sage Publications, 1997), 177.

17 Douglas Rushkoff, *Media Virus: Hidden Agendas in Popular Culture* (New York: Ballantine Books, 1996).

18 Ibid., 28.

19 Ibid., 7.

20 Ibid., 3.

21 Ibid., 29.

22 Ibid., xv.

23 Neil Gabler, *Life: The Movie: How Entertainment Conquered Reality* (New York: Vintage Books, 1998), 57.

24 Johann Gottfried Herder, "Ideas toward a Philosophy of History," in *Against Pure Reason*, trans. and ed. Marcia Bunge (Minneapolis: Fortress Press, 1993), 51.

25 Ibid., 56.

26 Ibid., 58.

27 As a theologian reflecting on culture, my sympathies lie with Herder. It is not off-limits to speak of culture, and of diverse cultures, in terms of divine providence or as embodiments of God's ideas. But this will have to be developed in a future chapter.

28 Edward B. Tylor, *Primitive Culture: Researches into the Development of Mythology, Philosophy, Religion, Language, Art and Custom*, vol. 1 (New York: Henry Holt, 1874), 1.

29 Terry Eagleton, *The Idea of Culture* (London: Blackwell Publishers, 2000), 2.

30 Karl Marx and Friedrich Engels, *The German Ideology* (New York: International Publishers, 1956), 64.

31 Leo Lowenthal, "Historical Perspectives of Popular Culture," in *Mass Culture: The Popular Arts in America*, eds. Bernard Rosenberg and David M. White (Glencoe, IL: The Free Press, 1957), 55.

32 Theodor Adorno, "On Popular Music," in *Studies in Philosophy and Social Science* 9/1 (1941), 42.

33 Ibid., 48.

34 Theodor Adorno, *Aesthetic Theory*, trans. C. Lenhardt (London: Routledge & Kegan Paul, 1984), 72.

35 Theodor Adorno, "Television and the Patterns of Mass Culture," in *Mass Culture: The Popular Arts in America*, eds. Bernard Rosenberg and David M. White (Glencoe, IL: The Free Press, 1957), 476.

36 Adorno, "On Popular Music," 22.

37 Max Horkheimer, "Art and Mass Culture," in *Studies in Philosophy and Social Science* 9/2 (1941), 294. Other avant-garde artists who are singled out for praise by members of the Frankfurt School and their American counterparts, the Mass Culture theorists, include the painters Braque, Mondrian, Miro, Kandinsky, Klee, Matisse, Cézanne; movements: Dadaism, Cubism, Futurism, and Expressionism; the composer Stravinsky; the filmmaker Charlie Chaplin; and the poets Rimbaud, Rilke, and Yeats.

38 Adorno, *Aesthetic Theory*, 337.

39 Ibid., 340.

40 One of the most colorful illustrations of this is the famous account of painter Jackson Pollack urinating in art collector Peggy Guggenheim's fireplace

during one of her elegant parties. Mass Culture theorist and art critic Clement Greenberg was present for this living parable.

41   Horkheimer, "Art and Mass Culture," 291–4.

42   Luminaries among this group of critics include Clement Greenberg and Dwight Macdonald. Like those in the Frankfurt School, the "New York intellectuals" were Marxist critics of developments in the Soviet Union, and of the Popular Front socialists who were embracing the New Deal policies of the Roosevelt administration.

43   Dwight Macdonald, "A Theory of Mass Culture," in *Mass Culture: The Popular Arts in America*, ed. Rosenberg and White, 60.

44   Ibid., 69.

45   Eagleton, *The Idea of Culture*, 24.

46   Ibid., 42.

47   See Habermas's two volume *The Theory of Communicative Action* (Boston: Beacon Press, 1985, 1989); Chomsky and Edward S. Herman's *Manufacturing Consent: The Political Economy of the Mass Society* (New York: Pantheon Books, 1988); Postman's *Amusing Ourselves to Death: Public Discourse in the Age of Show Business* (New York: Viking Press, 1986); and Ellul's *Propaganda: The Formation of Men's Attitudes* (New York: Random House, 1973) and *The New Demons* (New York: Seabury Press, 1975).

48   See David Kirkpatrick, "Shaping Cultural Tastes at Big Retail Chains," *New York Times* (May 18, 2003), business section: 1.

49   Michael Dawson, *The Consumer Trap: Big Business Marketing in American Life* (Urbana, IL: University of Illinois Press, 2003).

50   See his *Distinction: A Social Critique of the Judgment of Taste*, trans. Richard Nice (Cambridge, MA: Harvard University Press, 1984).

51   Tyler Cowan, *In Praise of Commercial Culture* (Cambridge, MA: Harvard University Press, 1998), 186. See also Martha Bayles, *A Hole in our Soul: The Loss of Beauty and Meaning in American Popular Music* (Chicago: University of Chicago Press, 1994).

Chapter 2

1   The Centre was abruptly decommissioned in the summer of 2002 by the University to the shock and consternation of many. The official reason given was a low rating on the Research Assessment Exercise by which the University evaluates the rigor and reputation of research done in its academic departments. Given the international reputation of the Centre, the results of this RAE are puzzling.

2   See Stuart Hall and Paddy Whannel, *The Popular Arts* (London: Hutchinson, 1964); Paul Willis, *Profane Culture* (London: Routledge & Kegan Paul, 1978); Angela McRobbie, *Feminism and Youth Culture* (London: Unwin Hyman, 1991); Dick Hebdige, *Subculture: The Meaning of Style*

(London: Methuen & Co., 1979); and John Hartley, *Uses of Television* (London: Routledge, 1999).

3   Richard Hoggart, *The Uses of Literacy* (London: Penguin Books, 1957), 340.

4   Ibid., 245.

5   Michael Bérubé, *Public Access: Literary Theory and American Cultural Politics* (New York: Verso, 1994), 141.

6   Antonio Gramsci, *Selections from the Prison Notebooks* (London: Lawrence & Wishart, 1971), 161.

7   John Storey, *An Introduction to Cultural Theory and Popular Culture*, 2nd edn (Athens, GA: University of Georgia Press, 1998), 126.

8   Hebdige, *Subculture*, 92f.

9   Hebdige, *Subculture*, 94.

10 Thomas Frank, *The Conquest of Cool: Business Culture, Counterculture, and the Rise of Hip Consumerism* (Chicago: University of Chicago Press, 1997), 227.

11 Thomas Frank, *One Market under God: Extreme Capitalism, Market Populism, and the End of Economic Democracy* (New York: Doubleday, 2000), 259f.

12 Willis, *Profane Culture*, 1.

13 Note also Angela McRobbie's study of the fashions and leisure activities of teenage girls in her *Feminism and Youth Culture*, cited above.

14 Hebdige, *Subculture*, 18.

15 Hebdige, *Hiding in the Light*, 74.

16 Hebdige, *Subculture*, 18.

17 Michel de Certeau, *The Practice of Everyday Life*, trans. Steven Rendall (Berkeley: University of California Press, 1984), 31.

18 Ibid., 174.

19 See <http://www.adbusters.org/information/who_are_we/>. See also the book, *Culture Jam* by Kalle Lasn, one of the founders of Adbusters (New York: HarperCollins, 2000). And Naomi Klein's *No Logo* (New York: Picador, 2002).

20 Umberto Eco, *Theory of Semiotics* (Bloomington, IN: University of Indiana Press, 1979), 150.

21 Jean Baudrillard, "The Evil Demon of Images and the Precession of Simulacra," in *Postmodernism: A Reader*, ed. Thomas Docherty (New York: Columbia Univ. Press, 1993), 194ff. See also, Baudrillard, *Simulations* (New York: Semiotext(e), 1983), 1–36.

22 Jane Addams, "The House of Dreams," in *The Spirit of Youth and City Streets* (New York: MacMillan, 1909), 75f, 82f. <http://www.boondocksnet. com/editions/youth/youth4.html>.

23 Baudrillard shares this view of America as the leading edge of hyperreality: "Yes, California (and America with it) is the mirror of *our* decadence . . . It is hyperreal in its vitality, it has all the energy of the simulacrum. 'It is the world centre of the inauthentic.' Certainly it is: that is what gives it its originality and power. The irresistible rise of the simulacrum is something you can simply feel here without the slightest effort." Baudrillard, *America*

(London: Verso, 1988), 104. This book, too, is a tour of America to verify the hypothesis of its full-force plunge into hyperreality.

24   Umberto Eco, *Travels in Hyperreality*, trans. William Weaver (New York: Harcourt Brace, 1986), 19.

25   Ibid., 44.

26   Ibid., 46.

27   Anne Raver, "Fooling with Nature," *New York Times* (July 11, 1993), travel section, p. 5.

28   Eco, *Travels in Hyperreality*, 8.

29   Jennifer Daryl Slack and Laurie Anne Whitt, "Ethics and Cultural Studies," in *Cultural Studies*, eds. Lawrence Grossberg et al. (New York: Routledge, 1992), 571–592.

30   Frank, *One Market under God*, 294.

31   Quoted in Adam Kuper, *Culture: The Anthropologists' Account* (Cambridge, MA: Harvard University Press, 2000), 230.

32   Dick Hebdige, "Postmodernism and 'The Other Side'," *The Journal of Communication Inquiry*, vol. 10/2 (1987), 85.

33   Dick Hebdige, "The Bottom Line on Planet One: Squaring up to *The Face*," *Ten-8*, vol. 19 (1987), 44.

Chapter 3

1   One fascinating aspect of this is that the sides do not follow the old fault line of conservative/liberal. Both camps are themselves divided internally in their estimations of the value of cultural studies, and particularly postmodernist elements within it. Among Evangelicals are found some of the most uncritical readers of postmodernism; among Liberals some of the most dismissive. Much has to do with attitudes toward the Enlightenment – those who believe it marginalized their communities and beliefs tend to have a friendly attitude toward the subaltern sympathies and deconstructionist irreverence that characterize so much of cultural studies. The enemy of your enemy is your friend.

2   A good analysis of this can be found in Sheila Greeve Davaney, "Theology and the Turn to Cultural Analysis," in *Converging on Culture: Theologians in Dialogue with Cultural Analysis and Criticism*, eds. Delwin Brown, Sheila Greeve Davaney and Kathryn Tanner (Oxford: Oxford University Press, 2001), 3–16.

3   See Anthony Pinn, *Why Lord?: Suffering and Evil in Black Theology* (New York: Continuum, 1995); *Varieties of African American Religious Experience* (Minneapolis: Fortress, 1998); "Rap Music and Its Message," in *Religion and Popular Culture in America*, eds. Bruce David Forbes and Jeffrey Mahan (Berkeley: University of California Press), 258–75.

4   See James Cone, *The Spirituals and the Blues: An Interpretation* (New York: Seabury Press, 1972); Michael Eric Dyson, *Between God and Gangsta Rap: Bearing Witness to Black Culture* (Oxford: Oxford University Press,

1996); Jon Michael Spencer, *The Rhythms of Black Folk: Race, Religion and Pan-Africanism* (Trenton, NJ: Africa World Press, 1995).

5   Pinn, *Why Lord?*, 141.

6   Pinn, "Rap Music and Its Message," 271.

7   Jürgen Moltmann, *God for a Secular Society: The Public Relevance of Theology* (Minneapolis: Fortress Press, 1999), 5. Emphasis is mine.

8   Robin Lane Fox, *Pagans and Christians* (New York: Alfred A. Knopf, 1986), 578–82.

9   Ibid., 55. See also Carlin A. Barton, *The Sorrows of the Ancient Romans: The Gladiator and the Monster* (Princeton: Princeton University Press, 1993), 11–46.

10 Tertullian, "The Shows, or de Spectaculus," trans. S. Thelwall, in *The Ante-Nicene Fathers*, vol. III, eds. Alexander Roberts and James Donaldson (Grand Rapids: Wm. B. Eerdmans Publishing Company, 1956).

11 Circuses in the second century had many elements that are still found in circuses today – sword swallowers, tightrope walkers, jugglers, clowns mimicking gladiatorial battles. The theater, too, resembled theater today, with actors performing tragedies and comedies, elaborate scenery, costumes, and special effects. Many of the great Greek dramas that are still performed today were part of their repertoire. Races would include chariot and horse races, as well as human athletes competing in various sports.

12 Tertullian, "The Shows, or de Spectaculus," 79.

13 Ibid., 87.

14 Ibid., 86.

15 Ibid., 87f.

16 John Chrysostom, "New Homily No.7," from *John Chrysostom*, eds. Wendy Mayer and Pauline Allen (London: Routledge, 2000), 122.

17 Ibid., 87, 89.

18 Ibid., 90.

19 Ibid., 79f.

20 Ibid., 80.

21 Tertullian, "On Idolatry," trans. S. Thelwall, in *The Ante-Nicene Fathers*, vol. III, eds. Alexander Roberts and James Donaldson (Grand Rapids: Wm. B. Eerdmans Publishing Company, 1956).

22 Ibid., 91.

23 H.R. Niebuhr, *Christ and Culture* (New York: Harper & Row, 1951), 55.

24 Augustine, *Confessions*, trans. R.S. Pine-Coffin (New York: Penguin Books, 1961), III/2.

25 Ibid., VI/8.

26 Augustine, *On Christian Doctrine*, trans. D.W. Robertson, Jr (Indianapolis: Bobbs-Merrill, 1958), II/40.

27 *City of God*, X/27.

28 *Confessions*, III/6.

29 *City of God*, XXII/24.

30 Ibid., XVIII/54.

31 Ibid., I/35. See also XI/1.

32 *City of God*, VII/30.

33   Ibid., VII/1,2,5.

34   Augustine, *Epistle 55*, trans. Wilfrid Parsons, in *The Fathers of the Church*, vol. 12 (New York: Fathers of the Church, 1951), 220.

35   *On Christian Doctrine*, II/18.

36   Ibid.

37   Ibid., II/40.

38   *Epistle 55*, 293.

39   *On Christian Doctrine*, III/10.

40   Ibid., I/4.

41   Ibid., I/35.

42   Augustine, *Epistle 91*, trans. Wilfrid Parsons, in *The Fathers of the Church*, vol. 18 (New York: Fathers of the Church, 1951), 45. Augustine cites the same example in *Confessions* I/16, and in *City of God*, II/7.

43   *City of God*, II/4.

44   Augustine, *Confessions*, X.34.

45   Ernst Troeltsch, *The Social Teachings of the Christian Churches*, trans. Olive Wyon (Chicago: University of Chicago Press, 1931).

46   See, for example, Stanley Hauerwas, *After Christendom: How the Church Is to Behave if Freedom, Justice and a Christian America Are Bad Ideas* (Nashville: Abingdon Press, 1991); Hauerwas and William Willimon, *Resident Aliens* (Nashville: Abingdon Press, 1989); and, following in this line, Martin Copenhaver, Anthony Robinson and William Willimon, *Good News in Exile: Three Pastors Offer a Hopeful Vision for the Church* (Grand Rapids, MI: William B. Eerdmans, 1999).

47   Hauerwas and Willimon, *Resident Aliens*, 46f.

48   Ibid., 22.

49   Stanley Hauerwas, *Vision and Virtue: Essays in Christian Ethical Reflection* (Notre Dame, IN: Fides Publishers, 1974), 241ff.

50   Augustine, *City of God*, XIX/13.

51   Martin Luther, "That These Words of Christ, 'This Is My Body,' etc., Still Stand Firm against the Fanatics" (1527), in *Luther's Works*, vol. 37, ed. Robert H. Fischer (Philadelphia: Muhlenberg Press, 1961), 59.

52   Paul Tillich, "One Moment of Beauty," in *On Art and Architecture*, eds. John Dillenberger and Jane Dillenberger (New York: Crossroad Publishing Co., 1987), 235. The essay was written in 1955.

53   For good background on this period of Tillich's life and the influences on his thinking at the time, see Wilhelm and Marion Pauck, *Paul Tillich: His Life and Thought* (New York: Harper & Row, 1976), 40–94; and, Ronald Stone, *Paul Tillich's Radical Social Thought* (Atlanta: John Knox Press, 1980), 32–58.

54   Paul Tillich, "On the Idea of a Theology of Culture," trans. William Baillie Green, in *What Is Religion?*, ed. James Luther Adams (New York: Harper & Row, 1969).

55   This is a device first suggested by John P. Clayton, in his book, *The Concept of Correlation: Paul Tillich and the Possibility of a Mediating Theology* (Berlin: Walter de Gruyter, 1980), 88f.

56   Paul Tillich, "Religious Style and Religious Material in the Fine Arts" (1921), trans. Robert Scharlemann, in *On Art and Architecture*, 54.

57   Tillich, "On the Idea of a Theology of Culture," 169.

58   Ibid., 174.

59   Paul Tillich, *The Religious Situation*, trans. H. Richard Niebuhr (New York: Henry Holt & Co., 1932), 37.

60   Paul Tillich, "Kairos" (1922), in *Writings in the Philosophy of Religion*, ed. John P. Clayton (Berlin: De Gruyter-Evangelische Verlagwerk GmbH, 1987), 66.

61   Paul Tillich, "Religion and Secular Culture," in *The Protestant Era* (Chicago: University of Chicago Press, 1957), 60.

62   Paul Tillich, "Existentialist Aspects of Modern Art," in *On Art and Architecture*, 95f.

63   A roster of better-known theologians whose use of culture reflects Tillich's influence includes James Luther Adams, Langdon Gilkey, Bernard Meland, Richard Kroner, Julian Hartt, Harvey Cox, David Tracy, Tom Driver, James Wall, Robert Scharlemann, Nathan Scott, Jr, Peter Hodgson, John MacQuarrie, Sallie McFague, Gibson Winter, Max Stackhouse, William Schweiker, David Klemm, Ronald Stone, and Ralph Wood.

64   A good account of Tillich's connection to the Institute for Social Research may be found in Ronald H. Stone, *Paul Tillich's Radical Social Thought* (Atlanta: John Knox Press, 1980).

65   Tillich, *On Art and Architecture*, 132, 152, 223.

66   Tillich, *Protestant Era*, 60.

67   Paul Tillich, "The Political Meaning of Utopia" (1951), in *Political Expectation*, ed. James Luther Adams (New York: Harper & Row, 1971), 170.

68   Paul Tillich, *Systematic Theology, I* (Chicago: University of Chicago Press, 1951), 39f.

69   Ibid., 40.

Chapter 4

1   Clifford Geertz, *The Interpretation of Cultures* (New York: Basic Books, 1973), 29.

2   Augustine, *Confessions*, trans. R.S. Pine-Coffin (London: Penguin Books, 1961), X.6.

3   Augustine, *On Christian Doctrine*, I.7.

4   Jack Kerouac, *On the Road* (New York: Viking Press, 1979), 48.

5   Tillich, *Dynamics of Faith* (New York: Harper & Row, 1957), 4.

6   Ibid., 13.

7   Havelock Ellis, *The New Spirit* (1890), 232, quoted in William James, *Varieties of Religious Experience*, 56.

8   Tillich, *Dynamics of Faith*, 10.

9   James, *Varieties of Religious Experience*, 298f.

10   Tillich, *Dynamics of Faith*, 12.
11   Paul Tillich, *Systematic Theology, I* (Chicago: University of Chicago Press, 1951), 13.
12   Edmund Burke, *A Philosophical Enquiry into the Origin of our Ideas of the Sublime and Beautiful* (1757), ed. Adam Phillips (Oxford: Oxford University Press, 1990); Immanuel Kant, *Observations on the Feeling of the Beautiful and Sublime* (1764), trans. John Goldthwait (Berkeley: University of California Press, 1960).
13   Philip Hallie, *Tales of Good and Evil, Help and Harm* (New York: HarperCollins, 1997), 124. Emphasis is his.
14   Kant also posits the experience of the sublime as the spring from which flows our most primordial sense of moral duty. In his *Critique of Practical Reason*, he writes: "Two things fill the mind with ever new and increasing admiration and awe, the more steadily we reflect on them: the starry heavens above me and the moral law within me. . . . The former . . . annihilates, as it were, my importance as an animal creature which must give back to the planet the matter from which it came. . . . The latter, on the contrary, infinitely raises my worth . . ." trans. Lewis White Beck (New York: Bobbs-Merrill, 1957), 166.
15   Friedrich Schleiermacher, *The Christian Faith* (1830), eds. H.R. MacKintosh and J.S. Stewart (Edinburgh: T&T Clark, 1928, 1986), §63.
16   Augustine, *Confessions*, trans. R.S. Pine-Coffin, XII.14.
17   Tillich, *Systematic Theology, I*, 216.
18   Ibid., 110.
19   The Greek root of the word "ontology," *onta*, means "existing beings."
20   Tillich, *Dynamic of Faith*, ch. 4.
21   See Friedrich Nietzsche, *The Birth of Tragedy*, trans. Francis Golffing (New York: Doubleday Anchor Books, 1956), 42.
22   Roger Shattuck, *Forbidden Knowledge: From Prometheus to Pornography* (New York: St Martin's Press, 1996), 319.
23   Paul Tillich, *Ultimate Concern: Tillich in Dialogue*, ed. D. MacKenzie Brown (New York: Harper Colophon Books, 1965), 179.
24   James, *The Varieties of Religious Experience*, 80f.
25   Tillich, *Systematic Theology, I*, 110.
26   Tillich, *Dynamics of Faith*, 6.
27   Paul Tillich, *The Protestant Era*, 78.
28   While his account of revelation lends itself to flattening out the difference between biblical revelation and any ecstatic experience, Tillich is careful to draw a distinction. He gives the name of *original* revelation to those outpourings of new awareness that are witnessed to in the Bible, and by extension, to the prophetic experiences that became the founding events of other religions. Once a religion$_2$ has been established, the continuing ecstatic experiences of those who conform their lives to it falls under the category of *dependent* revelation. The sacred texts, rituals, laws, sacraments, doctrines, institutions, prayers, clerics, saints, and ethical systems that flow from the original revelation are instances of a continuing ecstatic reception. The original revelation remains fresh in the lives of communities as long as it is renewed through ecstatic experiences in the lives of individuals, and this

is understood in the history of the church as the work of the divine Spirit, but it is a different order of revelation that is *dependent* upon the original event. Religion$_2$ has revelatory power, but it is the power of "illumination" in contrast to that of "inspiration," which is characteristic of occasions of original revelation. See Tillich, *Systematic Theology, I*, 126f.

29 Tillich, *Systematic Theology, I*, 140.

30 Tillich offers different variations on this list. See his *Dynamics of Faith*, 41–54; *Systematic Theology, I*, 239–41; and *Theology of Culture*, 53–67.

31 Clifford Geertz, *The Interpretation of Cultures* (New York: Basic Books, 1973), 127.

32 Ibid., 129.

33 Beginning with Friedrich Schleiermacher, theologians have used the expression "the picture of Jesus" to describe this magnetic quality of Jesus to accumulate ascriptions over time. For a historical survey of a succession of images that have been attached to Jesus, see Jaroslav Pelikan's *Jesus through the Centuries: His Place in the History of Culture* (New York: Harper & Row, 1985). On Jesus as CEO, see Bruce Barton's 1925 classic, *The Man Nobody Knows*, or the more recent book by Laurie Beth Jones, *Jesus CEO: Using Ancient Wisdom for Visionary Leadership* (New York: Hyperion, 1995).

34 Tillich, *Theology of Culture*, 58.

35 John Calvin, *Institutes of the Christian Religion*, ed. John T. McNeill (Philadelphia: Westminster Press, 1960), 1.9.8.

36 Tillich, *Theology of Culture*, 60.

37 Tillich, *Ultimate Concern: Tillich in Dialogue*, 180f.

38 Mircea Eliade, *Patterns in Comparative Religion* (New York: New American Library, 1958), 2.

39 Mircea Eliade, *The Sacred and the Profane* (New York: Harcourt Brace Jovanovich, 1959), 138.

40 Mike Featherstone, *Undoing Culture: Globalization, Postmodernism and Identity* (London: Sage Publications, 1995), 8.

41 Johann Gottfried Herder, "Fragment of an Essay on Mythology" (c. 1782–92), in *Against Pure Reason*, ed. Marcia Bunge (Minneapolis: Fortress Press, 1993), 80f.

42 Tillich, *Dynamics of Faith*, 50.

43 Ibid., 49.

44 Eliade, *The Sacred and the Profane*, 98.

45 Eliade, *Myth and Reality* (New York: Harper & Row, 1963), 5f.

46 Eliade, *Patterns*, 411.

47 Mircea Eliade, *Myths, Dreams, and Mysteries* (New York: Harper Torchbooks, 1960), 186.

48 Eliade, *Patterns*, 345.

49 Eliade, *Myths, Dreams and Mysteries*, 27.

50 This was the mantra of the Unabomber, Ted Kaczynski.

51 For more on this phenomenon, see the account of "religion$_3$" below.

52 Arnold van Gennep, *The Rites of Passage* [1908] (Chicago: University of Chicago Press, 1960), 20ff.

53   Ibid., 21.

54   Ibid., 71–5.

55   See Victor Turner, *The Ritual Process: Structure and Anti-Structure* (Ithaca, NY: Cornell University Press, 1969); and *The Forest of Symbols: Aspects of Ndembu Ritual* (Ithaca, NY: Cornell University Press, 1967).

56   Victor Turner, *Blazing the Trail: Way Marks in the Exploration of Symbols* (Tucson, AZ: University of Arizona Press, 1992), 49.

57   Turner, *Forest of Symbols*, 95–7.

58   Turner, *Blazing the Trail*, 50.

59   Turner, *Forest*, 103–10.

60   Ibid., 98.

61   Ibid, 127ff.

62   Paul Tillich, "Kairos" (1922), in *The Protestant Era*, 43.

63   Paul Tillich, *Systematic Theology, III* (Chicago: University of Chicago Press, 1963), 248f. Similarly, and under Tillich's influence, Margaret Miles wrote, "Religion without artistic images is qualitatively impoverished; art without religion is in danger of triviality, superficiality, or subservience to commercial or political interests." See her *Image as Insight* (Boston: Beacon Press, 1985), 152.

64   Tillich, *Systematic Theology, I*, 15. Similarly, Augustine pointed out that "those who exult in divine assistance...should calm themselves for this reason: they should remember that they have learned at least the alphabet from men." See his *On Christian Doctrine*, Prologue.4.

65   On this often neglected history, see James Morone, *Hellfire Nation: The Politics of Sin in American History* (New Haven: Yale University Press, 2003); Carol Hymowitz and Michaele Weissman, *A History of Women in America* (New York: Bantam Books, 1978); Michael J. Perry, *The Idea of Human Rights: Four Inquiries* (Oxford: Oxford University Press, 1998); Walter Rauschenbusch, *Christianizing the Social Order* (Boston: Pilgrim Press, 1912); Lezak Kolakowski, *Modernity on Endless Trial* (Chicago: University of Chicago Press, 1990); Max Stackhouse, *Creeds, Society, and Human Rights: A Study in Three Cultures* (Grand Rapids, MI: William B. Eerdmans, 1984); Rodney Stark, *One True God: Historical Consequences of Monotheism* (Princeton: Princeton University Press, 2001), and *For the Glory of God* (Princeton: Princeton University Press, 2003); and Benson Bobrick, *Wide as the Waters: The Story of the English Bible and the Revolution It Inspired* (New York: Simon & Schuster, 2001).

66   On religion and sports in the US, see Robert Higgs, *God in the Stadium* (Lexington: University Press of Kentucky, 1995); Joseph Price, ed., *From Season to Season: Sports as American Religion* (Macon, GA: Mercer University Press, 2001); Christopher Evans and William Herzog II, eds., *The Faith of 50 Million: Baseball, Religion, and American Culture* (Louisville, KY: Westminster John Knox Press, 2002); Michael Novak, *The Joy of Sports: End Zones, Bases, Balls, and the Consecration of the American Spirit* (New York: Basic Press, 1976); and Charles S. Prebish, *Religion and Sport: The Meeting of Sacred and Profane* (Westport, CT: Greenwood Press, 1993).

67 Two admissions are in order here to cover a multitude of sins in what lies ahead: First, the selection of artifacts from popular culture is not comprehensive. There is probably no escaping the fact that this selection reflects, for the most part, samples of popular culture that fall on the radar screen of my own generational location. Born in 1958, I straddle the line between baby boomers and Generation X. Consequently the materials that catch my attention as worthy of analysis favor these two generations, and, inescapably, a host of other biases (gender, race, social class). Second, while factors like *bricolage* and the consumers' sometimes oppositional use of popular culture do figure into some of the analyses, I have tended to favor intentions and values that can be located in the "texts" themselves (whether the texts be movies, ads, songs, wall art or TV shows). Where possible, I have investigated statements made by creators of these texts to better understand their intentions. But my primary interest here is not in the creators of the texts nor in their reception, but in the artifacts themselves and the world as they construe it. To do justice to the *use* consumers make of popular culture would require a more ethnographic approach than has been attempted here. This is certainly worth doing to supplement a consideration of the values built into artifacts, but not if it negates the discernible way of valuing the world that can be found in the artifacts themselves.

Chapter 5

1 Nikos Kazantzakis, *Zorba the Greek* (New York: Simon & Schuster, 1952), 270.
2 Douglas Coupland, *Life after God* (New York: Pocket Books, 1994), 273.
3 The resulting scar is clearly an allusion to the wounds of Christ and the stigmata of St Francis and other Catholic saints.
4 As Chuck Palahniuk, the author of *FightClub*, is clearly aware, there is a line to be drawn connecting our experience of our fathers and our image of God. In his background commentary on this scene in the DVD version of the movie, Palahniuk comments, "It has really struck a chord (with the audience) and I have to wonder . . . people without a presence of father, if they can ever have a presence of God."
5 "God," by Tori Amos, from *Under the Pink*. © 1994 Sword and Stone Publishing, Inc. Reprinted by permission.
6 Joan Osborne, "One of Us," from *Relish*. Song written by Eric Bazilian © 1995 Warner Bros. Music Corp. All rights reserved. Used by permission of Warner Bros. Publications US Inc., Miami, Florida 33014.
7 Distributed in the US under the title, *Don't Tempt Me*, directed by Agustin Diaz Yanes (First Look Films, 2001).
8 From Franchise Pictures, written by Roger Rueff, directed by John Swanbeck, 2000.
9 Wim Wenders, *On Film: Essays and Conversations* (London: Faber & Faber, 2001), 236, 277.

10   There was a surge of attention to angels in popular culture beginning in the 1990s. There was an emergence of television shows like *Touched by an Angel* (CBS), *Promised Land* (CBS), and *Wonderfalls* (Fox), and of movies like *Michael* (1996), *The Preacher's Wife* (1996), *City of Angels* (1998), and *Dogma* (1999). Paralleling this were bestselling books like Joan Webster Anderson's *Where Angels Walk* (1993), a collection of stories about people who attest to angels intervening in their lives. It remained for 55 weeks on the *New York Times* bestsellers' list, and still outsells Tillich's most popular books. It was followed by Anderson's *An Angel to Watch over Me* (1994) and *Angels We Have Heard on High* (1997). Publishing bonanzas by other authors include Sophy Burham's *A Book of Angels* (1990); Doreen Virtue, *Messages from Your Angels: What Your Angels Want You to Know* (2002) and *Angel Therapy: Healing Messages for Every Area of Your Life* (1997). Add to this angel calendars, guardian angel kits, angel oracle cards, wall prints and tote bags with the image of Raphael's angels, etc. Victoria's Secret has even introduced a line of erotic undergarments called "Angels." A more recent development circumvents the messenger role of angels and has God speaking directly to individuals – see *Joan of Arcadia* (CBS, 2003), and *Bruce Almighty* (Universal Pictures, 2003).

11   Wenders, *On Film*, 237.

12   Paul Ricoeur, "The Function of Fiction in Shaping Reality," in *Man and World* 12/2 (1970), 134.

13   Paul Ricoeur, "On Interpretation," in *From Text to Action: Essays in Hermeneutics, II*, ed. Kathleen Blamey and John B. Thompson (Evanston, IL: Northwestern University Press, 1991), 6.

14   Franco Ferrucci, *The Life of God (as Told by Himself)*, trans. Raymond Rosenthal and Franco Ferrucci (Chicago: University of Chicago Press, 1996), 7.

15   Ibid., 8.

16   Ibid., 25.

17   Ibid.

18   Ibid., 32.

19   Ibid., 33.

20   Ibid., 43.

21   Ibid., 67.

22   Ibid., 84f.

23   Ibid., 87.

24   Ibid., 119.

25   Ibid., 124.

26   Ibid., 124.

27   Ibid., 143.

28   Ibid., 142.

29   Ibid., 189.

30   Ibid., 225.

31   This notion that God is engaged in a project of self-discovery is also found in the very popular non-fiction book, *God: A Biography*, by Jack Miles (New York: Vintage Books, 1995). Miles proposes that a literary reading of

the Hebrew Bible displays a God who creates humans in order to find out something about himself, to clarify whether his deepest wish is to be known, to be loved, or to be served (see p. 403). Like Ferrucci's God, Miles's God is surprised by the consequences of his actions, and is chastened over time as one thing after another fails to go according to plan. This God gradually withdraws from intervening in human affairs, again, like the God we meet in Ferrucci's world.

32   Ibid., 239. This brings to mind the colorful charge of David Hume, who in 1760 chided theologians who anthropomorphize God: "[This world is the] first rude essay of some infant deity, who afterwards abandoned it, ashamed of his performance." See Hume's *Dialogues Concerning Natural Religion*, ed. Henry Aiken (New York: Hafner Publishing, 1948), 41.

33   Ferucci, *The Life of God*, 280.

34   James Morrow, *Towing Jehovah* (New York: Harcourt Brace & Company, 1994); *Blameless in Abaddon* (New York: Harcourt Brace & Company, 1996); and *The Eternal Footman* (New York: Harcourt Brace & Company, 1999).

35   James Morrow, *Towing Jehovah*, 138.

36   Ibid., 135.

37   Ibid., 181.

38   Fyodor Dostoevsky, *The Brothers Karamazov*, trans. Constance Garnett (New York: New American Library, 1957), 573.

39   Morrow, *Towing Jehovah*, 171.

40   Morrow, *Blameless in Abaddon*, 29.

41   Morrow, *Towing Jehovah*, 62.

42   Morrow, *The Eternal Footman*, 33f.

43   Ibid., 237. This is a near verbatim quote from Bonhoeffer's *Letters and Papers from Prison* (London: SCM Books, 1953), 122. But it is worth noting that Ockham (Morrow) has omitted one key sentence in the passage which would otherwise reinforce the underlying theism of Bonhoeffer's point. In the position where I have inserted the bracketed asterisks, Bonhoeffer includes the sentence, "The God who is with us is the God who forsakes us (Mark 15:34)."

44   This view that God is good but religion is bad is a recurring one. Both inside and outside of the religious community one can overhear the complaint that religion is somehow to blame for the thinness of the divine in our lives. In the words of rock artist Sinead O'Connor, who has recently made her peace with God after a very public display of shredding the Pope's photograph on NBC's *Saturday Night Live* ten years ago, "I believe in rescuing God from religion. Religion has God held hostage and hidden behind bars. If God were alive he or she would be suing a lot of people for libel." From interview with Sinead O'Connor, "O Mother, Who Art Thou?" *Sunday Herald* (Edinburgh) (January 12, 2003) <http://www.sundayherald.com/30497>.

45   H. Richard Niebuhr, *Radical Monotheism and Western* Culture (New York: Harper & Row, 1960), 29.

46   Ibid.

47   Laurence Cossé, *A Corner of the Veil*, trans. Linda Asher (New York: Scribner, 1999), 79.

48   Ibid., 30.
49   Ibid., 31.
50   Ibid., 31. Emphasis mine – note the Grand Inquisitor theme.
51   Ibid., 107.
52   Laurence Cossé, *A Corner of the Veil*, trans. Linda Asher (New York: Scribner, 1999), 261.
53   Ibid., 146f.
54   Ibid., 211.
55   Ibid., 233.
56   Ibid., 220.
57   As if they knew that effective marketing requires a myth, Needham Harper and Steers, an advertising agency, invented the McDonaldland campaign for McDonald's. For 6 years Ronald McDonald had been a free-floating mascot for the franchise, simply a clown who liked hamburgers. Then, in 1971, he was given a world of his own, where hamburgers could talk and french fries grew on bushes, and fellow inhabitants consisted of Mayor McCheese, Hamburglar, Officer Big Mac, Captain Crook, Grimace and CosMc, the hamburger-loving alien from outer space.
58   For more on this, see Sut Jhally, "Advertising as Religion: The Dialectic of Technology and Magic," in *Cultural Politics in Contemporary America*, eds. Ian Angus and Sut Jhally (New York: Routledge, 1989), 217–29.
59   Neil Gaiman, *American Gods* (New York: Harper Torch, 2001).
60   Albert Borgmann, *Technology and the Character of Contemporary Life* (Chicago: University of Chicago Press, 1984). See also his *Power Failure: Christianity in the Culture of Technology* (Grand Rapids, MI: Brazos Press, 2003).
61   On this, see Bill Joy, "Why the Future Doesn't Need Us," a highly confessional article Joy wrote for *Wired* magazine (April 2000), in which he worries over what long-term effects twenty-first-century technologies (robotics, genetic engineering, nanotechnology) will have on human beings and the planet. His primary concern is that through these technologies, machines will overtake humans, who may be the authors of our own demise. It will happen incrementally, he suggests, forwarded by scientists and consumers who think only of the next improvement in technologies they are currently using.
62   As reported by Thomas Friedman, in "Is Google God?" *New York Times*, commentary section (June 29, 2003) <http://www.nytimes.com/2003/06/29/opinion/29FRIE.html?8hpib>
63   Joy, "Why the Future Doesn't Need Us."
64   Scott Adams, *God's Debris: A Thought Experiment* (Kansas City: Andrews McMeel Publishing, 2001), 100.
65   Ibid., 52f.
66   Dick Hebdige, "Postmodernism and 'The Other Side'," *The Journal of Communication Inquiry*, vol. 10/2 (1987), 92.
67   Richard Rorty, *Contingency, Irony, and Solidarity* (Cambridge: Cambridge University Press, 1989), 93. Hebdige describes the aim of "the disciples of the Post" as an attack on all appeals to authority which are "seen to hover like the ghost of the Father behind all First World discourse guaranteeing

Truth, hierarchy and Order of Things." See his "The Bottom Line on Planet One: Squaring up to *The Face*," *Ten-8*, vol. 19 (1987), 43.

68 Rorty, *Contingency, Irony, and Solidarity*, 73f.
69 William Schweiker, *Theological Ethics and Global Dynamics: In the Time of Many Worlds* (Oxford: Blackwell Publishers, 2004), ch. 9.
70 Ibid., 187.
71 Jane Tompkins, *West of Everything: The Inner Life of Westerns* (Oxford: Oxford University Press, 1992), 220.
72 Schweiker, *Theological Ethics and Global Dynamics*, 188.
73 Tillich, *Shaking the Foundations*, 42–7.

Chapter 6

1 Walter T. Davis, Jr, Teresa Blythe, Gary Dreibelbis et al., *Watching What We Watch: Prime-Time Television through the Lens of Faith* (Louisville, KY: Geneva Press, 2001), 103. See also Elijah Siegler, "God in the Box: Religion in Contemporary Television Cop Shows," in *God in the Details: American Religion in Popular Culture*, eds. Eric Marzur and Kate McCarthy (New York: Routledge, 2001), 199–215.
2 David Samuels, "In the Age of Radical Selfishness," *New York Times Magazine* (October 17, 1999), 120ff.
3 Tom Beaudoin, *Virtual Faith: The Irreverent Spiritual Quest of Generation X* (San Francisco: Jossey Bass, 1998), 140.
4 Ibid., 141.
5 For a good analysis of this, see William Schweiker, *Theological Ethics and Global Dynamics: In the Time of Many Worlds* (Oxford: Blackwell Publishing, 2004).
6 Charles Taylor, *Sources of the Self: The Making of the Modern Identity* (Cambridge, MA: Harvard University Press, 1989), 211.
7 For a good history on the connections between gospel/jazz/soul/rhythm and blues and rock music, see Martha Bayles, *Hole in our Soul: The Loss of Beauty and Meaning in American Popular Music* (Chicago: University of Chicago Press, 1994).
8 John Mueller, *Capitalism, Democracy and Ralph's Pretty Good Grocery* (Princeton: Princeton University Press, 1999), 80.
9 Robert A. White, "Religion and Media in the Construction of Cultures," in *Rethinking Media, Religion, and Culture*, eds. Stuart M. Hoover and Knut Lundby (Thousand Oaks, CA: Sage Publications, 1997), 55.
10 David Lyon, *Jesus in Disneyland: Religion in Postmodern Times* (Cambridge: Polity Press, 2000), 89ff.
11 Ibid., 12.
12 Ibid., 79.
13 Ibid., 89.
14 Ian H. Angus, "Circumscribing Postmodern Culture," in *Cultural Politics in Contemporary America*, eds. Ian Angus and Sut Jhally (New York: Routledge, 1989), 99ff.

15 Herbert Muschamp, "Who Gets It?" *New York Times Magazine* (May 18, 2003), 13f.

16 Virginia Postrel, *The Substance of Style: How the Rise of Aesthetic Value Is Remaking Commerce, Culture, and Consciousness* (New York: HarperCollins, 2003), 117, 120.

17 A similar demographic study has been done in Britain by Experian Micromarketing, under a system called MOSAIC. Their research has identified 52 lifestyle clusters in the UK, including such stand-outs as "rising materialists," "graffitied ghettos," "rootless renters," and "chattering classes." On both PRIZM and MOSAIC, see Michael J. Weiss, *The Clustered World: How We Live, What We Buy, and What It All Means about Who We Are* (Boston: Little, Brown, & Co., 2000).

18 James Twitchell, *Lead Us into Temptation: The Triumph of American Materialism* (New York: Columbia University Press, 1999), 47.

19 Clive Thompson, "There's a Sucker Born in Every Medial Prefrontal Cortex," *New York Times Magazine* (October 26, 2004), 54–7.

20 Steven Watts, *The Magic Kingdom: Walt Disney and the American Way of Life* (Columbia, MO: University of Missouri Press, 1997), 104.

21 Alexander Wilson, *The Culture of Nature: North American Landscape from Disney to the Exxon Valdez* (Oxford: Blackwell Publishers, 1992), 120.

22 Michael Sorkin, "See You in Disneyland," in *Variations on a Theme Park: The New American City and the End of Public Space*, ed. Michael Sorkin (New York: Hill and Wang, 1992), 206. Or, as Eric Mazur and Tara K. Koda have suggested, "The American who can avoid contact with Disney must live in a cave; to reject Disney is to defy a major global force." See their essay, "The Happiest Place on Earth: Disney's America and the Commodification of Religion," in *God in the Details: American Religion in Popular Culture*, eds. Eric Marzur and Kate McCarthy (New York: Routledge, 2001), 300.

23 Lyon, *Jesus in Disneyland*, 3–6.

24 Ibid., 15.

25 Watts, *The Magic* Kingdom, 163.

26 As Neal Gabler puts it, because of its attractions, "entertainment conquers reality." See his *Life: The Movie* (New York: Vintage Books, 1998).

27 Alexis de Tocqueville, *Democracy in America*, ed. Richard D. Heffner, trans. Henry Reeve and Frances Bowen (New York: New American Library, 1956), 184.

28 David Gilbert Timothy Wilson and David Centerbar, "Making Sense: The Causes of Emotional Evanescence," in *Economics and Psychology*, eds. J. Carillo and I. Brocas (Oxford: Oxford University Press, 2002), 209–33; and David Gilbert and Timothy Wilson, "Miswanting: Some Problems in the Forecasting of Future Affective States," in *Thinking and Feeling: The Role of Affect in Social Cognition*, ed. J. Forgas (Cambridge: Cambridge University Press, 2000). Also good on this is Barry Schwartz, *The Paradox of Choice: Why More Is Less* (New York: HarperCollins, 2004).

29 Dick Hebdige, "The Bottom Line on Planet One: Squaring up to *The Face*," in *Ten-8*, vol. 19 (1987), 45.

30 Augustine, *Confessions*, X.8.

31 In addition to the films discussed here, one could add Kore-eda Hirokazu's *After Life* (1998) and Paul Verhoeven's *Total Recall* (1990).

32 Hebdige, "The Bottom Line on Planet One," 44.

33 Augustine, *Confessions*, X.17.

34 Wim Wenders, *On Film: Essays and Conversations* (London: Faber & Faber, 2001), 379.

35 Brenda E. Brasher, "Thoughts on the Status of the Cyborg: On Technological Socialization and Its Link to the Religious Function of Popular Culture," *Journal of the American Academy of Religion* 64/4 (Winter 1996), 809–30. This is an incisive and insightful review of the concept of the cyborg as a root metaphor in our evolving understanding of human nature, perhaps the best place to start in exploring the range of implications of this metaphor in relation to human nature. The pivotal thinker along these lines is, as Brasher points out, Donna Haraway. See Haraway's "Manifesto for Cyborgs: Science, Technology and Socialist-Feminist Perspective in the 1980's," in *Socialist Review* 80 (1985), 65–108; and *Simians, Cyborgs and Women: the Reinvention of Nature* (London: Free University Press, 1991). Graham Ward is also very good on this. See chapter 8 of his *Cities of God* (London: Routledge, 2000).

36 In a recent commercial for Nextel Wireless, an entire wedding is conducted in a great old gothic cathedral with all communications going through the flash idiom of instant messaging; bride, groom, minister and every guest in the pews all holding their accessorized personal handsets right in front of their faces: "Do you?" "I do?" "Do you?" "I do." "Kiss." Smooch. "Husband and wife." Organ plays opening bar of the "Wedding March." Then, "Next!"

37 Simon Frith, *Performing Rites: On the Value of Popular Music* (Cambridge, MA: Harvard University Press, 1996), 118–22.

38 In his typical promotion of the middle way, he concludes this passage glorying in the pleasures of sound by cautioning, "Yet when I find the singing itself more moving than the truth which it conveys, I confess that this is a grievous sin." Augustine, *Confessions*, X.33.

39 On this, see Hans Moravec's *Robot: Mere Machine to Transcendent Mind* (Oxford: Oxford University Press, 2000), and *Mind Children: The Future of Robot and Human Intelligence* (Cambridge, MA: Harvard University Press, 1988); also see Ray Kurzweil, *The Age of Spiritual Machines: When Computers Exceed Human Intelligence* (London: Penguin Books, 2000). For a theological view on artificial intelligence that is quite positive about the direction these technologies are headed, see Anne Foerst, *God in the Machine: What Robots Teach Us about Humanity and God* (New York: Dutton Books, 2004). Dr Foerst is a former research scientist at the Artificial Intelligence Laboratory at MIT, and the founding director of The God and Computers Project.

40 Moravec, *Mind Children*, 4.

41 Quoted in David Noble, *The Religion of Technology: The Divinity of Man and the Spirit of Invention* (New York: Penguin Books, 1999), 161.

42 Ibid., 162f.

43   Ibid., 164f.

44   Augustine, *City of God*, 10.29.

45   Augustine, *On the Soul and Its Origin*, in *The Nicene and Post-Nicene Fathers*, [first series] vol. V, ed. Philip Schaff (Edinburgh: T&T Clark, 1956), 4.3.

46   Ralph Wood, "John Updike's 'Rabbit' Saga," in *Christian Century* (January 20, 1982), 50.

47   George Lakoff and Mark Turner, *More than Cool Reason: A Field Guide to Poetic Metaphor* (Chicago: University of Chicago Press, 1989), 167f.

48   *A.I. Artificial Intelligence*, directed by Steven Spielberg (Warner Brothers, 2001).

49   *Blade Runner*, directed by Ridley Scott (Warner Home Video, 1982).

50   The same kind of endorsement of the human condition has come in from Wim Wender's angels in *Wings of Desire*. Recall angel Damien's expression of longing to be human, reported in chapter 1, who wanted "to be able to say, 'Ah!' and 'Oh!' and 'Hey!' instead of 'Yes' and 'Amen.' "

Chapter 7

1   "Woodstock," Words and music by Joni Mitchell, from *Ladies of the Canyon*. © 1969 Siquomb Publishing Corp. © Renewed and assigned to Crazy Crow Music. All rights reserved. Used by permission of Warner Bros. Publications US Inc., Miami, Florida 33014.

2   Neil Young with Crazy Horse, "Thrasher," from *Rust Never Sleeps* (Warner Bros, 1979).

3   Sting, "If I Ever Lose My Faith in You," from *Ten Summoner's Tales* (A&M Records, 1993).

4   Mircea Eliade, *Myths, Dreams, and Mysteries* (New York: Harper Torchbooks, 1960), 43, 60.

5   Clifford Geertz, *Interpretation of Cultures* (New York: Basic Books, 1973), 107.

6   Eliade, *Myths, Dreams*, 47f.

7   From the "Agganna Suttanta," in *The Dialogues of the Buddha*, Part III, trans. T.W. Rhys Davids (Oxford: Oxford University Press, 1921), 77–94.

8   Perry Miller, *The American Puritans: Their Prose and Poetry* (New York: Doubleday Anchor Books, 1956), 144.

9   John Winthrop, "A Model of Christian Charity" (1630), in ibid., 82f.

10   See Samuel Willard's "The Perils of the Times Displayed" (1700) in *The Puritans*, vol. 1, eds. Perry Miller and Thomas H. Johnson (New York: Harper Torchbooks, 1963), 369; and General Court of Massachusetts, "Provoking Evils" (1675) in *Puritan Political Ideas, 1558–1794*, ed. Edmund S. Morgan (Indianapolis: Bobbs-Merrill, 1965).

11   See Sacvan Bercovitch, *The American Jeremiad* (Madison, WI: University of Wisconsin Press, 1978); Perry Miller, *Errand in the Wilderness* (New York: Harper & Row, 1956).

12   James A. Morone, *Hellfire Nation: The Politics of Sin in American History* (New Haven, CT: Yale University Press, 2003), 45.

13 John A. Hall and Charles Lindholm, *Is America Breaking Apart?* (Princeton: Princeton University Press, 1999), 10.

14 Catherine L. Albanese, *America: Religions and Religion*, 2nd edn (Belmont, CA: Wadsworth Publishing Co., 1992), 486.

15 Ibid., 485–95.

16 Found on *The Best of Grandmaster Flash, Melle Mel & the Furious Five* (Rhino Records, 1994). Song originally recorded in 1982.

17 Walter M. Miller, Jr, *A Canticle for Leibowitz* (New York: Bantam Books, 1959), 200.

18 Ibid., 271ff.

19 Ibid., 101. For a book length treatment of GenX's list of grievances, see Geoffrey T. Holtz, *Welcome to the Jungle: The Why behind "Generation X"* (New York: St Martin's Press, 1995).

20 Tom Beaudoin, *Virtual Faith: The Irreverent Spiritual Quest of Generation X* (San Francisco: Jossey Bass, 1998), 104.

21 Mark Edmundson, *Nightmare on Main Street: Angels, Sadomasochism, and the Culture of Gothic* (Cambridge, MA: Harvard University Press, 1997), 8.

22 Ibid., 23, 26.

23 Ibid., 26.

24 Other landmarks of the Gothic genre include *Invasion of the Body Snatchers* (1956), *Psycho* (1960), *The Birds* (1963), *Rosemary's Baby* (1968), *Carrie* (1976), *Halloween* (1978), *Friday the Thirteenth* (1980), *The Shining* (1980), *Nightmare on Elm Street* (1984), *Silence of the Lambs* (1991), *Scream* (1997), *The Devil's Advocate* (1998), *Blade* (1998),*The Blair Witch Project* (1999), *The Others* (2001), *The Ring* (2002), *Panic Room* (2002). Better known practitioners of the genre include such writers and filmmakers as Steven King, Ann Rice, Dean Koontz, John Carpenter, David Cronenberg, Wes Craven, Roger Corman, and Tim Burton.

25 Edmundson, *Nightmare on Main Street*, 4, 15f, 28, 54, 81.

26 Ibid., 32ff.

27 Richard Stivers, *The Culture of Cynicism: American Morality in Decline* (Oxford: Blackwell Publishers, 1994), 143.

28 Edmundson, *Nightmare on Main Street*, 14.

29 Ibid., 63.

30 Ibid., 43, 62, 71.

31 Ibid., 67.

32 Ibid., 67–68.

Chapter 8

1 Jane Tompkins, *West of Everything: The Inner Life of Westerns* (Oxford: Oxford University Press, 1992), 228.

2 Ibid., 229.

3 Alex Wright, *Why Bother with Theology?* (London: Darton, Longman, and Todd, Ltd., 2002), 64.

4   Kenneth Kirk, *The Vision of God: The Christian Doctrine of the Summum Bonum* (New York: Harper & Row, 1932), 104.

5   Tom Beaudoin, *Virtual Faith: The Irreverent Spiritual Quest of Generation X* (San Francisco: Jossey-Bass, 1998), 76f.

6   *Catechism of the Catholic Church* (Liguori, MO: Liguori Publications, 1994), 417.

7   Walter T. Davis, Jr et al. *Watching What We Watch: Prime-Time Television through the Lens of Faith* (Louisville, KY: Geneva Press, 2001), xii.

8   On the role of advertising in shoring up the "meta-myth" of salvation through consumption, see Dell de Chant, *The Sacred Santa: Religious Dimensions of Consumer Culture* (Cleveland: Pilgrim Press, 2002); Leigh Eric Schmidt, *Consumer Rites: The Buying and Selling of American Holidays* (Princeton: Princeton University Press, 1995); and Vincent Miller, *Consuming Religion: Christian Faith and Practice in a Consumer Culture* (New York: Continuum, 2004).

9   Oscar Wilde, *The Critic as Artist*, in *Intentions* (London: Methuen & Company, 1913), 100.

10 Joe Strummer and the Mescaleros, "The Road to Rock 'n' Roll," from *Rock Art and the X-Ray Style*. Written by Joe Strummer and Antony Genn. © 1999 by Universal-Polygram International Publishing, Inc. on behalf of Casbah Productions, Ltd./ASCAP. Used by permission of the publisher and The Joe Strummer Foundation for New Music. International copyright secured. All rights reserved. Before going solo, Strummer was the lead singer and songwriter for The Clash.

11 Martin Luther, *Tischreden*, quoted by Roland Bainton in *Here I Stand: A Life of Martin Luther* (New York: New American Library, 1950), 267.

12 Charles Finney, *Revival Lectures* (Fleming H. Revell Co., n.d.), 5.

13 On the convergence of ring shouts and revivalist hymns, see C. Eric Lincoln and Lawrence H. Mamiya, *The Black Church in the African American Experience* (Durham, NC: Duke University Press, 1990), ch. 12; and Albert Raboteau, *Slave Religion* (Oxford: Oxford University Press), 66–75.

14 For good histories of this transfer of gospel into soul and rhythm and blues, see Jon Michael Spencer, *Theological Music: Introduction to Theomusicology* (Westport, CT: Greenwood Press, 1991); Martha Bayles, *Hole in our Soul: The Loss of Beauty and Meaning in American Popular Music* (Chicago: University of Chicago Press, 1994); and Steve Turner, *Hungry for Heaven: Rock 'n' Roll and the Search for Redemption* (Downer's Grove, IL: InterVarsity Press, 1995).

15 Another predecessor is the big top circus, which would roll in and set up outside of town and was well established by the middle of the nineteenth century. But the traveling circus itself borrowed elements from the earlier itinerant revival meetings. The Chautauqua movement, an important link between the camp meetings and the modern outdoor festival, began after the civil war. Originally a tent city on the shores of Lake Chautauqua in upstate New York organized for Methodist Sunday School teachers, it evolved into a college without walls where courses were offered in literature, science, economics and religion, with artists and musicians entertaining in

the evenings. A good history on the Chautauqua movement can be found in Andrew C. Rieser's *The Chautauqua Moment: Protestants, Progressives, and the Culture of Modern Liberalism, 1874–1920* (New York: Columbia University Press, 2003).

16   Although Turner was inclined to describe rock music with the more diminutive term "liminoid" than to grant it the full status of liminality. One way to understand the distinction: "The *liminoid* is more like a commodity – indeed, often *is* a commodity, which one selects and pays for – than the *liminal*, which elicits loyalty and is bound up with one's membership or desired membership in some highly corporate group. One *works* at the liminal, one *plays* with the liminoid." Victor Turner, *From Ritual to Theatre: The Human Seriousness of Play* (New York: Performing Arts Journal Publications, 1982), 55. See also Victor Turner, "Variations on a Theme of Liminality," in *Blazing the Trail: Way Marks in the Exploration of Symbols* (Tucson, AZ: University of Arizona Press, 1992), 55, where he identifies rock music as a liminoid phenomenon.

17   Victor Turner, *Dramas, Fields, and Metaphors: Symbolic Action in Human Society* (Ithaca, NY: Cornell University Press, 1974), 262.

18   The Burning Man Festival is a noteworthy exception. They don't accept corporate sponsorship. The event is funded through "participant sponsorship," and festival-goers are organized into rangers, drummers, art installers, bus drivers, journalists, greeters, and earth guardians to manage the event – reducing the need for the financial backing of corporate sponsors.

19   Jon Michael Spencer, *Theological Music: Introduction to Theomusicology* (Westport, CT: Greenwood Press, 1991), 81.

20   From a 1978 interview Dylan did with Marc Rowland: "'Blowin' in the Wind' has always been a spiritual. I took it off a song, I don't know if you ever heard, called 'No More Auction Block.' That's a spiritual. 'Blowin' in the Wind' follows the same feeling.... I've always seen it and heard it that way, it's just taken me...I just did it on my acoustical guitar when I recorded it, which didn't really make it sound spiritual. But the feeling, the idea, was always, you know, that's where it was coming from." See <http://www.fortunecity.com/tinpan/parton/2/blowin.html> accessed February 9, 2004.

21   "Blowin' in the Wind," by Bob Dylan, from *The Freewheelin' Bob Dylan*. © 1962 by Warner Bros., Inc. Copyright renewed 1990 by Special Rider Music. All rights reserved. International copyright secured. Reprinted by permission.

22   Joe Strummer and the Mescaleros, "Get Down Moses," from *Streetcore*. Written by Joe Strummer, Martin Slattery, Scott Shields, Simon Edward Stafford. © 2003 by Universal-Polygram International Publishing, Inc. on behalf of Casbah Productions, Ltd./ASCAP. Used by permission of the publishers and The Joe Strummer Foundation for New Music. International copyright secured. All rights reserved.

23   U2, "Where the Streets Have No Name," from *The Joshua Tree* (Island Records, 1987). Written by Paul Hewson, Adam Clayton, David Evans, Laurence Mullen.

24 "(Are You) the One That I've Been Waiting For?" by Nick Cave, from *The Boatman's Call* (Mute Records, 2003). © 1997 by Mute Song, Ltd. Reprinted by permission.

25 "Shelter from the Storm," by Bob Dylan, from *Blood on the Tracks*. © 1974 by Special Rider Music. All rights reserved. International copyright secured. Reprinted by permission.

26 "The Secret Life of the Love Song," by Nick Cave. © 1999 by Mute Song, Ltd. Reprinted by permission.

27 "Bring It On," by Nick Cave, from *Nocturama* (Mute Records, 2003). © 2003 by Mute Song, Ltd. Reprinted by permission.

28 These songs appear on Van Morrisons's 1979 album *Into the Music* (Warner Bros.). The lyrics of the first song, "It's All in the Game," were composed by Carl Sigman, © 1951 by Bug Music, Inc. Used by permission. "You Know What They're Writing About" is Morrison's own composition. © 1979 by Polygram Division Default on behalf of Essential Music/BMI. Used by permission. International copyright secured. All rights reserved.

29 St Bonaventura, *The Mind's Road to God*, trans. George Boas (New York: Liberal Arts Press, 1953), 18.

30 "The Healing Room," by Sinead O'Connor, from *Faith and Courage*. © 1999 Promostraat B. V. Netherlands, Warner/Chappell Music Ltd. All rights reserved. Used by permission of Warner Bros. Music Corp. Reprinted by permission of Warner Bros. Publications US Inc., Miami, Florida 33014.

31 The Waterboys, "Strange Boat," from *Fisherman's Blues*. Words and music by Michael Scott. © 1987 Dizzy Heights Music Publishing, Warner/Chappell Music Ltd. All rights reserved. Used by permission of Warner Bros. Publications US Inc., Miami, Florida 33014.

32 Moby, "Into the Blue," written by Richard Hall and Mimi Goese. © 1995 Warner-Tamerlane Publishing Corp., Richard Hall, Pub Designee and LMNO Music. All rights on behalf of Richard Hall Pub Designee administered by Warner-Tamerlane Publishing Corp. All rights reserved. Used by permission of Warner Bros. Publications US Inc., Miami, Florida 33014.

33 "Summertime in England," by Van Morrison, from the album *Common One*. © 1980 by Polygram Division Default on behalf of Essential Music/BMI. Used by permission. International copyright secured. All rights reserved.

34 "Take Me Back," by Van Morrison, from the album *Hymns to the Silence*. © 1990 by Polygram Division Default on behalf of Caledonia Publishing/BMI. Used by permission. International copyright secured. All rights reserved.

35 *Chocolat*, directed by Lasse Hallström (Miramax Films, 2000).

36 As McCarraher defines the term: "a mix-and-match collage of beliefs appropriated from various sources that is the signature religious consciousness of consumer society." See his *Christian Critics: Religion and the Impasse of Modern Social Thought* (Ithaca, NY: Cornell University Press, 2000), 6.

37 Paul Ricoeur, *The Symbolism of Evil* (Boston: Beacon Press, 1967).

38 Ricoeur, *The Symbolism of Evil*, 102.

39   *The Penitential of Cummean*, in *Medieval Handbooks of Penance*, ed. John T. McNeil (New York: Columbia University Press, 1938, 1990), 116.

40   Ralph Waldo Emerson, "On Self Reliance," in *Essays* (New York: Hurst & Company, 1885), 48.

41   Ibid., 53.

42   Ibid., 49.

43   Philip Rieff, *The Triumph of the Therapeutic: Uses of Faith after Freud* (New York: Harper & Row, 1966), 261.

44   Eva Moskowitz, *In Therapy We Trust: America's Obsession with Self-Fulfillment* (Baltimore: The Johns Hopkins University Press, 2001), 5.

45   Ibid., 280.

46   Ibid., 2f.

47   Kathleen S. Lowney, *Baring our Souls: TV Talk Shows and the Religion of Recovery* (New York: Walter de Gruyter, 1999), 30f.

48   Carl Rogers, "A Therapist's View of the Good Life: The Fully Functioning Person," from *On Becoming a Person: A Therapist's View of Psychotherapy* (Boston: Houghton Mifflin, 1961), 185.

49   Jack Kerouac, *On the Road* (New York: Penguin Books, 1957, 1979), 9.

50   Ibid., 11.

51   Lowney, *Baring our Souls*, 111.

52   On this, see Lauren Slater, "The Trouble with Self-Esteem," *New York Times Magazine* (February 3, 2003), 44ff.

53   Richard Mouw, *Consulting the Faithful: What Christian Intellectuals Can Learn from Popular Religion* (Grand Rapids, MI: Wm. B. Eerdmans, 1994), 61, 74. Mouw offers a poignant illustration of the legitimacy of therapeutic insight, describing neighbors of his in which father and son fought incessantly, shouting "I hate you" "I wish you would die." "Sometimes I would weep when I heard these exchanges. I wished desperately that they could sit down with a therapist. . . . It struck me that I could grasp the underlying dynamics of their conversations in ways that my forebears would not have been able to. Not because I am smarter . . ." but because "I have learned much from the therapeutic culture" (73).

54   Charles Taylor, *The Ethics of Authenticity* (Cambridge, MA: Harvard University Press, 1992), 23.

55   Ibid., 75.

56   Charles Taylor, *Sources of the Self: The Making of Modern Identity* (Cambridge, MA: Harvard University Press, 1992), 372f.

57   Taylor, *Ethics of Authenticity*, 65ff.

58   Alcoholics Anonymous, *Alcoholics Anonymous*, 3rd edn (New York: AA World Services, Inc., 1939, 1955, 1976), 82.

59   Ibid., 83.

60   Ibid., 62.

61   Ibid., 45. Emphasis in the original.

62   Ibid., 85.

Chapter 9

1   Victor Turner, *Dramas, Fields, and Metaphors: Symbolic Action in Human Society* (Ithaca, NY: Cornell University Press, 1974), 263.

2   Gary Laderman, "The Disney Way of Death," *Journal of the American Academy of Religion* 68/1 (March 2000), 39.

3   See their website at <http://www.eternalreefs.com>. Last accessed September 1, 2004.

4   See their website at <http://www.eternalascent.com>. Last accessed September 1, 2004.

5   Remains from psychic guru Timothy Leery and Star Trek creator Gene Roddenberry were sent into orbit by Celestis in 1997. See their website at <http://www.celestis.com>.

6   In a warning posted on the company's website regarding the color of the diamonds, which can range from "light to intense shades of yellow," there is a curious implication about the biblical metaphor equating sin and stain: "The elements and impurities in your loved one's carbon directly affect the resulting color of your LifeGem(s)." See their website at <http://www.lifegem.com>. Last accessed September 1, 2004.

7   Daniel Wojcik, *The End of the World as We Know It: Faith, Fatalism, and Apocalypse in America* (New York: New York University Press, 1997), 97. This is one of the most illuminating books on the contemporary apocalyptic – in both its popular religion and popular culture modes. Another perceptive analysis of the apocalyptic and eschatological as a germinative idea in culture is Paul S. Fidde's *The Promised End: Eschatology in Theology and Literature* (Oxford: Blackwell Publishers, 2000).

8   This is one of the central arguments of Paul Ricoeur's *Time and Narrative*, vol. I (Chicago: University of Chicago Press, 1984).

9   For an exemplary theological interpretation of the *Lord of the Rings*, see Ralph Wood's *The Gospel According to Tolkien: Visions of the Kingdom in Middle-earth* (Louisville, KY: Westminster John Knox Press, 2003).

10 Jane Tompkins, *West of Everything: The Inner Life of* Westerns (Oxford: Oxford University Press, 1992), 70.

11 John F. Sears, *Sacred Places: American Tourist Attractions in the Nineteenth Century* (Amherst, MA: University of Massachusetts Press, 1998), 12–15.

12 Ibid., 122.

13 Images of Kinkade's paintings may be found at <http://www.thomaskinkade.com>. Last viewed March 5, 2004.

14 Thomas Kinkade, quoted in "Thomas Kinkade's American Dream," *Saturday Evening Post* (May 1, 2003).

15 *Sharing the Light*, 3/2 (Summer 2000).

16 Thomas Kinkade, quoted in Tessa DeCarlo's "Landscapes by the Carload: Art or Kitsch?" *New York Times*, Art/Architecture section (November 7, 1999), 51.

17 A full record of the Poll-Art project can be found in *Painting by Numbers: Komar and Melamid's Scientific Guide to Art*, ed. JoAnn Wypijewski (Berkeley: University of California Press, 1997). Details of the project and digital images of all the paintings can also be seen at <http://www.diacenter.org/km/index.html> and at <http://www.komarandmelamid.org/chronology/1994_1997_peoples/index.htm>. Last viewed September 1, 2004.

18 Although Komar and Melamid claim they've borrowed the model for their landscape not from the Hudson River School, but from the seventeenth-century Italian Renaissance painter *Domenichino*. See *Painting by Numbers*, 31.

19 Ibid., 25, 32, 46.

20 Ibid., 13.

21 Wassily Kandinsky, *Concerning the Spiritual in Art*, trans. M.T. Sadler (New York: Dover, 1977), 38.

22 William Kennedy, *Ironweed* (New York: Penguin Books, 1984).

23 Sheri Reynolds, *A Gracious Plenty* (New York: Harmony Books, 1997), 33.

24 Alice Sebold, *The Lovely Bones: A Novel* (Boston: Little, Brown, and Company, 2002).

25 "The Room," episode #6, *Six Feet Under*, directed by Rodrigo Garcia (HBO, 2001).

26 "I'm Sorry, I'm Lost," episode #39, *Six Feet Under*, directed by Alan Ball (HBO, 2003).

27 See Peter Brown, *The Cult of the Saints* (Chicago: University of Chicago Press, 1981), 127. For his discussion of the origins of feasting at gravesites, see ch. 2.

28 R. David Arkush and Leo O. Lee, eds and trans., *Land without Ghosts: Chinese Impressions of America from the Mid-Nineteenth Century to the Present* (Berkeley: University of California Press, 1989), 177–80.

29 John S. Mbiti, *African Religions and Philosophy*, 2nd edn (Oxford: Heinemann International, 1989), 82f, 158f.

30 A few notable exceptions to this are Carol Zaleski, *The Life of the World to Come* (Oxford: Oxford University Press, 1996); Jerry Walls, *Heaven: The Logic of Eternal Joy* (Oxford: Oxford University Press, 2002); Peter Kreeft, *Heaven: The Heart's Deepest Longing* (San Francisco: Ignatius Press, 1989); and the recent book by my own former professor, Arthur O. Roberts, *Exploring Heaven: What Great Christian Thinkers Tell Us about Our Afterlife with God* (San Francisco: Harper & Row, 2003).

Conclusion

1 Nick Hornby, *About a Boy* (New York: Riverhead Books, 1998), 8.

2 Dick Hebdige, "The Bottom Line on Planet One: Squaring up to *The Face*," *Ten-8*, vol. 19 (1987), 48.

Bibliography

Annotated Bibliography of Books on Theology and Popular Culture

These are works that search for culturally influential religious or theological themes based upon a cross-referencing of (with a few exceptions) multiple avenues of popular culture, for example, film, novels, television, advertising, music. Books that do the same kind of analysis but limit themselves to a single medium are listed separately. By "background theorists," an attempt is made to single out the thinkers these authors favor or are consciously in conversation with. This is intended to provide reference points about the scholarly commitments, method, etc. of each of these authors and their analyses. To whom, in other words, do they feel answerable – theologians, sociologists, historians of religion, philosophers, cultural theorists; whose style of analysis is offered as most productive of insight?

Beaudoin, Tom, *Virtual Faith: The Irreverent Spiritual Quest of Generation X* (San Francisco: Jossey-Bass, 1998).
Based on surveys conducted with Generation Xers in the mid-1990s in combination with his own experience as a member of this cohort, Beaudoin's book begins with the premise that "popular culture is a major meaning-making system" that carries more weight for his generation than it has for any that precedes it. He writes: "We express our religious interests, dreams, fears, hopes, and desires through popular culture." Concentrating on three kinds of pop culture "texts" (music videos, cyberspace, fashion), he isolates four key themes of GenX religiosity: 1) suspicion of religious institutions, 2) stress on direct experience of the sacred, 3) preoccupation with suffering, and 4) comfort with ambiguity. He concludes that GenXers are irreverently reverent, given to expressing their religiosity through irony, and for this reason find Kierkegaard a particularly apt theologian for making sense of this generation. But, one wonders, is the "virtual religion" in which, according to Beaudoin, GenX feels most at home any more than Kierkegaard's aesthete who prefers pondering various quests to actually undertaking any. Still, this book contains wonderful thick descriptions

of representative music videos, fashion trends like tattoos, piercings and Gothic black, and the touristic experience of dwelling in cybercommunities.
Background theorists: Søren Kierkegaard, Jean Baudrillard, Douglas Rushkoff, Wade Clark Roof, Dietrich Bonhoeffer, Paul Tillich

Burridge, Richard A., *Faith Odyssey: A Journey through Lent* (Grand Rapids, MI: William B. Eerdmans Publishing Company, 2000).
A book of readings designed around Lent, with daily readings and a different theme for each week. Draws from fantasy and science fiction – films, television, and literature, e.g., *Star Wars, Star Trek, The Matrix*, C.S. Lewis's *Chronicles of Narnia, Harry Potter, Dune, The X-Files*, Arthur C. Clarke's Space Odyssey series, and *The Hitchhiker's Guide to the Universe*. Also weaves in some classics, e.g., Homer's *Odyssey*, and John Bunyan's *Pilgrim's Progress*. Each daily reading begins with a passage from scripture. Weekly themes include "The Mess," "The Conflict," "Finding the Way," "Greater Love," and, for Easter week, "To Infinity and Beyond." Includes appendices covering questions for group discussion for each chapter, popular culture resources, and an index of Bible passages.
Background theorists: Bible, *Book of Common Prayer*

Clark, Lynn Schofield, *From Angels to Aliens: Teenagers, the Media, and the Supernatural* (Oxford: Oxford University Press, 2003).
Explores how adolescents draw on shows like *Buffy the Vampire Slayer, Angel, X-Files, Touched by an Angel*, in their efforts to make meaning of their lives. This genre of shows emerged as the shadow side of the resurgence of Evangelicals into mainstream culture. Aware of their apocalyptic literature, media producers pulled together their own brand of supernatural tales, with angels, vampires, aliens, stories of good and evil. Clark bases her findings on extensive ethnographic research, interviewing teenagers about the use they make of these stories and characters. She develops a typology of consumer response to this material ranging from "Resisters," who resist organized religion but accept media supernaturalism uncritically, to "Traditionalists," who resist media supernaturalism and embrace their religious traditions. In the middle are "Mysticals," who can synthesize both sources. Clark teaches in the area of media, religion and culture at the University of Colorado School of Journalism. Her organizing theory is based in Pierre Bourdieu and Antonio Gramsci, so social practices and cultural populism inform her approach.
Background theorists: Pierre Bourdieu, Antonio Gramsci

Dean, William, *The American Spiritual Culture and the Invention of Jazz, Football and the Movies* (New York: Continuum, 2002).
For Dean, "God is a living, historical reality" in the pragmatic sense that God is a social convention that takes hold in a society, provides a general sense of the whole, and has real historical effects residing as it does in the springs of a society's desires, compulsions, and capacities for self-criticism. Conversely, whatever functions in these ways in a society is its living God. Once this doctrine of God is established, Dean observes that in our free time we engage in activities that offer insight into who we really are and what we really believe, and that a culture's

operative notion of God can be discerned in these activities. Three great American pastimes are jazz, football and movies. Dean analyzes what these three pastimes tell us about America's spiritual life, about our recommended regimens for enacting our religious lives – improvisation (jazz), "ambivalent negotiation with violence" (football), and "self-creation through fantasy" (movies). Each of these regimens is also a way of parsing an underlying mystery that is, in effect, the pragmatically-effective God evolving below the surfaces of our lives.
Background theorists: William James, John Dewey, Paul Tillich, Alfred North Whitehead, Flannery O'Connor

deChant, Dell, *The Sacred Santa: Religious Dimensions of Consumer Culture* (Cleveland: Pilgrim Press, 2002).
Drawing on an Eliadean account of religious phenomena, deChant analyzes the market economy as a "sacred canopy" under which we live out our lives, sorting out its cosmology, myths, rituals, shamans, sacraments, and disciplines. He examines the extent to which the cycle of acquisition-consumption-disposal has become the core of our self-definition in the West. DeChant digs down to the meta-myth of expanding prosperity that underlies our consumption, and discusses the secondary and tertiary myths and rituals that sustain it as a way of life. The book is about much more than Christmas, as the title implies, but the great potlatch of Christmas is one of the high holy days of the religion of consumerism, attended by ritualized acts of shopping, sacred texts (advertising inserts and mail order catalogues), feasting, etc. It has been appropriated from Christianity for the new religion – just as Christianity had appropriated the holiday from paganism centuries ago. In this sense, Santa Claus is a cultural deity, with powers of omniscience, omnipotence and omnipresence all in the service of our desires to consume.
Background theorists: Jacques Ellul, Mircea Eliade, Jean Baudrillard, Eric Voegelin, Peter Berger

Detweiler, Craig and Barry Taylor, *A Matrix of Meanings: Finding God in Popular Culture* (Grand Rapids, MI: Brazos Press, 2003).
This book is comprehensive and offers tantalizing namedropping and hundreds of specimens, but it is too uncritically dazzled by popular culture, both by its reach into our lives, with which these authors seem to have no problem, and by its content – it's all great stuff and quite spiritual. The theology is light and, following the tone of the book (with a few exceptions), seems to suffer from attention deficit disorder. The authors try to get away with profound sounding commentary like: "Philosophy teachers would be wise to use Richard Linklater's animated film *Waking Life* (2001) as an introduction to Nietzsche, Schleiermacher, and Hegel" (21). But there is no follow up. The next sentence moves onto promoting Tupac Shakur as a poet. The entire book contains no further references to Schleiermacher or Hegel, and mentions *Waking Life* again only in several of the endless lists that make up much of the book. Many such connections are drawn, but too infrequently explained or justified. This finally amounts to a "once-born" religion of popular culture, with virtually no sustained theological reflection. The theological pivot point of the authors' assessment seems to float in midair, although they continue to insist that it is there. The single strength of

the book is the spiritual biographies it offers of several producers of pop culture, such as musicians Nick Cave and Bono, filmmaker Paul Schrader, and artist Andy Warhol.
Background theorists: Neal Gabler, James Twitchell, Tom Beaudoin, Walter Brueggemann

Dyson, Michael Eric, *Reflecting Black: African-American Cultural Criticism* (Minneapolis: University of Minnesota Press, 1993); and *Between God and Gangsta Rap: Bearing Witness to Black Culture* (New York: Oxford University Press, 1996).
Both of these books are collections of articles Dyson has written for various journals and magazines in which he excavates the religious dimension of leading generators and expressions of African-American popular culture. He offers thoughtful interpretations of Michael Jordan, O.J. Simpson, Michael Jackson, Sam Cooke, hip-hop, gangsta rap, Bill Cosby, Toni Morrison, and the films of Spike Lee and John Singleton. Through each essay he offers what he describes as "an oppositional African-American cultural criticism" that takes Black culture seriously as internally diverse, representing a range of socio-economic interests, and laden with a frequently religiously driven creativity. He is good at making sense of elements of popular culture that can be alienating to mainstream audiences, and also at aiming internal criticisms when Black popular culture falls short of moral norms that Dyson articulates.
Background theorists: Cornell West, James Cone

Elshtain, Jean Bethke, *Who Are We? Critical Reflections and Hopeful Possibilities* (Grand Rapids, MI: William B. Eerdmans, 2000).
This book offers an analysis of contemporary literature, science fiction, film, advertising and public morality that finds American culture adrift because, as Elshtain puts it, "We are creatures who have forgotten what it means to be faithful to something other than ourselves." She parses this forgetfulness into the two traditional sins of pride and sloth – pride as the denial of dependence upon others, sloth as the unreflective acquiescence to the conventions of one's own time. The theological tradition is not exhausted, she argues, and can replenish us. But she also finds popular culture straining in hopeful ways with warnings and utopian longings that suggest it knows some of its errors.
Background theorists: Augustine, Martin Luther, Dietrich Bonhoeffer, John Paul II, Hannah Arendt

Forbes, Bruce David and Jeffrey H. Mahan (eds.), *Religion and Popular Culture in America* (Berkeley: University of California Press, 2000).
The editors of this compilation have been active in the American Academy of Religion for years, creating forums where scholars with twin interests in religion and popular culture may explore the seam where these two are knitted together and ponder which interpretive methods best illuminate it. This book is the fruit of that activity. In the introduction, Forbes sketches out what he finds along this seam: "Religion may be present in discussions of the roles superheroes play as deliverers, or reflections on the struggles of life, or in devotional acts to a celebrity,

or in ritual patterns of television viewers." He goes on to describe the diverse ways in which the contributors to this volume identify the religious dimension of popular culture – for some it is *beliefs* that are being carried in popular culture, for others it is the forms ordinarily identified with religion that crop up in popular culture (i.e., myths, symbols, rituals, icons), and for yet others it is the way that religion typically *functions*, providing people with encompassing systems of meaning to orient them in the universe, that popular culture appears to have appropriated. Highlights among the contributions include Gregor Goethals' argument that television advertising pulls all the levers once pulled by evangelists to promote salvation through their product, Michelle Lelwica's contention that traditional beliefs in human perfectibility now have a home in the fitness craze of what she calls "Culture Lite," and Joseph Price's delineation of the many ritual aspects of religion that have been inherited by professional sports.
Background theorists: Emile Durkheim, Victor Turner, Mary Douglas, Clifford Geertz, Catherine Albanese

Fox, Matthew, *An Inquiry into Religion and Culture by way of TIME Magazine* (East Dubuque, IL: Listening Press, 1971).
A real gem, this book begins with the suggestion that *TIME Magazine* is the Chartres Cathedral of the twentieth century, in that, like the prolific works of art that fill Chartres, it contains "the entire panorama of life" for a period – "from humor to superstition and horoscopes to politics . . . to advertising . . . to religious worship and spiritual aspirations." *TIME Magazine* is a distillation of American culture. Fox read every issue of *TIME* from 1958 and offers through what he finds in that slice an interpretation of the religious and spiritual aspirations that are expressed through political and economic affairs, professional pursuits, the arts and religion. He identifies a recurring tension between "living religion" and "dying religion" that is in keeping with Harvey Cox's conclusions in *The Secular City*, i.e., that religion is living wherever the struggle for justice is occurring, where freedom is valued and people are willing to question society honestly regardless of the risk, where artists are exuberant in their celebration of life's colors and tones. Religion's enemies are the over-industrialization and automation of life, war mongering, and the unbridled desire for consumer goods. This is a thick and thorough threshing of the newsmagazine as a religious artifact.
Background theorists: Paul Tillich, Mircea Eliade, Harvey Cox

Gardella, Peter, *Domestic Religion: Work, Food, Sex and Other Commitments* (Cleveland: Pilgrim Press, 1998).
This book offers an intriguing argument. Leaning on sociological definitions of religion and the emerging theorists who favor practice over ideas as to what constitutes the most salient feature of religions, Gardella argues that human beings have always practiced a kind of two-tiered religion. At the deepest level (where it matters most) is religion of daily concerns; closer to the surface is traditional religion with its explicit myths, rituals of worship, moral code and beliefs. Gardella calls the religion of daily concerns "domestic religion." Religion in this sense consists of all the routine practices that hold our lives together. In the context of the US, it is found in the "rituals and values [people] live by at home: the holiday things

that absolutely have to be done; the kinds of success for which no sacrifice or effort would be too much; the sports events that connect with the whole struggle of life; the songs that stand for transcendent love, sadness, and joy; the television shows that express exactly how life is, or should be; and the foods and drinks that can yield the last happiness of old age." Domestic religion is an aquifer that traditional religions draw from, and always have. What is new is that domestic religion, which used to be a universal phenomenon with highly localized elements, is being homogenized through mass media and popular culture. Gardella's book explores the domestic religion that is congealing in the US under the influence of popular culture.

Background theorists: Emile Durkheim, William James, Carl Jung, Joseph Campbell, Mircea Eliade, Robert Bellah, Colleen McDannell

Greeley, Andrew, *God in Popular Culture* (Chicago: Thomas More Press, 1988). This is a collection of essays on artifacts of 1980s' popular culture framed by a theory of the religious imagination. The basic idea here is that, according to Greeley, there is a "Catholic sensibility" that has always paid attention to the fears, loves, and aspirations of ordinary folk and "appropriated to Catholic worship and practice everything that was good, true, and beautiful in the pagan world around it." From this borrowing have come many of the most enduring symbols of God and faith. Attention to such popular culture forces as Madonna, Woody Allen, Clint Eastwood, Bill Cosby and Stephen King (among Greeley's favorites) is thus a form of "bottom up" theology, a version of liberation theology and a strong affirmation of the sacramentality of life. Some of popular culture, Greeley insists, "contains signals of the transcendent, the presence of grace, rumors of angels." The early chapters offer an account of the "religious imagination," drawing on the work of Catholic theologians Bernard Lonergan and David Tracy, but most of the chapters are examinations of particular artists and artifacts, written in a tone that is part journalistic review, part homily.

Background theorists: Bernard Lonergan, David Tracy, Northrop Frye

Hibbs, Thomas S., *Shows about Nothing: Nihilism in Popular Culture from the Exorcist to Seinfeld* (Dallas: Spence Publishing Company, 1999). This is a sustained examination of how the "dark God" of nihilism has evolved in popular culture over the last several decades, traced through film and television. After developing the idea of a universe bereft of providence, drawing on the work of David Hume, Alexis de Tocqueville and Friedrich Nietzsche, Hibbs identifies three stages in recent popular culture that track how this idea of "anti-providence" and the powers that desensitize us toward good and evil have become assumptions that pervade our culture. Hollywood, in effect, has come to "promote a debased, Nietzschean culture," a world in which there is no providence working behind the scenes to bring good out of evil. Far from being the standard rant against popular culture, this is a fresh and thoughtful reflection on our gradual desensitization to a benevolent universe and our embrace of an arbitrary universe that we, for whatever reason, actually seem to relish and demand. From horror films that dwell on the aesthetics of evil (*The Exorcist, Silence of the Lambs*), through light bemusement with evil (*Forrest Gump*), to an ironic acceptance of the meaninglessness of life as hip and comic (*Seinfeld*), we gravitate to stories that deconstruct the grand narratives of divine providence that once preferred good over evil. Along the way, Hibbs offers incisive interpretations of landmark films and television shows. This is a remarkable book, theological analysis of popular culture at its best.

Background theorists: Thomas Aquinas, Friedrich Nietzsche, Hannah Arendt, Roger Shattuck, Mark Edmundson

Lawrence, John Shelton and Robert Jewett, *The Myth of the American Superhero*
    (Grand Rapids, MI: William B. Eerdmans, 2002).
Tracing what they argue is a pervasive myth in the American experience, the "monomyth" of the American superhero, Lawrence and Jewett raise the question whether the fundamentally anti-democratic leanings of the myth serve as a safety valve for the frustrations of a democratic polity, as is generally held, or encourage a kind of "pop fascism" that undermines the patience required for democracy. The basic plotline of the monomyth is that Eden has been disrupted by external forces and none of the community's internal, democratically established institutions can cope with it. A superhero is required to restore peace and justice for the good folk of Dodge or Gotham City. This restoration necessitates a ferocious act of violence. In contrast to classical myths and jeremiads, the superhero myth feeds on a disdain for institutions and the due process of law, resorts to extra-legal means to restore justice, and depicts the world as divided between the innocent and their evil foes. It is uncompromising, and has little patience for what Reinhold Niebuhr called "proximate solutions for insoluble problems." The authors trace this superhero paradigm through Westerns, vigilante law enforcement plots, Disney characters, comic books, video games, *Star Trek* and *Star Wars*, disaster films, apocalyptic cinema, and post 9/11 politics.

Background theorists: Joseph Campbell

Mazur, Eric Michael and Kate McCarthy (eds.), *God in the Details: American
    Religion in Popular Culture* (New York: Routledge, 2001).
The contributors to this collection have agreed, according to the editors, on a Geertzian conception of religion, meaning that when certain "markers" are present, a "terrain worthy of religious analysis" has been entered. These markers include "the formation of communities of shared meanings and values, the presence of ritualized behaviors, the use of language of ultimacy and transcendence, the marking of special, set-aside 'sacred' times and spaces, and the manipulation of traditional religious symbols and narratives." A persistent idea throughout these essays is that myths, rituals, moralities, and our sense of sacred time and place – all things that were hatched and incubated in traditional religions – have been dislocated and are reasserting themselves in popular music, sports, festivals, television shows, movies, cyberspace and amusement parks. We can't seem to shake them, given their proven record at lending our lives meaning – even though they are broken apart and reassembled in novel, hardly recognizable ways in their new incarnations. The essays cohere with each other because their authors do share this combination of *bricolage* and Geertzian functionalism. Some of the chapters are better than others (especially good are McCarthy on Bruce Springsteen, Wade

Clark Roof on Southern barbecue, Elijah Siegler on cop shows, and Mazur and Tara Koda on Disney). One criticism, however, is that while most of the authors drop hints as to whether or not they condone the way meaning is construed in the artifact they are analyzing, few of them offer anything to justify these surreptitious normative judgments.
Background theorists: Emile Durkheim, Victor Turner, Clifford Geertz, Michel Foucault, Robert Bellah

Miller, Vincent, *Consuming Religion: Christian Faith and Practice in a Consumer Culture* (New York: Continuum, 2004).
Miller begins this book concurring that rampant consumerism has a corrosive effect on human well-being. But rather than offer another book-length rant against consumerism, he argues that the deeper problem is the *practice* by which consumption has become so central in our lives. He describes this practice as the commodifying of culture, drawing on the Marxist critique of commodity fetishism, whereby we conceptualize consumable products as abstract from their origins and processes of production, rendering them into objects toward which we have little accountability, and which, torn from their contexts, become pliable in their meaning. Consumerism is thus "a set of interpretive habits and dispositions" by which everything is wrenched from its context. His primary worry is how commodification transforms the religions we profess, how it engenders habits in us by which we sever belief and practice, and by which we break apart coherent traditions into discrete symbols, narratives, and rituals that can be mixed and matched in any manner we wish, i.e. made into objects that can be consumed. He offers a persuasive account of the many cunning ways in which this occurs. He then reflects on the way that consumerism cultivates human desire in a way that mimics the more traditional desire for transcendence, diverting and absorbing energies that would otherwise be used in the long, arduous journey of the spiritual life. In drawing this connection, Miller gains some sympathetic understanding for the desire that endlessly consumes, ever eluded by fulfillment. It is "hauntingly similar to Christian portrayals of desire as an endless, unquenchable seeking after an infinite God." With this discovery, he goes on to explore popular culture as a way of using commodities that sometimes contains seeds of resistance to the forces of commodification, thus subverting it and opening up a space in our culture for genuine transcendence. It is a supple argument, worthy of close reading.
Background theorists: Augustine, Karl Marx, Pierre Bourdieu, Michel de Certeau, Guy Debord, Zygmunt Bauman, Edward Schillebeeckx, Kathryn Tanner

Nelson, John Wiley, *Your God Is Alive and Well and Appearing in Popular Culture* (Philadelphia: Westminster Press, 1976).
Nelson is interesting because he wrote this book under the twin influence of his study of Tillich and his discovery in the early 1970s of the Bowling Green based Popular Culture Association, a branch of popular culture studies that developed in the US largely independent of the ideological critiques of the Frankfurt School and the Birmingham Centre. In this book he argues that American popular culture supports a coherent (if evolving) set of religious beliefs and values in the same

way that worship services support the beliefs and values of organized religions. With every exposure to popular culture, that is, "the dominant belief system of American life" is reaffirmed. And given the amount of time we spend in front of the TV, read fiction, go to movies, watch sports and listen to music, Nelson argues, popular culture is where most Americans worship and the site where they absorb most of their beliefs and values. Sometimes the beliefs and values of popular culture overlap with a Christian way of seeing and valuing life, but in many areas there is stark discordance. Early in the book, Nelson outlines what he takes to be the "American Cultural Belief System," with its basic elements of evil, salvation, and perfection: (1) meaningful social relations that make a community good are threatened by external evils, such as bad companions, illicit sexual partners, greedy landlords, criminals, selfish corporate interests and corrupt public officials; (2) the community and its institutions are too weak to resist these evil influences and must be delivered from them by an individual messiah-type figure who overcomes the source of evil through a dramatic act of violence; (3) the hero delivers us back to stable family-based communities, characterized by law and order and the civilizing influence of women, then disappears; and (4) a code of life that sustains us in the absence of the hero is conveyed through popular magazines that "generally equate fulfillment with certain physical appearances and with a breadth of social graces and *savoir-faire*." He develops this scheme through chapters on movies, country music, magazines, television, and crime fiction. He finds the archetype of the American Belief System in the classic western, with dissenting (if equally influential) beliefs in "Anti-Western" fiction such as *High Plains Drifter, McCabe and Mrs. Miller*, and many gangster and detective stories.

Background theorists: Paul Tillich, Jack Nachbar, John Cawelti, Robert Warshow

Ostwalt, Conrad, *Secular Steeples: Popular Culture and the Religious Imagination* (Harrisburg, PA: Trinity Press International, 2003).

The primary aim of this book is to challenge the unidirectionality of the standard secularization theory. Instead, Ostwalt argues, secularization takes place in two ways. First, overt religion adopts secular forms – like television and movies. Second, the religious sensibility is dispersed through other forms – not strategically, but because religion is irrepressible. It is actually an exchange; boundaries between sacred and secular dissolve: the sacred is secularized while the secular is sacralized. The religious and the secular "feed off one other." Religious striving is relatively constant in history, and at the moment its locus of authority is being dispersed and the cultural vehicles that carry it are being diversified. We have come to grant "the entertainment industry, the media, and the publishing industry" authority to express religious ideas and sentiments. At its best, religion is all about combating nihilism. In reference to literature, the author claims: "secular forms can supplement or even replace religious structures as vehicles for religious longings and conversations."

Background theorists: Peter Berger, Rodney Stark

Romanowski, William D., *Eyes Wide Open: Looking for God in Popular Culture* (Grand Rapids, MI: Brazos Press, 2001).

Romanowski offers this book as a guide for interpreting and evaluating popular culture as an evangelical Christian. On one level, it is an apology for popular culture, addressing readers he assumes are uneasy with it, even though they may consume it as a guilty pleasure. His message to them is that being artistically creative is a faithful way to be a Christian, given that Christians worship a creative God. As art has always done, popular "arts" can serve Christian purposes as vehicles of social criticism, social unity, and collective memory. On another level, he insists that popular culture does promote a worldview that is in many ways antagonistic to the Christian worldview. The solution, he proposes, is to view and listen to popular culture with a critical mind, endorsing it when it expresses values consistent with "biblical principles," berating it when it undercuts these principles. Some popular films and music approximate a "Christian" worldview, or exemplify important elements of it (Romanowski singles out such films as *Tender Mercies*, *Dead Man Walking*, *Titanic*, and *Gladiator* on this score), and when they do, their creators should be recognized and praised for their efforts. Minimally, he suggests, we should learn to encounter popular culture as an interpretation of our culture's values and struggles. He also calls upon Christians to learn the craft of producing popular culture so that they can insert their values into the public square. Lacking any citations, bibliography and index, however, the book does not lend itself to scholarly use – except as itself a specimen of evangelical apologetic literature that makes use of popular culture.
Background theorists: Bible

Ward, Graham, *Cities of God* (London: Routledge, 2000).
While not primarily an analysis of *popular* culture, this thick and rich book offers a more comprehensive assessment of culture, organized around the question: "what kind of theological statement does the city make today?" As he proceeds, however, Ward scrutinizes many artifacts of popular culture. With St Augustine's *City of God* whispering in his ear, Ward tunes into the semiology of the city through his reading of films, fiction, architecture, urban planning, employment patterns, sex shops and cyberspace – the places in the postmodern city where desire either pursues its object with abandon or is criticized for doing so. The key pathologies behind the ways we desire in the contemporary world are "social atomism" – which erodes our capacities for community – and a lust which is endlessly driven to own and accumulate (what Augustine once called concupiscence). In film and fiction, this latter pathology is often symbolized as killer viruses, parasitic creatures, and vampires – a motif to which Ward gives considerable, and enlightening, attention. Ward also surveys the surging popularity of angels in popular culture and interprets it as "the manufacture of new urban mythologies," the indication of a new "longing for transcendence," and an opening up of "new negotiations with the divine." At the center of this book, Ward sketches out what he calls a "systematic theology"; it is highly idiosyncratic and deeply dependent upon the surrounding analyses – very original, but barely in conversation with the genre of systematic theology *à la* Calvin, Schleiermacher, Tillich, MacQuarrie and Rahner, which is probably deliberate.

Background theorists: Augustine, Thomas Aquinas, Karl Barth, W.F. Hegel, Ludwig Wittgenstein, Jean Baudrillard, Jacques Derrida, Michel de Certeau, Jacques Lacan, Michel Foucault, Emmanuel Levinas, Slajov Žižek

Warren, Michael, *Seeing through the Media: A Religious View of Communications and Cultural Analysis* (Harrisburg, PA: Trinity Press International, 1997).
Warren mounts an argument in this book that electronic media, and particularly television, have a mesmerizing effect that encourages "cultural passivity," according to which while much of its content simply washes over us, much of it lodges within us and becomes reference points in our consciousness – without our awareness or consent. Because we cannot escape media, he argues for a "cultural agency" by which we become more conscious of this content and the means of its delivery, interrogating it for the picture of reality it is presenting to us and reflecting on it in light of counter messages found in the Bible (e.g., suspicion of the accumulation of wealth, taking the side of the victim). He offers guidance on frames of analysis that cultural agents can use to clarify the messages carried in the media, asking about the artifact itself (lyrics, narrative, images, performer), the layers of production (composer/writer, manufacturing process, marketing, intended audience), and the values that it conveys. He also offers an iconic interpretation of media images. Just as icons have always triggered within us ways of imagining ourselves, "inviting the viewer to imitate the qualities of the person or reality represented by the icon," media images have the same effect. Consequently it is a serious business to scrutinize what these images represent.
Background theorists: Gregory Baum, Paulo Freire, Raymond Williams, Stewart Ewen

Wright, Alex, *Why Bother with Theology?* (London: Darton, Longman and Todd, 2002).
Theology is on life support, Wright argues, as he surveys the British scene. It is as incomprehensible to those in the 17–35 age cohort as "the hieroglyphs in the British Museum." But he believes theology does remain relevant, a "secular theology" *à la* Bonhoeffer's "religionless Christianity." People are still hungry for meaning, but the churches have lost touch with them, speaking in archaisms that cannot be comprehended. Wright seeks a third way between liberalism and radical orthodoxy, favoring what he calls "cultural theologians." "God is to be found precisely in those places where churchpeople might often prefer that God is not. That is in places where people dream of liberation and release (whether through Lottery winnings, or promotion at work, or sex, or engagement with characters in a TV soap)." He favors novels and movies as barometers of significant thinking about meaning in our "postmodern" culture, and offers along these lines the novels of J.R.R. Tolkien, Ursula LeGuinn, Colin Thubron, and Hilary Mantel. In film he favors futuristic dystopias such as *BladeRunner* and *Alien*, and the metaphysical ponderings of Andrei Tarkovsky (esp. *Stalker* and *Solaris*).
Background theorists: Karl Rahner, Timothy Gorringe, Graham Ward, Slajov Žižek

Bibliography on Zones of Popular Culture

What follows is a list of books and articles organized around particular zones of popular culture. The selections are limited to works that deliberately employ some manner of religious or theological tools to understand the phenomena they interpret.

Architecture and sacred space

Chidester, David and Edward T. Linenthal, *American Sacred Space* (Bloomington, IN: Indiana University Press, 1995).

Gorringe, Timothy, *A Theology of the Built Environment* (Cambridge: Cambridge University Press, 2002).

Lane, Belden, *Landscapes of the Sacred* (Baltimore: The Johns Hopkins University Press, 2001).

Nye, David E., *American Technological Sublime* (Cambridge, MA: MIT Press, 1994).

Pahl, Jon, *Shopping Malls and Other Sacred Spaces* (Grand Rapids, MI: Brazos, 2003).

Zepp, Ira, Jr, *The New Religious Image of Urban America: The Shopping Mall as Ceremonial Center* (Niwot, CO: University Press of Colorado, 1997).

Civil religion

Bellah, Robert, *The Broken Covenant: American Civil Religion in Time of Trial* (New York: Seabury Press, 1975).

— "Civil Religion in America," in *Daedalus* (Winter, 1967).

Linenthal, Edward, *Sacred Ground: Americans and Their Battlefields* (Champaign, IL: University of Illinois Press, 1993).

Marvin, Carolyn and David Ingle, *Blood Sacrifice and the Nation: Totem Rituals and the American Flag* (Cambridge: Cambridge University Press, 1999).

Meyer, Jeffrey F., *Myths in Stone: Religious Dimensions of Washington, D.C.* (Berkeley: University of California Press, 2001).

Disney

Laderman, Gary, "The Disney Way of Death," *Journal of the American Academy of Religion*, vol. 68/1 (March 2000), 27–46.

Pinsky, Mark, *The Gospel According to Disney: Faith, Trust, and Pixie Dust* (Louisville, KY: Westminster John Knox Press, 2004).

Watts, Steven, *The Magic Kingdom: Walt Disney and the American Way of Life* (Columbia, MO: University of Missour Press, 1997).

Film

Journal of Religion and Film <http://www.unomaha.edu/~wwwjrf/>

Loughlin, Gerard, *Alien Sex: The Body and Desire in Cinema and Theology* (Oxford: Blackwell Publishing, 2004).

Lyden, John C., *Film as Religion: Myths, Morals, and Rituals* (New York: New York University Press, 2003).

Marsh, Clive and Gaye Ortiz (eds.), *Explorations in Theology and Film* (Oxford: Blackwell Publishing, 1997).

Martin, Joel and Conrad Ostwalt (eds.), *Screening the Sacred: Religion, Myth, and Ideology in Popular American Film* (Boulder, CO: Westview Press, 1995).

May, John R., *Nourishing Faith through Fiction: Reflections on the Apostles' Creed in Literature and Film* (Franklin, WI: Sheed & Ward, 2001).

Miles, Margaret, *Seeing and Believing: Religion and Values in the Movies* (Boston: Beacon Press, 1996).

Nathanson, Paul, *Over the Rainbow: The Wizard of Oz as a Secular Myth of America* (Albany, NY: SUNY Press, 1991).

Reinhartz, Adele, *Scripture on the Silver Screen* (Louisville, KY: Westminster John Knox Press, 2003).

Ruffles, Tom, *Ghost Images: Cinema of the Afterlife* (Jefferson, NC: McFarland & Company, 2004).

Scott, Bernard Brandon, *Hollywood Dreams and Biblical Stories* (Minneapolis: Augsburg Fortress Press, 1994).

Stone, Bryan P., *Faith and Film: Theological Themes at the Cinema* (St Louis, MO: Chalice Press, 2000).

Tompkins, Jane, *West of Everything: The Inner Life of Westerns* (Oxford: Oxford University Press, 1992).

Vaux, Sara Anson, *Finding Meaning at the Movies* (Nashville: Abingdon Press, 1999).

Film review websites

http://www.hollywoodjesus.com/
http://www.textweek.com/movies/themeindex.htm

http://www.spiritualityhealth.com/newsh/items/blank/item_238.html
http://www.thefilmforum.com/

The Internet and the World Wide Web

Brasher, Brenda E., *Give Me that Online Religion* (San Francisco: Jossey-Bass Publishers, 2001).
— "Thoughts on the Status of the Cyborg: On Technological Socialization and Its Link to the Religious Function of Popular Culture," *Journal of the American Academy of Religion,* vol. 64/4 (Winter 1996), 809–30.
Rosen, Jonathan, *The Talmud and the Internet* (New York: Farrar, Strauss & Giroux, 2000).

Music

Bayles, Martha, *Hole in our Soul: The Loss of Beauty and Meaning in American Popular Music* (Chicago: University of Chicago Press, 1994).
Cone, James H., *The Spirituals and the Blues* (San Francisco: Harper & Row, 1972).
Denselow, Robin, *When the Music's Over: The Story of Political Pop* (London: Faber & Faber, 1990).
Fillingim, David, *Redneck Liberation: Country Music as Theology* (Macon, GA: Mercer University Press, 2003).
Frith, Simon, *Performing Rites: On the Value of Popular Music* (Cambridge, MA: Harvard University Press, 1996).
Grossman, Maxine L., "Jesus, Mama, and the Constraints on Salvific Love in Contemporary Country Music," *Journal of the American Academy of Religion* 70/1 (March 2002), 83–115.
Joseph, Mark, *Faith, God, and Rock 'n' Roll* (London: Sanctuary Publishing, 2003).
Ricks, Christopher, *Dylan's Vision of Sin* (New York: Ecco/HarperCollins, 2004).
Rodman, Gilbert, *Elvis after Elvis: The Posthumous Career of a Living Legend* (London: Routledge, 1996).
Sample, Tex, *White Soul: Country Music, the Church, and Working Americans* (Nashville: Abingdon Press, 1996).
Schwarze, Bernd, "Religion, Rock, and Research," in John Michael Spencer (ed.), *Black Sacred Music: A Journal of Theomusicology* vol. 8/1 (Spring 1994), 78–91.
Spencer, Jon Michael, *Blues and Evil* (Knoxville, TN: University of Tennessee Press, 1993).

Spencer, Jon Michael, *Theological Music: Introduction to Theomusico-logy* (Westport, CT: Greenwood Press, 1991).

Strausbaugh, John. E., *Reflections on the Birth of the Elvis Faith* (New York: Blast Books, 1995).

Turner, Steve, *Hungry for Heaven: Rock 'n' Roll and the Search for Redemption* (Downers Grove, IL: 1995).

Veith, Gene Edward and Thomas L. Wilmeth, *Honky-Tonk Gospel: The Story of Sin and Salvation in Country Music* (Grand Rapids, MI: Baker Book House, 2001).

Outsider art

Bradshaw, Thelma Finster, *Howard Finster: The Early Years: A Private Portrait of America's Premier Folk Artist* (Birmingham, AL: Crane Hill Publishers, 2001).

Science fiction and fantasy

Fiddes, Paul S., *The Promised End: Eschatology in Theology and Literature* (Oxford: Blackwell Publishers, 2000).

Galipeau, Steven A., *The Journey of Luke Skywalker: An Analysis of Modern Myth and Symbol* (Chicago: Open Court Press, 2001).

Kraemer, Ross, William Cassidy and Susan Schwartz, *Religions of Star Trek* (Boulder, CO: Westview Press, 2000).

Neal, Connie, *The Gospel According to Harry Potter: Spirituality in the Stories of the World's Most Famous Seeker* (Louisville, KY: Westminster John Knox Press, 2002).

Porter, Jennifer E. and Darcee L. McLaren (eds.), *Star Trek and Sacred Ground: Explorations of Star Trek, Religion, and American Culture* (Albany: SUNY Press, 1999).

Wojcik, Daniel, *The End of the World as We Know It: Faith, Fatalism, and Apocalypse in America* (New York: New York University Press, 1997).

Wood, Ralph C., *The Gospel According to Tolkien: Visions of the Kingdom in Middle-earth* (Louisville, KY: Westminster John Knox Press, 2003).

Sports

Evans, Christopher and William Herzog II (eds.), *The Faith of 50 Million: Baseball, Religion, and American Culture* (Louisville, KY: Westminster John Knox Press, 2002).

Higgs, Robert, *God in the Stadium* (Lexington, KY: University of Kentucky Press, 1995).

Novak, Michael, *The Joy of Sports: End Zones, Bases, Balls, and the Consecration of the American Spirit* (Lanham, MD: Madison Books, 1993).

Prebish, Charles S., *Religion and Sport: The Meeting of Sacred and Profane* (Westport, CT: Greenwood Press, 1993).

Price, Joseph (ed.), *From Season to Season: Sports as American Religion* (Macon, GA: Mercer University Press, 2001).

Television

Davis, Walter T., Jr, Teresa Blythe, Gary Dreibelbis et al., *Watching What We Watch: Prime-Time Television through the Lens of Faith* (Louisville, KY: Geneva Press, 2001).

Fore, William F. *Television and Religion: The Shaping of Faith, Values, and Culture* (Minneapolis: Augsburg Publishing House, 1987).

Goethals, Gregor, *The Electronic Golden Calf: Images, Religion and the Making of Meaning* (Cambridge, MA: Cowley Publications, 1990).

Hoover, Stuart M. and Knut Lundby (eds.), *Rethinking Media, Religion, and Culture* (Thousand Oaks, CA: Sage Publications, 1997).

Lowney, Kathleen, *Baring Our Souls: TV Talk Shows and the Religion of Recovery* (New York: Walter DeGruyter, 1999).

McKibben, Bill, *The Age of Missing Information* (New York: Plume, 1992).

Pinsky, Mark, *The Gospel According to The Simpsons* (Louisville, KY: Westminster John Knox Press, 2001).

Tourism

Shaffer, Marguerite, *See America First: Tourism and National Identity, 1880–1940* (Washington, DC: Smithsonian Institute Press, 2001).

Sears, John, *Sacred Places: American Tourist Attractions in the Nineteenth Century* (Amherst, MA: University of Massachusetts Press, 1998).

Selwyn, Tom (ed.), *The Tourist Image: Myths and Myth Making in Tourism* (Hoboken, NJ: John Wiley & Sons, 1996).

Turner, Victor and Edith Turner, *Image and Pilgrimage in Christian Culture: Anthropological Perspectives* (New York: Columbia University Press, 1978).

Miscellaneous

Albanese, Catherine, *Nature Religion in America* (Chicago: University of Chicago Press, 1990).

Edmundson, Mark, *Nightmare on Main Street: Angels, Sadomasochism, and the Culture of Gothic* (Cambridge, MA: Harvard University Press, 1997).

Fuller, Robert, *Stairways to Heaven: Drugs in American Religious History* (Collingdale, PA: Diane Publishing Co., 2000).

Journal of Religion and Popular Culture <http://www.usask.ca/relst/jrpc/>.

Kittelson, Mary Lynn (ed.), *The Soul of Popular Culture: Looking at Contemporary Heroes, Myths and Monsters* (Chicago: Open Court Publishing, 1998).

Lardas, John, *Bop Apocalypse: The Religious Visions of Kerouac, Ginsberg, and Burroughs* (Champaign, IL: University of Illinois Press, 2001).

Lyon, David, *Jesus in Disneyland: Religion in Postmodern Times* (Cambridge: Polity Press, 2000).

Moore, Sally F. and Barbara G. Myerhoff (eds.), *Secular Ritual* (Amsterdam: Van Gorcum, 1977).

Moskowitz, Eva, *In Therapy We Trust: America's Obsession with Self Fulfillment* (Baltimore: The Johns Hopkins University Press, 2001).

Wilson, Charles R., *Judgment and Grace in Dixie: Southern Faiths from Faulkner to Elvis* (Athens, GA: University of Georgia Press, 1995).

Bibliography on Important Theoretical Texts on Popular Culture

What follows is a list of books and articles that are either landmark works or important reference points for the leading critical approaches to popular culture.

Frankfurt school and mass culture

Adorno, Theodor W., "On the Fetish-Character in Music and the Regression of Listening," in Andrew Arato and Eike Gebhardt (eds.), *The Essential Frankfurt School Reader* (New York: Continuum, 1982).

Benjamin, Walter, "The Work of Art in the Age of Mechanical Reproduction," in *Illuminations*, trans. Harry Zohn (London: Jonathan Cape Ltd, 1970).

Greenberg, Clement, "Avant-Garde and Kitsch," in *Art and Culture: Critical Essays* (Boston: Beacon Press, 1961).

Herman, Edward S., *Manufacturing Consent: The Political Economy of the Mass Society* (New York: Pantheon Books, 1988).

Horkheimer, Max, "Art and Mass Culture," *Studies in Philosophy and Social Science*, 9/2 (1941).

Lowenthal, Leo, "Historical Perspectives of Popular Culture," *The American Journal of Sociology*, 55 (1950), 323–32.

Macdonald, Dwight, "Masscult and Midcult" *Partisan Review*, 27 (Spring 1960), 203–33, and (Fall 1960), 589–631.

Sontag, Susan, "Notes on Camp," *Partisan Review*, 31 (Fall 1964), 515–30.

Cultural studies

Baudrillard, Jean, "The Evil Demon of Images and the Precession of Simulacra," in Thomas Docherty (ed.), *Postmodernism: A Reader* (New York: Columbia University Press, 1993).

— *America*, trans. Chris Turner (London: Verso, 1988).

Certeau, Michel de, *The Practice of Everyday Life*, trans. Steven Rendall (Berkeley: University of California Press, 1984).

Eco, Umberto, *Travels in Hyperreality*, trans. William Weaver (New York: Harcourt Brace & Co., 1986).

Featherstone, Mike, *Undoing Culture: Globalization, Postmodernism and Identity* (London: Sage Publications, 1995).

Fiske, John, *Reading the Popular* (London: Routledge, 1989).

— *Understanding Popular Culture* (London: Routledge, 1989).

Gramsci, Antonio, *Selections from the Prison Notebooks* (London: Lawrence & Wishart, 1971).

Grossberg, Lawrence, Cary Nelson and Paula A. Treichler (eds.), *Cultural Studies* (New York: Routledge, 1992).

Hall, Stuart and Paddy Whannel, *The Popular Arts* (London: Hutchinson, 1964).

Hartley, John, *Uses of Television* (London: Routledge, 1999).

Hebdige, Dick. *Hiding in the Light: On Images and Things*. London: Routledge, 1988.

— *Subculture: The Meaning of Style* (London: Methuen & Co., 1979).

Hoggart, Richard, *The Uses of Literacy* (New York: Penguin, 1957).

McRobbie, Angela, *Feminism and Youth Culture* (London: Unwin Hyman, 1991).

Willis, Paul E., *Profane Culture* (London: Routledge & Kegan Paul, 1978).

Market populism

Cowan, Tyler, *In Praise of Commercial Culture* (Cambridge, MA: Harvard University Press, 1998).

Frank, Thomas, *One Market under God: Extreme Capitalism, Market Populism, and the End of Economic Democracy* (New York: Doubleday, 2000).

Gans, Herbert, *Popular Culture and High Culture: An Analysis and Evaluation of Taste* (New York: Basic Books, 1974).

Heath, Joseph and Andrew Potter, *The Rebel Sell: Why the Culture Can't be Jammed* (Toronto: HarperCollins, 2004).

Hine, Thomas, *I Want That! How We All Became Shoppers* (New York: HarperCollins, 2002).

Holt, Douglas Bl, *How Brands Become Icons: The Principles of Cultural Branding* (Boston: Harvard Business School Press, 2004).

Klein, Naomi, *No Logo: No Space, No Choice, No Jobs* (New York: Picador, 2002).

Niedzviecki, Hal, *Hello, I'm Special: How Individuality Became the New Conformity* (Toronto: Penguin Canada, 2004).

Postrel, Virginia, *The Substance of Style: How the Rise of Aesthetic Value Is Remaking Commerce, Culture and Consciousness* (New York: HarperCollins, 2003).

Twitchell, James, *Lead Us into Temptation: The Triumph of American Materialism* (New York: Columbia University Press, 1999).

Media studies

Ewen, Stuart, *All Consuming Images: The Politics of Style in Contemporary Culture* (New York: Basic Books, 1988).

Gitlin, Todd, *Media Unlimited: How the Torrent of Images and Sounds Overwhelms our Lives* (New York: Henry Holt & Co., 2002).

Rushkoff, Douglas, *Media Virus: Hidden Agendas in Popular Culture* (New York: Ballantine Books, 1996).

Surveys

Storey, John, *An Introduction to Cultural Theory and Popular Culture*, 2nd edn (Athens, GA: University of Georgia Press, 1998).

Strinati, Dominic, *An Introduction to Studying Popular Culture* (London: Routledge, 2000).

— *An Introduction to Theories of Popular Culture* (London: Routledge, 1995).

Index

Note: "n" after a page reference indicates a note on that page; page numbers in italics refer to figures.